The New Global Politics of the Asia-Pacific

Now in its new and fully updated third edition, *The New Global Politics of the Asia-Pacific* continues to provide a compelling analysis of a region undergoing dramatic changes. Based on new research and offering fresh interpretation, this edition evaluates the prospects for continuing US dominance in the 'Asian Century'. It presents evidence of China's multifaceted 'Beijing Strategy', which aims to counter the US by building an alternative regional order. It also explains Japan's definitive departure from its limited military role. Providing an introductory guide for the main frameworks needed to understand the region, including realism, liberalism and critical theory, this new edition is reader-friendly, and offers sophisticated competing explanations. Key content includes:

- Intra-regional conflicts in the South China Sea and the Korean peninsula;
- The different responses within the Asia-Pacific to the globalization of Western ideas of democracy and political economy;
- The underappreciated success of the Association of Southeast Asian Nations in building a regional identity;
- The European Union's soft power in the region.

A highly topical account, which offers an overview of the main actors, institutions and contemporary issues in the Asia-Pacific, the book will be essential reading for undergraduate students of Asian Studies, International Politics, and anyone interested in the region.

Michael K. Connors teaches at the University of Nottingham, Malaysia Campus and is a Visiting Fellow at the Institute of Asian Studies, Chulalongkorn University. He is the co-editor of *Thai Politics in Translation: Monarchy, Democracy, Constitution* (forthcoming).

Rémy Davison holds the Jean Monnet Chair in Politics and Economics at Monash University. He is the author of *The Political Economy of Single Market Europe* (2011).

Jörn Dosch is Professor of International Politics and Development Cooperation at the University of Rostock, Germany, and Adjunct Professor at Monash University Malaysia. His recent publications include *Malaysia Post-Mahathir: A Decade of Change?* (2015).

The New Global Politics of the Asia-Pacific

Conflict and Co-operation in the Asian Century

Michael K. Connors, Rémy Davison and Jörn Dosch

Third edition

LONDON AND NEW YORK

Third edition published 2018
by Routledge
2 Park Square, Milton Park, Abingdon, Oxon OX14 4RN

and by Routledge
711 Third Avenue, New York, NY 10017

Routledge is an imprint of the Taylor & Francis Group, an informa business

First edition published by RoutledgeCurzon 2004

Third edition published by Routledge 2018

British Library Cataloguing-in-Publication Data
A catalogue record for this book is available from the British Library

Library of Congress Cataloging-in-Publication Data
A catalog record for this book has been requested

ISBN: 978-1-138-18957-7 (hbk)
ISBN: 978-1-138-64702-2 (pbk)
ISBN: 978-1-315-62566-9 (ebk)

Typeset in Times New Roman
by Saxon Graphics Ltd, Derby

Contents

Illustrations

Figures

Tables

Boxes

Preface to 3rd edition

Much has changed since the second edition of the *New Global Politics of the Asia-Pacific* appeared in 2011. These changes are documented and evaluated in the pages that follow. Readers of past editions will note extensive revisions to each chapter and perhaps a greater willingness to let our interpretative differences show on the page. In many cases, whole sections have been rewritten, and new sections added. Readers may also note the use of a subtitle in this edition. If the previous two editions tended to emphasise the possibilities of cooperation, it is now clear that conflict is in the ascendancy. Titles are often 'catchalls', but perhaps for the first time the title '*The Global Politics of the Asia-Pacific*' and reality substantively align. We also welcome on board Frederick Kliem, who has co-authored one chapter.

In updating and revising this third edition we have been ably and kindly supported by Georgina Bishop and the team at Routledge. We also owe thanks to anonymous colleagues who offered useful advice on improving the book.

Michael Connors thanks colleagues in the School of Politics, History and International Relations, University of Nottingham, Malaysia Campus for enabling a period of study leave that allowed him to work on this book. He also thanks the Institute of Asian Studies at Chulalongkorn University where he was a visiting fellow in 2017.

Rémy Davison would like to thank his best appointments: his life partner, defamation adviser and general solicitor-in-charge, Josephine Swiney, for her boundless support and encouragement throughout the writing of this book. He would also like to thank Professor Peter Shearman, his life tennis partner, for being (alternately) friend, supervisor, employer and editor. Special thanks are also due to the brilliant Monash team of Chris Arnel, Alfonso Martinez Arranz, Lucie Cadzow, Jessi Canny, Stephanie Carver, Bec Devitt, Samantha Kruber, James Paterson, Tim Rich and *Sensei* Theo Tsalamandris for providing invaluable teaching or research assistance that made the writing of this book possible.

Jörn Dosch would like to express his gratitude to his wife Ana Lucía and his children Nils-Mateo and Amelie for their continued love and support in all that he does.

Michael K. Connors, University of Nottingham, Malaysia Campus
Rémy Davison, Monash University, Australia
Jörn Dosch, University of Rostock, Germany

1 Introduction

Asia's 'Great Game'?

Rémy Davison

Donald Trump's victory in the 2016 United States (US) presidential election signalled a seismic shift in the international relations of the Asia-Pacific. The Trump administration also threatened to disrupt the complex network of security and trade institutions that successive US administrations have carefully constructed since 1945. During the 2016 US presidential campaign, Trump canvassed raising tariffs on Chinese goods from between 10 per cent and 45 per cent; and he accused Beijing of currency manipulation, imposing taxes on US exports, and of militarizing reefs and artificial islands in the South China Sea. Trump also asserted that the Chinese leadership was 'not helping' the US with North Korea. Prior to taking office, Trump took a call from Taiwanese President Tsai Ing-wen in December 2016, declaring subsequently that 'the US was not necessarily bound by the "one China" policy' (Reuters 12 December 2016). Japanese Prime Minister Shinzō Abe was forced to meet with Trump twice to obtain assurances that the US–Japan alliance was secure.

The Philippines' President Duterte declared his support for Trump, dismissing Obama with whom he had had a difficult relationship. In December 2016, the outgoing Obama administration found itself at odds with the transitional Trump team, as President Obama expelled 35 Russian diplomats from the US, sparking a diplomatic fracas. The Trump administration has challenged the orthodoxies that have governed US diplomacy in Asia for almost 50 years. Since 1971, US strategy in the Asia-Pacific has been built on a tripartite structure: containment of the People's Republic of China (PRC) and the USSR/Russia; maintenance of US hegemony in Asia via naval preponderance; and a system of formal and informal alliances throughout East and South Asia that enveloped Japan, South Korea, India, Pakistan, Singapore, The Philippines, Thailand and Indonesia. But the flashpoints that have now emerged in the East and South China Seas, as well as North Korea, represent some of the biggest international security challenges since 9/11. In 2016, Jane's Defence Budgets estimated that by 2025, China will outspend all other militaries in the Asia-Pacific region combined, while India in 2016 surpassed Russia and Saudi Arabia and ranked fourth in defence procurement expenditures (IHS Markit 2016).

In the first decade of the 21st century, three major events promulgated a profound reconfiguration of international politics. The first was the 11 September,

2001 attacks on the US; 9/11, it is widely agreed, 'changed everything'. The second event was the Iraq War of 2003; and the third event was the Global Financial Crisis (GFC) of 2008, the longer-term implications of which are still opaque. The three events are integrally linked; the 9/11 attacks drove the United States to develop forceful foreign and security strategies, redefining its relations with India, China and Russia in the global war on terror. The Iraq War divided both the Islamic world and the US's traditional allies, while simultaneously shifting the US budget from surplus to deep deficit. Finally, the 2008–09 Global Financial Crisis exacerbated the US debt spiral.

According to some analysts (Dadush and Stancil 2009, Fisk 2009), this period saw the balance of global financial power move in China's favour by 2010. By 2050, according to a widely cited Goldman Sachs (2005) report, the economic centre of gravity will have shifted decisively to the Asia-Pacific. Three of the world's four biggest economies will be Asian: China, Japan and India. By 2015, China's GDP of US$ 11 trillion was almost three times that of Japan (World Bank 2015). In 2016, South Asia was the world's fastest growing economy (World Bank 2016), while emerging Asia (the ASEAN-4) grew on average almost 7 per cent between 2013 and 2015 (IMF 2016). China now has more billionaires than the US, while Asia's billionaires now outnumber Europe's (*The Economist* 17 June 2015). In 2015, the Asia-Pacific region's share of global GDP was 40 per cent, with China accounting for 70 per cent of the total (ADB 2015).

Despite its modernization and expanding institutional architecture, there is still no regional security organization in Asia, no region-wide economic institution, and, indeed, no commonly held definition of what comprises 'Asia'. Thus, as recently as 2002, Hemmer and Katzenstein (2002: 575) could still ask, 'Why is there no NATO in Asia?' The answer is deceptively simple: in Europe, the United States built institutions; in Asia, it did not. The seductiveness of this answer fails to capture the complexity, uncertainty and instability of the Cold War era in the Asia-Pacific region. In 1949, no one could have predicted the endurance of the Beijing and Taipei regimes, the Sino–Soviet split, or America's ignominious withdrawal from Vietnam. Equally, few could have anticipated the rapid marketization of the People's Republic of China (PRC) economy after 1978, the extraordinary growth of the East Asian newly industrializing countries (NICs), or the equally extraordinary collapse of many of them in 1997–98.

The Asia-Pacific is such a fluid and dynamic region that it demands continual reappraisal and reconsideration. At the dawn of the 21st century, politico-economic instability, terrorism and security threats emerged as the key issues confronting the nations of East Asia. In parts of the region, the Cold War is far from over, evidenced by the re-emergence of a forceful North Korean regime, which embarked on an aggressive ballistic missile programme in the 1990s. Although Pyongyang's position appeared to soften following *rapprochement* with South Korea, and certain diplomatic guarantees from the US, tensions flared up once more during 2002–03, as the communist regime posed a new threat to its immediate neighbours, South Korea and Japan.

The Asia-Pacific has emerged as a region of global significance. It houses the world's two biggest economies, the world's largest military power and the world's most populous nation. The region is also home to eight of the world's ten largest military forces. The Asia-Pacific is also the most nuclearized region in the world, hosting six of the world's nuclear weapons states: the US, Russia, China, North Korea, India and Pakistan, and there is no regional consensus on arms control or WMD (see Kondapalli 2008). Communist, democratic and authoritarian regimes cohabit and co-exist within the region, if not always peacefully. Although the Yalta system, which divided the post-war world into US and Soviet spheres of influence, has disappeared, many Cold War relics remain scattered throughout the Asia-Pacific. Taiwan remains a point of friction between the US and China; the PRC remains a communist state politically, albeit one with many of the trappings of a capitalist market economy; the 1953 division of the two Koreas at the 38th parallel is still intact; Japan remains a military client state of the US; and US security dominance in the region persists, although serious challenges have emerged from Beijing and Pyongyang.

This chapter commences with a brief discussion of key developments in the Asia-Pacific during the Cold War. This is followed by an examination of the major paradigms in international relations – realism, liberalism, neo-Marxism and constructivism – which have been highly influential prisms through which both academic analyses, as well as policy-makers, have viewed international relations in the Asia-Pacific. We provide an overview of the book in the final section of this chapter.

Locating the Asia-Pacific region

As Hemmer and Katzenstein note, there is a great deal of confusion over what constitutes 'Asia', the 'Asia-Pacific' and the 'Pacific'. As Desker (2008: 56) notes, '"The Asia-Pacific region" includes the countries located on and within the edges of the Pacific Ocean, as well as India, which is beginning to play an important role in the politics of the region'. However, important, albeit artificial, geographical divisions are frequently drawn between East, South and Central Asia. For example, Palmer (1991: 21) asks whether the Asia-Pacific can be described as a region, due to its diffuse geography, ethnicity and culture. The first edition of *The New Global Politics of the Asia-Pacific* focused predominantly on what former Australian foreign minister Gareth Evans described as the 'East Asian hemisphere', comprising Northeast Asia (China, Japan, the two Koreas and Taiwan), Southeast Asia (the ASEAN 10), Australia and New Zealand. But the breadth of Asia, as well as the Pacific and Indian Oceans, means that Russia, Mongolia and Chile can rightfully claim membership of Asia-Pacific Economic Cooperation (APEC), while both Russia and India are members of the Shanghai Cooperation Organization (SCO). Russia has long been an Asian, as well as a Pacific and European power, while India's geostrategic location, in addition to its emerging status as a major economic power, make it a key player in the Asia-Pacific region. In the eastern Pacific and the Pacific Rim, both the US and

Australia, due to their respective strategic and economic interests, are heavily enmeshed with the East Asian region; however, due to their geographical locations and cultural backgrounds, they are not geographically located within the Asian region, although geopolitically and geo-economically, they are inseparable from Asia. Implicitly, APEC's very nomenclature recognized this fact in that it broadened the notion of Asian economic co-operation to encompass the Asia-Pacific, a form of transcontinental regionalism Keohane and Nye (2001: 2) term 'multicontinental interdependence'. In 2005, the promulgation of the East Asia Summit (EAS) saw Australia and India assume membership, with the US and Russia acceding in 2011.

Students of international politics confront a definitional minefield when attempting to determine the geographical boundaries of 'Asia' or the 'Asia-Pacific', and this is rendered all the more difficult by notions of 'Asian' versus 'Western' values. This encompasses a wide range of issues and models, a number of which we consider in Chapter 13: authoritarianism *v.* democracy; communitarianism *v.* human rights; and the capitalist development state *v. laissez-faire* capitalism.

APEC proves the exception, rather than the rule, in studies of East Asia. Unless the Trans-Pacific Partnership (TPP) is promulgated, APEC is the only Asia-Pacific economic organization that includes states from outside Northeast, Southeast or South Asia. ASEAN, the ASEAN Free Trade Area (AFTA), ASEAN Plus Three (APT) and Malaysia's 1990 East Asian Economic Caucus (EAEC) proposal comprise East Asian states exclusively. Conversely, security and dialogue fora, such as the Asia–Europe Meeting (ASEM) and the ASEAN Regional Forum (ARF), co-opt other states and regional actors, including the EU, Australia, Russia and the US, within a broad framework of mutual interests. However, it is notable that neither the ARF nor ASEM has developed the complex institutional framework of ASEAN, which became the ASEAN Community in 2015, while none of the other East Asian regional organizations, including the Southeast Asia Treaty Organization (SEATO), and the Asian and Pacific Council (ASPAC), remains.

This book investigates the transformation of the Asia-Pacific from regional to global actor. In the last 15 years, the region has become the centre of the global supply chain, the crux of the world's growth trajectory and home to 3.6 billion people, 51 per cent of the world's population (*Washington Post* 7 May 2013). That the region is of critical global significance, both strategically and economically, is beyond contestation. Of equal importance is the fact that both the US and Europe have developed such a level of interconnectedness with the Asia-Pacific that it arguably ranks foremost in the minds of American and European policy-makers, ahead of other potential flashpoints, such as the Middle East and Central Asian regions.

The making of the Cold War in East Asia

The Cold War may have been a battle between the US and Soviet Union, but its battlefields were to be found in East Asia: in China, Korea and Vietnam. In this respect, conflict, confrontation and co-operation in East Asia have provided rich empirical data for analyses of the region. In the immediate post-war period, international relations theory was dominated by realism, which monopolized national foreign policy agendas throughout most of the world.

Historians have debated the causes of the Cold War incessantly, but all concur that the Korean War was a pivotal moment in this emergent bipolar international system. Gaddis (1982: 110–15) argues that Korea was fundamentally an error of US foreign policy, driven by two imperatives: first, to atone for its early Cold War failures in Greece, Iran and Berlin; and, second, to restore US 'credibility' against the perceived threat of Soviet and Chinese communist expansionism. Gaddis asserts that despite US Secretary of State Acheson's assurances to Beijing that US interests extended only to preventing Soviet imperialism in China, in reality US policy was directed towards 'preventing the basis of a durable alliance between the Soviet Union and China'.

However, it was the Soviet Union's own diplomacy which destroyed the Sino–Soviet *entente cordiale* and divided the 'monolithic' communist bloc. Stalin's China policy in the 1940s was essentially motivated by realism, not international communism. Moscow sought to avoid a powerful communist state on its borders which might not only exhibit independence, but could also ultimately pose a challenge to the leading and guiding role of the Communist Party of the Soviet Union. In response, Mao's forces recommenced their insurrections against the Nationalists, leading to the virtual disintegration of the Nationalist government by 1948. Mao's suspicions of the Soviets deepened as Stalin urged him to concentrate his forces in northern China, leaving the south to the Nationalists. The damage to Sino–Soviet relations was permanent: in 1950, Stalin secured Mao's agreement that Mongolia would remain 'independent', albeit as a Soviet satellite. In return for some nominal financial and material assistance, Mao was also forced to cede to the Soviets some mining rights in Manchuria and Xinjiang.

If China could win concessions from the Americans while remaining in the Soviet camp, US Secretary of State John Dulles wrote in 1952, 'then there is little reason for her to change' (Gaddis 1992: 75). However, the Eisenhower Administration was uncertain about how to divide the communist bloc. Truman had viewed vigorous action in Korea as the only means by which to restore US credibility in the region, in an attempt to combat the perception that the US had 'lost' China. Conservative George Kennan had warned in 1947 that Soviet communist expansion had occurred much more quickly and successfully than the imperialist acquisitions of the fascist and Nazi regimes in the 1930s. Therefore, Kennan (1947) argued, both Communist China and the USSR needed to be contained, while the PRC could also be isolated from international affairs by continuing US support for the Nationalist regime in Taipei.

In East Asia, as well as Europe, Kennan's doctrine of the need to 'contain' the USSR became the linchpin of American policy. In Europe, the Soviet thrust was halted 80 miles west of Berlin; but in East Asia, the fall of the Nationalist Chinese government to Mao's communists in 1949 indicated that the US had underestimated the power of international socialism's 'second front'. Under a joint Soviet–American agreement, the two sides withdrew from the Korean Peninsula in 1949. However, North Korean forces' invasion of South Korea in 1950 provided the Truman administration with the justification for military re-engagement with the region. The US deployed the Seventh Fleet to Taiwan in June, ostensibly to protect the South Korean regime, as the Rhee government in the South had been quickly driven out of Seoul by North Korean forces by September 1950. The US's response was a United Nations Security Council (UNSC) resolution in October, calling for the establishment of UN-sponsored forces to restore stability in Korea. As the Chinese Nationalist government, now based in Taipei, was a permanent member of the UNSC, the PRC had no vote on the issue. The Soviet delegation absented itself, and the three other permanent members – the US, Britain and France – voted in favour of the resolution.

The US, Britain and Australia entered the war on the South's side with UN support for the intervention. In response, PRC 'Volunteers' covertly assisted the North. It has recently become apparent that the USSR also played a major covert role in the conflict. Although this was unclear at the time, the Korean War was the first armed conflict staged between nuclear powers. Despite the cessation of hostilities in 1953 with no decisive victory, the division of Korea, with a communist-dominated North, persists as one of the last remnants of the Cold War.

Throughout the Korean War, the American conservatives' view – that Mao's China and Stalin's USSR formed a monolithic communist bloc – appeared correct. The Soviets supplied China with over US$ 250 million in material assistance during the conflict, and relations were co-operative on issues such as Port Arthur and mineral resources in Manchuria and Xinjiang, which the Soviets returned to the PRC. Khrushchev's emergence as Soviet leader in 1957 initially maintained conciliatory policies towards China. However, the Soviets were disbursing a greater proportion of their foreign aid to satellites such as Egypt and, simultaneously, demanded China repay Korean War loans. Khrushchev also offered Soviet nuclear technology to Mao in return for virtually complete control over Chinese foreign policy. Mao, having witnessed the ruthlessness of the 1956 Soviet invasion of Hungary, rejected the overture. In 1959, Khrushchev abruptly cancelled nuclear co-operation with the PRC. However, China persisted with nuclear weapons development and exploded its first device in 1964.

During Khrushchev's leadership, the Sino–Soviet relationship moved from uneasy protagonism to an undeclared cold war, exemplified by military skirmishes on their common border (Bazhanov 1995: 160). Soviet Defence Minister Marshal Grechko warned of a potential PRC invasion of the USSR, and advocated the use of nuclear weapons to 'once and for all to get rid of the Chinese threat'. He was restrained by the Soviet Politburo leadership (Shevchenko 1985: 15). In an attempt to counter Soviet hegemony, Mao began to look westward for allies. In 1964,

France established diplomatic relations with the PRC when China was diplomatically isolated by American non-recognition and the Sino–Soviet split. Nevertheless, US administrations from Kennedy to Johnson continued to view the PRC as part of a contiguous communist bloc, a perspective that only underwent radical change with the election of President Nixon in 1968.

Unlike their predecessors, Nixon and, later, Kissinger viewed Sino–Soviet relations through the prism of realism, not conservatism. Both had seen the Sino–Soviet split as a potentially fundamental change in the balance of power. Equally, they saw no US national interest in continuing to sacrifice money and troops in Vietnam. Nixon's Guam Doctrine, announced in 1969, indicated that the US would no longer deploy ground troops in support of East Asian governments, a move which presaged the gradual withdrawal of the US from the Vietnam War.

After Guam: from Cold War to Asian regional security

Throughout the 1950s and 1960s, a number of regional agreements designed to ensure security and stability in the region were established in Southeast Asia. The Southeast Asia Treaty Organization (SEATO) was formed in Manila in 1954. SEATO was an American-inspired creation, rather than an endogenous form of regional integration, following the defeat of French forces in Indochina. SEATO broadly provided for the security of Southeast Asia, although its only members from the region were Thailand and the Philippines. The majority of its members were Atlantic and Pacific powers: the US, Britain, France, Australia and New Zealand, although newly independent Pakistan was also included. SEATO was designed to defend Southeast Asia from armed attack, which provided justification for future interventions by member states in Vietnam. In 1962, the US narrowed its interpretation of SEATO to provide specific commitments to Thailand, which was related to the crisis in Laos. US policy-makers argued that these commitments served to prevent communist aggression only, a clear indication that US foreign policy was primarily directed against PRC and Vietnamese influence in the region.

Although Washington viewed Moscow as a global competitor, the USSR failed to make serious inroads into East and Southeast Asia after the Sino–Soviet split, except in Vietnam and North Korea. Certainly, the Soviets were critical in supplying the North Vietnamese with training, weapons and other material support, but there were limits on the types of weapons Moscow would deliver. Soviet decision-makers achieved their strategic goals: US combat forces withdrew from Vietnam from 1972 after suffering the loss of over 50,000 troops, while communist North Vietnam rapidly overcame the South by 1975. However, the Soviets had no connection with the Khmer Rouge in Cambodia under Pol Pot (1975–79), which was largely supported by Beijing. As in Europe, the international communist movement was fragmented and disunited in Asia as national movements gave priority to their own immediate political objectives.

Washington and Moscow could not limit their attentions to East and Southeast Asia; the USSR was an Asian power, sharing a common border of almost 7,500km with China, separated from India and Pakistan only by Afghanistan. For the US, as for the British a century earlier, protection of the vital sea lines of communication (SLOCs), stretching from the Persian Gulf, through the Indian Ocean, across the Malacca Strait to the East China Sea and the Pacific, ensured the passage of energy supplies. Consequently, from the 1950s, the US built alliances and partnerships with Iran, Pakistan, South Vietnam, Thailand, Indonesia, the Philippines, Singapore, South Korea and Japan. India was different; on gaining independence in 1947, New Delhi co-founded the Non-Aligned Movement (NAM), eschewing overtures from both Moscow and Washington. However, by formalizing a mutual defence treaty with Islamabad in 1954, and co-opting Pakistan into SEATO, Washington raised deep suspicions in New Delhi. Following its defeat in the 1962 Sino–Indian War, which coincided with the Cuban Missile Crisis, Indian leaders realized that Moscow would not intervene militarily, despite India's informal alignment with the USSR, and the Soviets' recent split with the PRC. Moreover, Pakistan, India's main antagonist, had the security of a military guarantee from the US, which ultimately compelled New Delhi to 'tilt' towards Moscow and sign a formal partnership with the USSR in 1971. These circumstances also prompted New Delhi to implement significant military modernizations that, by 1974, culminated in the first Indian nuclear test. Consequently, by the mid-1970s, the number of nuclear weapons states in the Asia-Pacific region had increased to four. By the end of the 20th century, Asia would add two more nuclear weapons states to its number.

Following the failure of the Association of Southeast Asia (ASA) (1962), and the abortive South Korean-led Asian and Pacific Council (ASPAC) (1966), a key initiative was the formation of the Association of Southeast Asian Nations (ASEAN) in 1967. Its original members – Indonesia, Thailand, Singapore, the Philippines and Malaysia – eschewed the structure of a traditional military alliance, preferring instead to develop a set of principles aimed at ensuring non-interference in the internal affairs of ASEAN countries. Exemplifying 'old regionalism', ASEAN took many cues from the European Community (EC), establishing a large number of committees dealing with common interests such as banking, financial affairs, jurisprudence, shipping and employer organizations, as well as cultural organizations. From 1976 – notably, following the fall of Saigon – the Treaty of Amity and Co-operation provided a forum for the peaceful resolution of disputes between ASEAN member countries. However, unlike their EC counterparts, the ASEAN states did not introduce stringent regulatory frameworks; in fact, the 'ASEAN way' was the reverse of the European integration experience. ASEAN remained essentially a forum for regional dialogue, rather than an attempt at supranational institutionalism.

ASEAN has proven an enduring body, which has developed as an umbrella group for a wide range of important regional economic and security initiatives. These include the 1992 ASEAN Free Trade Agreement (AFTA); the Asia–Europe Meeting (ASEM) (1996); the ASEAN Regional Forum (ARF) (1994) and the ASEAN Community (2015). ASEAN has also expanded considerably, encompassing Brunei (1984), Vietnam (1995), Laos and Myanmar (1997) and Cambodia (1999). More recently, it has developed closer links with Japan, China and South Korea separately, with dialogue meetings under the auspices of ASEAN Plus One, as well as ASEAN Plus Three (APT), comprising ASEAN meeting with Japan, China and South Korea collectively. All of the original ASEAN-6, as well as Vietnam, are also members of Asia-Pacific Economic Co-operation (APEC) (1989).

Outside ASEAN, an important initiative of the early 1970s was the Five-Power Defence Arrangements (FPDA) (1971), comprising Malaysia, Singapore, Britain, Australia and New Zealand. The FPDA was primarily designed to ensure stability in Malaysia–Singapore relations, particularly following Singapore's expulsion from the Federation of Malaysia in 1965. As a strategic base during times of conflict, and as an important commercial centre in peacetime, Britain and Australia in particular saw the preservation of Singapore's autonomy from Malaysia – or any other state – as intrinsic to defence in the region, a posture explained partially by the successful Japanese invasion of the British fortress of Singapore in 1942.

For much of the Cold War, Europe was viewed as the geostrategic epicentre of superpower conflict; however, war took place in the East Asian theatre, not Europe, with both the US and USSR fighting proxy wars in the region. Soviet–American intervention in the region from 1945 divided the East Asian hemisphere into allies of either the capitalist West or the socialist East. Revolution in China in 1949 meant there were effectively 'four Chinas': the People's Republic of China; the Republic of China; British Hong Kong; and Portuguese Macao. Self-determination movements created newly independent states in the form of Indonesia, Malaysia and Singapore from old European colonial empires.

War has not been an uncommon phenomenon in the region. The victory of Mao Zedong over the Kuomintang Nationalist government itself sparked a conflict between American and British and Sino–Soviet forces on the Korean Peninsula in 1950, culminating in a bloody stalemate which left Korea bifurcated into North and South by 1953, a geographical and national division which remains today. French defeat at Dien Buen Phu in 1954 led to increased US intervention in Indo-China, resulting in the Vietnam quagmire that only ended with the fall of Saigon in 1975. The legacy of the Sino–Indian War of 1962 persists in the 21st century, as many border issues remain unresolved. The four India–Pakistan wars between 1947 and 1999 not only provided the impetus for nuclear weapons development in New Delhi and Islamabad, but also contributed, ultimately, to the development of an anti-Indian radical Islamist movement in South Asia. Revolution, coups and conflict in Cambodia, Indonesia, Singapore and Malaya demonstrated the volatility of the region in the Cold War climate. The story of post-1945 East Asia appeared to suggest that states in the region had conflict and proximity in common, but little else.

Yet, from the 1960s, both exogenous and endogenous factors contributed to a gradual stabilization of the international politics of the Asia-Pacific. The reasons for this were complex, but the emergence of a number of security regimes, such as the Association of Southeast Asian Nations (ASEAN) (1967), the Five-Power Defence Arrangements (FPDA) (1971), and the ASEAN Regional Forum (ARF) (1994) suggests that co-operative security, which envisages international consensus developed and managed through multilateral institutions and regimes, is becoming embedded in Southeast Asian diplomacy (Leifer 1998, Conetta 2002). Sino–American *rapprochement* from 1971, following the 1957–61 Sino–Soviet split, indicated that the US, the most powerful military actor in the region, was prepared to countenance a much less confrontational role in East Asia, particularly in light of the Vietnam debacle. President Nixon's articulation of the Guam Doctrine in 1969 meant that the US was no longer prepared to commit ground forces to the defence of allies and satellites in the region. Sino–American reconciliation also paved the way for the emergence of the PRC as a regionally significant, and potentially globally significant, power, evidenced by the seating of Mao's China as a permanent member of the United Nations Security Council (UNSC).

During the 1980s and 1990s, East Asia became the hub of global economic growth, and a key destination for foreign direct investment (FDI). The emergence of the 'four tigers' (South Korea, Taiwan, Hong Kong and Singapore) and the 'little dragons' (Indonesia, the Philippines, Thailand and Malaysia) as first- and second-tier 'newly-industrialized countries' (NICs), respectively, suggested that the 'East Asian' capitalist developmental state had succeeded, while 'Anglo-Saxon', 'Colbertist' and 'Third Way' Western models of capitalism were floundering.

However, the enormous development gains made by the 'little dragons' were damaged badly by the Asian Financial Crisis (AFC) of 1997–98, which wiped billions of dollars from East Asian stock markets, decimated currencies and shattered savings. The prescription of harsh medicine, administered largely by the US and its Western IMF partners, imposed heavy burdens on Indonesia, Thailand and South Korea in particular, from which they have yet to fully recover. Indeed, Waldon Bello (2002: 1) asks whether East Asia's future involves 'strategic economic co-operation or marginalization'. East Asian states have been forced to endure this form of Western interventionism for the best part of 500 years, represented most recently by the IMF and World Bank structural adjustment programmes and loans. But since the AFC, the Asia-Pacific has experienced extraordinary growth, driven by China's economic emergence, to the point where the region now forms the largest part of the global economy.

But the Asia-Pacific region is also home to many potential flashpoints, a number of which are discussed in this book, including the South China Sea, the East China Sea, and North Korea; the Taiwan Strait, US–China, Japan–China and China–India strategic rivalry; separatist movements; and terrorism in Indonesia and the Philippines. Given the legacy of political and economic instability in the region, one of the key questions in this book is: how are international relations (IR) in the Asia-Pacific to be understood? Broadly speaking, three main paradigms can be identified as relevant to both scholarly research into IR and foreign policy. These are realism, liberalism and critical theories. The latter can be said to encompass a wide range of theories, including varieties of neo-Marxism, constructivism and world order/global governance studies. As Peou (2002: 119) notes, 'The post-Cold War debate among positivist and post-positivist theorists of international security – particularly realists, liberals and constructivists – has not diminished'.

Approaches from international relations: realism, liberalism, neo-Marxism and constructivism

Realism and neorealism

Realism was the dominant paradigm in international relations for most of the 20th century, and it arguably remains the guiding logic in foreign policy decision-making among policy elites. For realists, a key attribute of the international system is war, which they argue is a natural condition. The central actor in international relations is the state, which is a unitary, rational, utilitarian entity, that has relative autonomy in decision-making, within the constraints imposed by other, competing states within the international system. Realists argue that the international system is essentially anarchic, in that there is an absence of central authority. They assert that whereas domestic systems are centralized and hierarchic, international systems are *de*centralized and anarchic (Waltz 1979). As central authority is lacking, states in the system are forced to provide for their own survival and security. Thus, the realist conception of the international system is one of self-help. Within this self-help system, states interact strategically, with each vying to maximize both their own security and interests.

Power accumulation is the key axiom in the realist conception of international relations. In realist theory, the structure of the international system is determined by the distribution of capabilities. A state's capabilities are measured by the extent to which it can project its power and influence. For Waltz, the only thing one need know about a state is the extent of its military power. According to Morgenthau (1948), power depends on a state's access to resources – financial, natural, human – and these will determine the extent of a state's capabilities. The only constraints placed on a state are imposed by the capabilities of the state itself, together with the structure of the system, i.e., the relative power of other states within the system.

Order in an anarchical system is a third key realist concern. Hedley Bull (1977: 53) asks: How is order maintained? The answer is via a balance of power. To avert the onset of general war, states will act militarily, often in coalition with others, in order to prevent the rise of a hegemonic power. Therefore, the general rule of balance of power theory is that should an individual state have the potential to overwhelm all the rest (Napoleon's France; Hitler's Germany), then states will form a counter-hegemonic coalition in order to restore the power balance.

In realist international theory, states seek only one goal: the maximization of their security. For neorealists, such as Waltz, at a minimum states seek security and, at a maximum, global domination. All means available to the state are directed towards one end: relative power gains at the expense of other actors in the system. The realist conception of world order regards international economic transactions as subordinate to the political interactions which take place between states. Although realists accept the importance of economic power and trade linkages between states, these are viewed as ancillary adjuncts to politico-military power. Naturally, economic strength is crucial to state power. But economic power is a means, not an end, to military power. To this extent, the realist paradigm suggested that states were relatively autonomous units, with exclusive sovereignty within their own territorial borders. Sovereignty has had formal status in international law since 1648, and the 1945 United Nations Charter confirmed the legal precept of state sovereignty. Consequently, both national sovereignty and the balance of power system have co-existed and developed symbiotically over 350 years.

The Cold War introduced a new balance of power structure. Whereas the multipolar European balance of power system (1648–1945) comprised a number of major powers, roughly equal in their capacities, the emergence of two superpowers – the USSR and US – after the Second World War introduced a *bipolar* structure, with the UK, France, West Germany, China and Japan relegated to the status of second-order powers, due to their vastly inferior military capabilities compared with the superpowers.

The extent to which the US and USSR could project their power was truly global. As a result, there was no continent that the Cold War left untouched. Although the military and financial dominance of the US was not seriously challenged by the USSR in the 1945–48 period, the emergence of Communist China in 1949 threatened to tip the power balance in the favour of the communist states. Although both China and the Soviet Union claimed to practise 'socialist' foreign policy, both exhibited realism in practice in their diplomacy, exemplified by the Sino–Soviet split of 1957–61, as the USSR sought to gain control of the overall direction of Chinese foreign policy, a feat it had already achieved throughout Eastern Europe. As a major power, China was able to resist Soviet attempts to transform the PRC into a client state.

What compels states to form regional security alliances? Why do they break down? Realists argue that regional co-operation takes place because of common external threats. Relative weakness is also an important precondition of co-operation, as weakness tends invite control. According to Waltz (1979: 201), 'The perils of weakness are matched by the temptations of power'. From a realist perspective, it would be impossible to leave South Korea or Taiwan without a credible defensive capability, as this could provide North Korea or China with the opportunity to annex or, at least, exercise considerable leverage over these territories.

As deterrence depends on the credibility of a serious conventional or nuclear capability, the trend throughout most of the Cold War was an increase in the level of military capabilities among the major powers of the region, although this was not restricted to the superpowers. China, India, Pakistan and North Korea became nuclear weapons states. Waltz (1993) predicted that in a multipolar world, Japan would develop an independent nuclear deterrent. With its civilian nuclear reactors, Japan has the capability to produce hundreds of nuclear weapons. As Japanese Defence Minister Ozawa stated in 2002:

> It would be so easy for us to produce nuclear warheads – we have plutonium at nuclear power plants in Japan, enough to make several thousand such warheads….If we get serious, we will never be beaten in terms of military power.
>
> (Lampton 2008: 198)

Even within ASEAN, Singapore's defence spending in the 1990s increased military capabilities at a rate vastly outpacing that of its rival, Malaysia. Due to the realist emphasis on the importance of military power, critics argue that the search for military invulnerability has led to a *security dilemma*. This thesis asserts that security is relative: because states compete for power and influence, this competition ultimately results in arms races. The security dilemma is, in reality, a vicious circle of security and power accumulation that emerges as a consequence of the combination of anarchy, a self-help system and competitive military strategies. In other words, one cannot improve one's own security without reducing that of others. As Jervis (1978) notes, the entire basis of the system is premised on making other states feel insecure. At the height of the Cold War, the Soviets and the Americans each possessed well over 20,000 nuclear warheads. More recently, the US commitment to the development of theatre missile defence (TMD), a strategy which the PRC claims is designed to 'encircle' China, has led the PRC to implement new countermeasures, such as the rapid development of multiple independently targetable re-entry vehicles (MIRVs), in response to US TMD. A security dilemma emerges when it is impossible to distinguish between defensive and offensive capabilities, and states are arguably no less vulnerable with massive arsenals at their disposal than they are without them. However, realists argue that this is an oversimplified view of the defence doctrine; they assert that counterforce and massive retaliation, two key doctrines of Cold War strategic thinking, provided stability in Soviet–US relations and rendered Chinese nuclear capabilities irrelevant (Glaser 1990: 302). For realists, conventional and nuclear deterrence has kept the peace in Korea and Taiwan, and even prevented the war in Vietnam from escalating into conflicts between the US and the USSR/China, due to the overwhelming dangers of direct nuclear confrontation.

Realists also differ considerably from liberals in their approach to co-operation. For realists, the incentive to co-operate is weak, and will usually be confined to 'low politics' areas, such as trade and investment. In realist theory, co-operation also denotes relative weakness; states seek co-operative security (for example, the ARF) because they are unable to provide adequately for their own security. This is clearly the case for Japan, South Korea and Taiwan, and explains why they have sought and accepted regional security under an American military umbrella. In this respect, realists are fundamentally at variance with liberals: whereas liberals argue that the incentives for regional and international co-operation and interdependence are strong, realists counter that states co-operate only because they are weak, and cannot guarantee their own security in the face of external threats.

Interdependence: liberal perspectives

Interdependence theory, a widely cited explanatory logic in an era of widespread industrial and technological modernization in the 1960s and 1970s, emerged as a challenge to the realist orthodoxy in the 1970s, primarily as an explanation of the failure of US military power to achieve its objectives in the Vietnam War. While Cooper's (1968) model of interdependence focused primarily on macroeconomic integration between states, Keohane and Nye (1977) argued that linkages across a range of issue areas reflected a growing 'web' of interdependence between states. For liberal theorists, interdependence existed at the level of the firm, between economies, through military coalitions and even in cultural linkages between states. For Keohane and Nye, interdependence meant a growing level of *mutual dependence*; the greater the level of interdependence, the higher the propensity for international co-operation.

Keohane and Nye argued that international interdependence had developed such complexity that it was impossible for states to ignore the potential impact of their domestic and foreign policies on other states. As a result, Keohane and Nye asserted that under conditions of complex interdependence, there was no longer any clear hierarchy of issues. Issues such as foreign *economic* policy were arguably of equal or greater importance than traditional foreign policy diplomacy. Moreover, as states developed enhanced levels of interdependence (for example, in areas such as trade and investment), they would be less likely to come into conflict, and more likely to identify common policy interests.

However, Keohane and Nye concede that interdependence is unlikely to be symmetrical; more often, relationships – such as trade, security or investment – are generally asymmetrical. For example, Southeast Asian states need Japanese investment, but Japanese firms also need Southeast Asia as a manufacturing base and a source of inexpensive labour. Thus, despite the inequalities in the relationship – Japanese corporations own many of the ASEAN states' productive assets, while ASEAN firms have few investments in Japan – ASEAN and Japan have achieved a certain level of interdependence, albeit asymmetrical. The incentive for increased co-operation between these two interdependent actors, Keohane and Nye argue, is high, as mutual benefits accrue if levels of interdependence increase. Therefore, complex interdependence is not merely a liberal theory of international integration, but also an explanation of international political co-operation.

Neoliberal institutionalism

Neoliberalism retains the key features of liberalism. For example, Grieco (1995) distinguishes between *liberal* and *neoliberal* forms of institutionalism. The original liberal thesis was in diametric opposition to realism's central propositions. Liberals rejected realist claims that the state was a unitary and rational agent. It also rejected the key tenet of realist thought: that the international system was an anarchic and decentralized realm where power was measured by the distribution of capabilities. In orthodox liberal theory, states were merely one of many actors in world politics, with non-state actors such as firms and international organizations playing at least an equal, if not more important, role than states.

Neoliberal institutionalism has its basis in regime theory, which points to the proliferation of institutions in the post-war world. In international politics, institutions were frequently, but not exclusively, the product of US hegemony which provided the international public goods (security, financial, trading systems) necessary for the establishment of regimes. After 1944, the US sponsored the Bretton Woods system (the GATT, IMF, World Bank), as well as NATO, the UN and SEATO. For neoliberals, regimes establish the institutions, frameworks and norms, the so-called 'rules of the game'. These are reflected in East Asian regimes, such as the institutional structure of ASEAN, and the ARF's objectives, which include promotion of confidence-building measures (CBMs), preventative diplomacy mechanisms and conflict resolution mechanisms (Ball 2000: 35).

Neoliberal institutionalist approaches essentially accept many of realism's key premises (the state as the central unit in the international system; the state as rational actor). However, despite this, neoliberals argue that, due to the existence and capabilities of international organizations, co-operation between states is not only possible, but also more likely. In realist theory, international co-operation *is* possible under conditions of anarchy, but only if states conclude that their national interests are served by engaging in co-operation.

From a realist perspective, complex interdependence does not necessarily result in increased international co-operation, but rather quite the reverse. Due to the increased sensitivity associated with close bilateral relationships, realists argue that interdependence creates 'a mutuality of suspicion' (Waltz 1970: 220). States with vital interests beyond their borders watch the activities of others warily, as variations in policy may affect their firms, their trade or their investments. Interdependence and globalization appeared to be the dominant logics governing the East Asian region throughout the 1980s, and for most of the 1990s, as it became the hub of global economic activity. For proponents of interdependence, the exponential growth experienced by the first- and second-tier NICs for almost two decades demonstrated the dominance of transnational forces, such as production and finance, over traditional realist concerns, such as security and military power. The enmeshment of the enormous Chinese economy with the post-Cold War global economy of the 21st century appears to demonstrate the ascendancy of market forces, which, to some extent, relegated regional security to a second-order issue.

Dominance and dependence: Neo-Marxist perspectives

Whereas liberals argue that interdependencies between states may be asymmetrical, dependency theorists claim that asymmetries reflect not interdependence, but *dominance* and *dependence*. Frank (1967, 1975) and Wallerstein (1979) posit that the structure of global capitalism creates international stratification between states of the developed industrial core and the underdeveloped periphery. Between the two lies a partially developed semi-periphery. For Frank, economic relations between states can never be in a state of mutual dependence, as inter-state relations are fluid and capitalist forces perennially readjust to altered market conditions. To this extent, any form of symmetry can exist only in a theoretical vacuum and without reference to a broader range of conditions which determines the structure of inter-state relations. Frank criticized capitalist development theories and argued that comprador elites formed a nexus with core elites producing a structure of dependent underdevelopment. States' relations, therefore, reflect dominance and dependence and, in a number of instances, dependent underdevelopment and capital accumulation by the core at the expense of the periphery. Wallerstein's world-systems analysis takes this core–periphery relationship a stage further by suggesting that dependent underdevelopment is reflective of a world capitalist economy which is characterized by an international division of labour. Yoshihara (1988) develops the Frank–Wallerstein dependency thesis further in his study of Southeast Asia. Yoshihara argues that the form of capitalism developed in Southeast Asia represents 'ersatz' (or inferior), replacement capitalism, exemplified by growth without economic development. For Yoshihara, Southeast Asia will be unable to break out of its dependency on foreign capital and technology as core firms (from Japan, the US and Europe) continue to control the key factors of production. Alternative neo-Marxist approaches employ Antonio Gramsci's critique of capitalism, which argues that hegemony is created by a ruling capitalist class. The overthrow of capitalism depends on a successful counter-hegemonic struggle.

Although dependency and neo-Marxist theories were largely discounted in the early 1990s, due to East Asia's explosive growth and the dramatic increase in living standards in the region, dependency theory developed renewed momentum in the wake of the 1997 Asian Economic Crisis which appeared to empirically validate many radical critiques of economic interdependence and globalization. However, some liberal economists have also emphasized the importance of the international division of labour. For Krugman (1979), the 'new economic geography' of the global political economy determines why clustering or agglomeration among states occurs. In his 'new trade' thesis formed during the 1980s, Krugman argued that states sought to perpetuate the international division of labour through 'strategic trade policy'; i.e., combining government market interventionism to avoid relying exclusively on a free trade system. Dependency and liberal theorists agree broadly on the power of transnational forces in international politics to affect and constrain states' national policy preferences. Where they diverge is how to counter the power of major states. For liberals, the answer lies in increased levels of interdependence and regional and global governance via institutions; for neo-Marxists, the answer is much more radical in that nothing less than the overthrow of the capitalist world economy will result in the destruction of the structure of dependency.

Constructivism

In Chapter 8, we provide a discussion of the comparative strengths and weaknesses of social constructivist, realist and liberal explanations of the 'ASEAN way'. Since its emergence during the 1990s, the 'constructivist turn' in IR has come to exert significant influence over the discipline. Contributions have been extensive, particularly in areas such as human security paradigms in international politics, the evolution of strategic culture, and the role of domestic forces in moulding foreign policy decision-making. Although constructivism has a number of variants, its proponents assert that it reveals much about the role of ideas, identities, and ideologies in shaping the structure of international politics. These theories represent a significant portion of the 'landscape' of IR theory in the late 1990s. Constructivism originated largely with the work of Alexander Wendt in the early 1990s. Baylis and Smith (2001: 165–90) note that constructivists make three central claims:

1 states are the principal actors in international politics;
2 the structure of the international system is ideational, rather than material; and,
3 state identities and interests are the product of this structure, rather than driven exogenously.

Constructivism focuses on ideational factors; that is, 'ideas', such as identity, culture and domestic politics, rather than material or structural factors, such as the power projection capabilities of great powers or the balance of power. For example, a number of scholars have explored ideational factors in analysing security behaviour in the Asia-Pacific region (Kahl 1998, Booth and Trood 1999). Berger (2000: 405) describes these factors as 'intangibles', because they are at the core of beliefs and values. These factors are thought to constitute the real sources of instability and conflict in regions such as the Asia-Pacific. Constructivists argue that they aim to supplement realist theory, rather than supplant it, by focusing on situations where structural material notions fail to adequately explain a particular behaviour (Deist 1998). By examining the normative dimension of politics, Hopf (1998: 171) argues that constructivism offers an alternative account of foreign policy decision-making to neorealism and neoliberalism, which are dominated by the concepts of anarchy, power balances, national interest, state security and institutions.

One of the main elements of constructivism is the focus on culture, which gives new meaning to state identity and security behaviour (Hopf 1998: 194). The study of 'strategic culture', a term first coined by Jack Snyder for a 1977 RAND report (Booth and Trood 1999: 4), examines the manner in which normative and domestic-level factors, such as historical experience and social identity, shape national attitudes and security behaviour. This approach provides an alternative to neorealist and neoliberal explanations for state behaviour. Security is conceptualized in terms of who or what represents the dominant culture or society, rather than purely in terms of considerations of military power. Constructivists regard war as a cultural phenomenon, and state behaviour as a product of identity and the manner in which this influences the assumptions made by individual decision-makers. Consequently, constructivists regard *internal* influences, rather than exogenous factors, such as international interdependence or the logic of global military competition, as the driving forces behind states' national foreign policy choices. For constructivists, state-based actors are no longer the sole determinants of foreign policy as, constructivists posit, sub-national ethnic, religious and cultural groups influence national policy-making.

Constructivists also focus on the changing nature of politics in the Asia-Pacific. In 2003, David Kang (2003) incited a robust debate by arguing that Western IR theorists had been 'wrong' about Asia and that the traditional lenses employed in foundational IR – realism, liberalism and Marxism – were inappropriate tools with which to analyse the politics of Asia. This includes the emergence of 'co-operative security' and the transformation from a sharply competitive zero-sum game, as viewed by realists, to a combination of competition and co-operation. Within this context, Alagappa (1998: 658–9) describes ASEAN as a 'partial pluralistic security community', one characterized by increasing co-operation and broader security concerns, including economic and socio-cultural issues. Dialogue assumes a central importance from this perspective. Alagappa sees it as a powerful agent for change, able to transform the normative context of the region, for example, over such principles as the legitimacy of force.

Yet, in reality, to what extent has constructivism contributed to our understanding of international relations in the Asia-Pacific? Is it helpful, for instance, in analyses of the behaviour of great powers? Does it prove incisive when assessing the forces behind major transformative events at the systemic level? Constructivism has been criticized harshly by both realists and some liberals, who view ideational perspectives on foreign policy decision-making as empirically unverifiable. Neorealists assert that system-level and structural constraints inhibit the implementation of specific policies that constructivists deem unit-level attributes. In neorealism, structural variables will always override cultural variables in international politics. For example, regionalism in ASEAN and the EU, both of which are seen as fertile ground for constructivist studies of integration, based on ideational coherence, has led realists (Jones and Smith 2006, 2007) and neoliberal institutionalists (Moravcsik 1999), to criticize constructivism on both empirical and theoretical grounds. In their forceful critique of ASEAN's regional role, Jones and Smith (2006) argue ASEAN does not represent the convergence of ideas, made possible by the proximity of the political cultures in the region, as Acharya (1997) claims; rather, ASEAN comprises merely uncertainty and incoherence, rather than a distinct regional order. Jones and Smith (2007: 184) further argue that constructivism attempts to veil the weakness of regional entities, such as ASEAN, by casting regional co-operation as collective strength and cohesion, rather than weakness relative to the major powers: 'Ultimately, ideational and normative constructivism conceals how weak states making a virtue out of the necessity of weakness cannot transform the practices of more powerful actors'.

For Moravcsik (1999: 673, 2001), constructivism simply 'evades theoretical analysis' and develops 'few testable hypotheses' in relation to foreign policy-making. Kang (2003: 67) argues that 'some scholars have smuggled ancillary and *ad hoc* hypotheses about preferences into realist, institutionalist, and constructivist theories to make them fit various aspects of the Asian cases'. Moreover, one leading neorealist, John Mearsheimer (2005: 145–7), charges that constructivists are merely seeking intellectual pre-eminence in order to dislodge realism as the dominant paradigm in IR.

There are several problems with constructivist analyses of strategic culture. First, as strategic cultures are unit-level attributes, logically, there should be considerable differentiation in how states approach strategic questions. However, strategic culture explanations do not explain why states view, and react similarly to, strategic challenges, such as military threats (Johnston 1995: 3). Commentators frequently write loosely of 'ASEAN' policy in a collectivist or holistic vein. However, realists are more concerned with determining which states wield the most power and influence within international organizations; naturally, they focus on the most powerful states in Asia. Or, as Jones and Smith (2007) put it aptly, 'Norms are what great powers choose to make of them'.

Structure of the book

The impact of the major powers' policy choices on the Asia-Pacific cannot be understated. Chapter 2 considers the United States' pre-eminent role in the Asia-Pacific region. Despite emerging new security and economic challenges in the post-Cold War regional order, the general pattern of US interests and policy strategies towards East Asia has been remarkably consistent over time because it is embedded in a persistent, multidimensional structure that has defined Washington's relations with the region since the early days of American involvement in the Asia-Pacific. Arguably, the US has had the most influence on the strategic environment and economic construction of the region over the past 60 years. Indeed, US troops have been stationed in the region since the 1940s, fighting major wars against Japan (1941–45), North Korea (1950–53) and North Vietnam (1965–73). Hot wars aside, the Asia-Pacific became the central geostrategic focus for the Cold War, with the region divided between American allies (ASEAN, Japan, South Korea, Taiwan) and the Communist quadrangle comprising the Soviet Union, the People's Republic of China, North Korea and Vietnam. Unlike Europe, where nuclear weapons kept the temperature of the Cold War cool (Waltz 1988), hot wars, and the precarious structure of the balance of power in the Asia-Pacific, saw the US presence become a permanent one.

While the main structures of Washington's regional engagement have largely remained unchanged, American standing in the region suffered significantly during the presidency of George W. Bush (2001–09) partly due to a widespread perception that the US preoccupation with conflicts in Southwest Asia and the Middle East (Afghanistan and Iraq) relegated US relations with the rest of Asia to secondary importance. The succeeding administration of Barack Obama

(2009–17) was quick to correct this widely held view of a weakened US position in the region. In one of his central foreign policy decisions Obama opted to 'pivot' or rebalance to the Asia-Pacific, a move which involved a more systematic and consistent reliance on diplomatic, economic and military instruments in an attempt to create a solid and durable basis for Washington's relations with regional states. Given his strong 'America first' rhetoric during the campaign, the election of Donald Trump and the scrapping of the Trans-Pacific Partnership (TPP) on the new president's first day in office created uncertainties about the future course of US–East Asia relations. However, only a few months later US foreign policy towards the Asia-Pacific, while still lacking a clear strategic direction, had normalized by reaffirming Washington's alliances and stressing the US commitment to defend South Korea under a growing threat from the North as well as reassuring Beijing that the US would not break away from its diplomatic acknowledgement of the People's Republic position that there is only one Chinese government.

The post-Cold War period has seen China emerge as an actor of both regional and global significance, due not only to its transformation into the workshop for the world, but also due in part to its massive foreign debt holdings, exceeding US$ 3 trillion in 2017. The exact composition of China's debt holdings is opaque, but Beijing owned approximately US$ 1.05 trillion in US Treasury bonds in February 2017 (US Department of Treasury 2017). It is less well known that the PRC's financial importance extends to the Japanese and South Korean economies. In October 2010, China's State Administration of Foreign Exchange (SAFE) sold off over US$ 20 billion in yen-denominated debt holdings as Sino–Japanese relations deteriorated following a minor boat collision in the East China Sea (ECS). Nevertheless, even as frictions increased over the ECS, the Bank of China still purchased considerable Japanese debt bonds (*Nikkei Asian Review* 23 October 2016). In summary, China's wealth has translated into economic power and leverage over its competitors, and Beijing's 'soft power' diplomacy is paying dividends as it attempts to extend its reach beyond East Asia to South Asia. Beijing's increasing wealth has also permitted its leadership to devote an increasing proportion of GDP to military expenditures, with over US$ 146 billion committed to defence procurement in 2015 (CSIS 2016), outspending Britain, France and Germany combined. In Chapter 3, we examine the PRC's relations with its regional neighbours, with particular reference to its relations with Taiwan, Hong Kong, Japan and North Korea. This chapter also discusses the 'Beijing strategy', and how it may challenge the traditional US dominance in the Asia-Pacific.

Japan performed a significant *volte-face* in the 1990s, from client state of the US to cautious military power. As we argue in Chapter 4, the transformation of Japan from Cold War ally into a key politico-strategic partner of the US has occurred gradually; the Diet has taken a piecemeal approach to legislative reform, which permits Japan to play a greater role in both regional and global security. Its constitution – which renounces war as an instrument of policy and commits Japan to a purely 'defensive' posture – has been largely circumvented by recent legislative initiatives, that are likely to make Japan a much more potent military force in the region. The end of the Cold War meant the end of Soviet containment of Japan, while the rise of China as a rival to Tokyo's economic ascendancy in East Asia, combined with the US's limited military disengagement with the region under the Clinton administration, indicated that a major power would need to fill the power vacuum. However, realist perspectives suggest that the US has not resiled from its dominant military role in East Asia; more accurately, since the 1991 Gulf War, the US has sought to end 'free riding' on the US's global defence capabilities, of which Japan has been a beneficiary since 1945. As this chapter argues, it is difficult to predict how Japan will react strategically to the dramatically altered security environment of the Asia-Pacific, given its proximity to an emergent China and an aggressive North Korea, although Japanese anti-terrorism legislation and co-operation with the US on ballistic missile defence (BMD) give some indication. The brief rule of the Democratic Party of Japan (DJP) saw Prime Minister Hatoyama reiterate Tokyo's co-operation with Washington in 2009–10, although his inability to relocate the US base at Okinawa cost him the premiership in 2010. The ascendancy of the Liberal Democratic Party (DJP) under Shinzō Abe has seen seismic changes in Japan's ability to deploy its military, as the DJP circumvented the 'peace constitution' with controversial legislation that passed the Japanese Diet in 2015. Chapter 4 explores how Japan dealt with the imposition of a pacifist constitution after the Second World War and used the opportunity of a US security guarantee to develop a formidable economy. By the end of the Cold War, facing considerable US pressure to contribute more to the Japan–US alliance, domestic political currents to expand its military capacity, and perceived threats from its security environment, Japan's security and military posture was no longer recognizably 'pacifist' despite rhetorical appeals to 'proactive pacifism'. Chapter 4 pays particular attention to the constitutional limits placed on Japan's military and explores the possibility of constitutional revision, as part of a longer-term process of Japan's 'normalization'.

Since the end of the Cold War, Russia and India have performed their own pivots to Asia. In military trade alone, China and India are Asia's most voracious consumers of defence materiel, while Russia is their biggest supplier. The renewed Sino–Russian relationship dates back to 1996, with the formation of the Shanghai Five, which quickly transformed itself into the Shanghai Cooperation Organization in 2001. In 2017, India and Pakistan formally joined the SCO. India, Russia, China, Brazil and South Africa also held the ninth BRICS summit in Xiamin, China in 2017, while in April 2017, Beijing refused to attend the annual China–Russia–India trilateral foreign ministers' meeting, following the Dalai Lama's visit to Arunachal Pradesh. Russia and India have made their own 'pivot to Asia' and have become increasingly integrated into the institutional and economic architecture of the Asia-Pacific region, via their respective participation in the East Asian Summit (EAS), the SCO, the Bay of Bengal Initiative for Multi-Sectoral Technical and Economic Cooperation (BIMSTEC) and the BRICS, as well as Moscow's membership of APEC. As Chapter 5 argues, New Delhi effectively abandoned over 50 years of non-alignment and strategically 'tilted' towards Washington as it forged new partnerships with the US's traditional regional allies: Japan and Australia. Russia arrested the decline it experienced in the 1990s, and re-emerged as an energy superpower by the early 21st century. Nevertheless, Moscow remains very much a second-tier power: despite its enormous natural resources and technological capabilities, its GDP is little over 10 per cent the size of China's. Russia and the PRC also compete for strategic and economic influence in Central Asia, but it is Moscow that wields the most leverage in the former Soviet republics. Moreover, Russia's invasions of Georgia (2008) and Crimea (2014) have compelled Moscow to turn back to Asia to forge closer strategic partnerships with China and India. Significant sanctions imposed by the US and the EU against Russia have badly damaged its economy. India and China need Russian energy and military technologies and, as Moscow's Western markets have closed, it is scarcely surprising that it has become Asia's chief supplier of weapons.

Australia (Chapter 6) appears to most observers a relatively minor player in international relations. It has a modest population and is geographically located on Asia's periphery. Yet, Australia is close to being one of the global top ten in terms of both defence expenditures and GDP. It also plays a significant role in the Asia-Pacific's security architecture through its alliance with the US, and its security engagements with significant actors, such as Japan and Indonesia. During the first decade of the 21st century, Australia's economic performance – amongst the OECD's best – became increasingly dependent on resources exports to China, principally black coal and iron ore. Canberra concluded FTAs with Japan and South Korea (2014) and China (2015), consolidating its network of Asia-Pacific FTAs with the US, Hong Kong, New Zealand, Singapore and Thailand. An FTA with India is currently under negotiation (DFAT 2015). However, as evidenced by its participation in the Iraq War (2003) and its troop deployments to Afghanistan, Australia's first-order strategic priorities lie with the US alliance, as Washington remains its chief weapons supplier. Equally, the US system of alliances and partnerships in the Asia-Pacific, comprising principally Japan, South Korea, Singapore and India, have heavily influenced Australian defence and security doctrines. As Chapter 6 notes, closer defence relations between Australia and Japan may presage the evolution of some form of 'JANZUS' alliance in the relatively near future.

The case of Australia is used to explore how a state with 'middle-power' (Cooper *et al.* 1993) aspirations negotiates its relationship with the United States, an alliance that arguably embeds Australia in a realist foreign policy world. Middle power and alliance diplomacy in relation to Australia are presented in Chapter 6 as 'squabbling siblings'. But the potential for middle power diplomacy to emerge as a more substantive challenge to the alliance relationship if Australian and US perceptions of international order significantly diverge is explored. Chapter 6 also considers how a subordinate partner in an alliance relationship is able to manipulate that relationship for its own gains.

In Southeast Asia, ASEAN is one of the few remaining relics of Cold War 'old regionalism' that has survived into the 21st century. Unlike its European counterpart the EU, ASEAN eschews major treaties and rigid institutional and jurisprudential frameworks, preferring an evolutionary, consensual and confidence-building approach to regional organization and security. The success of this approach for 50 years has meant that ASEAN has not only expanded its membership, but can also claim to be the hub of Southeast Asian integration. On 31 December 2015 the establishment of the ASEAN Community – based on the three pillars of political security, economic and socio-cultural co-operation – marked a new phase and higher level of institutionalization in the association's development. As Chapter 7 argues, ASEAN represents a challenge to realist and liberal analyses of international relations in terms of its approach to institution-building, which was not under the auspices of a hegemonic power, a characteristic of EU and global institutions. This chapter argues that 'identity politics' has been at least as strong an influence on the development of ASEAN as national self-interest and interdependence. ASEAN has evolved as a 'hub' around which a number of Asian regional organizations have emerged, such as the ASEAN Regional Forum (ARF) and the ASEAN Plus Three (APT).

Europe – particularly the EU – was slow initially to recognize the importance of East Asia to the global economy in the 1980s and 1990s. Despite the EU's rapid economic growth during the late 1980s, the bloc was inwardly focused on the completion of its internal market programme by 1993. In some respects, there were connections between the development of East Asian regionalism and the completion of the single market in the EU. Due to fears of 'Fortress Europe' (i.e., a protectionist trade bloc), APEC and AFTA were, to varying degrees, examples of 'reactionary regionalism', which were designed to buffer Asia-Pacific states from some of the negative implications of a more insular EU market.

The Asia–Europe Meeting, founded in 1996, signalled that East Asia was a key priority for the EU, given growing trade and investment links between the EU and both Northeast and Southeast Asia. Individual EU states, such as France, not only initiated over 90 ministerial visits to the Asian region after 1995, but also signed 'global partnership' agreements with China and Japan (Davison 2004). As Chapter 8 argues, unlike the United States, the EU and its individual member states cannot traditionally be viewed as major players in Asia. However, the role of European actors in the Asia-Pacific region is important in that they are said to exert a decisive influence on a wide range of politically relevant activities and issues. The key argument is that the EU has gained importance as a soft power, an accepted source of ideas in the sense that central elements of ASEAN as well as wider Asian debates on human rights, democracy and governance bear a European signature.

In Chapter 9, the discussion shifts to issues of intra-regional security, with particular reference to potential flashpoints in the region. Case studies such as the PRC–Taiwan conflict, the Korean Peninsula and the South China Sea are discussed in the context of changing concepts of security, unresolved Cold War conflicts and new rivalries. The main pillar of the regional security architecture is the US-led largely bilateral 'hub-and-spokes' system. Washington is the principal regional security guarantor, the hub of a complex arrangement of mostly bilateral security relationships (spokes). Its allies and partners contribute within their often limited means. In East Asia this is operationalized via a complex web of formal alliances with traditional allies including Japan and South Korea as well as informal, often intentionally ambiguous agreements and security guarantees, in particular but not exclusively with partners where ambiguity serves a wider strategic goal, such as Taiwan. This is supplemented by several treaties, short of formal alliances, supporting US efforts by granting access to military bases, offering logistic support, conducting joint exercises, etc. There has been a particular surge in such arrangements under the Obama administration as part of a strategy for navigating a more complex security situation in Asia. In addition, bilateral co-operative networks among individual East- and Southeast Asian countries, such as the Philippines and Vietnam, in particular in reaction to the South China Sea threat originating in China, have expanded in recent years. The chapter concludes with a brief discussion of how ASEAN and institutions such as the ARF may be able to build consensus on questions of mutual security. However, we argue that the main state-based actors in the Asia-Pacific – the US, China and Japan – will wield the most influence over the regional security agenda. Resolving these problems demands regional co-operation, but the absence of binding 'hard' security institutions in the Asia-Pacific may prevent regional actors from responding to these issues decisively.

The final four chapters of the book focus on transnational forces and their impact on the region. In Chapter 10, the intensification of globalization and the growth of regionalism are viewed as concomitant forces that have produced outcomes such as 'reactionary regionalism' and 'open regionalism'. Regionalism and globalization have also raised important questions concerning the complexity of the web of interdependence between Northeast, Southeast and South Asia, as well as the role of the 'Asian developmental state' (ADS).

Commencing with an introduction to some of the contending approaches in international political economy, Chapter 11 explores how these different approaches comprehend Asia's political economy. The chapter focuses on debates surrounding the role of the ADS. As Chapter 11 illustrates, debates about the Asian Financial Crisis (AFC) of the late 1990s are not technical debates about economic models, but intrinsically political debates about the impact of the state–firm nexus on the distribution of power in the international system. This chapter considers how Western attempts to restructure the Asian political economy after the crisis have largely failed and that the Asian Developmental State, in national variations, continues to structure the relationship between politics and the economy, both domestically and internationally.

The influence of transnational actors on national, regional and global politics is a strongly contested area in international relations. Chapter 12 assesses the significance of non-state actors in the Asia-Pacific region, with specific reference to transnational corporations (TNCs) and non-government organizations (NGOs). The TNC has become the main vehicle for the expansion and growth of national economics, market integration, capital liberalization and technology transfer. Conversely, NGOs play an increasingly important role in advocating issue areas such as human rights, fair trade and environmental protection. The chapter concludes that although it is difficult to quantify 'influence', it presents a number of case studies which suggest that some transnational actors have had an important impact on the direction of national policy.

The liberalizing effects associated with globalization are clearly not restricted to economics and finance. Asia's 'economic miracle' created a new and growing middle class in both Northeast and Southeast Asia. The debate over 'Western democracy' and 'Asian democracy' persists, particularly as corruption (the Philippines in 1986; South Korea in 1988 and 2016–17) and political instability (Thailand in 2006–07 and 2014; Indonesia in 1998) led to the downfall of long-established regimes, which were replaced by transitional democracies. During the post-Cold War period, Western countries aggressively promoted liberal-democratic models around the world. Chapter 13 reframes this activity as a project to restructure states in Asia so as to develop market access, and also create states that would support the US-led liberal international order. This reframing enables a rethinking of the so-called Asian values debate from the 1990s and its continued resonance today. Asian states have typically resisted the project, and more recently as China's authoritarian model has gained legitimacy, variants of the Asian values position are resurgent. Chapter 13 also considers how the rising tide of populist authoritarianism in the West may impact the sustainability of Western democracy promotion.

China's economic transformation, the nuclearization of Asia, regional security and the future role the United States will play in Asia are central to the debates about a new 'great game' unfolding in the Asia-Pacific. American hegemony and, concomitantly, the *Pax Americana* has dominated the Asia-Pacific since 1945. But the emergence of China and India as major economic powers, the rise of the 'Beijing Consensus' as a challenge to the 'Washington Consensus', combined with a more isolationist and protectionist US under the Trump administration has compelled some analysts to proclaim the end of the 'American century' and the commencement of the 'Asian century' (Layne 2008, ADB 2011). This book attempts to address a number of these questions, although it notes that the long-term strategic and economic architecture of the Asia-Pacific region remains opaque. China's rise, the US's, India's and Russia's respective 'pivots to Asia', North Korea's nuclearization, Japan's insecurity and the militarization of the Asia-Pacific all point to an increasingly unpredictable region. To paraphrase Bill Clinton, despite its growing prosperity, Asia has become one of the most dangerous places in the world.

References

Acharya, A. (1999) 'Realism, institutionalism, and the Asian Economic Crisis', *Contemporary Southeast Asia*, 21: 1–17.

Alagappa, M. (ed.) (1998) *Asian Security Practice: Material and Ideational Influences*, Palo Alto, CA: Stanford University Press.

Asian Development Bank (ADB) (2011) *Asia 2050: Realizing the Asian Century*, Manila: ADB.

Asian Development Bank (ADB) (2015) *Key Indicators for Asia and the Pacific 2015*, Manila: ADB.

Ball, D. (2000) *The Council for Security Co-operation in the Asia-Pacific: Its Record and Its Prospects*, Canberra Papers on Strategy and Defence No. 139, Canberra: Australian National University.

Baylis, J. and S. Smith (2001) *The Globalization of World Politics*, 2nd edn, Oxford: Oxford University Press.

Bazhanov, E. (1995) 'Russian policy toward China' in P. Shearman (ed.), *Russian Foreign Policy since 1990*, Boulder, CO: Westview.

Bello, W. (2002) 'East Asia's future: strategic economic co-operation or marginalization?' Transnational Institute, September, www.tni.org/reports/asia/crosspoints/paper6.htm.

Berger, T. U. (2000), 'Set for stability? Prospects for conflict and cooperation in East Asia', *Review of International Studies*, 26: 405–28.

Booth, K. and R. Trood (eds) (1999) *Strategic Cultures in the Asia-Pacific Region*, London: Macmillan.

Bull, H. (1977) *The Anarchical Society*, London: Macmillan.

Centre for Strategic and International Studies (CSIS) (2016) 'What does China really spend on its military?' Washington, DC: CSIS, http://chinapower.csis.org/military-spending/.

Conetta, C. (2002) 'World order, and cooperative security: a research and policy development agenda', Project on Defense Alternatives, *Briefing Memo*, 24, 9 September.

Cooper, A., R. Higgott and K. Nossal (1993) *Relocating Middle Powers: Australia and Canada in a Changing World Order*, Vancouver: University of British Columbia.

Cooper, R. (1968) *The Economics of Interdependence*, New York: McGraw-Hill.

Dadush, U. and B. Stancil (2009) 'The G20 in 2050', *International Economic Bulletin*, November, www.carnegieendowment.org/publications/index.cfm?fa=view&id=24195.

Davison, R. (2004) 'French security after September 11: Franco–American discord' in P. Shearman and M. Sussex (eds), *European Security after 9/11*, Aldershot: Ashgate.

Deist, M. (1998) 'Culture clash: assessing the importance of ideas in security studies', *International Security*, 23: 1.

Department of Foreign Affairs and Trade (DFAT) (2015) 'Australia–India Comprehensive Economic Cooperation Agreement', 25 October, http://dfat.gov.au/trade/agreements/aifta/pages/australia-india-comprehensive-economic-cooperation-agreement.aspx.

Desker, B. (2008) 'New security dimensions in the Asia-Pacific', *Asia-Pacific Review*, 15: 56–75.

Fisk, R. (2009) 'Economic balance of power shifts to the East', *The Independent*, 7 October.

Frank, A. G. (1967) *Capitalism and Underdevelopment in Latin America*, New York: Monthly Review Press.

Frank, A. G. (1975) *On Capitalist Underdevelopment*, Oxford: Oxford University Press.

Gaddis, J. L. (1982) *Strategies of Containment: A Critical Appraisal of Post-war American National Security Policy*, Oxford: Oxford University Press.

Gaddis, J. L. (1992) *The United States and the End of the Cold War*, Oxford: Oxford University Press.

Glaser, C. L. (1990) *Analyzing Strategic Nuclear Policy*, Princeton, NJ: Princeton University Press.

Goldman Sachs (2005) 'How solid are the BRICs?' Global Economics Paper No. 134.

Grieco, J. M. (1995) 'Anarchy and the limits of co-operation: a realist critique of the newest liberal institutionalism' in C. W. Kegley (ed.), *Controversies in International Relations Theory: Realism and the Neoliberal Challenge*, New York: St Martin's Press.

Hemmer, C. and P. Katzenstein (2002) 'Why is there no NATO in Asia? Collective identity, regionalism, and the origins of multilateralism', *International Organization*, 56: 575–607.

Hopf, T. (1998) 'The promise of constructivism in international relations theory', *International Security*, 23: 171–200.

IHS Markit (2016) '2016's $1.57 trillion global defence spend to kick off decade of growth, IHS Markit says', 12 December, http://news.ihsmarkit.com/press-release/2016s-15-trillion-global-defence-spend-kick-decade-growth-ihs-markit-says.

International Monetary Fund (IMF) (2016) 'Regional Economic Outlook (REO), October 2016: Asia and Pacific', 6 October, https://www.imf.org/external/Pubs/FT/REO/2016/apd/eng/pdf/areo1016.pdf.

Jervis, R. (1978) 'Cooperation under the security dilemma', *World Politics*, 30: 167–214.

Johnston, A. I. (1995) *Cultural Realism: Strategic Culture and Grand Strategy in Chinese History*, Princeton, NJ: Princeton University Press.

Jones, D. M. and M. L. R. Smith (2006) *ASEAN and East Asian International Relations: Regional Delusion*, Cheltenham: Edward Elgar.

Jones, D. M. and M. L. R. Smith (2007) 'Making process, not progress: ASEAN and the evolving East Asian regional order', *International Security*, 32: 148–84.

Kahl, C. H. (1998) 'Constructing a separate peace: constructivism, collective liberal identity, and democratic peace', *Security Studies*, 8: 94–144.

Kang, D. (2003) 'Getting Asia wrong: the need for new analytical frameworks', *International Security*, 27: 57–85.

Kennan, G. F. (1947) 'The sources of Soviet conduct', *Foreign Affairs*, 25: 566–82.

Keohane, R. and J. Nye (1977) *Power and Interdependence: World Politics in Transition*, Boston, MA: Little, Brown.

Keohane, R. and J. Nye (2001) 'Introduction' in J. Nye and J. D. Donahue (eds), *Governance in a Globalizing World*, Washington, DC: Brookings Institution Press.

Kondapalli, S. (2008) 'Weapons of mass destruction transfers in Asia: an analysis', *International Studies*, 4: 45–73.

Krugman, P. (1979) 'A model of innovation, technology transfer, and the world distribution of income', *Journal of Political Economy*, 87: 253–66.

Lampton, D. (2008) *The Three Faces of Chinese Power: Might, Money and Minds*, Berkeley: University of California Press.

Layne, C. (2008) 'China's challenge to US hegemony', *Current History*, January.

Leifer, M. (1998) 'The ASEAN Regional Forum: a model for cooperative security in the Middle East', Department of International Relations Working Paper No. 1998/1, Australian National University, Canberra.

Mearsheimer, J. (2005) 'E. H. Carr vs. idealism: the battle rages on', *International Relations*, 19 (2): 132–52.

Moravcsik, A. (1999) 'Is something rotten in the state of Denmark? Constructivism and European integration', *Journal of European Public Policy*, 6: 669–81.

Moravcsik, A. (2001) 'Bringing constructivist theories of the EU out of the clouds: have they landed yet?' *European Union Politics,* 2: 231–49.

Morgenthau, M. J. (1948) *Politics among Nations*, New York: Knopf.

Palmer, N. (1991) *The New Regionalism in Asia and the Pacific*, Toronto: Lexington Books.

Peou, S. (2002) 'Realism and constructivism in Southeast Asian security studies today: a review essay', *The Pacific Review*, 15: 119–38.

Shevchenko, A. (1985) *Breaking with Moscow*, New York: Knopf.

US Department of Treasury (2017) 'Major foreign holdings of US Treasury securities', 15 March, http://ticdata.treasury.gov/Publish/mfh.txt.

Wallerstein, I. (1979) *The Capitalist World Economy*, Cambridge: Cambridge University Press.

Waltz, K. (1970) 'The myth of national interdependence' in C. P. Kindleberger (ed.), *The International Corporation*, New York: MIT Press.

Waltz, K. (1979) *Theory of International Politics*, Reading, MA: Addison-Wesley.

Waltz, K. (1988) 'The origins of war in neo-realist theory', *Journal of Interdisciplinary History*, 18: 615–28.

Waltz, K. (1993) 'The emerging structure of international politics', *International Security*, 18: 44–79.

World Bank (2015) 'Gross domestic product 2015', World Development Indicators database, 31 August, http://databank.worldbank.org/data/download/GDP.pdf.

World Bank (2016) 'South Asia remains world's fastest growing region, but should be vigilant to fading tailwinds', press release, 10 April, www.worldbank.org/en/news/press-release/2016/04/09/south-asia-fastest-growing-region-world-vigilant-fading-tailwinds.

Yoshihara, K. (1988) *The Rise of Ersatz Capitalism in South-East Asia*, Oxford: Oxford University Press.

2 The United States in the Asia-Pacific

Still the hegemon?

Jörn Dosch

The United States' involvement in the Asia-Pacific is affected by two structural factors deeply rooted in history. The first, in a general sense, is the claim to American primacy in international relations, embedded in the strong belief in exceptionalism and moralism, or 'the deep and lasting faith in the singular, unique, "unprecedented" and "unrepeatable" character of the United States' (Hoffman 1978: 6). The second variable is the perception of the Pacific Ocean as a natural zone of American influence, as 'our lake'. This concept dates back to the late 19th century when most strategic points of the North Pacific rim came under US control, culminating in the takeover of the former Spanish colonies in the Philippines and Guam in 1898. Unlike the European powers, the Americans emerged as 'reluctant imperialists' (Kalb and Abel 1971) who built an 'empire by invitation' (Lundestad 1999) in an initially more unplanned than strategically envisioned process. For more than a century the Pacific Ocean has been perceived as a prime area for American opportunity. As an oft-repeated aphorism has it, 'the Mediterranean is the ocean of the past, the Atlantic is the ocean of the present and the Pacific is the ocean of the future' (quoted in Wardhana 1994: 174). Secretary of State John Hay's early 20th century account sounds strikingly similar to the prophecy of James Hodgson, then the US ambassador to Japan, about 80 years later: 'The now flourishing Pacific Region…constitutes nothing less than one of the great developments in human history – from now on the words "Pacific" and "future" will be synonymous' (ibid.). At the same time the US has acted as a stabilizer and balancer in the Asia-Pacific, a role embedded mainly in Washington's security alliances with Japan and South Korea, as well as close relations with ASEAN and individual member states, and a continuous strong military presence throughout the region.

It is therefore unsurprising that the election of each new US president regularly creates uncertainties in many of the region's capitals about the future direction of Washington's foreign policy towards the Asia-Pacific. During his 2016 presidential campaign Donald Trump repeatedly referred to South Korea and Japan as allies that were free riding on US security commitments, accused China's trade policy of 'raping the US' and being 'the greatest theft in the history of the world' (*The Guardian* 2 May 2016) and in early December 2016, as President-elect, had a phone conversation with the Taiwanese President Tsai Ing-wen which immediately raised questions about Washington's commitment to the 'One China' policy. One of the first major assessments of Trump's early foreign policy begins with the words, 'The United States has been on the same policy course for seventy years. This course is now being challenged more strongly than ever before' (Mills 2017: 2). However, only a few months into office, the president had reversed most of his earlier positions. US foreign policy towards the Asia-Pacific, while still lacking strategic direction, had normalized by reaffirming Washington's alliances and stressing the US commitment to defend South Korea under a growing threat from the North as well as reassuring Beijing that the US would not break away from its diplomatic acknowledgement of the People's Republic position that there is only one Chinese government.[1] There can be little doubt that Washington's strong political security and economic emphasis on the Asia-Pacific will continue.

American standing in the region suffered severely during the presidency of George W. Bush (2001–09) partly due to a widespread perception according to which the US preoccupation with conflicts in Southwest Asia and the Middle East (Afghanistan and Iraq) relegated US relations with the rest of Asia to secondary importance (Pempel 2008, Sutter 2009). Although empirical data did not support the assertion of any devastating decline in Washington's position, eminence and leadership in the Asia-Pacific under Bush (Green 2008), the succeeding administration of Barack Obama (2009–17) was quick to correct the widely held view of a weakened US position in the region. Immediately after taking office, Secretary of State Hillary Clinton proclaimed, 'The United States is back [in East Asia]' (quoted in *The Times & Transcript* 2009). Assistant Secretary of State for East Asian and Pacific Affairs, Kurt Campbell referred to Obama as 'our first Pacific president' (Davies 2009). The fact that Obama was raised and schooled for many years in Indonesia, and grew up for most of his life in Hawaii, seemingly made him the cheerleader for a structural overhaul of US–Asia-Pacific relations. Indeed, in one of his central foreign policy decisions Obama opted to 'pivot' or rebalance to the Asia-Pacific, a move which involved a more systematic and consistent reliance on diplomatic, economic and military instruments in an attempt to create a solid and durable basis for Washington's relations with regional states.

Two analytical perspectives dominate the debate on the US role in the Asia-Pacific. Neorealists describe the United States as a hegemonic stabilizer and honest broker that provides the necessary military power to bolster the security of the Southeast Asian states and acts as the regional balancer vis-à-vis an increasingly assertive China (a popular outlet for this discourse is the journal *Foreign Affairs*). While not disputing the existence of American primacy in the Asia-Pacific, the competing social constructivist argument stresses the incompleteness of US balancing due to the ambivalent nature of Washington's foreign policy and highlights the additional significance of soft-security multilateralism centred on the Association of Southeast Asian Nations (ASEAN) for the state of relative regional stability (for example, Acharya and Tan 2006). Few would deny the merits of five decades of intergovernmental co-operation in Southeast Asia and the basis it has provided for an emerging broader approach to regional multilateralism, most prominently the East Asian Summit. At the same time, it is difficult to imagine any alternative model of regional order which does not involve a dominant US position and role. US administrations have come and gone, and some were more coherent and consistent in their approaches to the Asia-Pacific than others. None ever developed any strategically sound long-term blueprint for Washington's relations with the region. Yet, the set of parameters that shape US policies towards the Asia-Pacific have largely remained unchanged. 'Continuity is the leitmotiv of US foreign policy, and the unilateral pursuit of national interests… has strong precedent' (Gurtov 2005: 1). The fundamental structures on which American policies in the region are based have persisted for many decades.

This chapter argues that despite emerging new security and economic challenges in the post-Cold War regional order, the general pattern of US interests and policy strategies towards East Asia has been remarkably consistent over time because it is embedded in a persistent, multidimensional structure that has defined Washington's relations with the region since the early days of American involvement in the Asia-Pacific. Five core objectives define this overarching strategy which aims at, first, preventing the emergence of a competing power capable of challenging American regional pre-eminence; second, keeping open and protecting the vital sea lines of communication in the area; third, strengthening commercial access to the economics of the region and sustaining the peace and stability that trade and investment relations require; fourth, maintaining and extending security ties with allies and friends in the region; and fifth – but only if it does not stand in the way of the other four goals – the promotion of democracy and human rights. These strategic aims will be explained by delving into the policy fields of security and economy.

The Cold War era

The first American trade activities date back to 1784 when the *Empress of China* set anchor in the Chinese port of Canton. The *Empress* was the first American merchant ship ever to cross the Pacific. In the early 1840s the US intensified its commercial engagement in East Asia. Under the terms of the Treaty of Wanghia (1844), the US gained the right to trade with Chinese ports. More decisively in 1853 Commodore Matthew Perry terminated Japan's self-imposed isolation and forced the country to enter into trade with the US. Both events paved the way for Washington's later colonial involvement in the region that took shape with the takeover of the former Spanish colonies in the Philippines and Guam in 1898. Within only a few decades the US had experienced a metamorphosis from a colony to a colonial power. Since the late 19th century the United States has held onto a pre-eminent position in the Asia-Pacific, only briefly interrupted by Japan's imperialistic attempts to establish a 'Greater East Asia Co-Prosperity Sphere' during the Pacific War. The defeat of Japan in August 1945 was followed by the emergence of an Asia-Pacific *Pax Americana* in the post-Second World War era. Although the Cold War in the Asia-Pacific was characterized by a tripolar structure with the US, China and Soviet Union as its poles and shifting power relativities within this triangular order, its central element was nevertheless American primacy or, as some argue, hegemony.

Unlike Western Europe where the United States' leading security role was integrated into a multilateral structure centred on NATO, a collection of bilateral alliances served as the ad hoc structure of security relations in the Asia-Pacific. The only attempt at multilateral alliance building during the Cold War failed: the Southeast Asia Treaty Organization (SEATO) was founded in 1954 and grouped Australia, UK, France, New Zealand, Pakistan (until 1973), the Philippines, Thailand and the US. Multilateral co-operation in the defence sector never got off the ground due to the high degree of diversity among the members and SEATO was finally dissolved in 1977. The system of bilateral security treaties that the United States initiated after the Second World War with its key allies in the Asia-Pacific, Japan, South Korea, Taiwan and the Philippines, has proved to be the more promising alternative to multilateralism. Among these alliances, the US–Japan axis emerged as the most important. In 1951 the United States and Japan signed the San Francisco Peace Treaty and the highly unequal Mutual Security Treaty. While the first formally ended the American occupation of Japan, the second enshrined Japan's position as Washington's military satellite. In 1960 a bilateral defence pact between the two nations increased Japan's profile because it eliminated earlier provisions allowing the United States to intervene in Japanese politics, provided a nuclear umbrella and obliged the US to defend Japan if attacked. The pact also required Washington to consult Tokyo for using military bases in Japan. At the same time the defence pact further integrated Japan as a key player on the chessboard of America's global Cold War security and defence strategy.

The Cold War security architecture of the Asia-Pacific was strikingly different from the one in Europe, not only in terms of its structure but even more with regard to the implications. While the American–Soviet balance of power kept Europe relatively secure and stable, the ideological-political antagonism between the two superpowers resulted in armed conflict in the Asia-Pacific. In fact, the two 'hot wars' of the Cold War were fought in East Asia, in Korea (1950–53) and Vietnam (1965–73). From about 1949 to 1975, the American presence in the Asia-Pacific region was dominated by its overall global anti-communist strategy. Maintaining military superiority over the Soviet Union and China was the highest priority. A first attempt to do this was the support given to the Nationalist Kuomintang (KMT) in the Chinese Civil War, which ended in bitter failure and recriminations. The US was again involved in military action in Korea, where it came to a stalemate in 1953. These failures persuaded both Democrats and Republicans in the US of the need for massive military strength, and subsequent administrations all authorized huge investment in submarines, aircraft carriers, nuclear and conventional weapons, and the maintenance of over 100,000 US troops in Asia, mostly based in Japan and Korea.

Another aspect of the strategy of containment was to support almost any regime that was perceived as anti-communist. This was promoted in the early 1950s by Secretary of State John Foster Dulles among others. First, anti-communist governments were supposed to prevent the spread of communism by clamping down on communist political movements in their territories. Second, US aid would make them prosperous, democratic countries that would have a 'demonstration effect' on neighbours, and also on the populations of communist countries themselves. The key countries that benefitted from US support in this context were Japan, South Korea, Taiwan, the Philippines and several countries in Southeast Asia. The results were mixed. The Philippines degenerated into the extremes of political decadence and corruption under President Ferdinand Marcos, who nonetheless received steadfast US support. Other states guilty of abuse of human rights and with few democratic freedoms were also beneficiaries of US aid, and the US exposed itself as simply supporting authoritarian regimes provided they were anti-Soviet. On the other hand, it may be argued that Japan and some other countries evolved into successful, prosperous, democratic states under US tutelage.

The greatest disaster of US policy was the war in Vietnam. By the early 1960s, US Asian policy was extremely rigid, doctrinaire and probably ill-informed. Ignoring the great diversity of the Asia-Pacific region, the military appeared to believe in a 'domino theory' whereby a successful communist movement (for example, in North Vietnam) would inevitably spread and overthrow pro-US governments in the whole region. This was the pretext for the massive bombing of Hanoi in 1965, leading to a ten-year war that devastated much of Indochina, and finally ended in humiliating defeat.

However, there was a third player in the situation: the People's Republic of China (PRC). The trilateral relationship tended to work in a 'two-against-one formation' and all three powers utilized the structure to their own advantage. The US manoeuvred between the PRC and USSR by strengthening or neglecting bilateral alliances in response to perceived shifts in relative power. Similarly, the Chinese utilized the conflict between the other two powers quite skilfully. Briefly, China was an ally of the Soviet Union during the 1950s, and gained economic and military assistance from Moscow. However, relations seriously degenerated as both claimed to be legitimate leaders of the world communist movement, and for a time war along China's northern borders seemed imminent. In 1960, the split became open and acrimonious, and the USSR withdrew all aid to China. The Sino–Soviet split resulted in a decade of anti-Soviet and anti-US Chinese foreign policy. In 1972, both Beijing and Washington significantly changed their strategic outlook and embarked on negotiations about a bilateral alliance directed against Soviet hegemony. Following the 'ping-pong diplomacy' between the two architects of *rapprochement*, Henry Kissinger and Zhou Enlai, the US and China re-established diplomatic relations in 1978. After this, China rather profited from the deadlock between the two superpowers, which allowed it relative freedom from military threat to pursue its own modernization goals. From the US point of view, the Soviet Union was consistently perceived as the major threat until 1990, by which time China had in fact acquired a very secure status in Asia due to its successful economic development. In the early 1990s, US reaction to the new power of China appeared to be rather mixed, reflective of the transition from Cold War to the new global arena.

The post-Cold War strategic setting

When the era of bipolarity came to an end it was clear from an American perspective that any new world order would have to be built along the lines of US supremacy and thereby mirroring abroad American values and beliefs. However, the United States entered the immediate post-Cold War era as a weaker power than it used to be, especially in economic terms. The relative decline in US economic power had two causes: the trade deficit and the budget deficit. The US trade deficit with Japan in the early 1990s was in the region of US$ 50 billion, and with other Asian countries around US$ 25 billion. At the same time, the US government was running a massive fiscal deficit, which necessitated a further reduction in spending on welfare programmes and the military. While within a few years the US had balanced the budget and rode a wave of tremendous growth, Japan drifted deeper and deeper into crisis, followed by the collapse of other East Asian economies during the 1997–98 meltdown, to many the scenario of the early 1990s nevertheless pointed to a continued decline in US influence in the region (Okimoto *et al.* 1996). It is important to note that not all analysts subscribed to the 'declinist' argument, as most prominently put forward by Paul Kennedy (1987). Nye (1990) and Rapkin (1994) promoted the counter-hypothesis based on the assumption that global US primacy was unchallenged. Still, the emergence of a strong neo-isolationalist impulse in some sections of the US political elite further contributed to the perception of significant changes to America's global role (Schlesinger 1995). Among Washington's East Asian allies, Japan and South Korea and other governments in the region, there was great concern that, 'with the ending of the Cold War and the US domestic reaction brought on by the trade deficit, the United States might "withdraw" from Asia' (Krauss 2000: 482). Such a scenario has never materialized and bilateral alliances have been strengthened rather than weakened. What was true for the administration of George W. Bush also applied to the Obama presidency and is likely to continue under Donald Trump: 'America's bilateral alliances…remain the foundation for its engagement in the Asia-Pacific; they remain indispensable to managing traditional security challenges and provide the basis for dealing effectively with new non-traditional security issues' (Cossa *et al.* 2009: 5).

Bilateralism versus multilateralism: real alternatives?

Of the existing treaties, The US–Japan alliance – revisited and renewed in 1996–97 – remains the foundation for US engagement in the Asia-Pacific, followed by the US–South Korea alliance in a close second position in terms of overall strategic importance. From 2012 onwards the Obama administration sought to upgrade the bilateral alliances under the umbrella of a 'strategic rebalancing' to the Asia-Pacific region. Beyond its immediate purpose of protecting Japan, the alliance has been widely interpreted as a safeguarding mechanism against an increasingly assertive China, although such a position is seldom officially stated.[2] In a rare exception a paper by the US Congressional Research Service highlights the importance of the alliance as 'a vehicle for enhancing security ties with Southeast Asian countries, especially since maritime territorial disputes in the East and South China Seas began to intensify in the late 2000s' (Chanlett-Avery and Rinehart 2016: 6). Equally, if more important, US strategic interests, Japan's position within the alliance and the North Korean threat are closely intertwined, as Christopher Hughes (2009: 293) explains: 'In certain cases, these alliance commitments are designed to directly counter the threat from North Korea. But in others they are designed to demonstrate a willingness to support the U.S. in dealing with regional and global contingencies that are more important to Washington than to Tokyo, in the hope that this will ensure U.S. reciprocation to support Japan against North Korea'. Tokyo's support of the US-led 'war on terror' through the dispatch of the Japanese Self-Defense Forces (SDF) to Iraq between 2004 and 2006, the related willingness to play a greater global security role and Prime Minister Shinzō Abe's strong promotion of the alliance as a means of strengthening Japan's national security posture are cases in point (Hughes 2015).

At the same time the US has not managed to find a sustainable strategic approach towards North Korea. Washington's North Korea policy since the early 2000s has been driven by trial and error. While George W. Bush emphasized the need for regime change in Pyongyang and displayed a tendency for unilateralism by refusing to talk directly to the North Korean regime (a policy that only resulted in growing North Korean defiance as well as antipathy in China and other countries), the Obama administration based its North Korea policy on the use of 'smart power', a combination of hard and soft power that was firmly embedded in international diplomacy. In this context Washington abstained from making any overly provocative references to the North Korean regime, even though several rounds of nuclear testing since 2006 have regularly heightened tensions on the Korean Peninsula. Obama's attempt to establish a direct dialogue in US–North Korea relations, to which Pyongyang initially responded reasonably well (Bahng 2009), proved ineffective. At the same time North Korean threats of violence against the US and its South Korean ally had become so common that they were 'rarely taken seriously in the United States, more frequently serving as a source of fodder for late night comedians than a credible national security threat' (Jackson 2016: 2). This, however changed in 2017 when a new policy approach of the Trump administration, based on sabre rattling and strong rhetoric, increased the pressure on North Korea and moved the United States 'closer to nuclear war than at any other time since the Cold War' (Li 2017) in the perception of some observers. Robert Litwak described the events as 'the Cuban missile crisis in slow motion' (quoted in Sanger and Broad 2017).

Northeast Asia regularly gets the most prominent – and often sole – attention in discourses on the Asia-Pacific security architecture. However, some of the most visible developments in US–Asia relations have taken place in Southeast Asia. Until the early 1990s the Philippines – hosting Clark Airbase and Subic Naval Base – represented the Southeast Asian cornerstone of Washington's bilateral alliance system. Despite ASEAN's official pro-neutrality rhetoric as manifested in the Declaration on the Zone of Peace, Freedom and Neutrality (ZOPFAN) of 1971 and other documents, Southeast Asian *realpolitik* has always welcomed the US presence in the region as a decisive contribution to the maintenance of peace and stability. When the Philippine Senate, reflecting strong nationalist sentiments at the time, decided against a renewal of the Military Bases Agreement (MBA) in 1991, the US intensified its relations with Singapore. The city state granted the United States considerable access to its seaports and airfields, thereby becoming a key American partner in the region. Since 2000, the US has been using Singapore's newly built Changi Naval Base as its logistics hub in the region. Other ASEAN states, particularly Malaysia, initially greeted the flirtation between Singapore and Washington with hostile scepticism as far as official political rhetoric was concerned but soon intensified their military relations with the United States too.

By 1998, Thailand, Indonesia and Malaysia had also signed military access arrangements, followed in 1999 by the implementation of the US–Philippines Visiting Forces Agreement. These arrangements form part of a broader set of military co-operation and training activities in Washington's relations with Southeast Asian states, which follow a new approach of a 'places not bases' policy in the region. In 2003, the US granted the Philippines and Thailand 'major non-NATO ally' status, which entitles the two governments to special access to US intelligence, among other privileges. In 2005 Singapore and the US signed a Strategic Framework Agreement for closer partnership in defence and security co-operation based on the explicit premise that 'a strong United States military presence is vital for regional peace and stability' (Strategic Framework Agreement 2005: Art. 1a). Since 2008, Vietnam and the US have significantly stepped up their security relations, which now include a formal 'policy, defence and security dialogue' on political-military issues (Thayer 2010). In 2016, Barack Obama announced the removal of all remaining US restrictions on sales of weapons and related services to Vietnam, marking the final step in the process of normalizing relations between the two countries. This fuelled speculation that the US would seek access to Cam Ranh Bay, a deep-water harbour in central Vietnam on the coast of the South China Sea that Washington had used as a base during the Vietnam War before the Soviet Union leased it following the end of the war in 1975 (Parameswaran 2016).

The rapid expansion of military ties in US–Southeast Asia relations has been feasible because the process is perceived as a three-fold positive sum game in both Washington and Southeast Asia. First, intensified defence co-operation enables the US to balance China's growing influence in the region while it forms an important element of a hedging strategy on the part of many Southeast Asian nations. Second, Washington and most Southeast Asian governments see a strong US naval presence as the most important contribution to securing the commercial sea lanes, especially the Malacca Strait and the South China Sea. Third, at least during the Obama presidency, security and the international political economy became increasingly intertwined as part of a quid-pro-quo strategy in which economic benefits, such as access to the US market via free trade agreements, were tied to the willingness of Southeast Asian governments to engage in military co-operation.

Robert Sutter (2008: 93) links China's rise to the potential emergence of 'an "inside-out" model of regional governance [which might be] displacing the past half century's "outside-in" model led by the United States through its regional allies'. While such a model has not emerged yet as China is still a one-dimensional power, based on economic strength, which cannot match the multidimensional power (hard and soft power) of the United States, Washington is preparing for the materialization of such a scenario. The key to balancing China's regional influence is mainly bilateralism, supplemented by multilateralism where and when deemed appropriate. The promotion of institution-building and more specifically multilateral co-operation in East Asia as a central element of President Bill Clinton's neo-Wilsonian 'Engagement and Enlargement' strategy (particularly between 1992 and 1994, the first half of his first term) has often been misunderstood and misinterpreted. Neither burden-sharing nor responsibility-sharing in the Asia-Pacific has ever implied a substitute for American leadership and primacy. The Clinton administration had always viewed the endorsement of ASEAN-type co-operation in the region as a means of securing American superiority within the – compared to the previous era – less clear-cut structure of post-Cold War international relations in the Asia-Pacific, as well as a strategy of delegating and diversifying financial and political responsibilities. The differences between the administrations of Bill Clinton, George W. Bush, Barack Obama and Donald Trump are one of form, not substance. While President Clinton rendered substantial political support to the multilateral dialogue diplomacy based on the so-called ASEAN way of informal, non-binding and consensus-oriented intergovernmental co-operation in the Asia-Pacific that had mushroomed since the early 1990s, George W. Bush openly demonstrated a lack of interest in multilateral organizations in the region such as ASEAN itself, the ASEAN Regional Forum (ARF) or the Asia-Pacific Economic Cooperation Forum (APEC). Secretary of State Condoleezza Rice decided not to attend the ARF meetings in 2005 and 2007, sparking criticism in Southeast Asia. Bush's Washington viewed the ARF 'as an overly large, underperforming "talk shop" that does not merit significant bolstering – even though it is the only region-wide security institution that includes the U.S.' (Mauzy and Job 2007: 631).

Hopes for a post-Bush revival of multilateralism and upgrade in US–ASEAN relations were not disappointed. In February 2009 Hillary Clinton not only included Indonesia on her first overseas trip in office but also paid the first ever visit of a US Secretary of State to the ASEAN Secretariat, even followed by a return visit in 2012. During his two terms in office President Obama regularly attended the ASEAN summit meetings. As one of the most visible acknowledgements of ASEAN's important role in the Asian-Pacific security architecture, in 2009 the US signed an agreement to accede to the ASEAN Treaty of Amity and Cooperation (TAC) after 17 years of consideration, in an attempt to boost multilateral approaches to regional security. A total of 34 states have now signed the 1976 regional code of conduct, making the TAC one of ASEAN's most significant international successes.

Most importantly, the strategy of the Obama administration to 'pivot' or rebalance to the Asia-Pacific included the support for 'ASEAN centrality' understood as ASEAN's lead role in several regional institutions such as the ARF, the East Asia Summit, and the ASEAN Defence Ministers Meeting Plus. The rebalancing concept originated in Hilary Clinton's article 'America's Pacific Century' of October 2011 and is particularly known for the introduction of the term 'pivot toward Asia'. In November 2011, in an address delivered to the Australian Parliament, President Barack Obama stressed that he had made the 'deliberate and strategic decision' that the United States 'as a Pacific nation…will play a larger and long-term role in shaping this region and its future, by upholding core principles and in close partnership with our allies and friends' (The White House, Office of the Press Secretary 2011). The pivot strategy revolved around the objective of strengthening regional partnerships (and thus US pre-eminence in the Asia-Pacific) through the support of structural reforms (investment in education, labour market reforms, etc.); democracy and human rights, free trade, transparency and the rule of law, with the Trans-Pacific Partnership (TPP) as the principle vehicle (see below); and to win support for global agendas including climate change, arms control and the responsibility to protect (Campbell 2016). The Trump administration's approach has been a mix of continuity and discontinuity. While the strong focus on ASEAN as a key partner has remained unchanged, TPP became an immediate victim of Trump's declared ambition to end the era of multinational trade agreements. On his first full weekday in office, Trump signed a presidential memorandum to formally withdraw from the trade agreement (which at that point in time had not been ratified by Congress anyway).

However, while ASEAN-centred multilateral approaches to order-building have undoubtedly regained the geostrategic importance and priority on the US foreign policy and defence agenda they lost during the presidency of George W. Bush, the core of Washington's approach to the Asia-Pacific is likely to remain bilateral in mode. From a US angle a firm bilateralism is seen as the most promising insurance against the emergence of a structural situation that would hinder American access to the region. Hillary Clinton once reinforced the main credo of American involvement in East Asia by declaring that Washington 'is not ceding the Pacific to anyone' (quoted in Elliott 2009: 2) – in a forceful response to the perceived rise of China.

The ghost of terrorism

Beyond long-term strategic considerations, both the US and ASEAN states consider an American military presence as a decisive – probably the most important – contribution to securing the commercial routes in the region. US military power in the Asia-Pacific is based on the presence and mission of the Seventh Fleet, the largest of the Navy's forward-deployed fleets, including 40–50 ships, 200 aircraft and about 20,000 Navy and Marine Corps personnel. At a conventional day-to-day level of military activity, the core mission of the US naval forces includes the provision of humanitarian assistance; the enforcement of international sanctions, such as embargoes and no-fly zones; the participation in or support of peace operations and an active contribution to the security of the sea lines of communication (SLOC). Especially with regard to the latter, the navy has intensified its activities in order to guarantee a stable and secure regional order even in zones that are less immediately linked to vital US national security interests today than in previous decades. This is particularly the case for the 600-mile long Malacca Strait, one of the world's most important and the second busiest commercial shipping lane (second only to the Strait of Dover), the main corridor between the Indian Ocean and the South China Sea, with approximately 220 ship movements in both directions per day. The US is determined to ensure the freedom of navigation continues in Southeast and East Asia. The threat of terrorism in Southeast Asia has reinforced this approach.

Since the 11 September 2001 terror attacks in New York and Washington, and during the subsequent 'war on terror', the United States has viewed extremist movements in Indonesia, Malaysia, the Philippines and Thailand as a potential hazard to world commerce flowing through the region's important commercial sea lanes. Under George W. Bush, US military involvement in Southeast Asia markedly increased when concerns of Islamic terrorism were becoming more pronounced after the Bali bomb attacks in October 2002, which killed 202 people. In the first substantial deployment of American troops in the Philippines since the closure of the US military bases in 1991, some 600 military personnel have been deployed in Mindanao (Southern Philippines) since 2002 to assist the Philippine Armed Forces in their struggle to eradicate the Abu Sayyaf group, militant bandits with a radical Islamist agenda. In 2014 the US and the Philippines negotiated an 'Enhanced Defence Cooperation Agreement' (EDCA), which 'allows the expansion of rotational deployment of U.S. ships, aircraft and troops at five bases in the Philippines as well as the storage of equipment for humanitarian and maritime security operations' (Mogato 2017).

Like in Mindanao, the situation in southern Thailand, where thousands of people have been killed since the renewed insurgent violence broke out in January 2004, has promoted closer US–Thai military ties. Bush's Washington tended to see this conflict almost exclusively through the lenses of the global fight against terrorism (Connors 2006). The succeeding Obama administration markedly watered down the American anti-terrorism rhetoric. Indonesia, for example, is no longer described as a terrorist haven but praised as a model democracy – and indeed 'a model for the Muslim world' (Solomon 2009: A8) – that deserves close and mutual beneficial relations with the United States as part of Washington's strategy to reinvigorate ties with the Islamic world. While the threat of terrorism as a destabilizing factor in US–Asia relations is less pronounced today than it was a decade ago, the new co-operation structures that were created in a joint effort to counter terrorism are here to stay.

Economic relations: the other side of the security coin?

Since the early 2000s Washington's initiatives to negotiate free trade agreements (FTA) with a range of countries in the Asia-Pacific have been driven as much by economic incentives as by security imperatives. The starting point and strategic framework was outlined by the George W. Bush administration under the title 'Enterprise for ASEAN Initiative' (EAI), which offered free trade negotiations to the Southeast Asian states based on a concept of 'countering terror with trade' (Zoellick 2001: A35). Bush announced the EAI in October 2002 shortly after the Bali bomb attack. From a US perspective, not only are free trade agreements aimed at intensifying moves towards closer economic integration of East Asia, but they are also intended to bind the United States more tightly to the region from a geostrategic and security point of view.

This new emphasis on expanding economic relations with the Asia-Pacific was first highlighted by the US–Singapore free trade agreement, which came into force in January 2004 and served as the blueprint for other possible FTAs in Southeast Asia under the EAI. Modelled on the successful Enterprise for America Initiative, launched by then President George H. W. Bush in 1990, the EAI was a vision for a web of bilateral FTAs linking the United States to the region. Under the EAI, the United States and individual ASEAN countries could jointly determine if and when they were ready to launch FTA negotiations. The EAI allowed ASEAN countries the flexibility to move at their own speed towards an FTA with the United States. A precondition for any negotiations, though, was WTO membership and the conclusion of a trade and investment framework agreement (TIFA) with the US. Washington signed TIFAs with Brunei, Cambodia, Indonesia, Malaysia, the Philippines, Thailand and Vietnam and was negotiating FTAs with Thailand and Malaysia. Preliminary free trade talks had been conducted with the Philippines and Vietnam. As already hinted, the EAI not only aimed to expand US trade ties with the region, but was also seen as a way to maintain a US presence in Southeast Asia and to enhance US security interests. The FTA with Singapore was called a step to anchor the United States in Southeast Asia 'in terms of business, economics *and security*' (US–ASEAN Business Council 2003, emphasis added). More explicit statements to this effect were made with regard to Malaysia.

> By solidifying our economic relationship, an FTA with Malaysia will advance other important policy goals, including supporting our partnership on security. Malaysia is a moderate Muslim country in a critical part of the world and has been an important partner in the war on terror. The United States and Malaysian militaries participate in extensive joint training, and Malaysia is an important purchaser of American defense systems.
>
> (Office of the United States Trade Representative 2006)

Seen from a different angle, 'the United States has used FTAs as political rewards for countries that support US foreign and security policies' (Pang 2007: 2). Similar strategic considerations apply to Northeast Asia where the US and South Korea successfully completed negotiations for a free trade agreement in 2007 – after the idea had been in the pipeline for some two decades. After a long and difficult ratification process the agreement entered into force in March 2012. In addition to the FTAs with South Korea and Singapore, the US has a free trade agreement with Australia (since 2005). While none of the other negotiations started by the George W. Bush administration yielded results, they nevertheless paved the way for the Trans-Pacific Partnership, one of President Obama's key foreign policy initiatives.

In October 2015 – after five years of negotiations – the US and 11 Asian-Pacific countries (Japan, Malaysia, Vietnam, Singapore, Brunei, Australia, New Zealand, Canada, Mexico, Chile and Peru) announced the successful conclusion of negotiations for TPP, the most extensive trade deal in history, representing roughly 800 million people and 40 per cent of the world's economic output. In February 2016 the trade and economy ministers from the member states signed the treaty in Auckland, New Zealand. Throughout the negotiation process the Obama administration argued that the strategic value of TPP paralleled its economic value, contending that the agreement would both strengthen US alliances and partnerships and reaffirm American economic pre-eminence in the region. Obama repeatedly highlighted the importance of maintaining US leadership in establishing and developing global trade rules, notably with reference to potentially alternative Chinese initiatives (Fergusson *et al.* 2016: 2). 'Many participants in the TPP talks, most notably Japan, made serious economic restructuring efforts. Countries like Vietnam had to improve its human rights conditions to gain a seat in at the TPP table. Given that the Trump administration…abandoned the TPP, countries like Japan and Vietnam are dismayed' (Lee 2017). Washington's withdrawal from TPP marked a discontinuity in US–Asia-Pacific policy which, for several decades, had been based on the premise of economic integration as the main contributing factor to prosperity and ultimately regional stability.

Conclusion

This chapter has tried to show that despite changing actors in US foreign policy-making and significant alterations to the structures of global and regional order, in sum both American interests and strategies towards the Asia-Pacific have been remarkably persistent over the past decades. Specific policies are embedded in Washington's approach to the wider Asia-Pacific area, which aims at preventing the emergence of a competing regional hegemon; keeping open the sea and air routes that transit the area; maintaining commercial access to the economies of the region and the peace and stability that commerce requires; and preserving and strengthening security ties with allies and friends in the region.

The Obama administration's rhetoric of realignment followed these objectives and was best summarized as pro-multilateralism and pro-engagement. TPP and the acknowledgement of ASEAN's central role in regional order-building were perhaps the most visible materializations of this strategy. There is no reason to believe – particularly when China's growing role and increasing status in the

Asia-Pacific and the ongoing crisis on the Korean Peninsula are taken into account – that the Trump administration will substantially depart from the previous co-operative approach. The withdrawal from TPP marked a small change in priority but given widespread opposition within Washington's political establishment even before the presidential elections of November 2016, the agreement's ratification by Congress had always been questionable. Overall, the parameters that determine Washington's international relations with the region remain largely unchanged. The dawn of a new security architecture is not in sight. The question needs to be asked: would anyone be interested in any substantial structural changes to the existent and persistent regional security order? A foreign policy strategy based on flexible bilateralism can be described as the default pattern of Washington's relations with the region – in line with the interests and expectations of most East and Southeast Asian governments.

Recent developments suggest that the United States will not drastically change its strategic approaches towards the Asia-Pacific. Absent irrational leadership or a catastrophic attack, the most likely mid-term scenario for the US role in the region is a continuation of bilateral patterns in economic and security relations characterized by economic partnerships (but not necessarily new free trade agreements) and increasing defence ties based on both the military alliances with Japan and South Korea and a 'places not bases' strategy with other partners in the region, particularly in Southeast Asia. Opposition to the US global and regional role has been relatively low-key in the Asia-Pacific in recent years and the Obama administration further boosted Washington's image as a benign hegemon.

If any single actor was to challenge the American pre-eminent position in the Asia-Pacific, China is the most likely candidate. Predicting China's future regional position and its relations with the US has exercised an uncounted number of pundits. While some believe that China's military potential is significantly overestimated, others see China as a military superpower in 10 to 20 years' time. Regardless of the likelihood or soundness of the latter scenario, there can be little doubt about the fact that both the United States and most Asian governments are preparing themselves for a more assertive China. This is where the strategic interests of the United States and most Asian states meet and overlap. While strengthened economic and defence relations with East and Southeast Asia enable Washington to balance China's emerging hard and soft power in the region, they help ASEAN governments to keep their international options open and hedge against the prospect of Chinese hegemony.

Alongside the question marks behind China's mid- and long-term grand strategy in the Asia-Pacific (and global international relations in general), and the future of the Korean Peninsula, the most uncertain move on the chessboard of US–East Asia security relations continues to be the one involving Taiwan as a key figure in any scenario for regional order. Again, continuity, not change, is the main characteristic of Washington's approach. In the post-Cold War era this has been a policy of strategic ambiguity (for example Kastner 2006) under which succeeding administrations have left deliberately unclear if and how Washington would intervene in the case of a cross-Strait conflict.

A concluding word on theory: IR theories in general and the main schools of thought, neorealism, idealism and liberal institutionalism in particular, do not solely explain observed reality. In addition to their purpose of providing a framework for academic analysis, very often they gain importance as foreign policy recipes. In this regard, IR theories are different from other social science hypotheses because academic analysis and foreign policy-making are intertwined in a reciprocal relationship. Over the decades the ideas developed by the father of realism Hans Morgenthau and his many academic followers have had a significant impact on the conduct of foreign policy, especially in the United States. The realist concept of 'balance of power' even became a self-fulfilling prophecy during the Cold War. At the same time, the way policy-makers perceive the international environment and react to challenges posed by it constantly refines IR theory. The most striking example is probably George Kennan's famous 'Long Telegram' of 1946 that best illustrated American anti-communism and general suspicion of Soviet aspirations, and laid the foundation for Washington's containment strategy towards Moscow. The 'Long Telegram' was perhaps the most cited and most influential statement of the early years of the Cold War. At the time he authored the telegram Kennan was chief of mission at the American embassy in Moscow. In 1947 the essence of the document was published in *Foreign Affairs* under the title 'The sources of Soviet conduct' and signed by 'X', although everyone knew that Kennan was the author. For Kennan, the Cold War gave the United States its historic opportunity to assume leadership of what would eventually be described as the 'free world'. Although US foreign policy seems to follow realist patterns due to the strong influence of the realist/neorealist school on policy-making, idealists (sometimes also called Wilsonians, referring to President Woodrow Wilson, the architect of the League of Nations and model idealist) and liberal institutionalists have equally put their mark on Washington's foreign policy interests and strategies. On the one hand there 'is the gulf between academic IR theorists and foreign policy practitioners.... Policy practitioners appear to find little of value in the canonical IR texts relating to the day-to-day conduct of diplomacy'. On the other hand,

> there have been exceptions to this rule – predominantly in the US – where the IR theorist has assumed the role of policy maker: Henry Kissinger, Madeleine Albright, Joseph Nye, G. John Ikenberry, Robert Kagan and Condoleezza Rice all possess substantial backgrounds in academic IR. All have served in major roles in US foreign and defence policy making for both Democratic and Republican US administrations.
>
> (Davison 2008)

With regards to the Asia-Pacific, one of the best examples is Harvard Professor Joseph Nye, who served in both the Carter and Clinton administrations. As Clinton's Assistant Secretary of Defence for International Security Affairs he drafted the US–Asia-Pacific Security Strategy of 1995 (even dubbed the 'Nye Report'), which put the main emphasis on multilateral co-operation and significantly changed, for a short period, Washington's foreign policy and defence approach towards the Asia-Pacific.

In the United States more than 1,000 private, non-profit think-tanks try to contribute their expertise to the governmental decision-making process. The influence of think-tanks and academics in the foreign policy process grows the more they are integrated in so-called epistemic communities or 'Track Two' activities which bring them together with government officials who often attend these kinds of meetings in their private capacity. In sum, the reciprocal relationship between theory as an analytical instrument and theory as a foreign policy recipe or even self-fulfilling prophecy is often ignored in the IR literature, but should be kept in mind when we try to analyse international relations and the conduct of foreign policy.

Notes

1 Under the 'One China' policy, a cornerstone of Sino–US relations, Washington formally recognizes the People's Republic of China rather than Taiwan. This policy is distinct from the 'One China principle', whereby Beijing insists Taiwan is an inalienable part of one China to be reunified one day.

2 For a stimulating and critical discussion of the concept of Chinese assertiveness see Johnston 2013.

References

Acharya, A. and S. S. Tan (2006) 'Betwixt balance and community: America, ASEAN, and the security of Southeast Asia', *International Relations of the Asia-Pacific*, 6: 37–59.

Bahng, T.-S. (2009) 'Prerequisites to upgrading the ROK–US Alliance: North Korea and wartime operational control', *SERI Quarterly* (Seoul), 2 (4) (October): 112–18.

Campbell, K. (2016) *The Pivot: The Future of American Statecraft in Asia*, New York: Twelve.

Chanlett-Avery, E. and I. E. Rinehart (2016) *The U.S.–Japan Alliance*, 9 February, Washington, DC: Congressional Research Service.

Clinton, Hillary (2011) America's Pacific century, *Foreign Policy*, November, http://foreignpolicy.com/2011/10/11/americas-pacific-century/.

Connors, M. (2006) 'Thailand and the United States: beyond hegemony?' in M. Beeson (ed.), *Bush and Asia: The US's Evolving Relationships with East Asia*, London: Routledge.

Cossa, R., B. Glosserman, M. A. McDevitt, N. Patel, J. Przystup and B. Roberts (2009) *The United States and the Asia-Pacific Region: Security Strategy for the Obama Administration*, Washington, DC: Center for a New American Security.

Davies, A. (2009) 'China climate talks take centre stage in Obama's first Asia visit', *The Age* (Melbourne, Australia), 2 November.

Davison, R. (2008) *Foreign Policies of the Great and Emerging Powers*, Frenchs Forest, NSW: Prentice Hall.

Elliott, G. (2009) 'Clinton firmly commits the US to Asia-Pacific security', *The Australian*, 21 May: 2.

Fergusson, I. F., M. A. McMinimy, and B. R. Williams, (2016) *The Trans-Pacific Partnership (TPP)*, 9 February, Washington, DC: Congressional Research Service.

Green, M. J. (2008) 'The United States and Asia after Bush', *The Pacific Review*, 21 (5): 583–94.

Gurtov, M. (2005) 'American crusades: unilateralism, past and present' in M. Gurtov and P. Van Ness (eds), *Confronting the Bush Doctrine: Critical Views from the Asia-Pacific*, London: RoutledgeCurzon.

Hoffmann, S. (1978) *Primacy or World Order: American Foreign Policy since the Cold War*, New York: McGraw-Hill.

Hughes, C. W. (2009) '"Super-sizing" the DPRK threat: Japan's evolving military posture and North Korea', *Asian Survey*, 49 (2): 291–311.

Hughes, C. W. (2015) *Japan's Foreign and Security Policy under the 'Abe Doctrine': New Dynamism or New Dead End?* London: Palgrave Macmillan.

Jackson, V. (2016) *Rival Reputations: Coercion and Credibility in US–North Korea Relations*, Cambridge: Cambridge University Press.

Johnston, A. I. (2013) 'How New and Assertive Is China's New Assertiveness?', *International Security*, 37 (4) (Spring): 7–48.

Kalb, M. and E. Elie Abel (1971), *Roots of Involvement: The US in Asia 1784–1971*, New York: W. W. Norton.

Kastner, S. L. (2006) 'Ambiguity, economic interdependence, and the US strategic dilemma in the Taiwan Strait', *Journal of Contemporary China*, 15 (49) (November): 651–69.

Kennedy, P. (1987) *The Rise and Fall of the Great Powers: Economic Change and Military Conflict From 1500 to 2000*, London: Random House.

Krauss, E. S. (2000) 'Japan, the US, and the emergence of multilateralism in Asia', *The Pacific Review*, 13: 473–94.

Lee. B. (2017) 'Trump's first 100 days in Asia: continuities and discontinuities in Trump's Asia policy', *The Diplomat*, 28 April, http://thediplomat.com/2017/04/trumps-first-100-days-in-asia/.

Li, E. (2017) 'Trump's tough talk about North Korea might actually end the crisis', *The Washington Post*, 5 May, https://www.washingtonpost.com/posteverything/wp/2017/05/05/trumps-tough-talk-about-north-korea-might-actually-end-the-crisis/?utm_term=.63530a696c65.

Lundestad, G. (1999) 'Empire by invitation in the American Century' in M. Hogan (ed.), *The Ambiguous Legacy: U.S. Foreign Relations in the 'American Century'*, Cambridge: Cambridge University Press.

Mauzy, D. K. and B. Job (2007) 'U.S. policy in Southeast Asia: limited re-engagement after years of benign neglect', *Asian Survey*, 47 (4): 622–41.

Mills, D. Q. (2017) *The Trump Phenomenon and the Future of US Foreign Policy*, New Jersey: World Scientific.

Mogato, M. (2017) 'Philippines says U.S. military to upgrade bases, defense deal intact', *Reuters*, 26 January, www.reuters.com/article/us-philippines-usa-defence-idUSKBN15A18Z.

Nye, J. S. (1990) *Bound to Lead: The Changing Nature of American Power*, New York: Basic Books.

Office of the United States Trade Representative (2006) Free Trade Agreement: U.S. – Malaysia Key Player in Southeast Asian Market, www.ustr.gov/assets/Document_Library/Fact_Sheets/2006/asset_upload_file510_9123.pdf.

Okimoto, D., H. Rowen, M. Oksenberg, J. Raphael, T. Rohlen, D. Emmerson and M. Armacost (1996) *A United States Policy for the Changing Realities of East Asia*, Stanford, CA: Asia/Pacific Research Center.

Pang, E.-S. (2007) 'Embedding security into free trade: the case of the United States-Singapore free trade agreement', *Contemporary Southeast Asia*, 29 (1): 1–32.

Parameswaran, P. (2016) 'US–Vietnam defense relations: problems and prospects. A closer look at what lies ahead for cooperation between Washington and Hanoi', *The Diplomat*, 27 May, http://thediplomat.com/2016/05/us-vietnam-defense-relations-problems-and-prospects/.

Pempel, T. J. (2008) 'How Bush bungled Asia: militarism, economic indifference and unilateralism have weakened the United States across Asia', *The Pacific Review*, 21 (5): 547–81.

Rapkin, D. E (1994) 'Leadership and cooperative institutions in the Asia-Pacific' in A. Black and J. Ravenhill (eds), *Pacific Co-operation?* St Leonards: Allen & Unwin.

Sanger, D. E. and W. J. Broad (2017) 'A "Cuban Missile Crisis in slow motion" in North Korea', *New York Times*, 16 April, https://www.nytimes.com/2017/04/16/us/politics/north-korea-missile-crisis-slow-motion.html.

Schlesinger, A. Jr (1995) 'Back to the womb?' *Foreign Affairs*, 74: 2–8.

Solomon, J. (2009) 'Clinton says U.S. will expand Southeast Asia ties', *Wall Street Journal* (Eastern edition), New York, 19 February: A8.

Strategic Framework Agreement between the United States of America and the Republic of Singapore for a Closer Cooperation Partnership in Defense and Security (2005) http://se2.isn.ch/serviceengine/FileContent?serviceID=23&fileid=D147CAFD-9C40-FB05-2DEF-ED4873138430&lng=en.

Sutter, R. (2008) 'China's rise, Southeast Asia, and the United States: is a China-centered order marginalizing the United States?' in E. Goh and S. W. Simon (eds), *China, the United States, and Southeast Asia: Contending Perspectives on Politics, Security, and Economics*, New York: Routledge.

Sutter, R. (2009) 'The Obama administration and US policy in Asia', *Contemporary Southeast Asia*, 31 (2): 189–216.

Thayer, C. A. (2010) 'US–Vietnam relations: a scorecard', *Asia-Pacific Bulletin*, 67, 14 September.

The Times & Transcript (New Brunswick) (2009) *The U.S. is back: Clinton; Remarks made in Asia as she prepares to join regional security conference*, 22 July.

The White House, Office of the Press Secretary (2011) *Remarks By President Obama to the Australian Parliament*, 17 November, https://www.whitehouse.gov/the-press-office/2011/11/17/remarks-president-obama-australian-parliament.

US–ASEAN Business Council (2003) Statement of the US–ASEAN Business Council on the signing of the US–Singapore Free Trade Agreement, www.us-asean.org/press_releases/2003/singapore_fta_signing.asp.

Wardhana, A. (1994) 'The Pacific Rim challenge' in H. Soesastro (ed.), *Indonesian Perspectives on APEC and Regional Cooperation in Asia Pacific*, Jakarta: CSIS.

Zoellick, R. (2001) 'Countering terror with trade', *Washington Post*, 20 September: A35.

3 The Chinese century?

Rémy Davison

Introduction

The People's Republic of China (PRC) is now a global power with a major economic presence on every continent. China accomplished its transformation into the world's second-biggest economy without shedding its communist leadership; without democratizing; and without fighting a single major war. More importantly, it achieved its economic success without being a US satellite, as Germany and Japan were compelled to do following the Second World War. China should no longer be referred to as an 'emerging power'; the PRC's emergence phase is complete and China is now a great power. Like all great powers past and present, the PRC is now seeking to consolidate and extend its power projection both regionally and globally. To accomplish this, Beijing is in the midst of constructing a series of 'Great Walls' (Osawa 2013): the 'Great Firewall' of cyberspace; the 'Great Wall at Sea' in the South and East China Seas (Cole 2001); and, potentially, a network of Air Defence Identification Zones (ADIZ), forming a 'Great Wall in the Sky'.

China's transformation into a global economic power is well known, but its military modernization is also well advanced. In 2015, China officially spent US$ 146 billion on defence, an 11 per cent increase over 2014. However, most analysts put a higher figure (US$ 165–US$ 214 billion) on the PRC's military spending (CSIS 2016). Moreover, in 2012, Asia's defence spending overtook Europe's for the first time, driven principally by China's expansionary military budget and Europe's austerity-induced defence programs. This was not a one-off event: by 2015, Asia was outspending European militaries by 36 per cent (Stanley-Lockman and Wolf 2016: 1).

Nevertheless, China's military power remains concentrated in the Asia-Pacific region for the time being. This chapter examines the main actors in the Asia-Pacific region with which the PRC interacts: Taiwan, North Korea, Japan and the US. The national security interests of these states are integrally linked; tensions between the PRC and Taiwan persist; and North Korea's nuclear weapons capabilities pose a renewed threat to regional security. Concomitantly, the PRC has developed extensive economic linkages with its Asia-Pacific neighbours, which has not only made China the centripetal economic force in the region, but has also transformed Asia into a global production powerhouse. The depth of China's regional and global engagement is evidenced by the fact that Beijing has now concluded over 40 regional economic and security agreements in the Asia-Pacific and 15 free trade agreements (FTAs) worldwide, with a further 15 either under consideration or under negotiation (PRC Ministry of Commerce 2017). This includes the much-vaunted, plurilateral Regional Comprehensive Economic Partnership (RCEP), between ASEAN, India, China, Japan, Australia and New Zealand (see Chapter 10). The centrality of China to the global economy represents almost half a century of engagement with the West and industrial modernization, in stark contrast with Cold War China's political isolation and economic atrophy.

The emergence of the People's Republic of China

Mao Zedong's accession to power in 1949 represented a seminal moment in China's history, particularly as the formation of the PRC came at a pivotal point of the Cold War. In 1948, the Soviet Union had effectively completed its takeover of most of Eastern Europe. Mao's revolution, and his alliance with the USSR, suggested that international communism was in the ascendancy. The result was a freezing of relations between the PRC and the West for almost a quarter of a century. The Nationalist Kuomintang (KMT) regime, which retained control over Taiwan, was recognized as the *de jure* government of the Republic of China (ROC), and remained a permanent United Nations Security Council (UNSC) member until 1971.

However, the relationship between the Soviet Union, the 'senior partner' in the relationship, quickly turned frosty, culminating in the Sino–Soviet split of 1957–61. Nevertheless, it took another decade before US policy-makers appreciated the depth of the split, and the PRC remained a pariah state in international relations. Effectively, 1949 meant the separation of China into the 'four Chinas': British Hong Kong, Portuguese Macao, the PRC and the Republic of China (ROC), Taiwan. Within months of its formation, the PRC became embroiled in the Korean War.

Box 3.1 Summary of key events in China, 1925–2017

1925	Nationalist government established under Kuomintang.
1931	Japan occupies Manchuria.
1937	The Manchurian 'incident' results in the massacre of over 100,000 people.
1949	Mao Zedong's Chinese Communist Party assumes power and establishes the People's Republic of China (PRC). The Kuomintang Nationalist government occupies Taiwan and forms the Republic of China (ROC). ROC retains China's Permanent Membership of the United Nations Security Council (UNSC).
1950	Korean War commences, UNSC authorizes intervention, resulting in fighting between multinational forces, led by the US, and communist-backed North Korean forces. 200,000 PRC 'volunteers' cross border to assist North Korean forces.

1958 Second Five-Year Plan: the 'Great Leap Forward'.
1959 Soviets cease nuclear development assistance programme with PRC.
1964 France establishes diplomatic relations with the PRC, Soviet leader Khrushchev overthrown. PRC explodes first nuclear device.
1966 Commencement of the Cultural Revolution.
1971 Australian Labor leader Gough Whitlam visits Beijing during US Secretary of State Henry Kissinger's secret visit. US President Nixon announces that the US will support the PRC's entry into the UN. The UN General Assembly votes to admit the PRC to the UN and to expel the ROC. The ROC withdraws from the UN.
1972 US President Nixon visits Beijing.
Japan recognizes PRC and establishes diplomatic relations, PRC renounces all war reparations claims against Japan.
Whitlam government establishes diplomatic relations between Australia and PRC, and recognizes PRC as government of China.
1973 PRC seated as a Permanent Member of the UNSC.
1976 Death of Mao. End of the Cultural Revolution. Ascendancy of Deng Xiaoping.
1977 Deng establishes 'open door' trade and investment policy and Special Economic Zones.
1979 US normalizes relations with PRC.
Deng initiates economic reforms integrating 'socialism with Chinese characteristics'.
1989 Deng orders suppression of Tiananmen Square uprising.
1994 Jiang Zemin assumes effective control of government.
1995 Jiang releases 'Eight-Pronged Plan' on China–Taiwan relations.
China occupies Mischief Reef in South China Sea.
1996 PRC recommences nuclear tests. PRC conducts a series of weapons tests in Taiwan Strait.
1997 Death of Deng. Formal succession of Jiang Zemin. PRC reassumes sovereignty over Hong Kong.
Jiang and Russian President Boris Yeltsin issue the 'Joint Declaration on a multipolar world and the formation of a new strategic order'.
2000 US President Clinton signs China Trade Relations Act.
2001 PRC and Taiwan enter the World Trade Organization.
US spy plane crashes on Hainan Island.
PRC, Russia, Kazakhstan, Kyrgyzstan, Tajikistan and Uzbekistan form Shanghai Cooperation Organization (SCO).
2002 US government grants permanent normal trade status to PRC.
2003 Retirement of Jiang Zemin. Hu Jintao assumes presidency, with Wen Ziabao as prime minister.
PRC, North Korea, South Korea, US, Russia and Japan commence Six-Party Talks.
2005 France and Germany make abortive attempt to lift EU arms embargo on PRC.
2006 Hu Jintao and Manmohan Singh sign '10-Pronged Strategy'.
2008 Beijing Olympics. Riots in Tibetan capital Lhasa, 21 killed.
Hu Jintao visits Washington.

2009	Ethnic riots in Urumqi, Xinjiang region, 400 killed. President Obama visits Beijing. First BRIC summit, Yekaterinburg, Russia.
2010	PRC overtakes Japan to become world's second largest economy.
2012	Xi Jinping assumes presidency of the PRC. China seizes Scarborough Shoal in South China Sea. Chinese government protests Japanese purchase of Diaoyu/Senkaku islands.
2013	Construction of artificial reefs and islands commences in the South China Sea. China declares Air Defence Identification Zone (ADIZ) in East China Sea.
2014	Asian Infrastructure Investment Bank (AIIB) launched.
2015	BRICS' New Development Bank (NDB) promulgated.
2016	China rejects Permanent Court of Arbitration's ruling on the South China Sea.
2017	China warns Trump administration that 'One China' policy is non-negotiable.

Rapprochement: China turns West

The US dilemma of how to contain their communist adversaries represented a classic case of the policy divergence between conservatives and realists. For realists, such as Hans Morgenthau, a state was a state was a state; it made little difference whether it was communist or capitalist; totalitarian or democratic. All states, Morgenthau (1948) asserted, had similar interests: security and survival. Conversely, conservatives, such as Kennan (1947), argued that communism was an inherently aggressive ideology that required active containment. However, conservatives failed to acknowledge that the Chinese military response to the Korean War was a realist response to the threat on its border, not a consequence of its alliance with the USSR.

The conservative ascendancy within the US foreign policy establishment led to no significant policy shift towards China until 1969, when Richard Nixon assumed the presidency. Both Nixon and his National Security Advisor (later Secretary of State), Henry Kissinger adopted realist responses to the 'China question', as conservatives had not treated the 1957–61 Sino–Soviet split with sufficient seriousness. Realists argued that Chinese and Soviet interests were *national* interests, driven by security agendas, rather than socialist ideology; conversely, conservatives tended to regard all communist states – the USSR, China, North Vietnam, North Korea and Cuba – as a monolithic socialist bloc. All were notionally satellites of Moscow, rather than independent states with distinctly different national interests. Realists, by contrast, argued that if the US sought to advance its own national interest, it should align itself with China in order to balance Soviet power. Constructivists, such as Hemmer and Katzenstein (2002: 584), attribute this to the ideological distance between Washington and Beijing: 'Although conceivable in terms of material balance of power, for ideological reasons, communist China was not a plausible alliance partner for the United States after 1949'.

The turning point in Western relations with the PRC came in 1971–72, with the visit of Australian Labor leader (later prime minister) Gough Whitlam to Beijing in July 1971. Days later, US National Security Advisor Kissinger took a secret flight to Beijing, resulting in the announcement that US President Richard Nixon would visit the PRC in 1972. For both China and the US, this represented a critical turning point in China's relations with the world; for the US, it was a significant diplomatic victory over the Soviets. Some analysts credited the US's diplomatic *coup* with a thaw in Soviet–US relations, resulting in the 1972–79 period of *détente* between the superpowers.

Sino–American *rapprochement* resulted in the ROC's removal not only from permanent membership of the UN Security Council (UNSC), but also from the General Assembly. In effect, as a sovereign state, the ROC ceased to exist in 1971. In December 1972, the Australian government recognized the PRC, establishing diplomatic relations for the first time since 1949. In 1972, the PRC was also seated as one of the five permanent members of the UNSC. Nevertheless, the question of Taiwanese independence persisted. In response, the US developed the 'One China' policy, which meant that the US recognized the *de jure* sovereignty of the PRC. However, in practice, it did not mean an end to US support for Taiwanese political and economic independence from the mainland, which resulted in an increasingly complex triangular relationship between Beijing, Taipei and Washington by the end of the 20th century.

PRC–US relations

Nixon's remarkable *volte-face* on US–China relations led to the 1972 Sino–US joint communiqué which set out the principles of the US's 'One China' policy.

> The United States recognizes that all Chinese on either side of the Taiwan Strait maintain there is only one China and Taiwan is a part of China.

Although this statement satisfied Mao's government, by couching the 'One China' policy in deliberate ambiguity, the clear intent of the Nixon administration was to avoid offending Taipei, while simultaneously recognizing there were not two *de jure* governments of China. Concrete US confirmation of its recognition of the PRC's primacy came in 1971 with the removal of the ROC from its permanent seat on the UNSC and the seating of the PRC in its place.

Having stabilized relations with China following Nixon's 1972 visit, the US deprioritized the PRC, content with issuing three communiqués (1973, 1978, 1982) which dealt with US recognition of China, the 'One China' policy, and reductions in arms sales to Taiwan, respectively. Despite warmer relations, the US did not recognize the PRC until 1979, by which time Cold War hostilities with the USSR had recommenced. Simultaneously, the US passed the Taiwan Relations Act (TRA), which committed the US to 'oppos[ing] any effort to determine the future of Taiwan by other than peaceful means'. In practice, this meant that Washington would arm Taipei with an extensive array of increasingly high-tech weaponry. Furthermore, the 'Six Assurances' on Taiwan, issued by President Reagan in 1982, made it clear to Beijing that Washington would retain the freedom to determine its position on Taiwan's sovereignty. In 1994, Premier Jiang Zemin sought a fourth US–China communiqué which would eradicate any possibility that the US would either initiate high-level official visits to or from Taiwan, or countenance the establishment of diplomatic relations between Washington and Taipei. The Clinton administration ignored Beijing's overtures to develop a fourth communiqué and declined to host an official visit from Jiang, arguing that only democratic countries or states which shared the US's ideals were permitted state visits. Ultimately, a compromise was reached, with a Clinton–Jiang meeting at the fiftieth anniversary of the United Nations in New York in 1995 (van Kamenade 1997: 48–9), but the episode revealed that cracks were appearing in the Sino–American relationship.

Following the abortive conflict in the Taiwan Strait in 1996, the US launched several initiatives aimed at defusing tensions between Washington and Beijing. First, the Clinton administration opted to follow a 'national interest' approach to its China policy, abandoning the tepid attempts at containment of the early 1990s. US Secretary of State Warren Christopher argued that, 'We reject the counsel of those who seek to contain or isolate China.... That course would harm our national interests, not protect them. Demonizing China is as dangerously misleading as romanticizing it would be' (van Kamenade 1997: 51). Nevertheless, events such as the 1999 American bombing of the Chinese embassy in Belgrade, and the Hainan Island affair in 2001, demonstrated that Sino–American relations were easily ruptured.

During the 2000 US presidential election campaign, Bill Clinton and Vice President Gore argued that China was a 'strategic partner' of the United States. Conversely, Republican candidate George W. Bush and his future national security advisor, Condoleezza Rice, asserted that China was a 'strategic competitor', not a partner (Baum 2001: 191). However, despite the diplomatic hostilities in 2001 following the US spy plane crash over Hainan, Beijing's relationship with Washington during the administration of George W. Bush was stable, and Sino–American economic relations expanded at an unprecedented rate. Two significant events suggested US policy towards China was demonstrably conciliatory. First, neither Bush nor Congress sought to reverse or delay China's entry into the WTO in 2001. Second, the US granted China 'permanent normal trade status' from 2002 (Embassy of the PRC 2001a, 2001b, 2001c). However, China's WTO entry also meant that it would be subject to tighter monitoring by both the WTO and the US. Since its WTO entry, China has accumulated significant merchandise trade surpluses with the US. Despite the US's modest surplus in services trade with China, the PRC's traded goods surplus has grown from US$ 83 billion in 2001 to US$ 347 billion in 2016 (US Census Bureau 2017).

Considerable diplomatic differences remain in key areas of Sino–US relations. After 9/11, the Chinese government declared its public support for the US's 'war on terror' (Embassy of the PRC 2002); however, the two states were at significant variance over policy on Iraq, with Washington favouring military intervention, while Beijing argued that US military action in the absence of an explicit Security Council mandate was a gross breach of international law. The issue of US arms sales to Taiwan remains a persistent thorn in the Sino–American relationship. In December 2015, after four years of holding sales in abeyance, President Obama approved US$ 1.8 billion in arms transfers to the ROC (*New York Times* 17 December 2015). However, the Obama administration had already made clear its intention to contain China by implementing its 'Pivot to Asia' policy in 2010–11. The Pivot sought to redeploy the bulk of American military power away from the Middle East to the East Asian region (see Chapter 2).

The PRC's integration into the global economy

Since 1993, China has been the largest recipient of inward foreign direct investment (FDI), with total stock of FDI reaching US$ 2.33 trillion in 2015. The PRC dominated inward FDI flows in 2014 (totalling US$1.23 trillion) with over 10 per cent of total global investment hosted by China (US$ 129 billion) (IMF 2015). Two caveats should be noted. First, FDI volumes have been directed, increasingly, at the PRC's services and advanced manufacturing sectors, while low-cost manufacturing investment has declined in recent years. Second, almost half of China's inward FDI is sourced from Hong Kong, evidencing the territory's centrality (Jin 2016).

Moreover, the PRC has emerged in the last decade as a significant source of outward FDI, which increased over 20-fold, from US$ 44.7 billion in 2004 to over US$ 1 trillion in 2015. However, its net stock of global outward FDI is dwarfed by flows from the EU (US$ 9.2 trillion), the US (US$ 5.9 trillion) and Japan (US$ 1.2 trillion) (UNCTAD 2016: Table 4).

Japan and the US have emerged as China's most important trade partners, with US–China trade totalling approximately US$ 665 billion in 2015 while Japan was second with US$ 303 billion (US Census Bureau 2016, JETRO 2016). Hong Kong, although formally a special administrative zone of the PRC, is the country's third largest exporter (US$ 283 billion in 2015) to both the Chinese mainland and the rest of the world (HKTDC 2017). Taiwan is also critical to China's economy; it is the mainland's seventh largest trading partner and bilateral trade exceeds US$ 100 billion annually (*South China Morning Post* 24 September 2016). One of the key factors driving China's integration with the global economy was its entry with Taiwan into the WTO in 2001. Although WTO membership led to a tremendous increase in FDI and trade with China, WTO accession also compelled China to follow more stringent regulations. These included not only sweeping anti-piracy measures in accordance with WTO agreements on trade in intellectual property services (TRIPS), but also structural reforms to asset ownership and financial services deregulation. Of even more significance has been the partial lifting of the restriction on foreign ownership of Chinese financial sector assets. Fifty per cent is the current maximum permissible level of ownership, although despite government assurances, 49 per cent FDI caps remain in the majority of the financial services sector, with the exception of some securities trading companies (*Fortune* 30 December 2016). Moreover, even under the WTO regime, China's regulation of pension funds and securities remains tight, despite recent reforms; most FDIs are still restricted to 49 per cent ownership.

Exchange-rate policy reform has proven fractious in China–US relations. Beijing abandoned its fixed-exchange rate regime in 2005 and adopted a 'crawling peg' for the yuan renminbi (RMB), allowing the currency to appreciate against the US dollar. Nevertheless, China is frequently subject to accusations of currency manipulation by deliberately undervaluing the RMB in order to retain export competitiveness. In 2010, the US Treasury considered whether to sanction Beijing over currency manipulation, which pushed the People's Bank of China (PBOC) to abandon its RMB–US dollar peg (*Businessweek* 1 April 2010, CNN 2010). In part, this was belated recognition of the considerable depreciation of the US dollar and the US Federal Reserve's quantitative easing operations between 2009 and 2014 to pump liquidity into the US economy (Davison 2016). However, Beijing's reluctant concession on RMB–US dollar exchange rates merely represented an attempt to stave off the inflationary pressures wrought by the US dollar glut caused by the 2008–09 Global Financial Crisis (GFC). In 2016, Donald Trump described China as 'the grand champions at manipulation of currency', promising to label the PRC a currency manipulator on day one of his presidency. However, US Treasury Secretary Steven Mnuchin announced only regular reviews of foreign exchange markets, while the IMF's 2016 annual report noted that the yuan RMB's value 'remain[ed] broadly in line with fundamentals' (Bloomberg 2017). Moreover, after the first summit between Trump and Xi Jinping in April 2017, Trump stated that the Chinese '[were] not currency manipulators' (Reuters 2017b).

The PRC is the biggest holder of US Treasury bonds, making Beijing Washington's largest foreign creditor. In January 2016, the PRC held almost US$ 1.24 trillion in US Treasury securities, 10 per cent more than the second largest bond holder, Japan (US$ 1.12 trillion) (US Department of Treasury 2017). The key issue is whether China's amassing of US securities allows Beijing to exercise leverage over US policies it opposes. In February 2009, the PRC's increasing economic assertiveness was evidenced by Prime Minister Wen Jiabao's 'worries' over the security of US Treasury bonds (*Wall Street Journal* 24 March 2009), which implied that the US, by effectively printing money and accumulating record future deficits, would possess a decreasing capacity to meet its future financial liabilities. In March 2009, the governor of the Bank of China went further and called for the establishment of a new global reserve currency, effectively calling for an end to the dominant role of the dollar in the world economy, a position it has occupied since 1944. However, for all its financial sabre rattling, China remains heavily dependent on the US market; 21 per cent of PRC merchandise exports (including Hong Kong) went to the US in 2015 (WTO 2017). The US dollar has retained its status as the global reserve currency, with over 63 per cent of foreign reserves held in US dollars in the fourth quarter of

2016, accounting for 61 per cent of global holdings (IMF 2017); this was considerably higher than the dollar's lowest point as a reserve asset (59 per cent) in 1995 (ECB 2006: 19, IMF 2010). The relative vulnerability of the slowing PRC economy and the RMB was clearly apparent by 2015: in August 2015, the People's Bank of China (PBOC) sold off a record US$ 94 billion, reducing its foreign exchange reserves from a peak of US$ 4 trillion in June 2013 to US$ 3 trillion by early 2017. In August 2015, PBOC was forced to devalue the RMB by 2 per cent. Devaluation sent such shockwaves through global markets that it sparked off a brief, but unsettling, Chinese stock market sell-off. Panicked, PBOC sought to stabilize the yuan by selling off its foreign exchange reserves and buying the yuan in an effort to bolster the RMB. In an attempt to stem the flood of yuan exiting the economy, PBOC invoked capital controls in January 2017, requiring Chinese banks to match capital inflows with outflows. However, by April 2017, as liquidity became an issue in offshore RMB markets, such as Hong Kong, PBOC abandoned the policy (Reuters 2017c).

In reality, China is facing the inevitability of the globalization of its currency and its economy, despite the fact that the RMB is not a floating currency. By 2017, the PRC had signed over 30 bilateral currency swap deals, including deals with the EU, as well as offshore RMB currency trading in markets such as Tokyo. Consequently, the RMB has been thoroughly internationalized, albeit subject to limits. In addition, in September 2016, the IMF added the RMB to its basket of five reserve currencies, including the US dollar, the euro and the pound sterling, evidencing the transformation of both China's economy and currency over the past three decades (IMF 2016).

China and the Asia-Pacific region

China and Japan

Since the 1931 Japanese invasion of Manchuria, Sino–Japanese relations have been characterized by a mutuality of suspicion, which were exacerbated by Mao's accession to power in 1949 and the PRC's support for North Korea. The Japanese surrender in 1945 had resulted in the return of Taiwan and Penghu Islands to the Republic of China, and the Japanese government formally recognized the Nationalist government of Chiang Kai-shek. Japan's geostrategic location, together with its membership of the US-dominated Western alliance, meant it was much more vulnerable to potential attack from the communist triangle of the PRC, North Korea and the USSR.

Throughout most of the Mao era, Japan adopted a position of 'uncertainty' on jurisdiction over Taiwan. However, Sino–US *rapprochement* from 1971 forced Japan to assume a more conciliatory position towards China. In 1972, Japan recognized the PRC and established diplomatic relations, adopting the US's 'One China' policy at the same time. Article 3 of the Sino–Japanese Joint Statement on 29 September 1972 noted that:

> The government of the People's Republic of China reiterates that Taiwan is an inalienable part of the territory of the People's Republic of China. The government of Japan fully understands and respects this position of the government of the People's Republic of China, and shall firmly abide by the principles under Article 8 in the Potsdam Proclamation.

As a quid pro quo, the PRC renounced all war reparations claims against Japan. However, a number of issues remain outstanding. China continues to dispute the legality of the peace treaty signed between Japan and the ROC government at the conclusion of the Second World War. Moreover, China consistently raises objections to official contacts between Japanese governments and the Taipei regime.

The steady marketization of the Chinese economy from 1979 – which coincided with Japanese financial power reaching its zenith – saw Sino–Japanese trade and investment achieve impressive growth. As the engine of Asian financial and industrial growth, it was clear that modernization and industrialization in China would require strong links with Japan. Chinese loans from Japan peaked in 2000, but the PRC no longer required Japanese financing for its major projects; consequently, Tokyo terminated its ODA program for China in 2008.

However, difficulties in the Sino–Japanese relationship have remained, as China continues to be one of the key strategic actors in the region. Renewed attempts to remove or amend Article 9, the 'pacifist' article of the Japanese constitution, also causes alarm among Beijing elites, who view constitutional strictures as the key to maintaining Japan's largely defensive posture within the region. In 2014, Shinzō Abe's cabinet controversially 'reinterpreted' Article 9, circumventing constitutional reform, allowing Japanese forces to come to an ally's aid, a development without precedent since 1945. In 2016, Abe urged explicit constitutional reform, based on his draft amendments tabled in the Japanese parliament in 2012 (Richter 2016: 1225). In the draft, Abe sought to expand the role of the Self-Defense Forces (SDF), 'specif[ying] that Japan possesses the right to self-defense and stipulates that an organization will be set up for self-defense' (*Japan Times* 3 February 2016).

Interdependence theory would suggest that the economics of the close Sino–Japanese commercial relationship would spill over into political co-operation. However, 'hot economics' has resulted in 'cold politics' (Dreyer 2014), as Japan has increasingly sought to expand its military role in East Asia, while Beijing has grown increasingly assertive within areas considered as territorial waters by the Japanese government. Tokyo's formal acquisition of the Diaoyu/Senkaku islands in 2012 transformed the East China Sea (ECS) into a potential flashpoint. The islands, claimed by both China and Japan, lie only a few hundred kilometres from the US base at Okinawa, Taiwan and the Chinese mainland. Irrespective of oil, gas and fishing rights, the area is of critical strategic importance to the Japanese-American forces, Taipei and Beijing. Control of the ECS would not only give the PLA Navy (PLAN) the means to encircle and threaten Taiwan and Okinawa, but also allow the PLAN to break out into the Pacific Ocean.

In November 2013, tensions over the ECS saw Beijing declare an air defence identification zone (ADIZ). This in itself would have been routine and uncontroversial; however, Beijing established the ADIZ over the Diaoyu/Senkaku islands without any discussion with regional powers, an attempt, as Osawa (2013) describes it, to build a 'Great Wall in the sky', to implement the PLA's counter-intervention strategy of anti-access/area denial. In response, South Korea immediately declared its own ADIZ, which overlapped with China's zone. Within 48 hours, the US Air Force flew a nuclear-capable B52 bomber into the ADIZ without notifying the Chinese. Nevertheless, Washington did advise its civil aviation companies to identify themselves to the Chinese when traversing the ADIZ (Mahapatra 2014: 4). However, despite China warning a US bomber for entering the ADIZ in March 2017, this has not disrupted routine US military air operations (CNN 2017). The US recognizes Japan's control over the islands and the Trump administration has confirmed that the Senkakus fall within the ambit of the US–Japan Mutual Security Treaty (*Nikkei Asian Review* 13 February 2017).

Arguably, under Xi's presidency, China's growing assertiveness in the ECS and South China Sea (SCS) has served only to broaden military co-operation between Japan, the US and South Korea, thus increasing the likelihood of the encirclement of China, a strategic outcome Beijing wishes to avoid. Three dominant issues have emerged on the contemporary Sino–Japanese security and diplomatic agenda. These are: (i) the threat of a nuclear-capable North Korea; (ii) the US–Japanese military relationship; and (iii) Japan's relationship with Taiwan.

China and Taiwan

Tensions in the China–Taiwan relationship have their origins in the 1949 establishment of rival regimes in Taipei and Beijing. The ROC remained a permanent member of the UNSC until 1971, when it left the UN, rather than face a vote of expulsion. The PRC assumed Taiwan's UNSC seat in 1972. However, although Taiwan has moderated its claims regarding its legal jurisdiction over mainland China, it has largely conformed with the US-mandated doctrine of a 'One China' policy.

The 1950–53 Korean War saw an escalation in the PRC–ROC conflict as Beijing saw US intervention in Korea as a possible prelude to an invasion of the Chinese mainland in support of the Nationalist government. However, the stalemate in Korea, together with US policy-makers' conviction that the Moscow–Beijing–Pyongyang triangle formed a holistic communist bloc, froze relations between the US and China for almost twenty years, and American administrations continued to support the Taipei government. US–Chinese *rapprochement* from 1971 politically and diplomatically isolated the ROC. In international law, Taipei was no longer the *de jure* government of China. Taipei had supported a 'Dual Representation Complex' proposal, which involved keeping both Taipei and Beijing within the UN, while Beijing took over Taipei's seat on the UN Security Council (*Taipei Times* 12 September 2001: 3).

The security of Taiwan became – and remains – a linchpin of American policy in the region. The Taipei–Beijing relationship reached a flashpoint in 1996 during the Taiwanese elections, which threatened the introduction of a democratic Taipei government on China's doorstep. In March, Beijing provocatively announced surface-to-surface missile tests in close proximity to two Taiwanese ports; air force and naval exercises employing live ammunition in the Taiwan Strait; and a third set of air and sea-based exercises late in March (see Ross 2002). The US response was to send two aircraft carriers to the strait, purportedly both to monitor the PRC military exercises, as well to ensure regional stability during the Taiwanese elections. Although no confrontation took place, the crisis prompted a rethink of policy on both sides, which resulted in serious attempts at *rapprochement* during the second Clinton administration. In 2001, China's ambassador to the US said, 'The question of Taiwan has always been the most important and most sensitive issue at the heart of China–U.S. relations' (Jiechi 2001).

In 1995, Taiwan's president, Lee Teng-hui, made a strong speech calling for international recognition of Taiwan's legal independence of the PRC. The ROC has always rejected Beijing's 'One Country, Two Systems' doctrine, which implies that Taiwan lacks sovereignty. However, Lee's provocative stance did not go as far as rejecting official US or PRC policy concerning the 'One China' issue. In 1999, Lee clarified Taipei's position, stating that Taipei's position on the PRC was 'unchanged' and that peaceful unification with a democratic mainland China remained the objective. He consistently referred to Taiwan as a 'sovereign nation' and argued that the PRC should recognize Taiwan as a state (CNN 1999). However, US liberals argue that the very ambiguity of America's 'One China' policy is a strength, and encouraging Taiwanese independence merely gives the impression that the US is a threat to Chinese interests in the region (Bush 2002a). As Ross argues, 'rather than needlessly challenge Chinese security, the United States should use its strategic advantage to expand co-operation with China and maintain the security of Taiwan' (Ross 2002: 85). However, the Bush administration did not overturn the long-held US policy of 'strategic ambiguity' over Taiwan. But despite the considerable volume of US arms transfers to Taipei, President Bush explicitly ruled out support for Taiwanese independence. President Chen Shui-bian moderated his independence rhetoric in 2003, with the Taipei administration cautiously moving towards acceptance of a 'Hong Kong' model, albeit a strict Taiwanese interpretation, as a last-resort basis for negotiations with the mainland, should direct economic links between Taiwan and the mainland fail to be established (Christensen 2003). Nevertheless, Chen reasserted his 'two countries' doctrine in late 2003 as he sought re-election, with the rival KMT also supporting independence (*The Australian* 24 November 2003).

Tensions emerged between Beijing and Washington in 2004–05, following the re-emergence of the Taiwanese independence movement. Although the 2004 ROC election effectively ended short-term prospects for independence, the fourth-generation leadership in Beijing was sufficiently alarmed to introduce the Anti-Secession Law in 2005, which stated unequivocally that the PRC would use 'non-peaceful means' to ensure Taiwan did not become independent of China.

The law amounted to little more than a thinly amended version of Jiang's 'Eight Points' of 1995. However, it proved sufficient to discourage Taipei's pro-independence movement; indeed, during Hu Jintao's 2006 visit to Washington, President Bush reaffirmed the US's commitment to the 'One China' policy. Nevertheless, this commitment did not prevent the administration from canvassing the sale of further Aegis-class destroyers to Taipei. In the 1982 US–PRC joint communiqué, the US pledged to gradually reduce arms sales to Taiwan. However, the US continues to supply sophisticated weapons to Taipei, while the Pentagon co-operates with Taiwan on anti-ballistic missile research. In October 2008, Bush announced a US$ 6.4 billion arms package for Taiwan, including advanced PAC-3 Missile Defence Systems, which Washington also offered to Seoul. In response, Beijing suspended military-to-military contacts between the two countries. In 2009, the promulgation of the Obama administration did not see the realignment of US weapons exports policy towards Taiwan. In January 2010, the White House notified Congress of its first proposed arms sale to Taipei, resuscitating the 2008 Bush package; Obama had voted to approve the Taiwan arms sales in 2008. Beijing immediately responded by placing sanctions on US firms in China, such as Boeing, while protesting vociferously that 'the US decision seriously endangers China's national security and harms China's core interests' (*Los Angeles Times* 31 January 2010). Equally, however, Congress is suspicious enough of the PRC's Taiwan strategy to order annual studies of China's military modernization. The Pentagon alleges that China is not only developing short-range missiles capable of striking across the Taiwan Strait, but that the PRC may also be pointing missiles at American targets in an effort to prevent any attempt by US forces to block a possible future invasion (*International Herald Tribune* 31 July 2003, Office of the Secretary of Defense 2016).

Although US liberals may be less unambiguous about their support for the defence of Taiwan, they are united in their opposition to a stance on Taiwan that would commit the US to an armed conflict (Berry 2000). Richard Bush (2002b) argues that 'Beijing is willing to tolerate much about the United States' ties with Taiwan, but it cannot accept a public US rejection of its claims on this issue'. Liberals argue that the US should reiterate its commitment to the 1979 Taiwan Relations Act, which would compel the US to intervene only if China–Taiwan integration is not achieved by peaceful means, rather than damaging trade relations, deploying BMD or supplying military assistance to Taiwan. Cohen (2000: 10) argues that to 'reassure Taiwan and deter China, it will not suffice for Washington merely to transfer a few high-technology weapon systems, like Aegis-class cruisers for missile defence, to Taiwan'. He posits that although the US should continue supplies of military material to Taiwan, it should not use trade leverage as a means of deterring China from an assault on Taiwan. Further integration of China into the global economy might be more likely to achieve a peaceful resolution of the PRC–ROC issue. Arguably, the most revisionist aspect of PRC foreign policy remains its position on the Taiwan issue. In 2003, the CCP leadership under Hu Jintao vacillated between closer integration and hardline opposition to any semblance of independence from Taipei. Further complicating the situation were occasional *faux pas*, such as Major-General Zhu Chenghu's threat to strike 'hundreds of American cities' with nuclear weapons in the event of Sino–US conflict over Taiwan (Lieggi 2005). However, Beijing has quietly outmanoeuvred Taipei by employing its growing financial clout to reduce diplomatic recognition of the ROC (Wang 2007: 32–3); and it has blocked Taiwanese membership of UN agencies, such as the World Health Organization. In short, the PRC has succeeded in diminishing considerably the ROC's chances of achieving statehood, whilst ensuring that Taipei's forays into the rhetoric of independence remain unsupported by both the US and the broader UN membership.

Flashpoint: the South China Sea

No body of water is more hotly contested than the South China Sea (SCS). Seven littoral states have maritime claims in the SCS, the largest of which is that of the PRC, which claims the entire SCS as its 'historic waters', demarcated by a 'nine-dash line' drawn by the Chinese Nationalist government in 1947. Beijing currently asserts that 80 per cent of the SCS belongs to the PRC. The strategic importance of the SCS is undisputed: it houses arguably the world's most vital sea lines of communication (SLOC) and the largest volume of global trade navigates its maritime channels. Thus, freedom of navigation through the SCS is essential. Only the US has the capability to enforce freedom of passage through the SCS's international sea lines of communication. The US Seventh Fleet is headquartered and forward deployed at Yokosuka, and the fleet's 55 vessels patrol the disputed areas of the SCS. Nevertheless, as the PLA Navy has modernized, US strategists are increasingly concerned with Chinese 'carrier killers': warships equipped with Dong Feng-21 missiles designed to disable or destroy an aircraft carrier. Any confrontation between the two navies could seriously disrupt relations between Beijing and Washington.

The SCS is also critical to the energy security of China, Taiwan, South Korea and Japan, as it is the main transit passage for Persian Gulf oil to East Asia. Furthermore, its fishing grounds are central to the food security of Indonesia, Vietnam, Malaysia, China and the Philippines. Some analysts even characterize the SCS conflict as a 'fishing dispute', rather than an oil dispute (Schofield *et al.* 2016). Neither perspective is entirely accurate. China currently imports more than 40 per cent of its oil requirements and the SCS represents a potentially reliable source of oil and natural gas. Beijing's narrative has emphasized that its aim in the SCS is gas and oil exploration; however, exploration has shown that SCS oil and gas reserves are not as extensive as claimed, and are difficult to access. Both China National Offshore Oil Corporation (CNOOC) and China National Petroleum Corporation (CNPC) have cancelled oil exploration projects since 2014. PRC government estimates have also significantly exaggerated SCS energy reserves; it is more likely that the PRC could only obtain oil and gas supplies equivalent to a mere six months of Chinese imports (*Forbes* 25 April 2016).

The SCS issue came to a head when the Permanent Court of Arbitration (PCA) ruled in July 2016 on a maritime claim made by the Philippines. Beijing refused to recognize the jurisdiction of the PCA in this case, despite being a party to the Third United Nations Convention on the Law of the Sea (UNCLOS III). Seven years earlier, China had responded to rival exclusive economic zone (EEZ) claims by Vietnam and Malaysia. For the first time, China deposited the 'nine-dash line' map as a legal instrument with the UN, thus demonstrating the seriousness with which Beijing viewed its SCS claim. Prior to the PCA's judgment, China submitted an *amicus curiae* (friend of the court) brief via a Hong Kong NGO that outlined the legal arguments Beijing would have tendered in defence, had it been a party to the proceedings (APIIL 2016).

Neither Jiang Zemin during the 1995–96 Taiwan Strait dispute, nor Hu Jintao seriously tested the red lines implicit in the PRC's claims in the South China Sea. Instead, conflict was contained: Jiang backed down in the face of US naval power in 1996, while Hu argued in 2012 that it was essential for China to become a 'maritime power' in order to achieve its national goals. However, it is under Xi Jinping's leadership that China has constructed the 'Great Wall of sand' in the SCS, assembling artificial reefs, pouring cement into islets and building aircraft runways on islands. If China succeeds with this strategy, it will ultimately transform the SCS into a Chinese lake (Davison 2012a, 2012b).

Beijing's divide-and-rule strategy produced major divisions within ASEAN over the SCS issue. China successfully negotiated a four-point consensus with Brunei, Cambodia and Laos prior to the PCA ruling. However, the strategic milieu in the SCS and ECS has become more complex. ASEAN has suffered from the law of unintended consequences: the ARF and APT commenced as Asian dialogue fora, but have unwittingly given China an entrée into the geopolitics of Southeast Asia. As Davison (2006, 2008: 109) and Jones and Smith (2007) note, the Code of Conduct on the SCS (2002) commits APT to recognize non-binding precepts that consigned ASEAN claims in the SCS to Track II dialogue fora. In effect, Beijing has outmanoeuvred ASEAN with its soft power strategy, compelling its APT partners to accept that the SCS question will be resolved diplomatically. When the Philippines sought to utilize international maritime law to rule on the SCS, Beijing refused to respond to the case, and, instead, commenced using force to militarize the SCS unlawfully from 2014. As Jones and Smith (2007: 180) argue, 'it becomes clear that the APT and its unwieldy offshoot, the East Asian Community, has little to do with constructing a shared East Asian identity and a lot to do with the realist pursuit of state interests'. Beijing's 'Great Wall of sand' strategy worked: despite the Philippines' protestations at China's militarization of the SCS, President Duterte appeared to abandon his Washington partner and tilt towards Beijing, offering to develop SCS oil reserves jointly, demonstrating the effectiveness of China's coercive diplomacy (*Forbes* 4 January 2017).

China and North Korea

The 1953 armistice left the Korean Peninsula question unresolved. As South Korea developed into a tiger economy in the 1980s, North Korea remained a relic of the Cold War: a diplomatically isolated communist state with high levels of poverty. China has remained North Korea's largest trade partner and it supplies an estimated 70 per cent of Pyongyang's oil (*China Reform Monitor* 2003). By 2003, the North Korean regime of Kim Jong-Il had expelled UN weapons inspectors and announced the recommencement of the country's nuclear weapons programme. More ominously, Pyongyang's two ballistic missile tests over Japan and the Sea of Japan provoked alarm in Tokyo.

The Bush administration labelled North Korea part of the 'axis of evil', which included Iraq and Iran. However, Beijing proved to be conspicuously silent in the midst of North Korea's new-found assertiveness. The *Asian Wall Street Journal* (16 January 2003) editorialized,

> China is the one country most reluctant to dislodge Kim Jong-il. For all the giveaways in Seoul's 'sunshine policy', the amount of aid that flows from South Korea is still only a fraction of the support Beijing provides in propping up its faltering communist neighbour.

Despite Chinese protestations to the contrary, reports persist of Beijing's exportation of dual-use materials to Pyongyang, including materiel that could utilized in North Korea's nuclear weapons program (McDonald 2016). Although Beijing prefers 'No war, no instability, no nukes' (Glaser and Billingsley 2012: 1) on the Korean Peninsula, the PRC continues to support North Korea because it fears a refugee crisis if it ceases supplying Kim Jong-Un's regime. Moreover, Kim's regime would likely become even more unpredictable if Beijing withdrew material support, as the PRC accounts for almost 90 per cent of North Korea's trade (Gray 2016). However, despite Beijing's frustration with Pyongyang's nuclear weapons program, Chinese Foreign Minister Wang Yi reiterated China's commitment to North Korea, arguing the two countries were 'as close as lips and teeth' (Godemont 2017).

China's intercession as a mediator between the US and North Korea is largely designed to portray the PRC as an 'honest broker' in regional affairs. Beijing hosted trilateral talks between the US, North Korea and China in April 2003. However, it was clear that Beijing sought a quid pro quo on US–Taiwan relations as a result of its mediation efforts with North Korea. Until 2005, bilateral PRC meetings with the DPRK emphasized denuclearization issues. However, since North Korea's first ballistic missile test in 2006 the PRC leadership has abandoned this agenda and has not raised it again. Beijing has frustrated Washington by its refusal to take a harder line on North Korea. Although it is highly unlikely that Beijing would support North Korean military action against South Korea in the event of a pre-emptive attack, China's support for tough UNSC-sanctioned resolutions against Pyongyang is an even more remote possibility. However, there are strong incentives for Beijing to moderate North Korea's behaviour. As Christensen argues, 'Taiwan is not the most likely flashpoint for US–China relations in the near term…North Korea is' (Christensen 2003).

The test launch of two ballistic missiles by North Korea in 1998 created alarm in Japan, as one missile landed in the Sea of Japan while the other flew over the country. In May 2003, Japanese Prime Minister Koizumi sought Chinese President Hu Jintao's intercession over the North Korean issue to defuse tensions between the US and North Korea. Three days of talks took place between Chinese, North Korean and US officials, although China refused to include Japan, Russia or South Korea in the trilateral dialogue. Despite Beijing's claim that it is a mediator in the dispute, few doubt China's need to stress its great power status and its unrivalled influence over North Korean policy. Not only was Japan excluded, but China has kept the UN at arm's length, in marked contrast to its policy on Iraq.

Beijing and Pyongyang maintain an uneasy, yet interdependent, relationship. On the one hand, North Korea has proven a useful pawn in China's long-term regional strategy, which, ultimately, aims to denuclearize the Pacific and push US military forces out of the region. To this end, Pyongyang is a bargaining chip employed by Beijing to secure the Korean Peninsula to prevent it from becoming a launching pad for offensive operations against China (Liping 2009: 241).

China remains North Korea's most important partner, supplying the regime with significant material support. Indeed, it is unlikely that Pyongyang could survive without the infusion of Chinese supplies, which vastly exceed the aid donated by South Korea to the DPRK under the 'sunshine policy'. Beijing is also widely suspected of proliferating nuclear technologies to Pyongyang. In 2003, the CIA reported that China had supplied raw materials to the DPRK to aid the extraction of plutonium from spent uranium – and plutonium devices have proven to be the core element of North Korea's nuclear program. Following the CIA report, the PRC tacitly acknowledged its partial veracity at least by tightening export controls across the common border.

Nevertheless, US policy-makers have long been convinced that Beijing is not serious in its efforts to discourage North Korea's efforts to gain a nuclear weapons capacity. Washington diplomats generally view China's management of the Six-Party Talks as hypocritical and self-serving, arguing that China could reduce the volume of military and dual-use exports it routinely supplies the DPRK. Moreover, Beijing has done nothing to encourage more moderate elements within the North Korean leadership. Consequently, it is scarcely surprising that the Washington foreign and defence policy establishment largely regards Pyongyang as Beijing's proxy; China employs the DPRK's nuclear ambitions as leverage against its principal Asia-Pacific competitors – the US, Japan and South Korea; it achieves concessions and compliance when it seeks issue linkage. Indirectly, too, Beijing's policy destabilizes Western interests in other regions such as the Middle East; for example, Pyongyang has previously acted as a 'proxy nuclear proliferator' to Libya and Syria.

Beijing's strategic partnership: the Shanghai Cooperation Organization

Arguably, one of the most important developments in China's relationship with the Russian Federation was the 1991 Sino–Russian border agreement that ended decades of sporadic military disputation (see Chapter 5). Subsequent agreements in 1994, 1998 and 2004 resolved outstanding border issues and the North Korean border. Importantly, the demilitarization of 4,200 km of the Sino–Russian border allowed China to shift its force capabilities south, giving the PLA considerably more personnel on its south, west and eastern flanks. Given this context, it is unlikely that the SCO could have been formed without the initial 1991 resolution of the border issue. In 1996, China and Russia agreed to develop a strategic partnership of equality, mutual confidence and mutual co-ordination. Article 3 of the 2000 Beijing Declaration specifically noted Sino–Russian opposition to US hegemony:

> defy hegemonism, power politics and group politics, and oppose attempts to amend the basic principles of international law, to threaten others by force or to interfere in other countries' internal affairs.
>
> (People's Daily 2000)

The most important aspect of the Beijing Declaration was Russia's recognition of China's sovereignty over Taiwan, the acceptance of a 'One China' doctrine and an explicit rejection of Taiwanese independence. In this respect, the SCO has proven to be an influential diplomatic instrument with which China exercises leverage within a region where Beijing does not have significant force projection. The SCO has also proven to be a particularly useful tool to thwart the American presence in Central Asia, although, clearly, Russia remains the dominant strategic influence in Central Asia. The SCO has expanded both Beijing's and Moscow's influence in Central and South Asia. At the 2015 Ufa summit, members agreed to enlarge the SCO, admitting India and Pakistan; both states signed formal accession documents at the 2016 Tashkent summit, with entry taking place in June 2017.

The 1995–96 Taiwan Strait crisis had demonstrated that the US was prepared to deploy substantial military assets to the South China Sea in response to Beijing's show of force against the ROC. The timing was significant in that, only a month after this incident, a Sino–Russian *entente* produced the 'Shanghai Five' agreement, which drew together two great powers that found themselves decidedly short of potential alliance partners. Together with China and Russia, the Shanghai parties comprised Tajikistan, Kazakhstan and Kyrgyzstan, and the agreement, expanded in mid-2001 to include Uzbekistan, was renamed the Shanghai Cooperation Organization (SCO), which has the status of a permanent international organization (IO) (Lentini 2004). In 2004, Mongolia gained observer status to the SCO. At the 2005 Astana summit, Washington's application for SCO observer status was rejected, most likely as a result of the US's continued military presence in Central Asia. India and Pakistan formally acceded to the SCO in June 2017.

However, Iran, despite Russian backing, was refused membership by China in June 2016, a position that was at odds with Xi Jinping's joint statement with President Rouhani in Tehran in January 2016, where Xi expressed support for Tehran's application for full SCO membership.

From the outset, the impetus behind Shanghai and the SCO was China, rather than Russia, demonstrated by the headquartering of the SCO's secretariat in Beijing, with the counterterrorism centre in Shanghai, while the Regional Anti-Terrorist Structure (RATS) is based in Tashkent. However, China and Russia are the key actors in the Shanghai process; for example, in July 2015, the PBOC and the Central Bank of Russia signed an agreement on bilateral trade, expanding RMB–rouble payments between Chinese and Russian banks. The *rapprochement* between the PRC and Russia, a distinct departure from the frosty relationship between the two great powers throughout Gorbachev's presidency of the USSR, achieved new heights in 2005, with the first ever Sino–Russian joint military exercises. These were extended to the largest SCO drills hosted by China in 2014, together with the SCO's first joint exercises in Kyrgyzstan in 2016 (*The Diplomat* 29 August 2014, *Eurasianet* 19 September 2016).

The enlargement and consolidation of the SCO was a direct response to an expanded American and NATO presence in Uzbekistan, Tajikistan and Kyrghyzstan after 9/11, prior to the invasion of Afghanistan. US and NATO forces established bases in Uzbekistan, Kyrgyzstan and Tajikistan (Khodarenok 2002). Alarmed at the US-NATO forces' presence in Central Asia, Beijing and Moscow increasingly pressured governments in the region, particularly the Kyrgyz regime, to close the US base (Blank 2003). In 2005, the Chinese and Russian governments persuaded SCO members to request a formal deadline for US evacuation of bases in Kyrgyzstan and Uzbekistan, while in July 2005, Uzbekistan also demanded that US forces leave their base in Karshi-Khanabad. Beijing promptly attempted to gain control of the Uzbek base, but was thwarted by Moscow, which negotiated access rights. In 2014, the US closed its last base in Kyrgyzstan (*The Diplomat* 10 June 2014). In this respect, the Beijing–Moscow SCO axis proved extremely adept at pushing back American strategic expansion into Central Asia.

Within the SCO, Sino–Russian interdependence has also increased. Beijing needs stability, rather than competition, from Moscow, while Russia's military-industrial complex needs PRC capital. China has US$ 8 billion in arms contracts with Russia, including advanced Su-35 fighter aircraft and surface-to-air missiles. Despite close co-operation, Sino–Russian relations have experienced tensions due to China's reverse engineering and cloning of a number of Russian military technologies. However, this has not proven sufficient to disrupt the bilateral relationship, although Moscow will not sell Beijing its most sensitive military technologies (*Financial Times* 3 November 2016).

Rising China: contending perspectives

How do analysts approach the question of emerging Chinese power in the Asia-Pacific region? Should China be contained, balanced and encircled? Or should it be integrated into the global economy and economic institutions? Does China represent a new pole of politico-economic power, having outlasted the USSR and eclipsed Russia, while developing as a major competitor of Japan, both economically and strategically?

The questions surrounding China's rise continue to vex analysts of PRC foreign policy: Beijing's public diplomacy emphasizes 'multipolarism' and opposition to 'hegemonism', while official PRC foreign policy extols China's 'Five Principles of Peaceful Co-existence' and the 'New Security Concept'. The cumulative effect is designed to reassure the PRC's partners and rivals that Beijing seeks co-operation, not conflict, but the regime's lack of transparency renders its real policy objectives opaque. The concept of China's 'peaceful rise' was originally coined by the chair of the China Reform Forum, Zheng Bijian. Bijian (2005: 24) argues that 'as it emerges as a great power, China knows that its continued development depends on world peace – a peace that its development will in turn reinforce'. By contrast, Robert Kaplan's (2005) provocative article, 'How we would fight China', asserts that Beijing's challenge to Washington's power will likely be played out as a naval competition for control of the SLOC of Pacific Asia.

Offensive realists, such as John Mearsheimer, argue that China's objective, as it emerges as a regional power, is to drive US forces from the East Asian region. China does not possess the military capability to challenge the US in the Asia-Pacific currently, but it may achieve sufficient force strength to do so within the next 30 years. For Mearsheimer (2005), China 'cannot rise peacefully'. Conversely, 'liberal realists', such as Zbigniew Brzezinski, former National Security Advisor to President Carter, assert that China is unlikely to embark on a foreign policy strategy that would damage its economic growth. Moreover, Brzezinski (2005: 47) asserts, the PRC is 'clearly assimilating into the international system'.

The Mearsheimer-Brzezinski debate – one of many in a crowded field of conjecture on Chinese foreign policy – exposes the difficulties associated with predicting states' intentions. Realists and liberals essentially adopt different views of the 'power transition' theory, first advanced by Kenneth Organski. Organski (1958) argues that rising great powers which become dissatisfied with the status quo ultimately transform into military challengers of the dominant power. War is most likely, asserts Organski, when a challenger achieves relative military parity with the dominant power. Furthermore, a state's 'political capacity' – defined by Organski as the government's authority to control and allocate internal resources – renders the situation more volatile, as a challenger directs an increasing proportion of its GDP to the production of military materiel.

Realists assert that power transition theory provides an apt description of emerging China, particularly given its authoritarian governmental structure and high proportion of state ownership. For realists, threat equals capability plus intention. But the most important question is how to gauge China's intentions. Most China analysts believe Beijing's tactics involve predominantly soft power economic initiatives, backed by growing hard power military capabilities. Viewed through this lens, one can identify the likely ingredients of the 'Beijing strategy' (see Box 3.2).

US policy-makers tend to believe the international system works best with a single leader; conversely, China, together with Russia, has sought to balance US power through sponsoring multilateral initiatives, such as the Asian Infrastructure Investment Bank (AIIB) and the Regional Comprehensive Economic Partnership. We discuss these in more detail in Chapter 10. Realists argue that China's resort to multilateralism is merely an indication of weakness, not strength, and only by building bilateral and multilateral partnerships throughout Asia and beyond – such as the AIIB – can Beijing hope to galvanize sufficient support to oppose, modify or block the US's dominant politico-economic role in the Asia-Pacific and globally.

By contrast, liberal approaches stress co-operation, rather than conflict, and integration, rather than division, when dealing with China's emergence as a great power. The Clinton administration to some extent exemplified the liberal position, which sought to draw the PRC into the US-led multilateral trade and investment system. Economic liberals recognized the centrality of China to the US financial and manufacturing sectors, and encouraged Washington to see the PRC as a partner, rather than a rival, in the global economy. Clinton supported the inclusion of both the PRC and Taiwan as members of the WTO, as this would benefit both China and the US. WTO membership would also compel China to liberalize its markets and adhere to a rules-based international trade regime. China, liberals argued, would then become more heavily dependent on, integrated with and enmeshed into the Western liberal capitalist economic system. Conversely, the Obama administration excluded Beijing from its major 'mega-regional' free trade initiative, the Trans-Pacific Partnership (TPP), which included 12 members from East Asia, the Pacific and the Americas. Obama's deployment of the 'Pivot to Asia' policy underscored his realist assessment of strategic competition in the East Asian region. That said, President Clinton's 'liberal' orientation should not be overstated: it was on Assistant Secretary of Defence Nye's initiative that the concept of an expanded defence role for Japan was explored and implemented from 1997, clear recognition that containment of China in the Asia-Pacific remained a first-tier objective on the US strategic agenda; it was Clinton who sent overwhelming American naval force into the Taiwan Strait in 1996; and it was Clinton who approved and signed NMD into existence, a defence system widely viewed by the Chinese leadership as not only directed at containing China, but also providing a means of strategically encircling China.

From a dependency perspective, China's ability to transform itself from a first-tier NIC to become, potentially, a core state in the capitalist world economy is critical to its emergence as a power of global significance. In this respect, China will need to avoid the pitfalls of path-dependency that have befallen other significant actors, such as India. China arguably remains on the semi-periphery of

Box 3.2 The 'Beijing strategy'

'One Belt, One Road' initiative	The 'New Silk Road' initiative, announced by President Xi Jinping in November 2014, involves US$ 40 billion in infrastructural investment. It envisages an 'economic belt' from Xi'an, China, linking Turkmenistan and Tajikistan in Central Asia, to Iran, Turkey, Russia, Germany and the Netherlands. China's 'Maritime Silk Road' aims to link the ports of Fuzhou, Guangzhou, Haikou, Hanoi, Kuala Lumpur, Jakarta, Kolkata, Colombo, Nairobi, Athens and Venice. The 'China–Pakistan Economic Corridor' would link Chinese Kashgar to Pakistani Gwadar.
Counter US theatre missile defence in the Asia-Pacific	This strategy is centred around China's acquisition of a blue-water naval capability. Its main weapon to achieve this goal will be a number of aircraft carriers and nuclear submarines currently under development. Nuclear-powered and armed submarines will vastly enhance China's capability to threaten the efficacy of US and Japanese ship-based TMD, particularly with the deployment of the Dong Feng 'aircraft carrier killer' missiles.
Employ North Korea as a bargaining chip to denuclearize the Pacific	Although one of Beijing's own priorities is its nuclear weapons capabilities, a complementary objective is to ensure that Japan and South Korea do not develop into nuclear weapons states. To this end, China is likely to argue for a nuclear weapons-free zone on the Korean Peninsula and the East China Sea. However, at present, Pyongyang has damaged this strategy by withdrawing from the Six-Party Talks in 2009, and adopting a much more belligerent tone towards the US. North Korea has undertaken more than 10 missile tests since 2012. Any peaceful resolution of the North Korean question will require China's co-operation, as the Trump administration must secure Xi Jinping's co-operation to convene talks with Pyongyang.

Prevent Taiwanese independence	The Taiwanese independence movement has experienced considerable setbacks, and this, combined with the ambiguity of Washington's security guarantee to Taipei, has reassured Beijing that the US will not countenance support for a formal declaration of Taiwanese independence, although Trump's phone call with Tsai caused questions about Washington's commitment to the 'One China' policy. Taiwan has purchased advanced Patriot and Harpoon missiles. Washington has only permitted upgrades for Taiwan's F-16 aircraft, rather than replacements, in order to placate Beijing (*Defence News* 24 January 2017).
Form a major power concert	Hu Jintao's medium-term strategy demanded the maintenance of the current status quo. However, Xi Jinping has adopted a more coercive strategic stance in the SCS and ECS, and increasingly coercive diplomacy towards regional neighbours, such as the Philippines, Indonesia, Japan, Singapore and Taiwan (Ayson and Pardesi 2017, Glaser 2012). As ASEAN cannot prevent China's military aggrandizement of the SCS, Beijing's preference is to utilize 'concert diplomacy' as a security regime for the Asia-Pacific.
Separate India and Pakistan from the US via economic diplomacy	The PRC has traditionally co-operated with Pakistan in order to balance India's conventional and nuclear power. Substantial evidence documents China's covert nuclear assistance to Pakistan's nuclear program since the 1970s (see Corera 2006), with the clear objective of focusing India's military attention westward. More recently, however, the PRC has sought *détente* with India and closer economic co-operation with Pakistan. In 2001, Beijing committed US$ 620 million in economic aid to Islamabad, while in 2009, US$ 700 million of Chinese energy investments in Pakistan were signed. A Sino–Pakistani FTA was signed in 2007. As a key element of the 'One Belt, One Road' initiative, the US$ 46 billion China–Pakistan Economic Corridor (CPEC), commenced in 2016, links overland gas and oil exports from the Middle East to Pakistan and China.

Court Southeast and South Asian, African and Iranian diplomatic and economic co-operation through a combination of ODA, 'protective diplomacy' and in international organizations (IOs)	Pursue the 'String of Pearls' strategy to open up port access for PRC vessels in Southeast Asia and South Asia. Increase trade and investment partnerships with Africa. China is Africa's biggest trading partner, with merchandise trade totalling US$ 160 billion in 2014, The PRC's strategy in Africa has largely targeted energy-rich countries, and three regimes with poor human rights records – the Republic of Congo, Nigeria and Sudan – are Beijing's principal partners on the continent. China has also made rare use of its UNSC veto to protect its other partners, such as Zimbabwe, when Beijing vetoed sanctions against the Mugabe regime in 2008. The PRC also abstained four times in relation to the Darfur conflict in 2004–06. In 2009, the PRC also abstained on a UNSCR authorizing sanctions on Eritrea, a decade-long partner of Beijing. Eritrea, like Sudan, is resource rich, but it is also geostrategically important, as a littoral state of the Red Sea, and bordering Sudan. In the Gulf, China has a vested interest in supporting the current Iranian regime. Beijing is Tehran's chief arms supplier and the two countries have signed energy partnerships of considerable significance, such as the Yadavaran oil and gas field development (Davison 2008: 267). The Sino–Iranian deal on LNG output from Yadavaran is valued at US$ 100 billion, while by 2017, PRC oil firms were extracting up to 700,000 barrels of oil per day from Iran (Reuters 2017a).
Soft balance US via Moscow–Tehran axis	Neither China nor Russia can confront the US directly via hard, military means. Consequently, the strategic architecture of the 21st century is dominated by 'strategic partnerships', rather than formal, binding military alliances (Davison 2008: 4–5). Acting in concert, Beijing and Moscow can appear to be responsible international actors in multilateral and regional fora, rather than 'veto players' and 'spoilers'. North Korea cannot confront the US directly, but is a plausible threat to both the Korean Peninsula and Japan. Beijing has expended considerable effort in managing relations with Pyongyang and projects itself as the only government that can moderate North Korea's behaviour. Moscow provides significant assistance to the modernization of Chinese military technologies, but Beijing remains the senior partner in the SCO.

Draw SE Asia into PRC (and out of US and Japanese) sphere of influence via economic diplomacy	China's accession to the ARF (1993), the ASEAN Dialogue Process (1996) and the China–ASEAN FTA (2003) integrated the PRC more closely with Southeast Asia. However, although China threatens the viability of ASEAN primary and secondary industries, the ASEAN–China FTA offers Southeast Asian countries increased access to the world's largest single internal market. But China's recent denunciation of the Permanent Court of Arbitration's ruling on the SCS damaged the PRC's soft power diplomatic thrust into the region; most ASEAN members co-operate militarily with Washington. In Southeast Asia, Hu Jintao's cautious approach has been abandoned and Xi Jinping's coercive diplomacy, including the militarization of the SCS and the deployment of Chinese weapons systems to its islands, has led to severe tensions between the PRC and ASEAN. China's potential declaration of an ADIZ in the SCS could also rupture China–ASEAN relations.

the world economy; despite its rapid development, agriculture still provided employment to 30 per cent of the labour force in 2012 (ADB 2014: 1). Economic liberals advocate further privatization, financial sector deregulation and a private ownership-based society in order to avoid the 'middle-income trap' (Woo 2012: 332). Conversely, neo-Marxist perspectives frequently view China's emergence as a counter-hegemonic, countervailing force in the region as a direct response to US–Japanese military and economic dominance of the Asia-Pacific. However, Wallerstein (1997, 1998) argues that it is difficult to predict whether China will be able to displace Japan as the dominant Asian power in the region. Analyses, such as Deng's (1998: 316), argue that 'the post-Mao China seems to have turned dependency theory on its head', due to 'dense interdependence' in the global economic system (Deng 1998: 308). With US$ 3 trillion in foreign exchange reserves (*Trading Economics* 1 March 2017), US$ 1.23 trillion in a burgeoning share of global investment and export markets, together with emerging multinational firms, China has shifted from the semi-periphery in 1978 to become virtually a core economy in scarcely four decades. Indeed, the PRC's burgeoning economic linkages with Latin America and Africa are increasingly assuming the form of core–periphery relationships (Jenkins 2012, Kaplinsky and Morris 2009). Yet, Beijing still has major economic security concerns: it is heavily dependent on energy imports, particularly oil, gas and coal from Iran, Africa and Australia; 21 per cent of Chinese goods are exported to the US (more if one includes Hong Kong and PRC manufactures shipped from Taiwan); and it is also compelled to 'import' US inflation to some extent, given the artificial RMB–US dollar peg (NAB 2016, USTR 2016, WTO 2016: 137). China's dependency on an export-geared economy, predicated on trade surpluses, continues to cause friction, particularly in the US, where during the 2016 presidential election campaign, candidate Donald Trump threatened a 45 per cent tariff on Chinese goods (*Fortune* 24 November 2016). China's dependency on export markets was aptly illustrated in a World Bank report, which noted that China's declining trade surplus, due to surging imports and reduced global demand, has produced a major deterioration in its terms of trade in the wake of the GFC (World Bank 2010).

A 'Beijing consensus'?

The term 'Beijing Consensus' was coined by Joshua Ramo in the 1990s, and elements of it are discernible in the 'Beijing Strategy' outlined in this chapter. However, realists and liberals are deeply divided over whether the Chinese leadership possesses a 'grand strategy' to achieve pre-eminence in international politics. Proponents of the 'China threat' thesis point to the widely cited Goldman Sachs (2003) BRIC report, which predicted that Brazil, Russia, India and China would overtake the GDP of the world's six largest economies within 40 years; the PRC's growth rate would consistently outstrip that of the developed states; and China would overtake the US as the world's largest economy in 2045. Neoconservatives, such as Robert Kaplan (2010), cite China's expanding naval capabilities and its 'String of Pearls' or 'Pearl Harbours' strategy, designed, ultimately, to deny US forces access to ports and bases in Southeast Asia and the Indian Ocean. In addition, hawkish assessments of PRC maritime power, such as the RAND (2010) report, argue that the US will no longer be capable of defending Taiwan against Chinese aggression by 2020.

However, no analyst can predict with any certainty the business and economic cycles that China – and much less the world economy – will experience throughout the next four decades. Despite the advent of the NDB and leaders' summits, little has come of the BRICS initiative. Goldman Sachs itself closed its BRICS department in 2015, citing major losses (Bloomberg 2015). Beijing faces considerable challenges: an ageing population due to the lost generations under the 'one-child' policy; and rising urban incomes while rural wages atrophy, leading to a 'scissors crisis', where the chasm between urban and rural prices and incomes becomes unbridgeable. It is highly unlikely that China can sustain such high levels of inequality, particularly given that its regional development is also deeply uneven (Yao 2010). Western observers commonly view China's vast population as an asset to its international competitiveness; CCP elites view population issues differently: China's financial and material resources need to be divided, not multiplied, by 1.3 billion.

Conclusions

PRC foreign policy has been realistic in its implementation, if not its articulation. However, realists, neoconservatives and liberals differ markedly over how to deal with China's growing military and economic importance. Realists, in the Obama administration, emphasized alliance diplomacy and offshore balancing of Chinese power, exemplified by the 'Pivot to Asia' policy, while neoconservatives argue that China needs to be contained and constrained, as characterized by the Bush administration's attempts to develop reconfigured security alliances in the region with Japan and Australia. US liberal approaches to Asia-Pacific security are different again: the Clinton administration sought to integrate China into the globalization project, arguing that an economically interdependent PRC is less likely to threaten others by placing its own national interests in jeopardy. The Trump administration faces a formidable challenge, as it deals with an increasingly assertive Beijing that is prepared to defy international law and militarize the South China Sea. If China succeeds in occupying the South China Sea, annexing the Senkakus and implementing the 'String of Pearls' and 'One Belt, One Road' initiatives, then the American 'Pivot to Asia' will have failed.

The CCP leadership's lack of transparency renders assessments of its foreign policy intentions exceptionally difficult. Official documents, such as the PRC's 10th Defence White Paper (DWP), requires the PLAN to undergo a transformation from coastal to global force, evidencing an ambitious maritime strategy, exemplified by the PLAN's new nuclear submarines and aircraft carriers under development (PRC 2015). China is clearly serious about assembling a blue-water naval capability with the capacity to deploy well beyond China's coastlines and EEZs. In April 2017, the PLAN launched its first indigenously developed aircraft carrier (*New York Times* 25 April 2017). Defence spending has grown measurably to the point that, together with India, China is one of the world's biggest arms importers and exporters. However, China's published defence expenditures defy credulity, with independent analysts asserting that the genuine figures are considerably higher. Officially, China preaches multilateralism, but, in practice, it deals bilaterally with both its partners and rivals: it resists WTO multilateral liberalization initiatives – evidenced by the abortive 2003 Cancun talks – and strikes bilateral trade deals with ASEAN; it resists membership of the ARF, preferring to describe itself as a 'participant'; it claims to embrace globalization, yet prosecutes a vigorous censorship regime; and it forms uncritical economic partnerships with regimes with records of serious human rights abuses, such as Sudan, Iran, Nigeria and Zimbabwe (Davison 2014). In light of these facts, it is scarcely surprising that most strategic analysts are convinced that China's rise will be anything but peaceful. If the collective strategy of the US, Japan, India, South Korea and ASEAN has been to ensure that Beijing cannot implement a 'Chinese Monroe doctrine' in the three China seas, then this strategy is dangerously close to failing.

References

Asia Pacific Institute of International Law (APIIL) (2016) 'On the issue of the efficacy of the award on the merits and factual/legal errors existing in the jurisdictional award released on 29 October 2015', Amicus curiae submission by the Asia Pacific Institute of International Law, 6 June, www.fredkan.com/mavista/upload/File/APIIL%20 Amicus%20curiae%20brief%20&%20Appendix%20(1).pdf.

Asian Development Bank (ADB) (2014) 'The declining share of agricultural employment in the People's Republic of China: how fast?' *ADB Economics Working Paper Series*, no. 419.

Ayson, R. and M. Pardesi (2017) 'Asia's diplomacy of violence: China–US coercion and regional order', *Survival*, 59 (2): 85–124.

Baum, R. (2001) 'From "strategic partners" to "strategic competitors": George W. Bush and the politics of U.S. China policy', *Journal of East Asian Studies*, 1: 191–200.

Berry, N. (2000) 'Maintaining the one-China policy makes good sense: a commentary', Center for Defense Information, 24 August. www.cdi.org/asia/fa082400.html.

Bijian, Z. (2005) 'China's "peaceful rise" to great-power status', *Foreign Affairs*, 84 (5): 18–24.

Blank, S. (2003) 'Scramble for Central Asian bases', *Asia Times*, 9 April.

Bloomberg (2015) 'Goldman's BRIC era ends as fund folds after years of losses', 9 November, https://www.bloomberg.com/news/articles/2015-11-08/goldman-s-bric-era-ends-as-fund-closes-after-years-of-losses.

Bloomberg (2017) 'Mnuchin says he won't label China a currency manipulator...yet', 24 February, https://www.bloomberg.com/politics/articles/2017-02-23/mnuchin-sees-no-china-yuan-decision-until-at-least-april-report.

Brzezinski, Z. (2005) 'Make money, not war', *Foreign Policy*, 146: 46–7.

Bush, R. C. (2002a) 'China's leadership transition: implications for cross-Strait and US–China relations', Brookings Institution, Center for Northeast Asian Policy Studies, 16 November.

Bush, R. C. (2002b) 'American ambiguity on Taiwan's sovereignty increases the island's safety', *Insight*, 4 December, https://www.brookings.edu/opinions/american-ambiguity-on-taiwans-sovereignty-increases-the-islands-safety/.

Centre for Strategic and International Studies (CSIS) (2016) 'What does China really spend on its military?' Washington, DC: CSIS, http://chinapower.csis.org/military-spending/.

China Reform Monitor (2003) 'Beijing's Korea goal: remove U.S. military and political influence from Asia', 483, 6 February.

Christensen, T. J. (2003) 'Optimistic trends and near-term challenges: Sino–American security relations in early 2003', *China Leadership Monitor*, June.

CNN (1999) '"One-China" policy remains unchanged, Taiwan says', broadcast 14 July.

CNN (2010) 'U.S. delays report on alleged China currency manipulation', 4 April, http://edition.cnn.com/2010/WORLD/asiapcf/04/04/us.china.treasury/.

CNN (2017) 'Chinese officials warned US bomber during "routine" East China Sea flyover', 25 March, http://edition.cnn.com/2017/03/22/politics/china-us-aircraft-warned/.

Cohen, E. A. (2000) '"One China" policy is obsolete', *Wall Street Journal*, 21 March.

Cole, B. (2001) *The Great Wall at Sea: China's Navy Enters the 21st Century*, Annapolis: US Naval Institute Press.

Corera, G. (2006), *Shopping for Bombs: Nuclear Proliferation, Global Insecurity and the Rise and Fall of the A.Q. Khan network*, Oxford: Oxford University Press.

Davison, R. (2006) 'Dangerous liaisons: China, ASEAN, the U.S. and the South China Sea', Proceedings of the Fulbright Symposium on Maritime Governance and Security in the Asia-Pacific, Hobart, 28–29 June, http://pandora.nla.gov.au/pan/66596/20061222-0000/www.utas.edu.au/government/Fulbright2006/papers.html.

Davison, R. (2008) *Foreign Policies of the Great and Emerging Powers*, Frenchs Forrest, NSW: Prentice Hall.

Davison, R. (2012a) 'Australian appeasement: the slow boat to China', *The Conversation*, 25 May, http://theconversation.com/australian-appeasement-the-slow-boat-to-china-7224.

Davison, R. (2012b) 'Review: The China Choice: why America needs to share power', *The Conversation*, 31 August, http://theconversation.com/the-china-choice-why-america-needs-to-share-power-9196.

Davison, R. (2014) 'Between Beijing and Washington: Danger. Here be dragons' in D. Baldino, A. Carr and A. Langlois (eds), *Australian Foreign Policy: Controversies and Debates*, Melbourne: Oxford University Press.

Davison, R. (2016) 'Quantitative easing', *EcoDate*, 30 (1): 3–6.

Deng, Y. (1998) 'The Chinese conception of national interests in international relations', *The China Quarterly*, 154: 308–29.

Dreyer, J. (2014) 'China and Japan: Hot Economics, Cold Politics', *Orbis*, 58 (3): 326–41.

Embassy of the PRC (US) (2001a) 'US seriously violates international law', press release, 15 April.

Embassy of the PRC (US) (2001b) 'Bush hails China's entry into WTO', press release, 11 November.

Embassy of the PRC (US) (2001c) 'US president grants permanent normal trade status to China', press release, 28 December.

Embassy of the PRC (US) (2002) 'China welcomes US stance on anti-terrorism', press release, 26 August.

European Central Bank (ECB) (2006) *The Accumulation of Foreign Reserves*, Occasional Paper Series, no. 43, Frankfurt: ECB.

Glaser, B. (2012) 'China's coercive economic diplomacy: a new and worrying trend', Center for Strategic and International Studies, 6 August, https://www.csis.org/analysis/chinas-coercive-economic-diplomacy-new-and-worrying-trend.

Glaser, B. and B. Billingsley (2012) *Reordering Chinese Priorities on the Korean Peninsula*, Washington, DC: Center for Strategic & International Studies.

Godemont, F. (2017) 'China and North Korea: a test case for China's future international role', European Council on Foreign Relations, 17 March, www.ecfr.eu/article/commentary_china_and_north_korea_a_test_case_for_chinas_future_internationa.

Goldman Sachs (2003) 'Dreaming with BRICs: the path to 2050', Global Economics Paper, no. 99.

Gray, K. (2016) 'Sanctions haven't transformed North Korea – but trade with China might', *The Conversation*, 29 November, https://theconversation.com/sanctions-havent-transformed-north-korea-but-trade-with-china-might-68945.

Hemmer, C. and P. J. Katzenstein (2002) 'Why is there no NATO in Asia? Collective identity, regionalism, and the origins of multilateralism', *International Organization*, 56: 575–607.

Hong Kong Trade Development Council (HKTDC) (2017) 'Economic and Trade Information on Hong Kong', 27 January, http://hong-kong-economy-research.hktdc.com/business-news/article/Market-Environment/Economic-and-Trade-Information-on-Hong-Kong/etihk/en/1/1X000000/1X09OVUL.htm.

International Monetary Fund (IMF) (2010) 'Currency composition of official foreign exchange reserves', www.imf.org/external/np/sta/cofer/eng/cofer.pdf.

International Monetary Fund (2015) 'The coordinated direct investment survey guide 2015', 8 October, https://www.imf.org/external/pubs/cat/longres.aspx?sk=42945.0.

International Monetary Fund (2016) 'IMF launches new SDR basket including Chinese renminbi, determines new currency amounts', press release no. 16/440, 30 September, www.imf.org/en/News/Articles/2016/09/30/AM16-PR16440-IMF-Launches-New-SDR-Basket-Including-Chinese-Renminbi.

International Monetary Fund (2017) 'Currency composition of official foreign exchange reserves (COFER)' 31 March, http://data.imf.org/?sk=E6A5F467-C14B-4AA8-9F6D-5A09EC4E62A4.

Japan External Trade Organization (JETRO) (2016) 'JETRO survey: Analysis of Japan–China Trade in 2015', 17 February, https://www.jetro.go.jp/en/news/releases/2016/c52b1f3efe0aa231.html.

Jenkins, R. (2012) 'Latin America and China – a new dependency?' *Third World Quarterly*, 33 (7): 1337–58.

Jiechi, Y. (2001) 'Cold War mentality vs. warm hopes for the new century', speech to the US–China Policy Foundation, 23 April.

Jin, I. (2016) 'China's inward FDI flowing to service and advanced manufacturing sectors', Asia Pacific Foundation of Canada, 27 June, www.asiapacific.ca/blog/chinas-inward-fdi-flowing-service-and-advanced-manufacturing.

Jones, D. M. and M. L. R. Smith (2007) 'Making process, not progress: ASEAN and the evolving East Asian regional order', *International Security*, 32: 148–84.

Kaplan, R. (2005) 'How we would fight China', *The Atlantic*, June.

Kaplan, R. (2010) 'The geography of Chinese power', *Foreign Affairs*, 89: 3.

Kaplinsky, R. and M. Morris (2009) 'Chinese FDI in Sub-Saharan Africa: engaging with large dragons', *The European Journal of Development Research*, 21 (4): 551–69.

Kennan, G. F. ('X') (1947) 'The sources of Soviet conduct', *Foreign Affairs*, 25: 566–82.

Khodarenok, M. (2002) 'Russia surrounded by military bases', Nezavisimoye Voennoye Obozreniye, no. 10, reproduced by the Centre for Defence Information. Original CDI source not available; only internet source *Wikileaks*, https://wikileaks.org/gifiles/attach/176/176379_090709%20Soviet%20Bases%20in%20CA.doc

Lentini, P. (2004) 'The Shanghai Cooperation Organization and Central Asia' in M. Vicziany, D. Wright-Neville and P. Lentini (eds), *Regional Security in the Asia-Pacific: 9/11 and After*, Cheltenham: Edward Elgar.

Lieggi, S. (2005) 'Going beyond the stir: the strategic realities of China's no-first-use policy', NTI Issue Brief, December, www.nti.org/e_research/e3_70.html.

Liping, X. (2009) 'How China thinks about national security' in R. Huisken (ed.), *Rising China: Power and Reassurance*, Canberra: Australian National University E Press.

Mahapatra, C. (2014) 'China and air defence identification zone (ADIZ): cold confrontation with the US?' in T. Singh (ed.), *China and the Air Defence Identification Zone (ADIZ)*, New Delhi: Institute of Peace and Conflict Studies.

McDonald, J. (2016) 'Chinese company "sold North Korea nuclear bomb materials"', *The Independent*, 21 September. www.independent.co.uk/news/business/news/china-north-korea-nuclear-bomb-company-investigation-a7320266.html.

Mearsheimer, J. (2005) 'Better to be Godzilla than Bambi', *Foreign Policy*, 146: 47–8.

Morgenthau, H. J. (1948) *Politics among Nations*, New York: Knopf.

National Australia Bank (NAB) (2016) 'China economic update', December, http://business.nab.com.au/wp-content/uploads/2016/12/China-Economic-Update-161216.pdf.

Office of the Secretary of Defense (2016) *Annual Report to Congress: Military and Security Developments Involving the People's Republic of China 2016*, Washington, DC: Department of Defense, https://www.defense.gov/Portals/1/Documents/pubs/2016%20China%20Military%20Power%20Report.pdf.

Organski, A. F. K. (1958) *World Politics*, New York: Knopf.

Osawa, J. (2013) 'China's ADIZ over the East China Sea: a "Great Wall in the Sky"?' Brookings Institution, 17 December, https://www.brookings.edu/opinions/chinas-adiz-over-the-east-china-sea-a-great-wall-in-the-sky/.

People's Daily (2000) 'China, Russia Issue Beijing Declaration', 18 July, http://en.people.cn/english/200007/18/eng20000718_45780.html.

People's Republic of China (PRC) (2015) *China's Military Strategy*, The State Council Information Office, 27 May, http://english.gov.cn/archive/white_paper/2015/05/27/content_281475115610833.htm.

People's Republic of China (PRC), Ministry of Commerce (2017) 'China FTA network', 31 January, http://fta.mofcom.gov.cn/english/.

Ramo, J. (2004) *The Beijing Consensus*, London: The Foreign Policy Centre.

RAND Corporation (2010) *Questions of Balance: The Shifting Cross-Strait Balance and Implications for the US*, Santa Monica: RAND.

Reuters (2017a) 'China's Iran oil imports to hit record on new production: sources', 5 January, http://uk.reuters.com/article/us-china-iran-oil-idUSKBN14P15W.

Reuters (2017b) 'Trump backs away from labeling China a currency manipulator', 12 April, www.reuters.com/article/us-usa-trump-currency-idUSKBN17E2L8.

Reuters (2017c) 'China relaxes some cross-border capital curbs as yuan steadies: sources', 19 April, www.reuters.com/article/us-china-economy-capital-controls-idUSKBN17L0M2.

Richter, J. (2016) 'Japan's "reinterpretation" of Article 9: a Pyrrhic victory for American foreign policy?' *Iowa Law Review*, 101: 1223–62.

Ross, R. S. (2002) 'Navigating the Taiwan Strait: deterrence, escalation, dominance, and U.S.–China relations', *International Security*, 27: 48–85.

Schofield, C., R. Sumalia and W. Cheung (2016) 'Fishing, not oil, is at the heart of the South China Sea dispute', *The Conversation*, 16 August, http://theconversation.com/fishing-not-oil-is-at-the-heart-of-the-south-china-sea-dispute-63580.

Stanley-Lockman, Z. and K. Wolf (2016) 'European defence spending 2015: the force awakens', Issue Brief, European Union Institute for Strategic Studies, March.

United Nations Conference on Trade and Development (UNCTAD) (2016) *World Investment Report 2016*, 21 June, http://unctad.org/en/Pages/DIAE/World%20Investment%20Report/Annex-Tables.aspx.

US Census Bureau (2016) 'U.S. trade in goods and services by selected countries and areas – BOP basis', press release, https://www.census.gov/foreign-trade/Press-Release/current_press_release/exh20.pdf.

US Census Bureau (2017) 'Trade in goods with China', 4 April, https://www.census.gov/foreign-trade/balance/c5700.html.

US Department of Treasury (2017) 'Major foreign holdings of US Treasury securities', 15 March, http://ticdata.treasury.gov/Publish/mfh.txt.

US Trade Representative (USTR) (2016) 'The People's Republic of China', https://ustr.gov/countries-regions/china-mongolia-taiwan/peoples-republic-china.

van Kamenade, W. (1997) *China, Hong Kong, Taiwan Inc.: The Dynamics of a New Empire*, New York: Knopf.

Wallerstein, I. (1997) 'The rise of East Asia, or the world-system in the twenty-first century', keynote address at Institute of International Studies Symposium on Perspective of the Capitalist World-System in the Beginning of the Twenty-First Century, Meiji Gakuin University, 23–24 January.

Wallerstein, I. (1998) 'The so-called Asian crisis: geopolitics in the Longue Durée', paper delivered to the International Studies Association Meeting, Minneapolis, 17–21 March.

Wang, J. (2007) 'Hu Jintao's "New Thinking" on Cross-Strait relations', *American Foreign Policy Interests*, 29 (1): 23–34.

Woo, W. T. (2012) 'China meets the middle-income trap: the large potholes in the road to catching-up', *Journal of Chinese Economic and Business Studies*, 10 (4): 313–36.

World Bank (2010) 'China Quarterly Update', June, http://documents.worldbank.org/curated/en/126261468021847068/pdf/551310NEWS0Qua10Box349441B01PUBLIC1.pdf.

World Trade Organization (WTO) (2016) *World Trade Statistical Review*, Geneva: WTO.

World Trade Organization (WTO) (2017) 'Trade profiles – China', WTO Statistics Database, http://stat.wto.org/CountryProfile/WSDBCountryPFView.aspx?Country=CN.

Yao, Y. (2010) 'The end of the Beijing Consensus', *Foreign Affairs*, 2 February, www.foreignaffairs.com/articles/65947/the-end-of-the-beijing-consensus?page=show.

4 Between a doctrine and hard place

Japan's emerging role

Michael K. Connors

At a press conference in 2015 Japanese Prime Minister Shinzō Abe described Japan's then 62-year-old Japan–US alliance as the cornerstone of his country's national security. He went on to ask,

> If Japan is attacked, the U.S. Forces will spare no effort in defending it.... Even if those U.S. Forces on duty to protect Japan are attacked, we cannot do anything, we will not do anything, unless Japan itself is attacked. That has been Japan's position to date. Does this really make sense?
>
> (Abe 2015)

Abe's question has been posed in various forms since the 1950s. Can Japan maintain a military force? If so, can such forces be deployed overseas? Can they use weapons? Can they participate in collective defence? The answer to these questions depends on how one interprets Article 9 of the Japanese constitution, which states:

> Aspiring sincerely to an international peace based on justice and order, the Japanese people forever renounce war as a sovereign right of the nation and the threat or use of force as a means of settling international disputes.
>
> In order to accomplish the purpose of the preceding paragraph, land, sea, and air forces, as well as other war potential, will never be maintained. The right of belligerency of the state will not be recognized.

By the end of the 1950s a dominant interpretation of Article 9 had congealed and would hold good until the end of the Cold War. That interpretation allowed for a military force to exist that did not constitute war potential and which could not be deployed overseas or engage in collective defence. Subsequent interpretative disputes about Article 9 have centred on whether proposed legislation or policy would exceed the limits of minimal self-defence either by force used or area of application. Beginning in the early 1990s the dominant interpretation began to be challenged and by the early 2000s 'normalization' of a full Japanese military force was underway.

Central in these developments, especially after 2000, has been a political orientation described as neoconservativism, of which Abe is considered a main player. Neoconservatism seeks to overcome the military limitations imposed by Japan's pacifist identity. Neoconservatism, both in policy and ideological terms, is identified with a deepening of US–Japan ties to respond to perceived threats from China and North Korea and also involves a positive reappraisal of Japanese traditions and identity (Takahashi 2010). It views the post-Second World War regime – Japan's enforced pacifism – as debilitating. Significantly, expansion of Japan's security posture and in the role of the Japan Self-Defense Forces (JSDF) has accompanied the long tenure of two broadly defined neoconservative prime ministers – fellow traveller Junichiro Koizumi (2001–06) and adherent Shinzō Abe (2006–07; 2012–present).

Neoconservatives, among others, consider that the pacifist straightjacket imposed by Article 9 has infantalized Japan. During the early 2000s, amidst deteriorating relations with China and North Korea, Koizumi secured passage of legislation concerning terrorism, JSDF deployment to Iraq, national emergencies and enhanced US–Japan security co-operation. Like Koizumi before him, Abe has relied on constitutional reinterpretation rather than the politically troubling option of constitutional revision to extend Japan's military capacity and role. His speech cited above presaged an extensive legislative package enacted in 2015 which extends Japan's contribution to the Japan–US alliance and may be seen as a direct response to a perceived China threat. The 2015 legislation enhanced Japan's commitment to the international liberal order by legislating greater geographic reach and capacity in SDF involvement in UN peace-keeping, continuing a process begun in the early 1990s. It also allowed involvement in non-UN peace-keeping operations, enabling deployment when UN consensus is wanting and groups of states outside of a UN mandate decide to act. This represents a major change. Second, and most controversially, the legislation extended Japan's contribution to the power politics of the US–Japan alliance by allowing the SDF to engage in collective defence, under restrictive conditions, which hitherto had been proscribed.

For some ultra-nationalists Abe's speech and legislative program restored a modest measure of national prestige, but did not go far enough. For peace activists, it went too far, and marked the penultimate step towards full militarization of the Japanese state and the end of its pacifist commitments (which will presumably come with constitutional revision). As if this political divide could be bridged by a euphemism, Abe described his approach as 'Proactive pacifism', futilely attempting to assuage two irreconcilable forces to the right and left of him: 'pro-activism' as a salve for the insatiable impatience of ultra-nationalists for recovering Japan's place in the world, and 'pacifism' as a salve for the fears of anti-militarists who viewed the 2015 legislation, in combination with increased military budgets and revised 2014 guidelines on US–Japan military co-operation, as signs of further remilitarization.

These conflicting political perspectives are partly mirrored in ongoing theoretical debates about the meaning of Japan's post-Cold War military transformation. Is Japan stepping up to play a deepened role in supporting the international liberal order structured by US hegemony as a recalibrated 'international state' with peaceful intentions (Singh 2008), or has it become a 'reluctant realist' forced by circumstance to flex its muscle (Green 2001)? Or perhaps major ideological changes within Japanese politics have enabled a military 'coming of age' as realists would expect of a major economic power? A related question then is whether under Abe Japan has moved towards fulfilling realist predictions of engaging in self-help strategies to mitigate security dilemmas and anarchy, or whether it remains, as Drifte (1998: 5) describes, a 'paradox of unrealized power'. To explore these questions the chapter commences with a brief account of Japan's transformation from defeated empire to a so-called insular 'pacifist state' during the Cold War and the emergence of the Yoshida doctrine. Its post-Cold War trajectory towards greater regional and global engagement is then described, as are security dilemmas focused on China and North Korea. The chapter closes by returning to the politics of Article 9 and offers remarks on the how various theoretical stances impact interpretations of Japan's burgeoning role.

Opening Japan: black ships

The arrival in 1853 of Commodore Perry's 'black ships' (so called because of the black smoke of the coal engines) marked the intensification of Japan's modern engagement with the Western state system. Perry delivered an ostensibly polite request from President Fillmore that Japan extend its limited trading relationships to include the United States of America. The presence of warships indicated a more demanding posture. This event played a part in bringing an end to the Edo period (1600–1868) and stimulating modernization of the state and industry. From the 1870s to the 1940s Japan acted like similarly late industrializing states (Germany and Italy, for example), in that it adapted domestic conservative ideologies, such as the samurai code of ethics and emperor worship, to mobilize the population around industrialization, militaristic nationalism and imperial expansion (Pempel 1998: 4).

By a determined process of 'catching up' with the great powers of Europe, Japan acquired a significant military force. It was victorious in the Sino–Japanese war (1894–95), and the Russo-Japanese war (1904–05). In the wake of these victories Japan moved to take control of Formosa (Taiwan) and Korea respectively. As a colonial power its repression of independence movements and the imposition of legal and language policies was severe. Japan aimed at hierarchical assimilation of its colonial subjects. Speaking to a journalist in 1906 one Japanese official in Korea explained: 'If you ask me as an individual what is to be the outcome of our policy, I see only one end.... The Korean people will be absorbed by the Japanese. They will talk our language, live our life, and be an integral part of us' (cited in Townsend 2000: 128).

Japan became increasingly belligerent regarding China, extending its position in Manchuria into formal rule, and displacing Russian influence. Fearing the nationalist movement in China, in 1932 the occupying Japanese force declared the puppet state of 'Manchukuo' and maintained tight control of the region. In 1936 an alliance of Chinese Nationalist and Communist forces emerged and the second Sino–Japanese war followed (1937–45). The Japanese captured the capital of the Chinese Republic, Nanjing, in 1937. Grotesque and brutal massacres of civilian populations were widely reported, with some 200,000 to 300,000 people slaughtered (see Yang 1999).

Throughout the Second World War, the Japanese controlled the eastern coastal areas of the Chinese mainland. The war in Europe provided a window of opportunity for the seizure of more territories. In 1940 Japan allied itself with Germany and Italy (the Tripartite Pact), and entered a new period of expansionism. After bombing Pearl Harbor, Japan moved to 'liberate' the Western colonies of the Philippines, French Indochina, Malaya, Indonesia and Myanmar (1941–42) (Beasley 1991).

Lingering aftermath: Japanese imperialism

Japan's imperialism was in part a product of the international state system. The mid-19th century was the heyday of free trade, but from the 1880s onwards Western states began a scramble for empire in an effort to secure access to raw materials and markets for their commodities. Japan as a late-starter, and resource poor, thus confronted an Asia dominated by Western powers and found its modernizing ambitions of 'rich nation, strong army' frustrated.

In this context Japanese intellectuals and officials began to propagate the idea of pan-Asianism – the idea that all Asian peoples had a common interest in defying the 'white man'. The flavour of this sentiment is found in the writings of nationalist Tokutomi Soho:

> The countries of the white men are already extending to the forefront of Japan. They have encroached on China, India and Persia.... We, Japanese, should take care of the yellow man.... We should proclaim that the mission of the Japanese Empire is to fully implement an Asian Monroe Doctrine.
>
> (cited in Susumu 2001: 24)

The Japanese 'Asian Monroe Doctrine', an informal idea, legitimated Japan's move into China in the 1930s. By the early 1940s Japan's pursuit of a 'Greater East Asia Co-Prosperity Sphere' was accelerated by its entry into the Second World War. Ideally, occupied territories would be governed by the benign and civilizing Japanese elite who would assist in economic development. In constructing a Japanese-controlled region, Japan would form the industrial centre and colonies or puppet states would supply labour and raw materials. Despite the rhetoric of Asian solidarity and independence, Japanese colonialism and occupation, like European colonialism, was a bloody and traumatic experience. Potent remembrance of Japan's actions in former colonies and occupied territories remains a challenge in Japan's relations with its formerly subjected peoples, who view it as not having learned the lessons of its belligerence (Field 1997).

From surrender to economic power

The conventional view is that the dropping of atomic bombs by the United States in August 1945 on the cities of Hiroshima (6 August) and Nagasaki (9 August), killing over 150,000 people instantly, was necessary. It forced Japan's surrender on 9 August, saving the lives of thousands of Allied soldiers. A revisionist view is that the Japanese surrender was not a product of this mass killing, to which the Japanese command had become habituated, even if the new weapon was shocking. For example, conventional bombing of Tokyo on 9–10 March 1945 had killed over 120,000 people (Wilson 2013). Rather, surrender was forced by the Soviet Union abrogating its Neutrality Pact with Japan and invading Manchuria in the early morning of 9 August. This ended the Japanese government's hope of using Stalin to mediate settlement talks that would avoid US demands for unconditional surrender. Having invaded Manchuria, the Soviets were believed to be planning to invade Japan within two weeks through Hokkaido. Having already shifted troops south to defend against a US attack, the prospect of the opening of a second front forced Japan's hand (see Wilson 2013). Relatedly, some historians argue that the use of atomic bombs was primarily intended to signal US superiority to the Soviets and a warning to limit their advance; unlike Europe, Japan would not be divided. If so, this was the first instance of 'atomic diplomacy' (see Alperovitz 1996, Yagami 2009): a hot and murderous prologue to the Cold War.

For Japan, strategically, the consequences of surrender were two-fold. After years of Allied Occupation (1945–52) it emerged as a major ally of the United States with formal sovereignty, but one arguably reduced to a 'client state' by which it 'internalised the requirement to give preference to "other" interests over its own' (McCormack 2010: 25). Second, having largely forfeited sovereignty on questions of security and thus being marginal in the creation of new international structures, Japan's rulers perforce turned to statist economic development and in part adopted a trading state mentality and disavowed international political commitments (Johnson 1993: 215).

Initially, the US-led occupation had as its principal objective the creation of a new Japan that would never again threaten Western interests and international order. To that end Japan was to be democratized and demilitarized. Political prisoners were released, the ban on leftist parties lifted, land reform enacted, union rights recognized, and a purge launched against militaristic elements in the state. Amidst widespread hunger and depressing deprivation a formal liberal-democratic settlement was forged in 1946 (Dower 2000). During Yoshida Shigeru's first tenure as prime minister, Japan's new 'peace constitution' largely drafted by United States officials was almost unanimously adopted in slightly amended form by the Japanese parliament in late 1946, and came into effect the following year. Speaking of the draft, Yoshida declared that Article 9 even excluded the right to self-defence (Richter 2016: 1234). The constitution established constitutional monarchy in Japan along the lines of a Westminster democracy (Stockwin 1999). The Constitutional Preamble set a tone of pacific liberal internationalism, a concrete and utopian expression of which was Article 9. As the prospect of communist advance in Asia loomed large in China and Korea, US strategy shifted to firm Japan's status as a future ally. Former militarist elements returned to public life and in modified form the business–state relationships that had fuelled Japanese imperialism were revived. This 'reverse course' was deemed tolerable as long as Japan was on the side of the 'free world', supporting the US strategy of containment.

The reverse course culminated in the joint signing in 1951 (effective 1952) of the San Francisco Peace Treaty and the Security Treaty between the United States and Japan. These codified Japan's subordinate integration into US geopolitical strategy. Among other things, the peace treaty gave the US sovereign control over the Ryukyu Islands, which included the island of Okinawa (from which the US continues to control the Pacific). Even though returned to Japanese administration in 1972, Okinawa remains host to a majority of US bases in Japan, the US personnel of which enjoy effective extraterritoriality despite local political and civic opposition (see McCormack 2016). The Security Treaty forged an 'alliance' in which Japan, in return for security, allowed the United States use of bases and port facilities for the forward deployment of its forces. The bases provided a crucial staging post for operations in the Korean and Vietnam wars. The treaty also allowed mobilization of US troops for the purposes of putting 'down largescale internal riots and disturbances in Japan, caused through instigation or intervention by an outside power or powers'. Notably, the Treaty's introduction touched on the interim nature of this arrangement, stating that Japan 'desires as a provisional arrangement for its defence, that the United States of America should maintain armed forces of its own in and about Japan so as to deter armed attack upon Japan', while the US was 'willing to maintain certain of its armed forces in and about Japan, in the expectation, however, that Japan will itself increasingly assume responsibility for its own defence against direct and indirect aggression'. Article 4, the sunset clause, noted that when a satisfactory alternative arrangement emerged the treaty would expire.

The US's reverse course meant that by the 1950s the US was exerting considerable pressure for Japan to form a military force. Despite great debate centred on Article 9, Japan rearmed. Three relevant developments help illustrate why Article 9 did not stand in the way of Japan hosting foreign military 'war potential' and having a military force of its own. First, in 1952, a member of parliament took to the Supreme Court the issue of the constitutionality of the quasi-military National Police Reserve. These had been formed consequent to the redeployment of significant US forces stationed in Japan to Korea, and at the request of the US. The court dismissed the case not because it was influenced by the government's denial that the Reserve constituted a military force. Rather, the court reasoned that it could only rule on concrete legal disputes; to rule on abstract matters, it opined, would be an undemocratic aggrandizement of its power and contravene the principle of the separation of powers (Supreme Court of Japan 1952). This reasoning would be repeated in subsequent court cases concerning Article 9. Second, in 1954 the US and Japan Mutual Defence Assistance Agreement (MDAA) was signed. It required that Japan maintain a force level sufficient to contribute 'to the development and maintenance of its own defensive strength and the defensive strength of the free world' (cited in Law Library of Congress 2006). Legislation for the establishment of the Japanese Self-Defense Forces (SDF) followed. In preparing that legislation the government was advised by the Cabinet Legislation Bureau (CLB), an influential legal advisory body, that the phrase '"war potential" [used in Article 9] refers to a force with the equipment and organization capable of conducting modern warfare.... Determining what constitutes war potential requires a concrete judgment taking into account the temporal and spatial environment of the country in question.... It is neither unconstitutional to maintain capabilities that fall short of war potential nor to utilize these capabilities to defend the nation from direct invasion' (cited in Samuels 2004). During debates on the MDAA and the SDF legislation the government and the CLB attempted to calm fears that Japan's military was being re-established by pointing to its self-defence function and stating that Article 9 ruled out collective defence (Law Library of Congress 2006, Samuels 2004.) Even so, on the day that the SDF legislation passed, members of the upper chamber passed a resolution banning the dispatch of troops overseas to ensure that the SDF would not participate in overseas military engagements with the US. Third, in 1959 the Supreme Court quashed the Tokyo District Court's dismissal of criminal trespass charges against protestors who had objected to the building of a US military base in Tokyo. The District Court ruled that use of Article 2 of The Law for Special Measures Concerning Criminal Cases, which covered trespass on facilities used by US forces, against protestors was unconstitutional because, citing Article 9, the US–Japan Security Treaty was unconstitutional. The Supreme Court claimed the District Court had overreached its power:

> unless the said treaty is obviously unconstitutional and void, it falls outside the purview of the power of judicial review granted to the court. It is proper to construe that the question of the determination of its constitutionality should be left primarily to the Cabinet which has the power to conclude treaties and the Diet which has the power to ratify them; and ultimately to the political consideration of the people with whom rests the sovereign power of the nation.
>
> (Supreme Court of Japan 1959)

Relatedly, in an aside, it noted that the presence of US forces was not unconstitutional as they did not constitute *Japanese* 'war potential'. It reaffirmed that provisions for Japanese self-defence were in the spirit of pacifism.

In 1960 despite million strong anti-treaty protests and parliamentary opposition, the treaty was revised and renamed the Treaty of Mutual Cooperation and Security between the United States and Japan. The interim nature of the first treaty was now replaced with a more complex set of arrangements that allowed for automatic extension in 1970. The provision for deployment of US troops to quell domestic disturbances was removed. The UN system was restated as the foundational principles for dispute resolution, and the treaty was to end on the provision of an alternative UN system of collective defence securing Japan. Effectively, the revised treaty graduated Japan from a de facto protectorate to a junior alliance partner. The terms of mutual military co-operation were restricted to Japan's sovereign territory, as stated in Article 5: 'Each Party recognizes that an armed attack against either Party in the territories under the administration of Japan would be dangerous to its own peace and safety and declares that it would act to meet the common danger in accordance with its constitutional provisions and processes'. The American security guarantee was politically conditional on continued stationing of US bases in Japanese territory. In 1967 the government also adopted the three non-nuclear principles stating that it would never produce, possess or allow passage to nuclear weapons. The third principle has been routinely violated, with the alliance holding greater weight than the policy.

Accepting US hegemony entailed benefits for the Japanese economy. Japan was identified as a Western-oriented industrial power. The US supported Japanese entry into GATT and the United Nations in the mid-1950s, and entry into the OECD in 1964. By the 1960s, an elite consensus had largely emerged within Japan around pursuing economic growth under the security umbrella afforded by its close relationship with the United States. This posture became known, retrospectively, as the Yoshida doctrine to highlight the successful process by which Yoshida and others secured a conservative economic, security and political settlement. The doctrine's adherents distilled from the messy politics of post-war Japan three key ideas: concentrate economic rehabilitation through co-operation with the United States; maintain internal consensus on economic growth by not getting involved in international political and strategic affairs which were domestically divisive; and maintain minimal forces and depend on a US security guarantee in return for allowing US bases on Japanese soil (see Pyle 1996: 25). Broad support for this approach, which Pyle (1996) labels mercantile realism, was electorally enabled by conservative elites forging a coalitional pact between business (big and small), the bureaucracy and farmers. The pact took electoral form when two major parties merged to form the covertly US-funded Liberal Democratic Party in 1955 (see Johnson 1995), which ruled from then until 2009 (with an interruption of less than one year between 1993 and 1994). Such foundations, exclusions and longevity created a conservative regime that cohered around the Yoshida doctrine (see Pempel 1998).

In the 1960s opposition to the Yoshida line was largely marginalized, as Japan embarked on a massive programme of economic growth. In 1960, Prime Minister Hayato Ikeda, responding to mass demonstrations against the renegotiated Security Treaty and rising political radicalization, announced the Income Doubling Plan. This ideology of 'GNPism', as it became known, undercut radical politics and cohered the political and business establishment around a policy of economic nationalism and growth (Curtis 1999: 31). The state played a significant role in industrial policy, allocating credit to select industries and supporting Japan's technological advances and exports, leading Chalmers Johnson (1982) to describe it as a capitalist development state (CDS).

As Japan's economy grew to challenge the supremacy of Western economies, the close relationship between state and business that established in Japan was increasingly scrutinized. This led 'revisionist' commentators to argue that far from being on the road to Western-style liberalism, Japan's 'capitalist developmental state' devised mercantilist trade strategies that advanced national interest in relative terms over and above the absolute interests that might be forthcoming by engaging in a liberalized and interdependent trading regime (Johnson 1982). The argument was that while Japan had access to Western markets for its produce, it played the trading game unfairly; Japan's massive trade surpluses with the US in the 1980s and 1990s were taken as evidence of this. The trade surpluses were only one factor causing friction; sustained disputes between the two countries also broke out regarding market access, technology sharing and reciprocity (McDougall 1997: 66–71). Yet underlining all these tensions was a general strategic tolerance of Japan's political economy that found early expression in a 1960 US State Department paper that recommended 'Firm Executive Branch resistance of American industry demands for the curtailment of Japanese imports' (cited in Pyle 1996: 34).

Tensions also existed regarding the terms of the alliance, with the US pressuring Japan to increase its burden-sharing in the face of increased US–Soviet tensions in the 1980s. While Japan undertook to expand its defence of its sea lanes up to 1,000 nautical miles, from the previous vaguely defined 'several hundred miles', no significant logistical deployment or procurement occurred for years (Singh 2002: 82). Similarly, efforts by the staunch anti-communist Prime Minister Nakasone (1982–86) to revise Article 9 of the constitution came to naught. Further, his attempt to explicitly overturn the policy of a defence spending cap (1 per cent of GDP) led to threats of parliamentary boycotts. Nakasone retreated from an official policy change, and instead worked through budgetary announcements to achieve his objective for one year only (Chai 1997: 402). And even as the US Congress passed amendments to US defence legislation several times during the 1980s that stipulated that Japan increase defence spending from 1 per cent to 3 per cent of GDP (ibid.: 390), the spending cap has remained in place until the present (Abe has promised to lift it).

Conflict also surrounded the financial terms of the alliance. Beginning in 1978, and under US pressure, the Japanese government provided a relatively small 'sympathy budget' to defray US expenditure related to its bases in Japan. Constant US pressure to increase this, and secure other funds, has seen exponential increases, with the Japanese Ministry of Finance (*Mainichi Japan* 30 May 2016) estimating that the Japanese government contributes 75 per cent of the cost of the bases, while a US Congressional Research paper suggests the figure is closer to 50 per cent (Chanlett-Avery and Rinehart 2016: 21).

China and the region: new ideas

As is evident from the above, even as a subordinate partner in the alliance Japan was able to exercise independent agency. This is especially seen in its development of economic relations with China despite its formal anti-communist stance during the Cold War. Yoshida, speaking in 1951, was clear on this: 'Red or white, China remains our next door neighbour. Geography and economic laws will…prevail in the long run over any ideological differences' (cited in Mendl 1995: 78). Although there existed a strong pro-China lobby within business, the bureaucracy and among politicians, a condition of the peace treaty was that Japan establish diplomatic relations with Taiwan and submit to US containment policy on China. However, by arguing a case for the separation of politics from economics (*seikei bunri*), Japan was able to reach a substantial level of trade with China that steadily grew from 1950 to the mid-1960s after which trade relations were interrupted by China's cultural revolution. Although the US-opposed formalization of the relationship, senior LDP politicians helped promote private trade with China with considerable success (Burns 1999: 37–40, Edström 1999: 23). Following US engagement with China, in September 1972 Japan eagerly signed a communiqué recognizing the People's Republic of China, and broke off diplomatic ties with Taiwan. Despite various tensions, economic matters dominated the Sino–Japanese relationship into the late 1990s. The closeness of the relationship was evident in Japan's response to the Tiananmen Square massacre in 1989 when thousands of pro-democracy students were killed by government forces. China found itself internationally isolated and condemned, and subject to economic and diplomatic sanctions. Japan was the first country to resume aid, and the first G-7 country to have its head of state visit China after the massacre. Since that time, trade and investment has grown. By 2015 China was indispensable, being Japan's second largest export market, and its largest importer.

Japan also expanded its interests by developing ties with the economies of Southeast Asia in the 1960s and 1970s. These ties accelerated from the mid-1980s onwards. This was largely supported by the US, which as early as the 1950s recognized the importance of Southeast Asia for Japan's economic reconstruction. As William Nester notes, 'Washington promoted a triangular economic division of trade between the United States, Japan and Southeast Asia in which America would provide high technology and capital goods, Japan intermediate and consumer goods and Southeast Asia raw materials and energy' (1992: 121). Such openness to Japanese interests lay in a security logic moulded by the Cold War. According to a Joint Chiefs of Staff report in 1952:

> the United States must take into account Japan's dependence upon Southeast Asia for her economic wellbeing and…the loss of Southeast Asia to the Western world would almost inevitably force Japan into an eventual accommodation with the Communist controlled area in Asia.
>
> (cited in Nester 1992: 121)

If there was some degree of independence on economic matters, there was less regarding security in the early Cold War period. However, in the 1970s a series of developments including US withdrawal from Vietnam, the end of the Bretton Woods system, and US *rapprochement* with China against the backdrop of renewed hostilities between the US and the Soviet Union, led to a Japanese perception that the US capacity to act as Japan's security guarantor was compromised. It thus devised two key responses, one focused on the region and the other on developing a security doctrine that could serve Japan's international purpose.

Regarding its regional posture, on assuming the prime-ministership in 1976, Takeo Fukuda quickly moved to define Japan's foreign policy objectives and to restate Japanese pacifism in the face of the perceived partial US withdrawal from Southeast Asia and the rise of anti-Japanese nationalism in Southeast Asia. At the conclusion of a trip through Southeast Asia in 1977 Fukuda articulated an eponymous doctrine. The Fukuda doctrine committed Japan to peace and proclaimed that Japan would never pose a military threat to the region. Co-operative relations with ASEAN and for 'heart to heart' understanding were proposed. Fukuda also pledged to pursue relationships with the communist Indochinese countries based on mutual understanding. The doctrine effectively articulated a regionally specific policy of engagement that was to be underscored by the emerging economic interdependencies between Japan and the region (Edström 1988: 88–91). In subsequent years the rhetoric was to be backed by a massive flow of aid and FDI.

By the 1980s the idea of the flying geese model was being promoted by Japanese economic agencies, and may be seen as an early instance of Japanese 'soft power'. The model construed Japan as the 'lead goose', followed by the first-tier NICs and the second-tier NICs; this became a popular way of visualizing Japan's relationship with the region:

> As it flies forward, becoming more and more technologically advanced, Japan pulls the entire V formation along with it. It does so by successively shedding industries in which it no longer holds comparative advantage. Through FDI, these industries ultimately find a new home among the less developed countries (the follower geese) of Asia. Over time, these developing countries master the new technology, upgrade their own industrial structure, and themselves begin shedding outdated industries.
>
> (Hatch and Yamamura 1996: 27)

Japanese guidance, foreign direct investment and Japanese overseas development aid helped move the NICs forward and bring them into Japan's sphere of influence. Japan was in this period the predominant economic power in Asia. By the force of its economic power and ideology, it was able to win other states to its project of constructing a regional production alliance (Beeson 2001). This had the advantage of reducing Japan's controversial trade surpluses, as its FDI in Asia enabled Japan to enter new markets by jumping barriers to trade (see Hatch and Yamamura 1996).

Regarding its international posture, policy circles within Japan began to articulate the need for Japan's own security doctrine. What emerged was the amorphous concept of 'Comprehensive Security', adopted as policy in 1980 and about which there remains debate (see Sakai 2003). Notably, the 1980 *Summary of Report on Comprehensive National Security* observed that 'the era of the "Pax Americana" upheld almost single-handedly by the U.S. is over, and it has given way to a new era of "peace maintained by shared responsibilities", in which all countries cooperate in the maintenance and management of the international system' (cited in Barber 2016). Comprehensive Security envisioned an expanded concept of national security. The idea embraced resource security, including imported energy and raw materials. It also entailed provision of foreign aid as part of building international economic growth and stability. The idea of Comprehensive Security also allowed Japan to codify its regional and global role. By building up regional economic interdependencies, through investment, technology transfer and trade, Japan could claim to be a good international citizen, assisting in the growth of regional stability and thereby enhancing regional security; at the same time its budgetary commitments to the United Nations, second only to those of the United States, also signalled Japan's seeming commitment to peace and order. These claims were used to combat increasing pressure for it to develop its military capacity and reach.

The post-Cold War period

With the formal end of the Cold War imminent in 1990, Prime Minister Kaifu Toshiki noted that:

> with dialogue and co-operation now replacing missiles and tanks as the tools for achieving order, Japan has both the chance and the duty to apply its economic and technological strength, along with its store of experience and its conceptual ability, to the creation of a new framework for international relations.
>
> (cited in Kelly 2002: 109)

However, as is frequently noted, optimism for a new world order based on the principles of liberal internationalism, economic interdependency and rational dialogue soon faded. Facing up to this reality, Japan has attempted to steer a course that adequately takes account of an increasingly hostile security environment while at the same time pushing forward elements of a liberal foreign policy based on multilateral institution-building, trade and development activity through the UN.

The 1990s and 2000s were marked by an increased interest in multilateral initiatives by Japan. Japan sought to improve its security environment through the support of regional security dialogue, especially through the ASEAN Regional Forum, the body established by ASEAN to establish dialogue on security matters between members ranging from China, the US, South Korea and Japan. The Japanese rationale for such engagement is given in typically liberal tones in official documents, including commitments to interdependency, transparency, and confidence-building measures between states (Ministry of Foreign Affairs of

Japan 2002). Moreover, in a range of annual *Bluebooks* issued by the Ministry of Foreign Affairs, Japan's role in the UN is highlighted, including its high level of funding for the UN, its advocacy of human security and its role in peace-keeping operations. These indicate significant ideological investment in international order, beyond the logic of its alliance diplomacy with the US. It has also engaged in extensive economic bilateral and multilateral negotiations, securing free trade agreements or economic partnerships with the Philippines, Brunei, Thailand, Vietnam, ASEAN and Australia, and is engaged in negotiations with South Korea and China.

Japan's reach has also become global. Noted Japanese scholar Takashi Inoguchi proclaims that by the 21st century Japan had become a rule-maker rather than rule-taker in 'global governance in a number of policy areas' (Inoguchi 2007: 381). Some commentators note that in recent times Japan has more extensively hammered its own nationalist agenda in various global fora, and its attempt to shape the instruments of global governance and influence policy domains has grown significantly, as evidenced by its engagements in the G7 and G20 (Dobson 2017). The suggestion here is that there has been an accretion in diplomatic capacity by the Japanese state, and a willingness to insert itself into governance debates to shape their outcome. It is no longer marked by political dissociation. For Singh (2008) this indicated Japan's emergence as an international state.

Yet while successive volumes of the Ministry of Foreign Affairs' *Diplomatic Bluebooks* after the Cold War pay homage to peace and liberal institutions, present also is an underlying theme of emergent dangers in the post-Cold War world – also expressed in various Defence White Papers. Fears of an emerging China, and concerns about the nuclear capacity of North Korea contributed to Japan's strengthening of its alliance with the US from the 1990s onwards. Moreover, facing US criticism for a belated and inadequate response to requests for assistance in the 1990–91 Gulf War, and subsequently requests to take greater responsibility for areas surrounding Japan, governments began to reinterpret Article 9 in a fashion that enabled the SDF to break out of its 'pacifist straitjacket'. Second, in the 2000s US pressure resulting from the 'war on terror' and the rise of neoconservatism in Japan provided the conditions for the passage of legislation that expanded Japanese military involvement in international security affairs. For those supportive of these developments, Japan was becoming a 'normal state'.

As Hughes (2005: 49–51) notes, a discourse of normalization in the Japanese context emerged most prominently during debates about how Japan should respond to the Gulf War. The former LDP politician Ichiro Ozawa argued that to become a normal state Japan should be willing to play a combat role in line with UN collective security principles. Others have understood 'normal' to entail a more independent foreign policy furthered by the acquisition of nuclear weapons (autonomists), or more moderately the expansion of Japanese military capacity within the US–Japan alliance. It is the latter which has predominated. However conceived, the process of normalization has been accompanied by military hardware procurements and programmes to ensure greater interoperability between US and Japanese forces, enabling Japan to play a role well beyond its borders (Davison 2008: 218–21). The first stage of 'normalization' lasted 15 years. A schematic representation of Japan's normalization covering the years 1990 to the mid-2000s is given in Table 4.1.

The second stage of 'normalization' occurred after Abe returned as prime minister in 2012. When Abe first came to office (2006–07) he aimed to drive the first stage further. He transformed an existing defence agency into the Ministry of Defence, giving military officials greater say on policy. He appointed a panel to examine the amendment of laws to avoid constant ad hoc legal responses to security circumstances. Changes to be examined included enabling Japanese assistance to the US Navy in the event it was attacked at sea, using ballistic missile defence systems to destroy missiles aimed at the United States, and engaging in the use of military force during peace-keeping operations. The panel reported affirmatively that such changes should be made and suggested possible avenues, but Abe had already lost office. Then followed a turbulent five years in which a handful of prime ministers rotated office until Abe returned in 2012.

As if pent up coming-of-age frustrations could be released in one historical outpouring, significant legislation and policy was announced by the Abe government in December 2013. A peak security agency – the National Security Council – was established, quickly followed by the State Secrets Protection Law. A week later saw the adoption of Japan's first ever National Security Strategy announcing a 'proactive contribution to peace'. This was released with the periodic National Defence Program Guidelines 2014–2018, which reconfirmed earlier commitments away from a basic defence posture to a more dynamic one involving greater interoperability with US forces. The National Security Strategy (Government of Japan 2013) promoted a geographically expanded military partnership with the US parallel to the support of an international liberal order. Both approaches were advanced in the knowledge of the relatively declining US position and an emerging multipolarization, euphemistically presented in the Strategy document as 'unprecedented changes in the balance of power' (ibid., 6). Finally, following the 2015 speech with which this chapter began, the government submitted two pieces of legislation which were passed by parliament in September 2015 and came into effect in March 2016. The legislation is complex. One law, the Security Laws Amendment Law, in fact comprises revisions to ten existing laws as well as technical changes to a further ten laws, while the International Peace Support Law is new. The combined impact of the legislative package is transformative, leading one scholar to speak of Japan's 'security renaissance' (Oros 2017). A summary of significant changes is given in Table 4.2.

Such dramatic changes in Japanese military posture naturally invited regional criticism. On the Chinese state-run website *Xinhuanet* (29 March 2016) the legislation was described as enabling Japan to meddle in Asia while riding the coat-tails of Uncle Sam and risked the 'loss of regional geopolitical balance through triggering an arms race'. North Korea ranted. For its part, the (South) Korean Ministry of Foreign Affairs (*Korea Joongang Daily* 21 September) issued a statement that it would not countenance the presence of Japanese troops on the

Table 4.1 Japan's expanding domains of action 1990s–early 2000s

Context	*Action*	*Implications*
1990–91: The Gulf War and Peace-Keeping: In August 1990 the US requests Japanese minesweepers in the Persian Gulf. Japan sends them in April 1991. Japan bankrolls Gulf War effort to the tune of US$ 13 billion dollars. The then US Secretary of State James Baker criticizes Japan's 'checkbook diplomacy'. Japan is compelled to reassess its role in the post-Cold War environment.	October 1990: Japanese parliament debates the creation of non-SDF peace co-operation corps. The Bill lapses in the face of parliamentary opposition. In June 1992 parliament passes the 'Law Concerning Cooperation for United Nations Peace-keeping Operations and Other Operations' (known as the PKO law). This allows SDF participation in UN PKO and humanitarian operations.	Japan breaks through a decades-long constitutional interpretation that disallowed overseas dispatch of SDF forces. Japan is now in a position to play a greater international role, but one with strict conditions. The law requires that for forces to be deployed a ceasefire be in place, that Japan's presence be agreed to by rival parties and that use of weapons can only be in direct self-defence. Nevertheless, the PKO law is criticized by China, and others, as marking a departure from constitutional restraints on Japan's military role. Legislatively enabled, Japan engages in UN operations in Mozambique, Cambodia, Zaire and the Golan Heights. Later it participates in UN operations in Afghanistan and East Timor. This habituates Japan and the world to the mobilization of the Japanese Self-Defense Forces.
1996–99: Enhanced US–Japan Co-operation: In 1996 the US and Japan sign a Joint Declaration on Security that restates the primacy of the relationship in the post-Cold War context. In 1997 they renegotiate The Guidelines for Japan–US Defense Cooperation (unrevised since 1978), cognizant of the new security environment, and the possibility of conflict breakout (China–Taiwan and the Koreas).	The Revised Guidelines stipulate that Japan is responsible for defensive operations within Japanese territory, while the US provides support if Japan is attacked. They extend Japanese support to the US to 'situations in areas surrounding Japan that will have an important influence on Japan's peace and security'. The guidelines are legally codified in The Law Concerning Measures to Ensure Japan's Peace and Security in Areas Surrounding Japan (1999).	Japan's field of operations are extended outside of its own territory. The ambiguity of the term 'situations in areas surrounding Japan' is a thorn in the side of Sino–Japan relations, as China interprets it as sanctioning Japanese involvement in any US-led operations related to the defence of Taiwan. While the role of the SDF remains couched in terms of self-defence, the sphere of operability has been significantly extended. The involvement in regional contingencies is open to interpretation, and provides justification for operations that take place well beyond those previously sanctioned (1,000 nautical miles). The guidelines are criticized by North Korea and China as a staging post for the re-emergence of a militarized Japan.

1998 onwards: Missile Defence: After North Korea fires a test missile over Japan in August 1998, Japan and the US agree to initiate joint research and development of a theatre missile defence system that is capable of detecting and destroying incoming missiles.	Japan agrees to jointly fund research and development of the system. In 2002, the US withdraws from the Anti-Ballistic Missile Treaty of 1972. In 2003 the Japanese government signals support for the development of a missile defence system, which begins to be rolled out from 2007 onwards.	The deployment of a TMD system in East Asia is seen as a measure directed not just at North Korea, but at degrading China's nuclear stockpile; China is against the system, seeing it as directly related to a growing US–Japan pact to dominate the region. Some are concerned that the deployment of a missile defence system in the region will embolden Taiwan to declare independence. Thus the system is seen as heightening, rather than attenuating, existent security dilemmas for states involved.
2000s Terrorism: After the 11 September 2001 terror attacks, the US pressures allies to actively respond. President George Bush declares: 'You're either with us or against us in the fight against terror'. The US pushes for Japanese involvement in Afghanistan and later in Iraq.	In October 2001 an Anti-Terrorism Special Measures law allows for the dispatch of the SDF to Afghanistan. The anti-terrorism law provides for: co-operation and support of US and allies in 'war against terrorism', participation in search and rescue missions for foreign forces and relief operations.	The law sanctions, in unambiguous terms, the deployment of Japanese forces to foreign territory. Japan Maritime forces provide refuelling to US craft in the Indian Ocean in support of US operations in Afghanistan. Critics argue that the Terrorism Law is being used to transform the SDF into a regular armed force. South Korea and China express concern at the development. Indeed, the precedent set by the law allows Japan to pass further support laws relating to operations in Iraq (see below). When the law expired in 2003 it was re-enacted several times, and lapsed in 2007 after parliamentary opposition obstructed its extension. A new anti-terror law passes in 2008. Politicking over extension highlights the need for a general law.

Table 4.1 continued

Context	*Action*	*Implications*
Iraq 2003 and Emergencies: Facing further US pressure for involvement in Iraq, the Japanese government responds positively by pushing through legislation enabling SDF deployment. In 2003 as tensions between China and Japan escalate and with North Korea's withdrawal from the non-proliferation treaty, the government passes a range of Emergency Legislation covering responsibilities in the event of an attack.	In 2003 The Law concerning the Special Measures on Humanitarian and Reconstruction Assistance in Iraq is passed. In 2004 approximately 1,000 SDF personnel arrive in Iraq. The 2003 Law provides for a four-year deployment of the SDF for humanitarian and reconstruction purposes in Iraq. It forbids the use of force or entry into combat zones.	Reflecting on the 2003 Law and noting further amendments to the SDF Law, China's *People's Daily* (30 July 2004) comments: 'Japan's SDF has actually shifted ahead the time for its use of force from the previous "after being invaded by the enemy" to "being threatened by the enemy", and allowed itself the right to mount "pre-emptive strike" on the enemy. At the same time, the SDF's operation area has been expanded from its own territory to "surrounding areas" and then to farther regions'.

Source: adapted from Mulgan (2000), Iwamoto and Edirippulige (2002), Singh (2002) and Ishizuka (2002), Hayashi (2004) and from various articles in *Japan Times*, *Asia Times* and *People's Daily*.

Table 4.2 Japan: what's changed?

Before 2015	*After 2015*
*Need for new laws or extension of existing laws for deployment of SDF overseas for support purposes related to UN-supported peace-keeping, emergencies and other non-warlike contingencies. Highly limited terms of operation in non-combat zones.	*Permanent Law now in place. Parliamentary approval required for deployment. Allows logistical support in non-combat zones, but includes preparatory combat support including provision of ammunition and support for aircraft launching for combat.
*Self-defence allowed. See Table 4.1.	*May now protect by use of force foreign nationals under certain conditions.
*PKO limited to UN framework, election observance or international humanitarian assistance.	*Extends partnership to extended UN agencies, the EU, multilateral regional organizations based on treaties, or by request of country where operation is proceeding.
*Use of military force only permissible when Japan under direct attack. Support operations allowable in vaguely defined geographical areas.	*Geographic restrictions lifted. Military force now allowed '[w]hen an armed attack against Japan occurs or when an armed attack against a foreign country that is in a close relationship with Japan occurs and as a result threatens Japan's survival and poses a clear danger to fundamentally overturn people's right to life, liberty and pursuit of happiness'. Essentially, the new legislation permits collective self-defence operations under restrictive conditions: when no other option is available and only by the use of force as necessary for success.
*Only permitted to protect SDF weapons.	*Japan is able to protect weapons of foreign countries.

Source: adapted from Nasu (2016), Oros (2017), and the Government of Japan (2016).

Korean Peninsula under the principle of collective self-defence, a stance comprehensible because of historic tensions between Japan and its former colony. Given the history and proximity, the regional response was expected. Likewise, from the US perspective, Japan still has more to do, and in the words of two scholars it remains an 'exceptional ally', needing to do more before it may be considered a 'normal power' (Hornung and Mochizuki 2016).

Responding to regional tensions: constitutional revision?

Although Japan has succeeded in expanding its security capability beyond the limited 1950s interpretation, it has done so in a manner that dependently ties it to its alliance partner and the United Nations. Japan does not have self-reliant defence capacity as some 'autonomists' have demanded, nor does the 2015 legislation go as far as neoconservatives wish. For example, the terms of its engagement in collective defence remain highly restricted. Ideally, Abe wants more but is circumscribed by the constitution. The US also wants more. Two factors are relevant in considering whether Japan will move to revise its constitution, the first is the intensity of the security dilemmas it faces, particularly in regard to China and North Korea. The second is the obstacles that confront constitutional amendment.

Regarding China, Japan may be said to be facing the logic of an emerging rival power challenging its subdued regional leadership, and this expresses itself in occasional policy adventurism. Echoing Prime Minister Junichiro Koizumi's earlier willingness to entertain strained relations with China (Takahashi 2010: 29), is Abe's promotion of a 'democratic security diamond' that would push back against China's efforts to turn the South China Sea into, as Abe terms it, 'Beijing's lake' (Abe 2012). That diamond, composed of the democratic states of India, the United States, Australia and Japan, composing an Indo-Pacific strategy, would extend democratic preponderance for the purpose of protecting the 'maritime commons' from the Western Pacific to the Indian oceans. Apart from extending Japan's strategic partnership to India, the proposal was couched as a direct challenge to Chinese ambitions. Fuelling such activism is the clear-eyed Chinese objective to control the East and South China Seas and break out from the strategic encirclement it faces in the combined alliances of Japan, Australia, Taiwan and South Korea with the United States, as well as US-oriented states in Southeast Asia.

One sign of a combative China is the 2013 Chinese declaration of an air defence identification zone in the East China Sea (ECS), beyond its national airspace. The Chinese demanded that transiting civil and state aircraft provide their identity and location. The zone included airspace over the uninhabited Senkaku Islands, which are administered by Japan, but claimed by China (which calls them the Diaoyu islands). The declaration was quickly challenged when US, Japanese and South Korean military aircraft entered the zone without notification to indicate non-compliance. Also of note is that Chinese flights into the zone, parts of which overlap with Japanese national airspace, has led to increased incidents of scrambling by the Japan Air Self-Defense Force, in response to potential air incursions. Between 2001 and 2010 no year recorded more than 100 scrambles in response to Chinese aircraft. In 2011 that figure rose to 150 and by 2015 it had reached 571 (Pilger 2016: 2–6, *Japan Times* 23 April 2016). In March 2017 Japan and the US conducted a joint military exercise in the EAS in response to North Korean missile tests, but also to signal resilience to China (*South China Morning Post* 10 March 2017). Tensions also exist over China's extensive claims, disputed by four Southeast Asian states, over the South China Sea, through which over 85 per cent of Japanese oil supplies pass. In addition to a proposed 'security diamond', Japan has developed forms of maritime security assistance with two SCS claimants, Vietnam and the Philippines. Triggered by an increase in hostilities over rival claims, it may be only a matter of time before Japan joins the US in demonstrative freedom of navigation exercises in the SCS as well as surveillance patrols (*Guardian* 17 July 2015), although Abe's security diamond remains no more than an aspiration. Furthermore, the remote but possible US defence of

Taiwan against a Chinese attack may draw Japan, by virtue of its US alliance, into a regional conflagration.

Turning to North Korea, the failure of the 1994 Agreed Framework and the Six-Party Talks (commencing in 2003) that aimed at stopping North Korea's development of nuclear weapons capacity has led to a regional crisis (Habib 2011). For all its willingness to commit substantial aid and diplomacy, Japan now faces a hostile and belligerent neighbour. North Korea withdrew from The Treaty on the Non-Proliferation of Nuclear Weapons in 2003. And building on previous missile tests that landed in the Sea of Japan in 1998, 2006, 2014 and 2016, in March 2017 North Korea test-fired four ballistic missiles that landed approximately 300 kilometres – or just minutes short – of Japan's coastline. Famously, this occurred as Prime Minister Abe was dining with President Donald Trump at the 'southern White House'. The timing left no doubt as to the intended signalling regarding Japan's intensified relationship with the United States, a state with which North Korea effectively considers itself to still be at war. Bluff or not, North Korea's various threats against Japan meant that from 1998 onwards there has been support and development of ballistic missile defence in co-operation with the United States (Toki 2009; see Table 4.1). Relatedly, in 2016 South Korea and the United States also announced their intention to deploy a missile defence system on the Korean Peninsula, components of which began to arrive in early 2017 (*The Korea Times* 3 March 2017). Ostensibly a response to North Korea, it will also impact on China's strategic position. Thus, North Korea's race to nuclear power has destabilized the balance of power, and led to new regional security dilemmas that are felt intensely in Japan and China.

Faced with a rising China and an unpredictable nuclear-armed North Korea it is perhaps surprising from a realist perspective that Japan has not gone further to expand the role of the SDF. The developments outlined in Tables 4.1 and 4.2 reflect a strategy of constitutional reinterpretation. If during the heyday of the Yoshida doctrine those limits were functional to Japan's economic development, they are now experienced as frustration by revisionists in power. The imperative for revision is evident in that legal fault lines may yet await Japan's new international prominence. For example, in 2008 the Nagoya High Court ruled as unconstitutional the deployment of forces to Iraq and the use of Air Self-Defense Forces to transport coalition forces (*Japan Times* 18 April 2008, *Japan Times* 24 January 2010) because it judged Iraq to be a combat zone. The ruling reminded revisionists of the precarious legal standing of Japan's evolving normalization: even if the Supreme Court has previously ruled that interpretation of Article 9 is a political question and outside of its jurisdiction, rulings can change.

As early as 2001 the Japanese government established a Constitutional Review Committee to survey possible amendments to the Constitution. In early 2003 the committee tabled its report, surveying a range of possibilities. It was largely recognized that revision of Article 9 would almost certainly lead to a regional crisis, and expected that US allies such as South Korea and a number of Southeast Asian nations would interpret revision as the beginning of a new era of Japanese imperialism. Nevertheless, in May 2007 Abe pushed through a law that established procedures to enact a referendum on the constitution, but a decade later no referendum had been called. Apart from political considerations such as domestic and international opposition (McCormack 2008), one practical obstacle is the two-thirds parliamentary vote required to enact constitutional amendment. And even though the Abe-led coalition government had by mid-2016 secured that requirement, it was unclear if there was unanimity in the coalition. An additional obstacle is that constitutional revision politics do not concern Article 9 alone, and great disagreement and political mobilization can be expected. For example, the LDP presented a draft constitution in 2012 to great outcry. Predictably, it rewrote Article 9 to transform the Self-Defense Forces into a National Defense Force deployable for a range of reasons. This also provided for the establishment of military courts and intimated the need for national security laws. But the draft also proposed that wording surrounding human rights that echoed Western liberal theory be changed. The draft also elevated the status of the emperor (see *Japan Times* 2 July 2013). Constitutional revision then is about national purpose and identity, not only the already complicated issue of Article 9. Given what has been achieved through constitutional interpretation, constitutional amendment might appear imprudent insofar as it would open up fundamental debates on Japanese identity well beyond the narrower scope of Article 9.

Even so, increasing instability in North Korea and a souring relationship with China could lead to a dramatic sea change and the ascendancy of political forces seeking constitutional 'normalization'. Moreover, with the Trump administration exacting greater burden-sharing, greater pressure than previously may be exerted by the US state to revise Article 9. Such forces for revision would have to confront the popular opposition to amendment that has been indicated by numerous opinion polls. However, one cannot assume that pacifism is irrevocably embedded in Japan. As Miyashita (2007: 111, 113) notes, the embedding of Japanese pacifism has in part been contingent on the available supply of 'relative peace' during the Cold War. That supply has continued into the post-Cold War era, but any reading of the current play of international politics would posit that the supply is running out. And should belligerent threats turn to action even on Japan's periphery, the popular mood may well slip to support revision.

Making sense of Japan?

Eminent scholars support analytical eclecticism when it comes to understanding Japan in the post-Cold War era (Katzenstein and Okawara 2001/02). For them, no single theoretical perspective can account for the often muddled, contradictory and wide-ranging actions of the Japanese state across economic and security matters, nor can any theory capture the various levels at which states and other actors interact, nor determine the relative importance of structure and agency in outcomes. Be that as it may, it will be useful to discern in broad outline three interpretations of Japan.

At the most basic level a key question relating to the realist perspective is whether, given the assumed condition of anarchy, even if mitigated by balance of power strategies, the Japanese state has now 'normalized', as neorealist Kenneth Waltz expected at the end of the Cold War:

> For a country to choose not to become a great power is a structural anomaly. For that reason, the choice is a difficult one to sustain. Sooner or later, usually sooner, the international status of countries has risen in step with their material resources. Countries with great power economies have become great powers, whether reluctantly or not. How long can Japan and Germany live alongside other nuclear states while denying themselves similar capability?
>
> (Waltz 1993: 66)

From a realist perspective it can be argued that the cumulative expansion of the SDF's role represents a movement towards 'normality'. Japan may be moving to end the paradox of its unrealized power, or perhaps it already has, *sans* nuclear weapons. For the neorealist, Japan's behaviour is to be expected in the current security environment. Through its deepening alliance with the US, Japan is doing what all states do: balancing the power of potential rivals. Furthermore, the incremental expansion of the SDF's role may be taken as evidence of a classic self-help strategy in the specific circumstances of the constraints Japan faces (Singh 2002: 85). Calls within Japan, from right-wing nationalists and MPs for Japanese rearmament commensurate with its economic power, add force to the realist interpretation. Nevertheless, it is worth recalling that when faced with the North Korean crisis of 2003 (and again in 2006) the defence establishment made it clear that entering a nuclear arms race was not an option (Thompson 2003). Instead of nuclear normalization, Japan appears to have more forcefully embraced normalization within the alliance, even in the face of escalating tensions with China and North Korea.

A more sceptical argument comes from those who see Japan as a remnant neo-mercantilist state bent on economic supremacy and advantage (see Chapter 11). As it happens, the global resurgence of economic nationalism may well give greater credence to mercantilism as an acceptable policy. Historically, Japan's alliance with the US was seen as conveniently stripping Japan of military engagements that might hurt its economic interests. Japan, for example, was able to maintain good relations with Arab oil-producing countries, on whom it is heavily dependent, because it does not have to bear the cost of the US's unpopular Middle East policy centred on the defence of Israel. From this perspective Japan's incrementalism may be taken as shrewd 'dual hedging', in which it keeps up the alliance for the sake of its security in Asia, and yet downplays the importance of the alliance in the Middle East in order to maintain good relations with oil states (see Heginbotham and Samuels 2002). Some would see its role in Iraq as motivated by its energy interests. More recently, Japan's shift to free trade agreements, Abe's economic reforms and the government's willingness to join the now defunct Trans-Pacific Partnership would suggest a significant retreat from mercantilist policy.

For liberals, Japan's increased role in UN PKOs may be interpreted as a welcome sign of its engagement with emergent institutions of global security, while remaining under the leadership of what Ikenberry has termed US-constructed liberal hegemony (Ikenberry 1999). Japan has moved cautiously towards direct involvement in collective security; this, liberals can countenance. For liberals, Japan's constant engagement with the instruments of the UN (and its misplaced desire for a permanent seat) reflects an abiding concern with internationalism and the development of international law. Japan's ratification of the Kyoto Protocol is similarly seen in these terms. Further, its multilateral pursuits may be interpreted in terms of liberal institutionalism. By supporting the ARF and the EAS, Japan is seen as participating in an emergent regional security regime with the capacity to create new forms of order less dependent on power and self-help and more reliant on co-operation. In this light, Japan is an exemplar state, militarily defensive, a major contributor to global governance through its massive support of the UN budget, and its ODA programme. While recognizing the national interest that Japan pursues in all of these arenas, for liberals the logic of institution-building ties Japan into a liberal internationalist perspective supportive of global trade and peace. In 2006 the Japanese Foreign Minister announced that Japan's work with the US and the United Nations and its regional engagement would be buttressed by a renewed commitment to universal values, 'such as freedom, democracy, fundamental human rights, the rule of law, and the market economy and creating an Arc of Freedom and Prosperity' (Ministry of Foreign Affairs, Japan 2007: 2). Similar statements about values-oriented diplomacy are made in the 2013 National Security Strategy. Taken together with Japan's constant reference to efforts in preventative diplomacy, PKOs and Confidence Building Measures, the resilience of liberal rhetoric within Japanese discourse is evident. Even Abe's posture towards a democratic security diamond would, at most, place Japan's military developments within the liberally accepted principle of collective defence.

From a radical perspective Japan's failure to balance US power, and its continuing preference to augment US power in the region suggests that a structure of US-led hegemony is present (Kelly 2002, McCormack 2004, Mulgan 2006). The Japanese state ties the interests of Japanese capital to working within that structure. After all, Japan has enjoyed the twin benefits of economic growth and access to vital markets, as well as the security apparatus of the US machine (Van Ness 2001). In this perspective, Japan exists in a structured world system in which the rules of the game are set by US hegemony. Having accepted these rules, it is not driven to self-help strategies that would suggest nuclearization (an expectation of the neorealists).

To conclude on a speculative note, as US hegemony and unipolarity is now under challenge the US's demand for greater burden-sharing from its allies may lead to alliance weakening or a significantly depleted US security guarantee. This would open up space for the already evolving balance of power to shift rapidly. In that event, the contradictory postures that make up Japan's current strategy may collapse in a process of creative destruction. What emerges will depend on the balance of forces both internationally and domestically.

References

Abe, S. (2012) 'Asia's democratic security diamond', *Project Syndicate*, 27 December.

Abe, S. (2015) 'Speech and Statements by the Prime Minister', 14 May. http://japan.kantei.go.jp/97_abe/statement/201505/0514kaiken.html.

Alperovitz, G. (1996) *The Decision to Use the Atomic Bomb and the Architecture of an American Myth*, London: Fontana.

Barber, B. (2016) 'Comprehensive security 2.0: (re)applying a distinctive security concept to the 3/11 disasters', *Journal of Contemporary Japanese Studies*, 16 (2). www.japanesestudies.org.uk/ejcjs/vol16/iss2/barber.html.

Beasley, W. G. (1991) *Japanese Imperialism 1894–1945*, Oxford: Clarendon Press.

Beeson, M. (2001) 'Japan and Southeast Asia: the lineaments of quasi-hegemony' in G. Rodan, K. Hewison and R. Robison (eds), *The Political Economy of South-East Asia: An Introduction*, 2nd edn, Melbourne: Oxford University Press.

Burns, K. G. (1999) 'China and Japan: economic partnership to political ends' in M. Krepon and C. Gagnè (eds), *Economic Confidence-Building and Regional Security*, Washington, DC: Henry L. Stimson Center.

Chai, S. (1997) 'Entrenching the Yoshida defence doctrine: three techniques for institutionalization', *International Organization*, 51 (3): 389–412.

Chanlett-Avery, E. and I. Rinehart (2016) *The U.S.-Japan Alliance* (Congressional Report Number RL33740). Retrieved from Congressional Research Service, https://fas.org/sgp/crs/row/RL33740.pdf.

Curtis, G. (1999) *The Logic of Japanese Politics: Leaders, Institutions, and the Limits of Change*, New York: Columbia University Press.

Davison, R. (2008) *Foreign Policies of Great and Emerging Powers*, Frenchs Forest, NSW: Prentice Hall.

Dobson, H. (2017) 'Is Japan really back? The "Abe Doctrine" and global governance', *Journal of Contemporary Asia*, 47 (2): 199–224.

Dower, J. (2000) *Japan: Embracing Defeat*, New York: Norton & Company.

Drifte, R. (1998) *From Japan's Foreign Policy for the 21st Century: From Economic Superpower to What?* Basingstoke: Macmillan.

Edström, B. (1988) *Japan's Quest for a Role in the World*, Stockholm: Institute of Oriental Languages, University of Stockholm.

Edström, B. (1999) *Japan's Evolving Foreign Policy Doctrine: From Yoshida to Miyazawa*, Basingstoke: Macmillan.

Field, N. (1997) 'War and apology: Japan, Asia, the fiftieth, and after', *Positions*, 5 (1): 1–49.

Green, M. (2001) *Japan's Reluctant Realism: Foreign Policy Challenges in an Era of Uncertain Power*, New York: Palgrave.

Government of Japan (2013) *National Security Strategy, provisional translation*, http://japan.kantei.go.jp/96_abe/documents/2013/__icsFiles/afieldfile/2013/12/17/NSS.pdf.

Government of Japan (2016) 'Japan's legislation for peace and security: seamless responses for peace and security of Japan and the international community', www.mofa.go.jp/files/000143304.pdf.

Habib, B. (2011) 'North Korea's nuclear weapons programme and the maintenance of the Songun system', *The Pacific Review* 24 (1): 43–64.

Hatch, W. and K. Yamamura (1996) *Asia in Japan's Embrace: Building a Regional Production Alliance*, Melbourne: Cambridge University Press.

Hayashi, M. (2004) 'Japanese Law Concerning the Special Measures on Humanitarian and Reconstruction Assistance in Iraq: translator's introduction', *Pacific Rim Law & Policy Journal*, 13: 579–610.

Heginbotham, E. and R. J. Samuels (2002) 'Japan's dual hedge', *Foreign Affairs*, 81: 110–21.

Hornung, J. W. and M. Mochizuki (2016) 'Japan: still an exceptional U.S. ally', *The Washington Quarterly*, 39 (1): 95–116.

Hughes, C. (2005) *Japan's Re-emergence as a 'Normal' Military Power*, London, Routledge.

Ikenberry, G. J. (1999) 'Hegemony and the future of American post-war order' in T. V. Paul and J. A. A. Hall (eds), *International Order and the Future of World Politics*, Cambridge: Cambridge University Press.

Inoguchi, T. (2007) 'Are there any theories of international relations in Japan?' *Journal of International Relations of the Asia Pacific*, 7 (3): 369–90.

Ishizuka, K. (2002) 'The evolution of Japan's policy towards UN peace operations', paper presented at the 15th Annual Meeting for the Academic Council on the UN system, Cascais, Portugal, 21–23 June 2002.

Iwamoto, Y. and S. Edirippulige (2002) 'Japan's response to the war against terrorism', *New Zealand International Review*, 27: 9–12.

Johnson, C. (1982) *MITI and the Japanese Miracle: The Growth of Industrial Policy*, Stanford, CA: Stanford University Press.

Johnson, C. (1993) 'The state and Japanese grand strategy' in R. N. Rosecrance and A. Stein (eds), *The Domestic Bases of Grand Strategy*, Ithaca, NY: Cornell University Press.

Johnson, C. (1995) 'The 1955 System and the American connection: a bibliographic introduction', *JPRI Working Paper* No. 11, www.jpri.org/publications/workingpapers/wp11.html.

Katzenstein, P. J. and N. Okawara (2001/02) 'Japan, Asian-Pacific security, and the case for analytical eclecticism', *International Security*, 26: 153–85.

Kelly, D. (2002) *Japan and the Reconstruction of East Asia*, Basingstoke: Palgrave.

Law Library of Congress (2006) 'Japan: Article 9 of the Constitution' (prepared by Umeda Sayuri in February 2006).

McCormack, G. (2004) 'Remilitarizing Japan', *New Left Review*, 29: 29–45.

McCormack, G. (2008) 'Japan, through the US looking glass', *Asia Times*, 26 June, www.atimes.com/atimes/Japan/JF26Dh01.html.

McCormack, G. (2010) 'Obama vs Okinawa', *New Left Review*, 64: 5–26.

McCormack, G. (2016) 'Japan's problematic prefecture – Okinawa and the US–Japan relationship', *The Asia-Pacific Journal/Japan Focus*, 14 (17): 1–27.

McDougall, D. (1997) *The International Politics of the New Asia-Pacific*, Boulder, CO: Lynne Rienner.

Mendl, W. (1995) *Japan's Asia Policy*, London: Routledge.

Ministry of Foreign Affairs, Japan (2002–2010) *The Diplomatic Bluebook*, Volumes 2002, 2006, 2007, 2009, Ministry of Foreign Affairs of Japan, www.mofa.go.jp/policy/other/bluebook/index.html.

Miyashita, A. (2007) 'Where do norms come from? Foundations of Japan's postwar pacifism', *International Relations of the Asia-Pacific*, 7 (1): 99–120.

Mulgan, A. G. (2000) 'Beyond self-defence?' *The Pacific Review*, 12 (2): 25–48.

Mulgan, A. G. (2006) 'Japan and the Bush agenda: alignment or divergence' in M. Beeson (ed.), *Bush and Asia: America's Evolving Relations with East Asia*, London: Routledge.

Nasu, H. (2016) 'Japan's 2015 security legislation: challenges to its implementation under international law', *International Law Studies*, 92: 249–80.

Nester, R. W. (1992) *Japan and the Third World: Patterns, Power, Prospects*, Basingstoke: Macmillan.

Oros, A. (2017) *Japan's Security Renaissance: New Policies and Politics for the Twenty-First Century*, New York: Columbia University Press.

Pempel, T. J. (1998) *Regime Shift: Comparative Dynamics of the Japanese Political Economy*, Ithaca, NY: Cornell University Press.

Pilger, M. (2016) 'ADIZ update: enforcement in the East China Sea, prospects for the South China Sea, and implications for the United States', U.S.-China Economic and Security Review Commission, https://www.uscc.gov/sites/default/files/Research/ADIZ%20Update_0.pdf.

Pyle, K. (1996) *The Japanese Question: Power and Purpose in a New Era*, 2nd edn, Washington, DC: AEI Press.

Richter, J. (2016) 'Japan's "reinterpretation" of Article 9: a Pyrrhic victory for American foreign policy?' *Iowa Law Review*, 101 (3): 1223–62.

Sakai, H. (2003) 'The end of comprehensive security? The evolution of Japanese security policy in the post-September 11-terrorism world', *Indian Journal of Asian Affairs*, 16 (1/2): 71–98.

Samuels, R. J. (2004) 'Politics, security policy, and Japan's Cabinet Legislation Bureau: who elected these guys, anyway?' *JPRI Working Paper* No. 99.

Singh, B. (2002) 'Japan's post-Cold War security: bringing back the normal state', *Contemporary Southeast Asia*, 24: 82–105.

Singh, B. (2008) 'Japan's security policy: from a peace state to an international state', *The Pacific Review*, 21 (3): 303–25.

Stockwin, J. A. A. (1999) *Governing Japan: Divided Politics in a Major Economy*, 3rd edn, Malden, MA: Blackwell.

Supreme Court of Japan (1952) 'Judgment concerning the question of whether, in the absence of a concrete case, the Supreme Court has authority to determine the constitutionality of any law or the like in the abstract'. Case Number 1952 (Ma) 23, www.courts.go.jp/app/hanrei_en/detail?id=4.

Supreme Court of Japan (1959) 'Judgment upon case of the so-called "SUNAKAWA CASE"', Case number 1959 (A) 710, www.courts.go.jp/app/hanrei_en/detail?id=13.

Susumu, T. (2001) 'The global meaning of Japan: the state's persistently precarious position in the world order' in G. D. Hook and H. Harukiyo (eds), *The Political Economy of Japanese Globalization*, London: Routledge.

Takahashi, T. (2010) 'Japanese neo-conservatism: coping with China and North Korea', *Security Challenges*, 6 (3): 21–40.

Thompson, J. (2003) 'Japanese nuclear arsenal looks unlikely', *Japan Times*, 10 August.

Toki, M. (2009) 'Missile defense in Japan', *The Bulletin*, 16 January, www.thebulletin.org/web-edition/features/missile-defense-japan.

Townsend, S. (2000) *Yanihara Tadao and Japanese Colonial Policy: Redeeming Empire*, Richmond, Surrey: Curzon.

Van Ness, P. (2001) 'Hegemony, not anarchy: why China and Japan are not balancing US unipolarity', Australian National University, Department of International Relations, Working Paper 2001/4.

Waltz, K. (1993) 'The emerging structure of international politics', *International Security*, 18: 66.

Wilson, W. (2013) 'The bomb didn't beat Japan…Stalin did', *Foreign Policy*, 30 May.

Yagami, K. (2009) 'Bombing Hiroshima and Nagasaki: Gar Alperovitz and his critics', *Southeast Review of Asian Studies*, 31: 301–7.

Yang, D. (1999) 'Convergence or divergence? Recent historical writings on the rape of Nanjing', *American Historical Review*, 105: 1, www.historycooperative.org/journals/ahr/104.3/ah000842.html.

5 Looking East

India and Russia in the Asia-Pacific

Rémy Davison

Introduction

Two states in the Asian region – one an emerging power, the other a former superpower – have staked claims to be major actors in the Asia-Pacific. In an era of globalization and complex economic and military interdependence, it is no longer possible to make the artificial and arbitrary distinction between the 'East Asian hemisphere', and South Asia, Central Asia or Russian North Asia. Russia has long been an Asian, Pacific and European power, while India has developed into South Asia's regional hegemon. In the post-Cold War era, both countries have become increasingly enmeshed in the political and institutional structures of the Asia-Pacific; for example, Russia was a foundation signatory to the Shanghai Five agreement (1996), and entered the Asia-Pacific Economic Cooperation (APEC) in 1998, while both Russia and India are members of the ASEAN Regional Forum (ARF). Moscow and New Delhi were longstanding partners throughout much of the Cold War, while Beijing and New Delhi have gravitated towards cautious détente in the last decade. In 2009, three of Asia's major powers, Russia, India and China, held the first BRIC (Brazil, Russia, India, China) summit, with South Africa acceding in 2010. In 2016, India hosted the eighth BRICS summit in Goa, inviting the Bay of Bengal Initiative for Multi-Sectoral Technical and Economic Cooperation (BIMSTEC) members to attend a joint BRICS-BIMSTEC meeting for the first time.

India has long been an advocate of Asian economic regionalism, even proposing the formation of an Asian Council in 1967, the year of ASEAN's promulgation (Sridharan 1996: 46), and founding the South Asian Association for Regional Cooperation (SAARC) in 1996. In 1955, India was a foundation member of the Non-Aligned Movement (NAM), an international organization comprising most of the world's developing countries. However, during the 1990s and 2000s, New Delhi effected a profound shift away from the NAM principles that had sustained Indian foreign policy for almost half a century. In the last two decades, India has engaged vigorously in South and Southeast Asian regional integration; it has cemented strategic partnerships with Russia and the US; in 2005, it risked jeopardizing a US$ 20 billion gas deal with Iran and voted against Iran at the International Atomic Energy Agency (IAEA); it did so again in November 2009, marking a decisive break with its traditional policy of solidarity with NAM members. In 2016, Narendra Modi became the first elected Indian prime minister to miss a NAM summit, evidencing the declining importance of the movement, compared to the NDB and India's regional economic initiatives.

Soviet involvement in Asian conflicts profoundly affected the region for almost a century. From the Russo-Japanese war of 1904–05, through the Second World War, the alliance with Mao's China and the Korean conflict, to the Vietnam War, Soviet influence in Asia fermented communist insurgencies throughout the region. Thus, the implications for Asia of the collapse of the USSR were manifold. First, the belated collapse of the Council for Mutual Economic Assistance (CMEA) stripped Vietnam of important Soviet technical, military and economic aid. Second, the Soviet Union's disappearance compelled India to abandon its 'tilt' towards Moscow, for decades the cornerstone of New Delhi's foreign policy. Third, the power vacuum created by the breakup of the Soviet Union reconfigured the balance of power in Asia; Beijing no longer faced a direct security threat from Moscow; New Delhi could no longer rely on the USSR as a regional balancer; and, by the mid-1990s, the US, Japan and South Korea, jointly, sought to take advantage of Russia's weakness in the Pacific by consolidating their military presence in the region, which served the dual purpose of reinvigorating the US–Japan alliance, as well as containing the military rise of emergent China. The medium-term impact of the Russian retreat also extended to North Korea, long a Soviet client state, which could no longer rely on the security afforded by Moscow. In a period of flux in Pacific Asia in the 1990s, DPRK leader Kim Jong-Il signed the US–DPRK 'Agreed Framework' in 1994; but Kim was sufficiently perturbed by the assertiveness of US foreign policy, particularly after 9/11, to maintain a covert nuclear weapons program deliberately designed to threaten the security of two core US allies: Japan and South Korea.

The 1990s were characterized by Russian economic and political weakness in the Asia-Pacific, as much as they were remarkable for the concomitant rise of China and India. The early 21st century was similarly noteworthy because of Russia's re-emergence as a regional power under the leadership of Vladimir Putin. In the 2000s, the Russian Federation was transformed from a paralysed, bankrupt state in the wake of the 1998 Russian financial crisis, to an energy superpower, bolstered by burgeoning oil and gas revenues following the 2003 Iraq War. Moscow also became New Delhi's and Beijing's largest arms supplier, averaging US$ 5 billion in worldwide exports until 2008, when sales reached US$ 8 billion, despite a shrinking global market. In 2009, Russia's monopoly arms exporter, Rosoboronexport, claimed US$ 25–6 billion in contracts. (Abramson 2009, *The New York Times* 30 September 2008). For 2013–15, Russia exported US$ 5 billion in arms to India alone, comprising 75 per cent of all of India's military imports (*The Diplomat* 1 March 2016). Russia was also the world's second-biggest arms exporter in 2012–16, followed by China. India was not only Asia's biggest arms importer, taking 14 per cent of global exports in 2011–15, but also Russia's biggest customer. Seventy per cent of Russia's arms in 2012–16 went to four countries: China, India, Vietnam and Algeria (SIPRI 2017a, 2017b).

A widely cited 2003 Goldman Sachs report on the BRICS economies conjectured that, by 2025, these four countries would account for the equivalent of 50 per cent of the GDP of the G6 (US, Japan, Germany, Britain, France and Italy), and that the BRICS would overtake the G6 by 2041. A further prediction was that, by 2035, Russia would outperform Germany, France, Italy and the UK, while India would become the world's third largest economy (Goldman Sachs 2003: 3–8). India and Russia are two of Asia's – and the world's – most important emerging economies. India's GDP in 2016 was US$ 2.25 trillion, eclipsing Britain, while in purchasing power parity (PPP) terms, India ranked third globally in 2015, outranked only by China and the US (IMF 2016, World Bank 2017a). Indian military spending was only the 10th-highest in the world in 2008, totalling US$ 30 billion, but in projected budgetary allocations, by 2018, India will have the third largest defence expenditures ($ 56.5 billion), overtaking Britain (SIPRI 2009, *Financial Times* 11 December 2016). Despite a five per cent expenditure increase in 2017–18, some analysts labelled this 'grossly inadequate', given India's urgent need for force modernization (Behera 2017). The Russian economy had fallen to the world's 13th-largest by 2015. With a GDP of US$ 1.33 trillion in 2015, this represents little more than 10 per cent of China's output (US$ 11 trillion), and less than Australia (US$ 1.34 trillion) (World Bank 2017b). However, Russia remains a major military power, despite manifold problems associated with some obsolete defence systems, ill-equipped armed forces personnel, and a poorly maintained navy. Russian defence spending plummeted during the 1990s, but in President Putin's first two terms, military expenditures surged by 172 per cent between 1999 and 2008 (SIPRI 2009). However, the dual impact of sanctions and collapsing global oil prices saw Russia announce a 25 per cent defence spending cut in 2017, the biggest since the 1990s (*Jane's Defence Weekly* 16 March 2017). Moscow retains the world's largest stockpiles of nuclear warheads, and it has become the second largest arms trader globally with a 21 per cent worldwide market share in 2016, and customers throughout Asia, including Myanmar, Vietnam, Malaysia, Kazakhstan and Indonesia. Russia accounts for over 80 per cent of Vietnam's and Mongolia's total arms imports; however, New Delhi and Beijing are critical arms markets for Moscow. Almost 80 per cent of imported Chinese armaments and 72 per cent of Indian arms imports are sourced from Russia (Connolly & Sendstad 2017). However, both China and India have diversified their industrial bases sufficiently to develop their own indigenous arms technologies and production facilities. In addition, over the last decade, China has developed quickly into an arms exporter, albeit on a much smaller scale than Russia or the US.

Box 5.1 Key events in Russia and India, 1991–2017

1991	Sino–Soviet Border Agreement signed. USSR dissolved. Russian Federation becomes 'successor state' to Soviet Union, under presidency of Boris Yeltsin.
1992	Indian Prime Minister Narasimha Rao initiates 'Look East' policy.
1993	SAARC Preferential Trade Agreement (PTA) signed.
1996	Russia, China, Kazakhstan, Kyrgyzstan and Tajikistan sign Shanghai Five agreement.
1998	Nationalist BJP government under Atal Bihari Vajpayee elected in India. India undertakes Pokhran II nuclear tests. Russian foreign minister Yevgeny Primakov proposes a Russia–India–China 'strategic triangle'.
1999	US President Clinton visits New Delhi.
2000	Vladimir Putin succeeds Boris Yeltsin as president of the Russian Federation.
2001	Russia and China sign the Treaty of Good-Neighbourliness and Friendly Cooperation. Shanghai Five forms Shanghai Cooperation Organization (SCO). Uzbekistan accedes to SCO. Putin agrees to allow US to establish military bases in former Soviet Central Asia.
2002	Russian, Indian and PRC foreign ministers issue their first annual joint statement.
2003	Prime Minister Vajpayee and President Jiang conclude Sino–Indian border agreements.
2004	US–India Next Steps in Strategic Partnership (NSSP) initiative launched. Manmohan Singh assumes Indian premiership. India launches bid for permanent membership of the UNSC.
2005	Kyrgyz and Uzbek governments request that US set deadlines for evacuation of bases. Russia, India and PRC hold Vladivostok summit. Russia and PRC sign final border agreement. India commences US$ 15 billion defence procurement program.
2006	President Bush visits New Delhi. India and US conclude civilian nuclear agreement. Prime Minister Singh visits Beijing. Singh and President Hu Jintao sign '10-Pronged Strategy'.

2007	SCO conducts first joint military exercises. India, Pakistan and Iran reach in-principle agreement to build US$ 7 billion gas pipeline. India–EU free trade agreement negotiations launched.
2008	(May) Dmitry Medvedev replaces Putin as President. Putin becomes Prime Minister. (August) Russia invades Georgia. (October) Prime Minister Singh visits Beijing. Final passage of US–India nuclear agreement through Congress.
2009	India–ASEAN Free Trade Agreement signed.
2010	India and ASEAN commence talks on a Free Trade Agreement in services.
2013	Vladimir Putin accedes to third presidential term with Medvedev as prime minister.
2014	(March) Russia invades Crimea, Ukraine. Subsequent referendum results in Russian annexation of Crimea. (May) Narendra Modi becomes prime minister of India.
2015	Ufa SCO/BRICS summit approves Indian and Pakistani membership of SCO.
2016	First joint BIMSTEC-BRICS summit in Goa, India.
2017	India and Pakistan accede to SCO.

India in the Asia-Pacific

'Look East'

Strategic competition for influence in Southeast Asia has long involved India, Japan and China. Japan has sought to reassure ASEAN countries of its co-operative intentions through a combination of ODA, the establishment of the ASEAN–Japan Forum, and Prime Minister Fukuda's renunciation of nuclear weapons in 1977. As Japanese firms dramatically expanded their international production networks throughout Southeast Asia in the 1980s and 1990s, Indian Prime Minister Narasimha Rao made an abrupt break with New Delhi's traditional non-aligned status with the introduction of the 'Look East' policy. In 1992, India became a Sectoral Dialogue partner of ASEAN, and became a Full Dialogue Partner in 1996, a position it shares with China, Japan and South Korea. Moreover, whereas previous Congress Party governments had supported regional democratic movements (for example, in Sri Lanka and Myanmar), Rao brokered pragmatic agreements between New Delhi and Rangoon, developing closer relations with Myanmar's ruling military junta. New Delhi has always sought partners in South and East Asia, and the relatively untapped potential of Myanmar's considerable oil and gas resources also compelled Rao to seek closer economic integration with

Rangoon's ASEAN partners. Moreover, Myanmar is geostrategically important to India, providing the territorial link between South and Southeast Asia, and the fourth-largest military forces in Asia. A succession of short-lived Indian governments in the 1990s led to foreign and strategic policy incoherence from New Delhi, but the 'Look East' policy was revived under Vajpayee's government from 1998.

In South Asia, New Delhi was instrumental in initiating the South Asian Association for Regional Cooperation (SAARC) in 1985. The central objective of SAARC is principally economic and resources-related, including regional water management, monetary integration and the development of a South Asian Free Trade Area (SAFTA) and, ultimately, economic union. In 1993, SAARC signed a preferential trade agreement (PTA), while the South Asian Free Trade Agreement (SAFTA) was finalized at the 2005 SAARC Dhaka Summit, entering into effect in January 2006. Despite Prime Minister Singh's strong promotion of SAARC and SAFTA, the groupings largely failed to meet their commitments. However, at the September 2016 SAARC summit, finance ministers sought to reinvigorate South Asian integration by pushing for a South Asian Economic Union (SAEU), in order to maximize regional trade, remove barriers to imports and investment and operationalize an earlier SAARC agreement on trade in services (*Daily Times* 12 September 2016).

New Delhi's diplomatic thrust into Southeast Asia in the 1990s mirrored Beijing's rapid rise throughout the same period. In 1993, China became the second largest recipient of FDI globally and the largest in Asia (Wu *et al.* 2002: 97). Nevertheless, Beijing's maritime claims over the South China Sea (SCS), and the consequential disputes that persisted between the PRC and ASEAN countries, meant states such as Thailand, the Philippines and Singapore were pursuing partners that sought neither regional economic domination (such as Japan) nor military-strategic primacy, which appeared to be Beijing's objective.

The India–ASEAN relationship is increasingly characterized by rivalry with China for influence within Southeast Asia, although the main driving force behind deeper India–ASEAN relations was the internationalization of the Indian economy and the significant growth in trade between South Asia and Southeast Asia. Between 1993–94 and 2003–04, India–ASEAN trade grew by 350 per cent (Indian Ministry of External Affairs 2005). Nevertheless, trade volumes were relatively small – a mere US$ 15 billion in 2004, or 2 per cent of ASEAN's total trade – a surprisingly low figure, given that the combined GDP of India and ASEAN was US$ 1.5 trillion. The 2003 ASEAN–India Framework Agreement also sought to boost investment; Indian FDI in ASEAN in 2007 accounted for only 0.2 per cent of investment in Southeast Asia. The Framework provided not only for FTA negotiations, but also for an investment area under the auspices of the ASEAN–India Regional Trade and Investment Area (RTIA) (ASEAN Secretariat 2007). However, India was slow to develop strategic trade linkages with ASEAN, with FTA negotiations commencing only in 2003. Consequently, at the 2004 ASEAN–India Vientiane summit, Prime Minister Singh signed the India–ASEAN Partnership for Peace, Progress and Shared Prosperity. Vientiane also established a target of US$ 30 billion in ASEAN–India two-way trade by 2007. The Indian National Congress (INC) party, re-elected in 2009, faced an increasing backlash from the agriculture sector, which feared that millions of jobs would disappear as ASEAN exports drove Indian farmers out of business. Nevertheless, Singh pointed to the growth in India–ASEAN two-way trade, which increased more than six-fold between 2000–01 and 2007–08 to US$ 39.4 billion (*The Economic Times of India* 25 July 2009). The ASEAN–India FTA was ultimately signed in 2009 and promulgated in 2010. By 2015, two-way trade had expanded to US$ 58.5 billion, making India ASEAN's seventh largest trade partner (ASEAN 2016). In summary, New Delhi's burgeoning diplomatic activism with ASEAN demonstrates the serious intent of the 'Look East' policy, which has transformed India into a major economic and strategic competitor with the PRC in a region that remains wary of China's rapid emergence as a major economic and military power.

'Act East'

Writing in 2006, at the time of India's 'tilt' towards Washington, the strategic analyst C. Raja Mohan wrote that India was 'on the verge of becoming a great power' and a potential 'swing state' in the global balance of power. For Mohan, Indian grand strategy comprises three concentric circles of interest: the immediate neighbourhood; extended regional interests throughout Asia and the Indian Ocean; and global politics (Mohan 2006). This has begun to come to fruition under Prime Minister Narendra Modi. Modi's accession to the premiership has transformed Indian foreign policy. Under Modi, India has re-engaged with Asia and developed new strategic relationships with Japan and Australia. Rao's 'Look East' policy had resulted in the creation of BIMSTEC, the seven-member Bay of Bengal group (Bangladesh, Bhutan, Burma, India, Nepal, Sri Lanka and Thailand), which aimed to establish a free trade area by 2017. In June 2009, BIMSTEC signed an FTA covering goods trade, with two-way trade between India and BIMSTEC countries worth over US$ 31 billion (Mishra 2016). However, in 2015, India failed to achieve a consensus to move forward with the FTA in the face of BIMSTEC members' opposition. Nevertheless, India's 'Look East' policy – involving both bilateral and regional compacts – successfully matched China's FTA with ASEAN, while marginalizing Pakistan within SAARC. BIMSTEC also ties South Asia and Thailand to India, a regional grouping that excludes both China and Pakistan entirely. However, Modi's India's 'Act East' policy is a direct response to the expansion of PRC power and influence, as well as an attempt to isolate Pakistan both strategically and economically from Asia. Modi's commercial thrust into Asia does have its limits: despite Indian exporters' enthusiasm for an India–China FTA, the proposal has not gone beyond a 2003 feasibility study (*Business Standard* 21 August 2014). In 2017, China's ambassador to India, Luo Zhaohui, made two proposals: an FTA, as well as a 'Friendship and Cooperation' treaty. In addition, Luo said New Delhi should join China's 'One Belt, One Road' initiative (*Hindustan Times* 10 January 2017).

Under Modi, the policy emphasis has switched to 'Neighbourhood First, Act East'. For Modi, 'Neighbourhood First' means that South Asia is New Delhi's key priority. First, in 2014, Modi invited all of the SAARC leaders to his inauguration in order to conduct informal meetings. Second, he visited Nepal, Bangladesh, Bhutan, Seychelles, Mauritius and Sri Lanka during the first few months of his premiership. In some cases, these were the first Indian prime ministerial visits for decades, illustrating the extent to which Indian governments had neglected regional diplomacy (Roy-Chaudhury 2015: 1–2). Third, at the November 2014 SAARC summit, Modi pledged to revitalize the organization, although only one agreement was signed, while key items were blocked by Pakistan (Sidhu and Godbole 2015). Fourth, in order to arrest burgeoning Chinese influence in the region, exemplified by Beijing's US$ 40 billion 'One Belt, One Road' initiative, Modi authorized a US$ 2 billion line of credit for Bangladesh in 2016, extending this to US$ 4.5 billion in 2017, in addition to US$ 500 million for Bangladesh's defence procurement program (*The Times of India* 10 April 2017).

Modi sought to place foreign economic policy at the top of the agenda during his first term, proclaiming 'India means business'. To achieve this, Modi made 56 overseas visits within the first three years of his 2014 election victory, and pushed Indian diplomatic missions to promote business and investment under the 'Make in India' policy. The strategy worked: in 2015, India became the biggest destination for FDI globally (US$ 63 billion), surpassing China (US$ 56.6 billion) for the first time (*Economic Times of India* 7 March 2017). By pursuing a revitalized foreign economic policy, Modi differed considerably from his predecessors, who had regarded security and strategic challenges, such as Kashmir and relations with Pakistan and Beijing, as first-order issues. Modi indicated to Pakistani Prime Minister Nawaz Sharif that 'all outstanding issues' could be resolved between India and Pakistan, although relations between the two countries have been poor throughout the last decade.

Uneasy neighbours: India–China relations

The main impetus behind New Delhi's decision to develop nuclear weapons was the 1962 Sino–Indian war; however, US aid to its ally, Pakistan, was also a key factor (Yang 2016). China's clear conventional superiority in the conflict exposed India's relative military weakness, and the fact that Beijing, with Soviet assistance, had embarked on a rapid nuclear weapons program only encouraged Indian defence planners to join the race to build the first Asian bomb. Tensions between the two countries were exacerbated by increased diplomatic and technical links between Pakistan and China, as well as Beijing's client state, North Korea. Nevertheless, Mao's government refrained from intervening in the 1965 and 1971 Indo–Pakistani wars, even desisting from supplying Islamabad with arms until 1966, when relations between New Delhi and Beijing reached their nadir. However, Indian suspicions of the PRC's strategic intentions in Southeast and South Asia increased, as Beijing established closer relations with Burma (Myanmar) and Pakistan in the late 1960s. The South Asian security dilemma was exacerbated by the significant technical assistance China afforded Pakistan, particularly in terms of missile and nuclear technologies in the 1970s. Indian defence policy-makers increasingly saw the Sino–Burmese–Pakistani triangle as form of hostile encirclement, aimed at containing India's regional power and influence. Closer relations between Beijing and Islamabad also produced deep divisions within the Indian defence and foreign affairs establishments; traditionalists viewed Pakistan as the most serious and persistent threat to India's national security; conversely, Indian defence planners from the 1960s viewed China as the main threat to New Delhi's core interests. Their suspicions were confirmed by the Sino–Pakistani border agreement (1963) that saw Indo–Pakistani disputed territories in the Northern Areas ceded by Islamabad to Beijing. As a result of the 1962 war, China also gained control over the Aksai Chin region, which borders Indian-held Jammu and Kashmir.

Although Nixon and Mao achieved *rapprochement* in the 1970s, attempts at normalizing Sino–Indian relations failed. During External Affairs Minister Vajpayee's visit to Beijing in 1979, Deng ordered troops into Vietnam, which had close ties with India, forcing Vajpayee to return to New Delhi. Nevertheless, renewed diplomatic attempts were made to resolve existing border disputes in 1981, which saw Deng make minor concessions, such as the re-opening of the Kailash-Manasarovar route, which had been closed since the 1962 war. Exchange visits between foreign ministries also took place during Indira Gandhi's second administration (1980–84), but relations soured in 1986–7, as India engaged in military incursions across the common border, combined with a build-up of armour by both sides. However, by the late 1980s, Rajiv Gandhi's government sought détente, with Gandhi visiting Beijing in 1988. Two key Sino–Indian initiatives emerged from the working groups established following the 1988 Deng–Gandhi meetings: the Free Trade Protocol (1991), and the Sino–Indian border agreement (1993); the latter was signed by the Rao government. The more moderate governments of Vishwanath Singh (1989–90) and Chandra Shekhar (1990–91) paved the way for Sino–Indian reconciliation, which was in sharp contrast with the more hawkish and nationalist positions adopted by Indira and Rajiv Gandhi. In 1996, the Gowdra government hosted President Jiang Zemin's visit to New Delhi, the first by a Chinese leader since the 1962 war.

In May 1998, India undertook five nuclear tests, known as 'Pokhran II'. Following the tests, Vajpayee alluded to a 'China threat' in a leaked letter to President Clinton, leading to a distinct chilling of relations between New Delhi and Beijing. The situation worsened when Defence Minister Fernandes, embarrassingly, canvassed the 'China threat' publicly. Beijing roundly condemned the tests, labelling them 'nothing but outrageous contempt for the common will of the international community' (*Beijing Review* 1 June 1998: 7). Furthermore, the PRC charged that India was 'seeking hegemony in South Asia' and Beijing's ambassador to the UN demanded that India 'cease nuclear weapons development immediately' (*The Hindu* 15 and 17 May 1998). Nevertheless, when Pakistan concluded six nuclear tests two weeks after Pokhran II, Beijing merely 'regretted' Islamabad's actions, implying the Pakistani tests were a justifiable deterrent response to India's provocation (Yuan 2001: 980). Controversially, Ganguly (1998) argues that Vajpayee's strategic rationale for Pokhran II was not only to satisfy domestic interests and fire a warning shot at Islamabad, but also to improve US–India relations by demonstrating India's nuclear capabilities. Ganguly asserts that Vajpayee's objective was to convince Washington that India could be a strategic counterweight to China in Asia. However, the Pokhran II tests also meant that New Delhi, in the short term, discarded any prospect of fully normalizing Sino–Indian relations.

Vajpayee's 1998 letter to Clinton clearly implied that Indian hawks viewed China not only as an economic competitor, but also as a security threat, compelling New Delhi to prepare for contingencies on two fronts. Conversely, moderates, such as Shekar Gupta, viewed the 'China threat' as primarily economic, as the PRC's rapidly expanding share of world exports and investment has seen China outperform and out-compete Indian firms for global market shares, particularly in India's own region (*Asia Times* 18 January 2001). In contrast, Beijing's concerns extended not only to India's nuclear weapons program, but also to the significant resources New Delhi appeared to be devoting to weapons delivery systems and arms imports, particularly as Russia sold higher-technology weapons to India than it did to China. In 2005, India commenced a US$ 15 billion defence procurement program, comprising 126 fighter planes (including French Mirages, modified to carry nuclear weapons), six submarines, and mobile rocket launchers. In 2009, New Delhi launched its first nuclear submarine, took delivery of the Russian-built MiG-29K fighter aircraft, and commenced building the Vikrant-class aircraft carrier. India has also deployed the Agni II ballistic missile, which has a 2,500-km range and can strike major Chinese cities (see Raghuvanshi 2004). In December 2016, India's first ICBM, the Agni V, underwent its fourth test-firing; with a 6,000km range, this would give India a long-range nuclear force projection capability comparable with China's (*Economic Times of India* 26 December 2016). Indian defence planners have focused intently on increasing India's second-strike capacity, as a direct response to Beijing's own second-strike capacity improvements. Most Indian defence planners view Pokhran II as a success: irrespective of the displeasure it incited in Washington, Vajpayee had convinced the US that India was a serious and responsible nuclear weapons state; and he had restored the regional power balance.

Despite Pokhran II, Vajpayee and his successor, Manmohan Singh, commenced building India's security framework on a series of strategic partnerships, rather than depending exclusively on costly conventional and nuclear weapons systems. In this respect, India's military modernization program supplements, rather than substitutes for, India's securitization strategy, which is based on a number of pillars, including bilateral and regional trade, and investment and security initiatives, designed not only to expand New Delhi's soft power, but also to balance China's regional influence in ASEAN and South Asia. The Indian Navy's expanding blue-water capability gives New Delhi the ability to control the vast expanses of the Indian Ocean, which comprise its exclusive economic zone (EEZ), an area likely to expand if claims before the International Tribunal for the Law of the Sea (ITLOS) are upheld. In 2004, Vajpayee produced a new Maritime Doctrine, which was adopted by Singh's government. As Blank (2005: 24) notes, its significance lay in New Delhi's commitment to protect the Indian diaspora:

> Whereas earlier doctrine focused on inward-looking strategies, the new doctrine attempts to deal with 'conflict with [an] extra-regional power and protecting persons of Indian origin and interest abroad', points that clearly suggest action against China and in the Gulf where four million expatriates are living.

In 2006, Prime Minister Singh and Hu Jintao signed the '10-Pronged Strategy'. Known as the New Delhi Agreement, this document provided for continued deliveries of enriched uranium from the PRC for India's nuclear reactors. Singh also became the first Indian premier in five years to visit China, demonstrating the extent to which Sino–Indian relations had improved since Pokhran II. In a joint statement, Premier Wen Jiabao said that the PRC fully supported India's bid to become a permanent member of the UNSC; he further noted that the two countries were 'partners, not rivals' (*The Australian* 17 January 2008), a position which underpinned the Sino–Indian agreement in January 2008 on a 'Shared Vision for the 21st Century' (*China Daily* 15 January 2008). But in 2015, Beijing's support had become equivocal. During Modi's visit to China in 2015, the joint statement said only that China 'understands and supports India's aspiration to play a greater role in the United Nations including in the Security Council' (*The Diplomat* 3 June 2015). India's hegemonic status in South Asia, its economic interests in Southeast Asia, and its security partnerships in Northeast Asia mean that Beijing increasingly finds itself competing for influence in ASEAN, South Asia and the Indian Ocean. In the Mekong Delta region, India and China are in direct competition; India's Mekong Ganga Cooperation initiative (MGC) in 2000 linked India, Kampuchea, Laos, Myanmar, Thailand and Vietnam in an agreement covering education and tourism, with a view to expanding the MGC to encompass issues such as infrastructure and transport. In forming the MGC, New Delhi was merely mirroring China's diplomatic thrust into the region: earlier in 2000, Beijing had signed a co-operation agreement with Laos, Myanmar and Thailand governing commercial navigation along the Mekong River (Batabyal 2006: 188–9). Indian strategic analysts view this as a clear intent on Beijing's part to utilize Myanmar as the PLAN's passage to the Indian Ocean (Bhattacharya 2004: 359).

India's sphere of interest overlaps directly with that of China. India's exclusive economic zone (EEZ) encompasses more than 2 million square kilometres, covering almost 1,200 islands, some of which are 1,300 kilometres from the mainland, neighbouring ASEAN countries. In order to secure such a large EEZ, India has developed an advanced, blue-water naval capability, with the ability to project power into the Indian Ocean. In 2014, Modi responded positively to Japanese Prime Minister Shinzō Abe's concept of a 'Security Diamond', which articulated a 'confluence of the two seas' (Pacific and Indian Oceans) doctrine. Abe also offered to invest US$ 6 billion in a 'Bay of Bengal Industrial Growth Belt'

(BIG-B) (Matsuda 2014). Abe's 'confluence' doctrine raises the question of naval supremacy in the Asia-Pacific region. This has brought New Delhi into direct competition with Beijing, which has embarked on an ambitious blue-water naval modernization program of its own, centred around its 'String of Pearls' strategy, which necessitates Chinese port access throughout the major sea lines of communication (SLOC) (Yoshihara 2006, Yoshihara and Holmes 2007). This involves China employing its burgeoning diplomatic and economic power to gain naval access from the SCS, through the Malacca Strait and the Indian Ocean to the Persian Gulf. Consequently, Beijing has fêted a number of states within New Delhi's sphere of interest, including Bangladesh, Maldives, Mauritius, Myanmar, Nepal, Seychelles, Sri Lanka and Pakistan. In direct response to Beijing's naval strategy, New Delhi finalized an agreement with Myanmar in 2009 to contribute US$ 120 million to the construction of the port of Sittwe (Singh 2015). India's core objective is to prevent Chinese naval power from extending into the Indian Ocean; this is why Modi sought to deploy an unprecedented 'Neighbourhood First' diplomatic thrust into the region early in his government's term. India's ability to block or otherwise contain China's 'String of Pearls' strategy will depend on how much soft power influence it can wield throughout South Asia. China's port investments in Gwadar, Pakistan, Hambantota (Sri Lanka) and Maday Island (Myanmar) indicate the seriousness of Beijing's intent to penetrate and maintain a presence in the Indian Ocean, traditionally New Delhi's lake. A key aspect of China's 60-country 'Belt and Road Initiative' (BRI), the China–Pakistan Economic Corridor (CPEC), plans to build an access route via Pakistan-occupied Kashmir; however, it is unlikely that this would be acceptable to the Indian government (*Indian Express* 22 April 2017). China's financial clout means that Asia's power centre is shifting to Beijing. India can no longer assume that it has automatic influence in the region; equally, Washington's alliance with Pakistan has waned, resulting in Islamabad making a renewed 'tilt' towards Beijing.

Beijing's diplomacy has proven most successful in countries outside New Delhi's direct influence; for example, India has few interests in Cambodia. Under Modi, India has pushed back successfully against Chinese power in Southeast Asia, forging a comprehensive new relationship with Thailand. The oft-mooted Kra Canal project in Thailand, a proposed 50-km waterway, would bypass the Malacca Strait and core US ally Singapore, thus providing China with a direct link from the SCS through to the Indian Ocean. The Kra Canal initiative has stalled due to the enormous financial and technical challenges it presents, but it would provide a vital link in Beijing's proposed 'maritime Silk Road', as well as potentially marginalizing Singapore's status as the region's maritime hub. In January 2016, Thai Prime Minister Prayut Chan-ocha stated that the Kra Canal project would not proceed (Channel News Asia 2016), Nevertheless, owing to Thailand's geostrategic location, Bangkok finds itself in the unenviable position of having to balance the demands of its US ally, an emerging China, its ASEAN partners and its Indian neighbour, a position made all the more difficult due to India's control of the Andaman and Nicobar islands, which are only 700 kilometres northwest of the Thai coastline. However, India's 2009 trade and defence export agreements with Thailand demonstrate that New Delhi's diplomatic attentiveness to Bangkok is paying dividends.

'ChIndia' rising?

The term 'ChIndia' was popularized by the Indian Minister for Commerce (2004–09) Jairam Ramesh, and has since found wider application, particularly in international business studies (see Engardio 2006). In his book, *Making Sense of Chindia* (2005), Ramesh argues that India and China should engage in deeper economic and cultural integration. He argues that the two countries' economic complementarity makes them natural partners: in 2015–16, two-way trade totalled US$ 70 billion, making the PRC India's largest trade partner, although India runs a considerable trade deficit (US$ 52.7 billion) (*Economic Times of India* 1 August 2016). China has a surplus of foreign exchange reserves and investment capital, while India suffers from investment scarcity; Indian firms, particularly in IT, such as Tata Consulting Services (TCS), Infosys Technologies, Wipro and Satyam Computer Services, have established a strong presence in the PRC market. Moreover, Chinese firms increasingly outsource their IT and software requirements to Indian firms (Athreye and Kapur 2009, *China Daily* 17 January 2011).

In 2003, Prime Minister Vajpayee and Chinese President Jiang Zemin resolved a number of longstanding border disagreements involving the Indian state of Sikkim, and Chinese sovereignty over Tibet. Sikkim's 1975 accession to the Indian Union was not officially recognized by Beijing, but by 2003 the two countries agreed to open a trade route through Sikkim and Renqinggang in bordering Tibet. The Jiang–Vajpayee joint declaration noted that India

> recognizes that the Tibet Autonomous Region is part of the territory of the People's Republic of China and reiterates that it does not allow Tibetans to engage in anti-China political activities in India.
>
> (Embassy of China 2003)

By couching the Sikkim–Tibet issues in terms of a trade deal, Vajpayee and Ziang avoided complex sovereignty issues, while attempting to circumvent domestic unrest amongst their respective Tibetan populations. Effectively, both sides achieved their objectives, obtaining mutual, tacit acceptance of political positions long held by both countries. Arguably, economic liberalization was at the crux of the thaw in Sino–Indian relations: as both China and India liberalized their markets, their growing commercial interdependence found expression in the forging of new trade routes, which required *political* solutions. By opting for a quid pro quo on the Sikkim and Tibet questions, realists in New Delhi and Beijing adopted a pragmatic approach that would resolve outstanding political differences and lay the groundwork for more intensive commercial collaboration between the two Asian powers. For Ramesh (2005), this shift signalled that 'ChIndia' was a realizable possibility.

The 'ChIndia' thesis rests on the potential synergies and complementarities of the Sino–Indian markets. China possesses more mature manufacturing sectors and developed domestic traded goods markets than India, while India's financial system is much more globalized than China's. India has a distinct advantage in high-technology sectors, such as software, while China manufactures mature technologies, such as computers and smart phones. India has also ploughed resources into capital-intensive fields such as satellites. Thus, India's focus, as Ramesh (2005) argues, is on integration with other advanced economies and developing its firms' technologies and reach through foreign acquisitions. Both countries, but particularly India, are growing stronger in knowledge-based services: both, for example, are competing to lead the global telecommunications market (Paul and Mas 2016: 37–9). Recent appraisals of the ChIndia thesis point to the rise of both India and China as techno-industrial powers; the two countries may be rivals currently, but ultimately the logic of transnational production will lead to the integration of the Indian and Chinese value chains. Both countries' investments in research and development (R&D), higher quality tertiary education systems, producing increased numbers of science, technology, engineering and mathematics (STEM) graduates, combined with high volumes of patent registrations, are likely to result in ChIndia emerging as innovative, technically advanced powers (Kennedy 2015, Engardio 2006, Sheth 2008).

However, it is the logic of strategic competition that prevents the emergence of ChIndia for the foreseeable future. Both the Indian government and Indian firms are cautious about technology transfers to China, viewing intellectual property theft and product patent piracy as endemic to China. Similarly, Beijing has been hesitant in allowing Indian technology firms free rein in the PRC market, for fear that foreign firms may ultimately dominate China's high-technology sector. Moreover, Beijing's intrusions into India's sphere of influence, particularly its strategic partnership with Pakistan, are of utmost concern to New Delhi foreign and security policy-makers. Similarly, India's 'tilt' towards the US from 2006 – exemplified by the US–India nuclear deal – and its wariness of Beijing's regional strategic intentions means that the Sino–Indian economic relationship is likely to remain dominated by lukewarm politics.

Russia in the Asia-Pacific

For much of the 20th century, either directly or indirectly, Russia was deeply mired in Asian conflicts. In 1904–05, Russia suffered a humiliating defeat at the hands of Imperial Japan, which subsequently occupied Vladivostok until 1922. In August 1945, the USSR declared war on Japan; 70 years later, the two countries had yet to sign a formal peace treaty. During the Chinese Civil War, the Soviet Union covertly supported Mao, arming the Chinese Communist Party against the Nationalists. Following Mao's victory in 1949, Stalin initiated a formal alliance with the PRC. Covert Soviet intervention in Asian regional conflicts persisted with the outbreak of the Korean War in 1950. Stalin was careful not to provoke direct confrontation with UN forces on the Korean Peninsula, although Soviet fighter pilots secretly flew missions on behalf of North Korea. The Soviets' reach also extended to Indochina. Ho Chi Minh had long been backed by the Soviet-led

Communist International (Comintern), and the USSR recognized the Democratic Republic of Vietnam in 1950. Both the Soviet Union and the PRC provided considerable material and financial support to the North Vietnamese throughout the Vietnam War, during both its French and American phases. Following reunification in 1975, Vietnam became a member of the Soviet-led economic bloc, the Council for Mutual Economic Assistance (CMEA) in 1978.

In South Asia, New Delhi turned to Moscow for assistance following the First Indo–Pakistani war (1948), but the Soviets deliberately distanced themselves from the 1962 Sino–Indian conflict, as well as the Second Indo–Pakistani War (1965). The 1971 Soviet–Indian Treaty of Friendship was not a mutual security agreement in the manner of the US–Pakistan alliance, but it served notice to both the US and China that New Delhi had moved into the Soviet orbit. However, the Third Indo–Pakistani War (1971) again saw the USSR remain largely aloof in order to avoid confrontation with Pakistan, long a US military ally. As in the Middle East, the 1970s and 1980s were decades of decline for Soviet power in Asia.

Throughout much of the Cold War, Southeast Asia was also infiltrated by Soviet-backed communist groups. Recent evidence suggests that the USSR was behind the 1948 insurgencies in Indonesia, Malaya and Burma, as well as domestic unrest in the Philippines and Vietnam (see Efimova 2009). However, Soviet influence in Asia was short-lived: by 1961, the USSR and China had split permanently; by the 1970s, when Beijing achieved *rapprochement* with Washington, the only remaining areas of Soviet influence in the region were Mongolia, Vietnam and North Korea. With the Soviet economy collapsing in the late 1980s, Moscow's military, financial and energy assistance to the USSR's CMEA partners evaporated, marking the final disappearance of Soviet power in Asia.

The 1990s are widely viewed as Russia's 'lost decade'. Beset by a moribund economy, domestic political turbulence, an unpopular war in Chechnya, and a demoralized military, Moscow's fall from superpower status was epitomized by images of its Pacific Fleet rusting at anchor in Vladivostok. Less obvious was the rapidity of Russia's re-emergence in Asia under Boris Yeltsin's presidency. In 1991, Gorbachev had signed the Sino–Soviet Border Agreement, ending decades of fractious disputes between Moscow and Beijing, which had almost led to war in 1969. In 1994, the Russian Federation became a foundation member of the ASEAN Regional Forum (ARF), while in 1996, China and Russia formed the 'Shanghai Five', which broadened into the Shanghai Cooperation Organization in 2001. The 1990s also saw Russia and India renew an *entente* that had been neglected during the Gorbachev and Rajiv Gandhi governments of the 1980s. Moreover, Moscow's Asia-Pacific diplomacy was not limited to security regimes; in 1998, Russia acceded to the Asia-Pacific Economic Cooperation (APEC). Thus, in merely a decade, Russia re-emerged as a major actor in the Asia-Pacific, after more than 20 years of stagnation. Much of the impetus behind Moscow's renewed thrust into Asia came from foreign minister Yevgeny Primakov (1996–98), who envisaged, ultimately, a Moscow–Beijing–New Delhi strategic triangle that would link the three powers in a series of 'strategic partnerships', which would balance against the US which, in combination with its Japanese, South Korean and ASEAN partners, increasingly dominated the strategic landscape of the Asia-Pacific region.

Russia's re-emergence in the Asia-Pacific: the Shanghai Cooperation Organization

In 1995–96, the Sino–American confrontation across the Taiwan Strait saw Washington respond forcefully to Chinese military exercises designed to intimidate Taiwan and forestall Taipei's independence movement. In April 1996, only a month after the crisis ended, China and Russia, together with Tajikistan, Kazakhstan and Kyrgyzstan, signed the 'Shanghai Five' agreement. Notionally, the Shanghai Five merely expanded on, and consolidated, the 1991 Sino–Soviet Border Agreement, which demilitarized several thousand kilometres of common border areas. However, the Shanghai agreement established a formal institutional structure. In 2001, the agreement expanded to include Uzbekistan and was renamed the Shanghai Cooperation Organization (SCO), which is a permanent international organization (IO). In 2004, Mongolia became an official observer to the SCO, together with India and Pakistan in 2005. In 2017, India and Pakistan formally joined the SCO. From the outset, the Shanghai Five and SCO were Chinese initiatives, with the organization's secretariat based in Beijing and its counterterrorism centre headquartered in Shanghai. Although China has the largest economy of the SCO members, Russia is critical to the organization, given its status as the world's second-strongest military power, its Asian, Pacific and European interests, as well as its centrality as an energy superpower, and as a major global supplier of defence materiel. In 2016, 20 years after the promulgation of the Shanghai Five, Russia remained the biggest trading partner of Kazakhstan, Kyrgyzstan and Tajikistan, although China had become Central Asia's second or third largest trade partner. In addition, Moscow and Beijing have a shared interest in countering potential terrorist activity within their borders; consequently, both Russia and China have targeted Muslim separatist groups, such as the Chechens in Russia, and the Uighurs in western China, under the auspices of the SCO's counterterrorism measures.

The SCO represented a dramatic transformation in the Sino–Russian relationship. Under Gorbachev and Deng from 1985 until 1991, Sino–Soviet relations reached their nadir, while the nascent democracy and Westernized market economy established in Russia under Yeltsin was viewed by Beijing as a betrayal of the international socialist cause. Nevertheless, realism and pragmatism triumphed over ideological differences by 1996, when Yeltsin and Jiang signed the Shanghai Five agreement. Shanghai and the SCO proved to be only the foundation stones of a renewed Sino–Russian *entente*, with the signing of the Treaty of Good-Neighbourliness and Friendly Cooperation in July 2001, a raft of subsequent energy agreements, together with the first joint military exercises between Russia and the PRC in 2005. This developed into a full SCO joint exercise in 2007, while in 2009, there were 25 Sino–Russian joint military manoeuvres, including counterterrorism exercises (Shlapentokh 2009: 9). In 2014, the SCO conducted military exercises in Kazakhstan involving 7,000 troops from five member countries, which were the SCO's largest and most complex drill, involving an extensive range of military hardware (*The Diplomat* 29 August 2014). In 2000, Russia and China also canvassed the option of jointly developing a BMD system, if the US were to implement its National Missile Defence (NMD) program (Rahm 2001: 89). However, although both Russia and China are developing ballistic missile defence (BMD) systems, their joint opposition to the US and allied deployment of BMD has largely been limited to joint statements (Bloomberg 2016, CNN 2017, *The Diplomat* 2 August 2016).

The expansion of the SCO in 2001 was a direct response to Washington's establishment of bases in Kyrgyzstan, Tajikistan and Uzbekistan, as the US prepared to invade Afghanistan after 9/11 (Khodarenok 2002). By 2002, Moscow and Beijing grew increasingly concerned at the potentially permanent presence of US forces in former Soviet Central Asia (Blank 2003). Consequently, both the Putin and Hu governments pressured governments in the region to close US bases. The Kyrgiz regime was the first to bow to Russian pressure, giving Washington a formal deadline for the evacuation of its forces in 2005; shortly afterwards, Uzbekistan also demanded that US forces leave the base in Karshi-Khanabad. Washington complied with the Uzbeks' demand, which resulted in intense Russian and PRC competition for basing rights. However, Moscow's diplomatic influence in Uzbekistan proved decisive, giving Russian forces access to the base. Although this was a minor victory, the episode demonstrated that concerted and persistent diplomacy by the Moscow–Beijing axis within the SCO could halt Washington's steady advance into Central Asia. Russian leadership itself has vacillated on this issue. It cautiously welcomed US and NATO forces' presence in Central Asia after 9/11, broadly viewing them as strategic partners in the fight against Islamic extremism, a battle Russia had lost twice in Afghanistan (1979–88) and Chechnya (1991–2001). However, Moscow also held deep-rooted suspicions concerning the long-term presence of Western forces in the region, exemplified by the pressure it placed on Kyrgyzstan to close the US-leased Manas base, as well as its expanded force presence in Central Asia, comprising 6,000 troops in Tajikistan, with a planned increase to 9,000 in 2020 (Stratfor 2016). In mid-2009, the Kyrgyz government, despite its assurances to Moscow, abruptly approved an agreement to extend US use of Manas (BBC 2009a). Finally, Moscow's pressure on Kyrgyzstan prevailed, as the US vacated the base in 2014 (Reuters 2014).

Washington is not a plausible ally for Moscow; and Russia does not believe the Central Asian SCO states are reliable or durable partners. Consequently, as Shlapentokh (2009: 11) argues, Beijing is Moscow's 'least worst' option as a partner, principally as China does not pose the kind of threat to Russian influence in Central Asia that Washington would, if US and NATO forces were permitted to retain a presence in the region indefinitely. Nevertheless, Chinese expansion into the Russian Far East, and its growing influence in former Soviet republics, such as Tajikistan (see Peyrouse 2008), further exacerbates the mutual suspicion between Moscow and Beijing, which belies their public proclamations of partnership.

The very existence of the SCO is reflective of both the trade and security interdependence of Russia and China, as well as their relative weakness in the face of US military power. Beijing needs stability, energy and armaments, rather than competition, from Moscow, while Russia needs access to China's vast stock of investment capital, its energy market and its increasing importance as a customer for Russian military exports. Beijing emerged as Moscow's biggest armaments purchaser during the 1990s, as the PRC embarked on a rapid and ambitious program to modernize its armed forces. Notably, Russia and China's most significant trade, energy and armaments agreements have taken place under the rubric of the Shanghai process, which has largely resolved old disputes, while providing Moscow and Beijing with a platform for bilateral strategic co-operation. A clear example of the latter was Russia and China's opposition to Washington's plans to militarize the Asia-Pacific (see Tanter 2005).

In 1996, Yeltsin tilted towards China by signing the Shanghai Five agreement; however, after 9/11, Putin staged a major *volte-face*, supporting Bush on counterterrorism and raising no objections to US base installations in former Soviet Central Asia in late 2001, as Washington prepared to invade Afghanistan. Moreover, following the 1998 Russian financial crisis, Putin sought to avoid a situation where Moscow could become strategically irrelevant in Northeast Asia and dependent on Chinese capital (see Rozman 2005: 4–5). However, Putin publicly opposed the US-led invasion of Iraq in 2003, criticized NATO's 2004 enlargement and, by 2005, was actively pressuring Russia's Central Asian SCO partners to expel US bases from the region. Putin and Medvedev also forcefully opposed US BMD plans in East Asia and Eastern Europe, threatening to aim missiles at Poland if Washington proceeded. President Obama cancelled the Europe-based BMD system in 2009 and eliminated most of its development programs in 2013, demonstrating that Moscow's threats of retaliation were taken seriously in Washington. Moreover, unlike the Bush administration, which did not perceive the SCO's 'soft balancing' as credible, the Obama administration saw no advantage in strategically encircling Moscow and driving it closer to Beijing. Putin and Medvedev also had an additional bargaining chip: the expiration of the START I treaty in December 2009, and the Russian leadership exploited this to press Washington to cancel its European BMD system. Russia and the US agreed to negotiate a new treaty to replace START I; in the absence of a treaty, both states would be free to develop new, offensive strategic nuclear weapons, a threat both Putin and Medvedev reiterated in 2009, despite Obama's shift from land-based to sea-based BMD (Reuters 2009c, *Washington Times* 30 December 2009). However, this did not deter the Obama administration from moving ahead with plans to deploy the Terminal High Altitude Area Defense (THAAD) missile system with South Korea in 2016–17, which is viewed with alarm by both Moscow and Beijing, as neither currently possesses the means to counter it (CNN 2017).

Liberal perspectives on Sino–Russian interdependence emphasize the importance of trade and energy interdependence, as opposed to military competition, between Russia and China. For example, during her 2009 Moscow visit, Secretary of State Hillary Clinton stated that she

> believe[s] in a world in which our interdependence and interconnectedness is recognized…so it is far better to have…China and Russia cooperating commercially, looking for ways to support the economic growth and prosperity of their respective peoples. I think that's to the good not only of China and Russia, but to the world as a whole. The United States is not threatened or worried by relationships between other countries.
>
> (US Department of State 2009)

The SCO has also consolidated Sino–Russian co-operation in several controversial areas. Moscow did not endorse Beijing's aggrandizement of the SCS from 2013, due to its close relations with Vietnam and the Philippines, but it nevertheless co-operated in joint military drills in the East China Sea (ECS), due in part to its fractious relationship with Tokyo, which has several maritime disputes with Moscow. In addition, Russia's 2014 annexation of Crimea and its subsequent support for irredentist Russian populations in eastern Ukraine presented Beijing with a delicate balancing act; it wanted to retain solid relations with the West, but it could not afford to jeopardize the Russian relationship. Consequently, Beijing adopted a position of neutrality on Crimea, stating the issue should be resolved via 'political means' and 'inclusive dialogue', without endorsing the annexation (Fratolillo 2014, Nechepurenko 2014). Beijing needs Russia's co-operation to build its 'One Belt, One Road' initiative across Central Asia, where Russian influence remains dominant. New Delhi was equally silent on Crimea and Ukraine, refraining from any criticism of Moscow and not broaching the question of sanctions. Clearly, neither China nor India sees any diplomatic advantage in publicly criticizing Russian behaviour.

Analysts are divided on the implications and importance of the SCO. For Christopher Brown (2005) of the Hudson Institute, 'the SCO is perhaps the most dangerous organization that the American people have never heard of'. US conservatives, such as Ariel Cohen (2001), hold similar views, arguing that Russia and China are

> positioning themselves to define the rules under which the United States, the European Union, Iran, and Turkey will be allowed to participate in the strategically important Central Asian region…[the SCO] could undermine US influence in Central Asia.

However, most realists argue that the SCO amounts to 'soft balancing' that avoids hard military balancing, such as mutual defence commitments. Soft balancing equates to 'constraint actions' in the face of unipolarity (Brooks and Wohlforth 2005: 75). Washington adopted a forceful US foreign policy stance from the 1990s, particularly after 9/11, exemplified by the revitalization of the US–Japan alliance, NATO expansion and the establishment of bases in Central Asia after the 2001 invasion of Afghanistan. Since 2001, Russia and China, having few alliance choices, have sought to contain American military expansion, as first Kabul, then Baghdad, fell to US forces within weeks. Thus, for realists, the SCO is a product of unipolarity, US military dominance, and the relative weakness of Russia and China.

Russia: the Asian arms and energy giant

Much of the focus on Russia's emergence as an energy superpower has centred on Moscow's critical supply of oil and gas to Eastern and Western Europe. However, until recently, comparatively little attention has been paid to Russia's energy diplomacy in Asia. At the Beijing SCO summit in October 2007, Prime Ministers Vladimir Putin and Wen Jiabao signed US$ 3.5 billion in commercial contracts. Included was a framework agreement between Russia's Gazprom and China's National Petroleum Corporation to deliver 70 billion cubic meters of gas per annum to China from 2014–15, making Beijing Moscow's biggest gas customer. In return, Chinese banks agreed to underwrite over US$ 1.7 billion in loans to Russian financial institutions (Reuters 2009b). Russian oil exports were given a major boost in 2013 with the Rosneft agreement to supply $ 270 billion in oil to China (Reuters 2013). Even this agreement was dwarfed within months by two US$ 400 billion deals agreed in 2014 between Putin and Xi for Russia to supply almost 20 per cent of China's total gas requirements, via two Gazprom Siberian pipelines, to be completed by 2019–20 at the latest (Bloomberg 2014). These pipelines are strategically important to both sides for a number of reasons. First, in the wake of sanctions over Crimea, Moscow needs to ensure it has substitute energy markets, as exports to the EU became uncertain. Second, as global oil prices have slumped with the advent of surplus production, the Russian economy has experienced a severe downturn, thus increasing gas export revenue dependence. Third, Beijing sought to ensure its energy security did not remain reliant on the SLOC through the SCS, controlled by the US Navy. However, the pipeline's start-up may be delayed, and gas volumes may not be as large as envisaged initially, as China's gas demand has declined (Reuters 2016). Despite these developments, it is clear that Sino–Russian energy trade is becoming central to both countries' economies. But whereas China has diversified its energy sources, including a deal with Turkmenistan, Russian government revenues are heavily dependent on energy exports and Moscow finds itself in a position of vulnerability interdependence; if Beijing controls a major proportion of Russian gas revenues, it can also exercise considerable economic leverage over its SCO partner.

As Russia turns away from the West in the wake of the Crimean annexation, Moscow is making its own 'pivot' to Asia, which comprises both a geopolitical and resources pivot (Sussex 2015). In the first decade of the 21st century, the Asia-Pacific region emerged as the world's largest arms importer. Although the US remains the leading armaments supplier globally, Russia has marketed its industry aggressively throughout Asia, with China and India taking the bulk of Russian arms exports. In 2012, President Putin noted, 'We see active military technical co-operation as an effective instrument for advancing our national interests, both political and economic' (Putin 2012).

Deals struck with Indonesia, Malaysia and India saw Moscow agree to supply Sukhoi SU-30 advanced fighter aircraft to its Asian neighbours, predominantly Beijing and New Delhi. India ordered almost 300 SU-30MKIs, to be fully deployed by 2019 (*Business Standard* 22 April 2014). SU-30 production reached 1,000 units by 2008, with more to be manufactured by China and India under licence. The Indonesian deal sparked considerable unrest among Australian defence policy-makers in 2006, who perceived an increasing capabilities gap opening up between Australia and its immediate neighbours (*Defense Industry Daily* 20 March 2008). It also demonstrated how deeply Russia had become embedded in the arms modernization plans of Asia-Pacific states. In 2015, Russia promised to consider technology transfers to Indonesia if Jakarta purchased the Sukhoi SU-35 multirole fighter. In early 2017, Russia and Indonesia were reportedly at the draft contract stage for Moscow to deliver up to 10 SU-35s (*The Diplomat* 22 February 2017). Furthermore, as Bitzinger (2006) notes

> Recent arms transfers to the Asia-Pacific go beyond 'mere' modernization, and the introduction of new types of armaments promises to significantly upgrade and modernize the manner of war-fighting in the region. Many regional militaries are, for example, acquiring greater lethality and precision at greater ranges, increased power projection.... The addition of modern submarines and surface combatants, amphibious assault ships, air-refueled combat aircraft and transport aircraft have all extended these militaries' theoretical range of action.

Importantly, Russia is the biggest armaments supplier to both India and China, while New Delhi and Beijing are by far the largest arms importers globally. Nevertheless, Moscow continues to favour New Delhi with more technologically advanced weapons systems than those it permits Beijing to purchase. For example, in January 2010, Moscow signed a US$ 1.2 billion deal to deliver 29 MiG 29K fighter aircraft to India (*Economic Times of India* 10 January 2010). Russian armaments firms are currently India's biggest military suppliers, accounting for 70 per cent of New Delhi's arms imports, as well as supplying India with up to US$ 20 billion in civilian nuclear reactors (*World Nuclear News* 2014). Despite these major deals, Moscow has not allowed its partnership with New Delhi to obstruct its arms sales to Pakistan, India's primary security threat. In 2014, Russia lifted its arms embargo from Pakistan, brokering sales of four Mi-35M attack helicopters to Islamabad (Pant 2017). However, in the Indian market, Russia also faces increasingly strong competition from British, US, Franco–German and Israeli defence contractors. For example, Israel has displaced France to become India's second largest source of defence materiel, although French nuclear technology firms are dominant in the power generation industry (Bitzinger 2013, *New York Times* 20 February 2006, 30 September 2008). New Delhi's Israeli arms deals provoked a hostile reaction from Moscow, which abruptly cancelled joint army and navy exercises with India, even going so far as to turn away the Indian naval contingent from Vladivostok (Blank & Levitzky 2015: 74).

A Russia–India–China 'strategic triangle'?

The post-Cold War international order has become dominated by 'strategic partnerships'. The 1996 Sino–Russian Beijing Declaration and the subsequent Moscow Declaration (1997) established the PRC–Russia strategic partnership, while the US–India Next Steps in a Strategic Partnership (NSSP) initiative (2004), and the Russo–Indian strategic partnership (see Embassy of India 2004) all contain elements of co-operation, collaboration, trade and investment. However, unlike formal military alliances, strategic partnerships do not place formal obligations and costly commitments on participants; partnerships may be constructed relatively quickly and easily, and abandoned with equal facility, should circumstances require.

Russia first sought to develop a 'strategic triangle' with India and China in 1998, an initiative spearheaded by Prime Minister Yevgeny Primakov, a proponent of the doctrine of 'multipolarism'. Although Beijing welcomed the strategic partnership envisaged by the Shanghai Five agreement, Jiang rejected Primakov's overtures, even with specific guarantees that the triangle would not comprise a formal military dimension. Similarly, New Delhi, traditionally a non-aligned power, was distinctly cool towards Primakov's concept of implicitly balancing against US power. It was only after Pokhran II, with India isolated in the face of widespread international condemnation of its nuclear testing, that Vajpayee in 2000 affirmed that India and Russia would move towards a strategic partnership. In framing the new Russo–Indian accord, both states acted out of weakness. India had long suspected China of assisting Pakistan in developing a nuclear weapons capability; India also needed to modernize its armed forces, a task Beijing had already commenced with vigour; and New Delhi needed Russian technology and arms exports to bolster its indigenous conventional and nuclear capabilities. Russia in 2000 was also isolated, but for different reasons. Yeltsin and Primakov had opposed NATO air strikes on Yugoslavia in March 1999, while in the same month, former Warsaw Pact members Poland, Hungary and the Czech Republic acceded to NATO. The Russian economy was still reeling from the impact of the 1998 rouble crisis, while oil revenues were declining as the Iraqi oil-for-food program restored Baghdad's position as a major oil supplier. That the contemporary re-invention of the 1971 Soviet–Indian Treaty emerged in the form of a 'strategic partnership' was scarcely surprising.

For India, the advantages of the partnership relate primarily to military hardware, energy and nuclear fuels. Armaments agreements between New Delhi and Moscow include Sukhoi and MiG fighter aircraft, the purchase of a Russian aircraft carrier (finalized in 2008), tanks and semiconductors. In February 2009, Russia signed a US$ 700 million contract to supply India with nuclear fuels, while in December of the same year, a nuclear reprocessing deal was finalized. Russian firms will also build up to six nuclear reactors for civilian power generation in

Kudankulum, a contract expected to deliver around US$ 10 billion to Russia (Reuters 2009a, BBC 2009b). At the December 2009 Moscow summit, Medvedev and Singh signed a 10-year tripartite defence agreement, covering equipment modernization, maintenance, licenced production and advanced high-technology weaponry from Russia. A core element of the deal is developing India's defence industries' indigenous production capacity, to ensure increased Indian defence self-reliance (*The Hindu* 8 December 2009). For its part, Moscow agreed to refrain from supplying Pakistan with any military materiel.

Primakov's 1998 proposal for a Russia–India–China strategic triangle commanded considerable attention from commentators, even if the concept received a less-than-enthusiastic initial response from New Delhi and Beijing. A number of analysts (see Mahapatra 1999) argue that the antagonism between India and China will not last indefinitely and that the two states will ultimately normalize and further improve relations. In support of this argument is the fact that Russia and India have a long-established strategic partnership dating back to the 1971 treaty. Since 1991, Russia and China have progressively resolved their outstanding border issues and constructed a solid strategic partnership under the rubric of the Shanghai Five and SCO. India has not objected to this relationship. Moreover, all three countries are members of the ARF. More radical analyses (Ahmad 2006) argue that India, Russia and China have a fundamental interest in ensuring not only Asian energy security, but also in breaking the US's century-old grip on global energy markets. Russia, Iran and the Central Asian states bordering the Caspian Sea are the core elements of what Ahmad calls the 'Asian Energy Security Grid'; once in place, he argues, this would 'secur[e] the great industrial revolution of Asia'. The SLOC that connects India, China, Japan and the rest of Asia to Middle Eastern oil and gas supplies are controlled and policed by the US Fifth and Seventh Fleets (Persian Gulf and Indian Ocean/Western Pacific, including the SCS). By contrast, Russian, Iranian and Central Asian energy can be piped directly across land borders, eliminating the costs associated with maritime transport. The much-touted Iran–Pakistan–India (IPI) gas pipeline would supply Pakistan, India and, potentially, China. Abandoned in 2008 in the wake of sanctions against Iran, the Indian government considered reviving the project in 2017 (*Indian Express* 19 March 2017). In 2016, Russia and India agreed to study a project to deliver gas to India via a 4,500–6,000km pipeline, although this would be more expensive than the shorter IPI route (*Hindustan Times* 25 October 2016). China's Sinopec also has a 51 per cent stake in Iran's Yadavaran oil and gas project, valued at US$ 100 billion for its liquefied natural gas (LNG) alone (Davison 2008: 268). However, as sanctions were lifted from Iran in 2015, Tehran sought international tenders, sidelining Sinopec (*New Straits Times* 27 December 2016). Russia has emerged as an increasingly important energy supplier to India and China, while Iran is a major consumer of Russian civilian nuclear technologies and fuels. According to Buzan's (2008) 'regional security complex' theory, India and China are military rivals, but also have shared interests in the region, thus compelling them to manage their strategic rivalry.

Realists, such as Pant (2006: 55) argue that the Sino–Russian–Indian strategic triangle has gradually taken shape since 2002, when the three states' foreign ministers met informally at the UN General Assembly, a tripartite meeting that has since taken place annually. Conversely, Blank (2006) emphasizes the centrality of energy, arguing that the relationship between Russia, China, India and Central Asia constitutes a 'Eurasian security triangle', with the PRC as a principal customer of Russian and Central Asian energy. Blank asserts that Russian influence in Central Asia will largely determine the extent to which Central Asian energy exporters fulfil China's – and, to a lesser extent, India's – burgeoning energy demands. However, the emergence of an India–Russia–China 'strategic triangle' feared by US intelligence in 2000 has not emerged, due largely to strategic competition between the three states (National Intelligence Council 2000). For example, Schmidt (2014) notes that because China's interests are linked with Pakistan, this causes friction in the India–China–Russia strategic triangle. India's growing defence links with Vietnam, and its developing partnership with Washington since 2006, constrains the 'strategic triangle' from developing closer military co-operation. Moreover, as Lo (2017) argues, Putin's view of Russia as a global power is distinctly at odds with Beijing's view of China as a pole of power in an international system where Washington remains pre-eminent, while Russia is a third-order power.

Conclusions: Russia, India – and China: a new Asian 'great game'?

Neither Russia nor India wants to be a supplicant in a Sino-centric world. India and China have long been locked into a 'security complex', where Central Asia, Russia's traditional sphere of influence, is geo-economically important to China as part of the 'One Belt, One Road' initiative and as a source of, and transit region for, oil and gas. India has cautiously established a minor presence in Tajikistan as a counter to both Pakistan and China. For Russia, Central Asia provides Moscow with a geostrategic reach into South Asia and the Middle East, which it lost with the collapse of the USSR in 1991. However, Moscow's military focus on Ukraine and Syria has distracted it from Central Asia, and defence budget cuts have forced it to reduce its troop numbers in the region. Moreover, Uzbekistan has banned foreign bases and withdrawn from the Russian-led Collective Security Treaty Organization (CSTO) (Menelly 2016). From Washington's perspective, neither Russia nor China should dominate Central Asia. All four countries have a strategic interest in preventing Central Asia from becoming a recruiting ground for radical Islamist terrorists.

The shadow of non-alignment still looms large in Indian foreign policy; New Delhi has hedged, while forging partnerships with all the major powers in the Asia-Pacific, thus avoiding – for now – the hard strategic choices it will be forced indubitably to make. As Ambrosio (2005: 409) argues, 'If any of these three states were to defect and bandwagon with the US, then the chances for multipolarity to emerge will be significantly undermined or, quite possibly, staved off'. This is precisely the direction in which Manmohan Singh moved in 2006, following

Bush's visit to New Delhi. To counter Beijing's soft power strategy in South Asia, Modi renewed India's diplomatic thrust into the region with 'Neighbourhood First'.

Russia and India provide compelling case studies of how states respond to geostrategic and geo-economic challenges. Russian military and economic weakness in the 1990s forced Moscow to find new partners as its influence receded throughout Europe, Asia and the Pacific, while Washington consolidated its power in the unipolar post-Cold War international system. Among the few remaining weapons in Russia's arsenal were energy and arms exports, which found ready customers in the emerging markets of India and China. By comparison, India's 'Neighbourhood First' and 'Act East' policies are a direct response to China's economic and military rise. Beijing, already well established in Southeast Asia, and closely aligned with Pakistan and Iran to India's west, has effectively developed diplomatic and trade relationships deep within the sphere of India's geostrategic interest. Consequently, New Delhi's belated decision to seek a nuclear, economic and diplomatic partnership with Washington – the dominant power in East Asia and the Indian Ocean – was scarcely surprising.

Realists assert that, logically, regional power competition will drive military competition, prompting the development of counter balancing coalitions with external partners. Since 2006, India has given every indication of taking this path, by bandwagoning with the US, rather than explicitly endorsing a Beijing–Moscow–New Delhi axis. On the balance of probabilities, we may be witnessing the commencement of a new Asian 'great game', played out between Asia's three biggest nuclear weapons states.

References

Abramson, J. (2009) 'Arms exports fell in 2008, UN data say', Arms Control Association, November,www.armscontrol.org/act/2009_11/UNROCA.

Ahmad, A. (2006) 'Iran: imperialism's second strike', Centre for Research on Globalization, 29 January, www.globalresearch.ca/index.php?context=va&aid=1844.

Ambrosio, T. (2005) 'The third side? the multipolar strategic triangle and the Sino–Indian papprochement', *Comparative Strategy*, 24 (5): 397–414.

Association of Southeast Asian Nations (ASEAN) (2016) 'ASEAN trade by partner countries/regions, 2015', November, http://asean.org/storage/2016/11/Table24_as-of-6-dec-2016.pdf.

ASEAN Secretariat (2007) 'Overview of ASEAN–India relations', www.aseansec.org/5738.htm.

Athreye, S. and S. Kapur (2009) 'The internationalisation of Chinese and Indian firms: trends, motivations and policy implications', United Nations University, *Policy Brief*, no. 1, April.

Batabyal, A. (2006) 'Balancing China in Asia: a realist assessment of India's Look East strategy', *China Report*, 32 (2): 179–97.

BBC (2009a) 'US agrees deal for Kyrgyz airbase', 23 June, http://news.bbc.co.uk/2/hi/asia-pacific/8114500.stm.

BBC (2009b) 'India in nuclear deal with Russia', 7 December, http://news.bbc.co.uk/2/hi/8399647.stm.

Behera, L. (2017) 'India's defence budget 2017–18: an analysis', Institute for Defence Studies and Analysis, Issue Brief, 3 February, www.idsa.in/issuebrief/india-defence-budget-2017-18_lkbehera_030217.

Bhattacharya, A. (2004) 'The fallacy in the Russia–India-China triangle', *Strategic Analysis*, 28 (2): 358–61.

Bitzinger, R. (2006) 'Arms exports to Asia-Pacific region increase', International Relations and Security Network (ISN), 13 November, www.css.ethz.ch/en/services/digital-library/articles/article.html/52719/pdf.

Bitzinger, R. (2013) 'Israeli arms transfers to India: ad hoc defence cooperation or the beginnings of a strategic partnership?' Policy brief, S. Rajaratnam School of International Studies, April, https://www.rsis.edu.sg/rsis-publication/idss/219-israeli-arms-transfers-to-indi/#.WP2eJSN95GE.

Blank, S. (2003) 'Scramble for Central Asian bases', *Asia Times*, 9 April.

Blank, S. (2005) *Natural Allies: Regional Security in Asia and Prospects for Indo–American Strategic Cooperation*, Carlisle, PA: US Army War College.

Blank, S. (2006) 'The Eurasian energy triangle: China, Russia, and the Central Asian states', *Brown Journal of World Affairs*, 12 (2): 53–67.

Blank, S. and E. Levitzky (2015) 'Geostrategic aims of the Russian arms trade in East Asia and the Middle East', *Defence Studies*, 15 (1): 63–80.

Bloomberg (2014) 'Russia, China add to $400 billion gas deal with accord', 10 November, https://www.bloomberg.com/news/articles/2014-11-10/russia-china-add-to-400-billion-gas-deal-with-accord.

Bloomberg (2016) 'Russia says it's joining China to counter U.S. missile defense', 12 October,https://www.bloomberg.com/news/articles/2016-10-11/russia-says-it-s-joining-china-to-counter-u-s-missile-defense.

Brooks, S. G. and W. Wohlforth (2005) 'Hard times for soft balancing', *International Security*, 30 (1): 72–108.

Brown, C. (2005) 'Putin's power pact with China', *Front Page Magazine*, 30 May, http://97.74.65.51/readArticle.aspx?ARTID=8449.

Buzan, B. (2008) *People, States and Fear*, 2nd edn, London: Harvester & Wheatsheaf.

Channel News Asia (2016) 'Kra Canal project not on government agenda: Thai PM', 13 January, www.channelnewsasia.com/news/asiapacific/kra-canal-project-not-on/2421334.html.

CNN (2017) 'China, Russia fear the US is boxing them in', 14 January, http://edition.cnn.com/2017/01/13/asia/russia-china-thaad/.

Cohen, A. (2001) 'The Russia–China Friendship and Cooperation Treaty: a strategic shift in Eurasia?' The Heritage Foundation, Backgrounder no. 1459, 18 July, www.heritage.org/Research/RussiaandEurasia/BG1459.cfm.

Connolly, R. and C. Sendstad (2017) 'Russia's role as an arms exporter: the strategic and economic importance of arms exports for Russia', Chatham House Research Paper, March, https://reader.chathamhouse.org/russias-role-arms-exporter-strategic-and-economic-importance-arms-exports-russia#introduction.

Davison, R. (2008) *Foreign Policies of the Great and Emerging Powers*, Frenchs Forest, NSW: Prentice Hall.

Efimova, L. (2009) 'Did the Soviet Union instruct Southeast Asian communists to revolt? New Russian evidence on the Calcutta Youth Conference of February 1948', *Journal of Southeast Asian Studies*, 40 (3): 449–69.

Embassy of China (2003) 'Declaration on Principles for Relations and Comprehensive Cooperation Between the People's Republic of China and the Republic of India', 24 June, www.chinaembassy.org.zw/eng/xwdt/t149428.htm.

Embassy of India in Russia (2004) 'Russia and India: strategic partnership, oriented towards future', 3 December, http://indianembassy.ru/cms/index.php?option=com_content&task=view&id=345&Itemid=623.

Engardio, P. (ed.) (2006) *Chindia: How China and India are Revolutionizing Global Business*, New York: McGraw-Hill.

Fratolillo, O. (2014) 'The SCO's potential enlargement and the Asian Great Game', Aspenia, 10 December, https://www.aspeninstitute.it/aspenia-online/en/article/sco%E2%80%99s-potential-enlargement-and-asian-great-game.

Ganguly, S. (1998) 'India's pathway to Pokhran II: The prospects and sources of India's nuclear weapons program', *International Security*, 23: 148–77.

Goldman Sachs (2003) 'Dreaming with BRICs: the path to 2050', *Global Economics Paper*, no. 99, www2.goldmansachs.com/ideas/brics/book/99-dreaming.pdf.

Indian Ministry of External Affairs (2005) 'ASEAN–India Relations', July, http://meaindia.nic.in/onmouse/ASEAN%20-India.pdf.

International Monetary Fund (IMF) (2016) 'World Economic Outlook database', October, www.imf.org/external/pubs/ft/weo/2016/02/weodata/weorept.aspx?pr.x=73&pr.y=15&sy=2015&ey=2018&scsm=1&ssd=1&sort=country&ds=.&br=1&c=534&s=NGDPD%2CNGDPDPC%2CPPPGDP%2CPPPPC&grp=0&a=.

Kennedy, A. B. (2015) 'Powerhouses or pretenders? Debating China's and India's emergence as technological powers', *The Pacific Review*, 28 (2): 281–302.

Khodarenok, M. (2002) 'Russia surrounded by military bases', Nezavisimoye Voennoye Obozreniye, no. 10, reproduced by the Centre for Defence Information. Original CDI source not available; only internet source *Wikileaks*, https://wikileaks.org/gifiles/attach/176/176379_090709%20Soviet%20Bases%20in%20CA.doc.

Lo, B. (2017) 'China–Russia relationship key to the emerging world order', Lowy Institute for International Policy, 1 April, https://www.lowyinstitute.org/publications/china-russia-relationship-key-emerging-world-order?.

Mahapatra, C. (1999) 'India, China and Russia: strategic triangle is possible', *Strategic Analysis*, 22 (11): 1793–96.

Matsuda, T. (2014) 'Between Tokyo and Beijing: India's Modi strategy and Asia's future', 26 September, http://foreignpolicy.com/2014/09/26/between-tokyo-and-beijing-indias-modi-strategy-and-asias-future/.

Menelly, S. (2016) 'The geographical pivot of Central Asia', *Harvard International Review*, 37 (4), http://hir.harvard.edu/article/?a=14484.

Mishra, A. (2016) 'India softens stance on Bay of Bengal free trade agreement', *Live Mint*, 22 February, www.livemint.com/Politics/GxcCHglHmc5GelTo5GPLeI/India-softens-stance-on-Bay-of-Bengal-free-trade-agreement.html.

Mohan, C. R. (2006) 'India and the balance of power', *Foreign Affairs*, July/August, https://www.foreignaffairs.com/articles/asia/2006-07-01/india-and-balance-power.

National Intelligence Council (2000) 'Global trends 2015: a dialogue about the future with nongovernment experts', www.dni.gov/nic/NIC_globaltrend2015.html.

Nechepurenko, I. (2014) 'China's clever neutrality over Ukraine and the evolution of the Shanghai Cooperation Organization', Aspenia, 10 December, https://www.aspeninstitute.it/aspenia-online/en/article/sco%E2%80%99s-potential-enlargement-and-asian-great-game.

Pant, H. V. (2006) 'Feasibility of the Russia–China-India "strategic triangle": assessment of theoretical and empirical issues', *International Studies*, 43 (1): 51–72.

Pant, H. V. (2017) 'Rekindled Sino–Indian tensions roil geopolitics in Asia', YaleGlobal, 12 January, http://yaleglobal.yale.edu/content/rekindled-sino-indian-tensions-roil-geopolitics-asia.

Paul, J. and E. Mas (2016) 'The emergence of China and India in the global market', *Journal of East–West Business*, 22 (1): 28–50.

Peyrouse, S. (2008) 'China's recent advances in Central Asia', *Central Asia-Caucasus Analyst*, 10 (24): 6–8.

Putin, V. (2012) 'Meeting of the Commission for Military Technology Cooperation with Foreign States', President of Russia, official website, 2 July, http://en.kremlin.ru/events/president/news/15865.

Raghuvanshi, V. (2004) 'India's new government rethinks acquisitions', *Defence News*, 13 December.

Rahm, J. (2001) 'Russia, China, India: A new strategic triangle for a new Cold War?' *Parameters*, 31 (4): 87–97.

Ramesh, J. (2005) *Making Sense of Chindia: Reflections on China and India*, New Delhi: India Research Press.

Reuters (2009a) 'Russia, India sign $700 mln in nuclear fuel deals', 12 February.

Reuters (2009b) 'China, Russia bolster ties with gas, trade deals', 13 October.

Reuters (2009c) 'Russia to work on new nuclear missiles-Medvedev', 24 December.

Reuters (2013) 'Rosneft to double oil flows to China in $270 billion deal', 21 June, www.reuters.com/article/us-rosneft-china-idUSBRE95K08820130621.

Reuters (2014) 'U.S. vacates base in Central Asia as Russia's clout rises', 3 June, www.reuters.com/article/us-kyrgyzstan-usa-manas-idUSKBN0EE1LH20140603.

Reuters (2016) 'Exclusive: Russia likely to scale down China gas supply plans', 15 January, www.reuters.com/article/us-russia-china-gas-exclusive-idUSKCN0UT1LG.

Roy-Chaudhury, R. (2015) 'India's Neighbourhood Policy in the first year of the Modi government', International Institute for Strategic Studies, Washington, DC, 14 April, https://www.iiss.org/en/events/events/archive/2015-f463/april-09d7/indias-neighborhood-policy-in-the-first-year-of-the-modi-government-470c.

Rozman, G. (2005) 'Sino–Japanese competition over the Russian Far East: is the oil pipeline only a starting point?' in I. Akihiro (ed.), *Siberia and the Russian Far East in the 21st Century: Partners in the 'Community of Asia'*, Sapporo: Slavic Research Center, Hokkaido University.

Schmidt, J. D. (2014) 'The Asia-Pacific Strategic Triangle: unentangling the India, China, US relations on conflict and security in South Asia', *Journal of Asian Security and International Affairs*, 1 (2): 203–22.

Sheth, J. (2008) *Chindia Rising: How China and India Will Benefit Your Business*, New Delhi: India Professional.

Shlapentokh, D. (2009) 'China, Russia, and the risk of explosion in Central Asia', *Central Asia-Caucasus Analyst*, 11 (14): 9–11.

Sidhu, W. and S. Godbole (2015) 'Neighbourhood first: Bilateralism trumps regionalism', Brookings Institution, 26 May, https://www.brookings.edu/opinions/neighbourhood-first-bilateralism-trumps-regionalism/.

Singh, U. B. (2015) 'Maritime strategies of China and Southeast Asia', *Strategic Analysis*, 39 (1): 88–91.

Sridharan, K. (1996) *The ASEAN Region in India's Foreign Policy*, Aldershot: Dartmouth Publishing.

Stockholm International Peace Research Institute (SIPRI) (2009) 'SIPRI Military Expenditure Database', http://milexdata.sipri.org/.

Stockholm International Peace Research Institute (SIPRI) (2017a) 'Increase in arms transfers driven by demand in the Middle East, Asia, says SIPRI', 20 February, https://www.sipri.org/media/press-release/2017/increase-arms-transfers-driven-demand-middle-east-and-asia-says-sipri.

Stockholm International Peace Research Institute (SIPRI) (2017b) 'The state of major arms transfers in 8 graphics', 22 February, https://www.sipri.org/commentary/blog/2017/state-major-arms-transfers-8-graphics.

Stratfor (2016) 'Russia re-evaluates security ties in Central Asia', 3 March, https://www.stratfor.com/analysis/russia-re-evaluates-security-ties-central-asia.

Sussex, M. (2015) 'Putin's pivot: the Russians are coming to Asia', *Lowy Interpreter*, 9 June, https://www.lowyinstitute.org/the-interpreter/putins-pivot-russians-are-coming-asia.

Tanter, R. (2005) 'With eyes wide shut: Japan, Heisei militarization and the Bush Doctrine' in M. Gurtov and P. Van Ness (eds), *Confronting the Bush Doctrine: Critical Views from the Asia-Pacific*, New York: RoutledgeCurzon.

US Department of State (2009) 'Secretary Clinton's interview with Ekho Moskvy Radio', 14 October, www.state.gov/secretary/rm/2009a/10/130546.htm.

Wang, T. (2016) 'The Great Russia–China oil alliance is here (and why it matters)', *The National Interest*, 30 September, http://nationalinterest.org/blog/the-buzz/the-great-russia-china-oil-alliance-here-why-it-matters-17883.

World Bank (2017a) 'Gross domestic product 2015', 1 February, http://databank.worldbank.org/data/download/GDP.pdf.

World Bank (2017b) 'Gross domestic product 2015, PPP', 1 February, http://data.worldbank.org/data-catalog/GDP-PPP-based-table.

World Nuclear News (2014) 'Putin: Russia ready to build "more than" 20 reactors in India', 11 December, www.world-nuclear-news.org/NP-Putin-Russia-ready-to-build-more-than-20-reactors-in-India-11121401.html.

Wu, F., T. Poa, H. Yeo and K. Puah (2002) 'Foreign direct investments to China and Southeast Asia: has ASEAN been losing out?' *Economic Survey of Singapore*, third quarter, http://unpan1.un.org/intradoc/groups/public/documents/apcity/unpan010347.pdf.

Yang, X. (2016) 'China's perception of India as a nuclear weapons power', Carnegie Endowment for International Peace, 30 June, http://carnegieendowment.org/2016/06/30/china-s-perceptions-of-india-as-nuclear-weapons-power-pub-63970.

Yoshihara, T. (2006) 'Japanese maritime thought: if not Mahan, who?' *Naval War College Review*, 59 (3): 23–51.

Yoshihara, T. and J. Holmes (2007) *Chinese Naval Strategy in the 21st Century: the Turn to Mahan*, London: Routledge.

Yuan, J. (2001) 'India's rise of Pokhran II: Chinese analyses and assessments', *Asian Survey*, 41 (6): 978–1001.

6 Middle power and alliance diplomacy in Australia's foreign policy

Michael K. Connors

All fundamental security issues in Australian foreign policy are viewed through the prism of Australia's alliance with the United States of America. This was formed in 1951 with the signing of the Security Treaty between Australia, New Zealand and the United States of America (ANZUS). And while the relationship is subject to periodic scrutiny, this is mostly for celebratory affirmation rather than deep questioning, for who could deny the allure of 'great and powerful friends'? Such was the case during the tenure of John Howard, Australia's second-longest serving prime minister (1996–2007). Howard was once caricatured as a 'small thrifty shopkeeper' by a political opponent – a gibe that spoke to Howard's 'small picture' approach to government and his conservative temperament. It is fitting then that during the Howard years an accounting exercise on the alliance was conducted and published in the parliamentary report *Upside, Downside: ANZUS after Fifty Years* (Brown and Rayner 2001). That report eschewed sentimentality and presented a transactional balance sheet of the alliance – a 'what do we get' approach. The report's opening epigraph, from Lord Palmerston (1848), set the tone: 'We have no eternal allies and no perpetual enemies. Our interests are eternal and perpetual, and those interests it is our duty to follow'.

Upside, Downside reported how Australia's foreign policy community considered the benefits of the alliance to include: giving Australia a sense of security; 'giv[ing] pause to possible aggressors'; providing access to the US military and government; providing preferential access to military hardware, technology, and intelligence; providing opportunities for joint training exercising, enabling greater interoperability; allowing, through association with the US, for enhancement of Australia's power projection; and protecting against possible abandonment by its ally by engaging the US in the Asia-Pacific through the alliance and other means (ibid.: 2–15). Of course, like any unequal relationship there is obligatory flattery, pouting, mutual tributes, threats of separation, and post-breakup love-ins. But this is not simply the relationship rollercoaster of a celebrity coupling such as Brangelina or TomKat. By constituting a nuclear deterrence pact, ANZUS is so much more consequential.

Writing a decade after *Upside, Downside*, Australian scholar Nick Bisley (2013) dismissed speculation that declining US power would lead to a China-drift in Australia's security posture. Rather, he surmised, Australia had already chosen to stick with the US. He summed up mainstream policy and academic opinion by presenting, with some qualifications, the alliance in the same beneficial terms outlined by the authors of *Upside, Downside* (ibid.: 405–8). Bisley noted that even Australia's left-wing Prime Minister Julia Gillard (2010–13) described the US as an 'ally for all the years to come' (ibid.: 410). Others, across the political spectrum, view the alliance as a conduit of danger, entrapping Australia into the security logics of a superpower (see Brown and Rayner 2001: 16–26). As alliance critic Mark Beeson (2003: 117) put it some years ago: 'For a country with no obvious enemies, the main threats to Australian security since World War II have, paradoxically enough, actually resulted from its U.S. alliance'. Why critics would argue thus, and increasingly so with the rise of China, will be explored in this chapter.

The chapter begins with a historical overview of Australian foreign policy before examining two dominant strands in it: liberal middle power diplomacy and realist alliance diplomacy or 'national interest diplomacy'. Alliance diplomacy in this chapter is defined as the prioritizing of security alliances and a normative commitment to the necessity of power politics as the means by which to preserve national security and international order. Middle power diplomacy is defined as the pursuit by middle-sized states of national security and international order through a normative commitment to co-operative international institution-building that can regulate power politics. A state typically pursues alliance and middle power diplomacy simultaneously, as a strategic hedge, or more prosaically because the world is more complex than one strategy can capture and gains may be forthcoming from both approaches. But at moments of decision one approach will prevail, and resources will follow accordingly. Regarding Australia, the two approaches will be viewed as squabbling strategic siblings, with their differences being a matter of policy domain, rhetoric and a consequence of circumstance and political party ideology across the post-Cold War period. Each approach plays loyal opposition to the other. This chapter argues that as far as Australian foreign policy elites are concerned Australia's *eternal interest* is to maintain the US alliance in defiance of Palmerston's axiom. This has been so whether a middle power or alliance diplomacy logic is dominant in a government's rhetoric.

Pining for a great and powerful friend

With no regard to first people's sovereignty, the British Crown established colonies from the 1788 onwards on the southern (Latin: *australis*) land mass known to Europeans as New Holland, so named by a 17th-century Dutch explorer. The colonies federated to form the sovereign nation state of Australia in 1901, but that did not fully end colonial mentalities. For the first forty years of the 20th century Australia's foreign policy was devised in London and the federation's interests represented by British diplomatic missions. Australia's strategic culture in the early period was greatly marked by fear of its Asian neighbours. As Cheeseman (1999: 273) explains:

> Australia has always been a 'frightened country'. The constant fear of attack or conquest by external and predominantly Asian 'others', coupled with the belief that Australia cannot defend itself…has led Australia's policy makers to look to 'great and powerful friends' for reassurance and protection.

Such fears were to be realized with the opening of the Pacific War, and Australia would turn to a new powerful friend. In late 1941 in the wake of the bombing of Pearl Harbor and Japan's invasion of Southeast Asia Australian Prime Minister John Curtin warned of the need for a new war footing bearing directly on Australia's physical security:

> we refuse to accept the dictum that the Pacific struggle must be treated as a subordinate segment of the general conflict [the Second World War]…. The Australian Government, therefore, regards the Pacific struggle as primarily one in which the United States and Australia must have the fullest say in the direction of the democracies' fighting plan and the need for Australia and the US to work together…. I make it quite clear that Australia looks to America, free of any pangs as to our traditional links or kinship with the United Kingdom.
> (Curtin 1941)

The shift, uneven at first, marked Australia's entry into international relations without the obligatory British stamp of approval. And while Curtin's speech was celebrated as a strong statement of independence, it presaged a post-war dependency on the United States that grew stronger in the 1950s under conservative prime minister Robert Menzies.

Shortly after the Second World War, the Australian Labor government sought to promote an active security and ordering role for the newly established United Nations, believing that small and middle powers such as Australia were vulnerable to the consequences that would flow from great power conflicts. At the same time, the government saw itself as a regional leader, seeking the establishment of a regional grouping for security co-operation with the involvement of the United States and the United Kingdom (Gurry 1995). However, overtures on security regionalism were rejected by the United States, and instead the US brought into being a series of bilateral relationships, or the so-called hub-and-spoke system (see Chapter 2), of which Australia would be but one spoke. The two countries also differed on the terms of a peace settlement with Japan. Australia wanted Japan's demilitarization. The Truman administration, which initially shared this objective, began to take a softer line in the context of the Cold War, seeing Japan as a central ally in the region. Truman made it clear that the US would commit itself to Japan's defence, and support a defensively armed Japan. Australia succumbed to the loose bilateralism offered by the US, and when the Korean War broke out and fears turned towards Chinese communism, Australia consented to the 'soft' peace treaty with Japan. Partly in response, in 1951 Australia was rewarded with ANZUS, which promised consultation in times of need (Dalby 1996: 114). ANZUS was less than a security guarantee, as Article 4 spelled out:

> Each Party recognizes that an armed attack in the Pacific Area on any of the Parties would be dangerous to its own peace and safety and declares that it would act to meet the common danger in accordance with its constitutional processes.

Throughout the 1950s, the conservative administration of Robert Menzies made it clear that Australia was tied to both the United States and the United Kingdom, who he considered Australia's 'great and powerful friends'. Australian links with the Commonwealth led to military action with the British in Malaya against communist insurgency in the 1950s and in the 1960s Australia participated in action against Indonesian border incursions in the regions of Sabah and Sarawak in northern Borneo. The historical connection lives on today in the form of the Five-Power Defence Arrangements (FPDA), which involves Australia, New Zealand, Malaysia, Singapore and the United Kingdom in limited co-operation and intelligence sharing. As Russell Ward noted, until the mid-1960s white Australians largely saw themselves as having a dual identity and '[f]or most… national and imperial patriotism were complementary, not contradictory' (cited in Bell 1997: 195). A feature of this national-imperial patriotism was the maintenance of the White Australia Policy (WAP), which since the early 1900s had systematically blocked Asian migration into Australia. Australia only began to dismantle the WAP in 1966 when Asian trade more forcefully entered calculations (Meaney 1995: 178–9, Tavan 2005).

While national and imperial patriotism anchored Australian identity in Europe, in the 1960s that identity began to drift. First, the UK's strategic impotency and drift from Commonwealth commitments, marked respectively by the Suez Canal debacle and moves to enter the European Community, moved Australia closer to the United States. Australia's increasing entanglement with US global strategic objectives was evidenced by its involvement in the Korean and Vietnam wars, and its membership of SEATO (1954–77). As Australia's earlier 'race' fears of Asia were conflated with fear of communism, a deepening of the Australia–US alliance occurred. This was marked by the stationing of three important US bases in Australia from the 1960s onwards. For some observers, the establishment of the bases, which were crucial to nuclear strategy, were 'the real ties that bind' the US to protection of Australia, and which continue to do so (Ball 2001).

Towards Asia

While Australia integrated into the Cold War perspective of its ally, it also promoted its economic interests in the regional neighbourhood. The shift in Australia's trade patterns over the decades was dramatic. Even on the eve of troop commitments to Vietnam in 1964, Australia's external affairs minister expressed what would become a habitual incantation: 'Friendship with Asia, reciprocal trade, closer cultural relations and a clearer understanding of Asia and its people are in the forefront of Australian policy' (cited in Bell 1997: 198). Modestly paced at first, Australia's attempt to relate to the economic dynamism of the region gathered pace. The dominant focus in this shift was the growing economic powerhouse of Japan. The relationship was codified in the 1957 Commerce Treaty and the more wide-ranging Basic Treaty of Friendship and Co-operation and Protocol (1976), which set the tone for future relations as partners in the region sharing similar goals of economic integration and complementarity – a relationship that remains constant into the contemporary period (see Mackerras 1996, Tereda 2000).

Australia's relations with the region were also influenced by the gradual withdrawal of US troops from Vietnam in the light of the Nixon Doctrine of 1969, which compelled US allies to move towards defence self-reliance, thus raising the question of greater co-operation among states in the region. In the 1970s, the Australian government began to pursue regional diplomacy and engagement at a distance from the US. Australia established diplomatic relations with China in 1972, and entered intensive dialogue with ASEAN countries. These developments intensified in the 1980s as the Australian economy underwent profound change. In the 1980s the government responded to economic troubles and declining returns in trade by floating the Australian dollar and opening the country to greater foreign direct investment and capital flows. The aim was to end dependence on primary commodity exports and to graduate to the export school of elaborately transformed manufactures. Tapping into the 'Asian economic miracle' was a principal objective of this economic strategy, and increasingly defined the prime objectives of foreign policy.

Australia's 'post-Cold War' era

As has been much remarked, the end of the Cold War did not end the hub-and-spoke US alliance system. Indeed, despite emergent structures, the rise of ad hoc coalitions, and the joint Russian/Chinese push for multipolarity, the system remains largely intact nearly thirty years after the Cold War ended because it serves as an 'alliance for order insurance' (Park 2013). Australian governments had already viewed payments into the alliance as a form of security insurance, and this rationale continued into the post-Cold War era.

In the following sections, Australian foreign policy is approached analytically rather than chronologically. It is proposed that periods of emphatic middle power diplomacy are coterminous with governments led by Australia's left-centrist Labor Party, while periods of emphatic alliance diplomacy are coterminous with coalition governments led by the conservative Liberal Party. As foreign policy is driven as much by institutional pathways, decisions, regime domains and activist diplomats as it is by grand ideas and commitments, in each period both approaches co-exist in a hierarchical relationship. For example, it is notable that during Australia's non-permanent membership of the UN Security Council from 1 January 2013 to 1 January 2015 the Labor Party lost office to the conservative opposition. But Australia's role in the UN was not noticeably impacted by the change of government in terms of strategy related to humanitarian issues, or the pursuit of a more robust UN sanctions system (see Farrall and Prantl 2016), issues that are in the purview of middle power diplomacy. Centrally, despite ideational differences, both approaches align on the importance of the alliance, and diverge only on questions of the extent and conditionality of the US insurance-security guarantee.

Middle power diplomacy

It has been remarked that for Australia the end of the Cold War came well before the collapse of the Soviet Union in 1991. In the mid-1980s it was becoming clear that communist China was intent on economic modernization that would eventually entail integration into the international order. This reduced Australia's threat perception of China just as Soviet influence in the Pacific was declining too. With an easing security environment, the idea of 'middle power diplomacy' emerged as an influence on Australian foreign policy. The use of the term in Australia from the late 1980s was associated with Gareth Evans, Australia's 'liberally oriented' foreign minister from 1988–96. Evans argued that middle power diplomacy recognized that countries had 'a self-interested preference for the peaceful resolution of conflict, acceptance of international law, protection of the weak against the strong, and the free exchange of ideas, people and goods' (Evans and Grant 1995: 344).

If there is no consensus among scholars on what constitutes a middle power in international relations theory, all agree that size matters. Gilley and O'Neil (2014: 4–5) note the positional approach (the power states have), and identify as middle powers those states below the great powers (United States, China, Russia, Japan, Germany, France, India and the United Kingdom) which are counted as being in the top 30 in the world for GDP. In 2015 the World Bank ranked Australia's GDP the 12th largest in the world. Furthermore, there is some agreement that 'the use of the term assumes a state-centric conception of the international community in which "powers" are defined as geographically delineated' (Chapnick 1999: 73). Australian understandings of 'middle powers' has a 'behaviourist' flavour. Cooper *et al.* (1993: 19) define middle powers as those states that behave in a particular way: 'their tendency to pursue multilateral solutions to international problems, their tendency to embrace compromise positions in international disputes, and their tendency to embrace notions of "good international citizenship" to guide their diplomacy'. Combining both criteria, a middle power state is one recognized as possessing the substantive means to act like a middle power and which attempts to build international order through co-operative institution-building as a counterbalance to the security dilemmas and self-help strategies that crowd the system of international anarchy. In this respect, the idea of a country being a middle power is clearly associated with the institutionalist approaches to international relations. However, there is nothing dictating that a state with middle power means would act as a middle power in the behavioural sense. For middle powers may well favour alliance building for security at the cost of an ideal co-operative international order, or they may not possess the political skill or will to transform capacity into actuality (Beeson and Higgott 2014).

In Australian foreign policy and practice, a middle power orientation entails a moderation of alliance diplomacy so as to refocus on building a rules-based international order with other like-minded states in the hope that this order would gradually supplant power politics. Middle powers tend to display greater independence. Such endeavours have provoked resistance. For example, in the 1980s the Labor government contemplated linking the presence of the US bases to a future reform of America's export enhancement programme, that arguably hurt Australian farmers (Ravenhill 2001), but was rebuffed by the US. Also, following New Zealand's move to ban nuclear ships entering its waters, Australia also dallied with the idea. But in 1986, as a consequence of the ban the United States suspended its ANZUS treaty obligations to New Zealand, with Secretary of State Shultz stating, 'we part company. We part as friends, but we part company' (cited in Catalinac 2010: 319). The message was clear and repeated often. In 1986 a government-commissioned paper on Australian defence capabilities was released. The paper was deemed too 'Australian focused' by the US, which pushed for Australian conceptions of 'self-reliance' to be hitched more firmly and explicitly to the alliance. A mid-1980s drift too far from alliance diplomacy was averted. Henceforth the idea of self-reliance was understood as being 'set firmly within the framework of our alliances and regional associations' (Dibb 1997: 63). The same may be said of middle power diplomacy: it was henceforth to be pursued in the shadow of the alliance.

Even so, realist security logic was increasingly overshadowed by new, arguably liberal diplomatic initiatives relating to trade and security in the Asia-Pacific. In the 1990s Gareth Evans proposed the notion of co-operative security: 'consultation rather than confrontation, reassurance rather than deterrence, transparency rather than secrecy, interdependence rather than unilateralism' (Evans 1994: 7). In line with this new thinking, Australia began to voice ideas of building 'a sense of regional community' (Department of Defence 1993). In 1990 Evans proposed, at an ASEAN post-ministerial conference, the establishment in Asia of something like the European Conference on Security and Cooperation that would give life to co-operative security (Evans and Grant 1995: 116–17). The US rejected the idea, preferring to maintain the status quo. It feared that co-operative security arrangements would bring its own strategies and deployments into question. By 1994, as if to reassure its great and powerful friend that its middle power initiatives were not at the expense of the alliance, the Department of Defence 1994 *Defending Australia White Paper* sketched a security environment fraught with insecurities. Reporting on the volatility of the China–Taiwan issue, the Spratly Islands dispute and the Korean Peninsula stand-off, the paper argued that the US should remain as a stabilizing force in the region.

Australian engagement with Asia led to a bold refashioning of Australian identity. By the end of the 1980s Australia was a much transformed country. The final dismantling of the White Australia Policy had occurred in 1973, and Australia's ethnic composition was rapidly changing. As Australia turned its focus towards Asia, commentators spoke of the 'Asianization' of Australia. However, the government chose to see it as a matter of redefining Australia's sense of place in the world:

> for most of the two hundred years since European settlement, Australia has fought against the reality of its own geography. We thought of ourselves, and were thought of by just about everyone else, as an Anglophonic and Anglophilic outpost – tied by history, language, culture, economics and emotion to Europe and North America.
>
> (Evans and Grant 1995: 348)

Thus, a significant consequence of middle power diplomacy towards the Asia-Pacific was the effort to produce an 'Asia literate' population by the promotion of Asian studies and languages. There was a powerful reason compelling Australia to engage – the phenomenal growth Asia had experienced in the preceding decades. Rather than see this as a threat, Australians were urged to see it as an opportunity. Indeed, the influential report *Australia and the Northeast Asian Ascendancy* written by Ross Garnaut (1989) called for Australia to open itself to more investment from Asia and to learn from Asia's economic success.

Middle power diplomacy found expression in a number of areas. Australia was, with Japan, a frontrunner in the establishment of the Asia-Pacific Economic Cooperation grouping, which eventually tied over 20 countries into a multilateral organization, promoting open regionalism in accord with GATT prescriptions of non-discrimination (McDougall 2001). It supported the formation of the ASEAN Regional Forum, seeing this as an important initiative in regionalizing security issues.

Yet significant bilateral diplomacy was also embraced in this period. Australia signed the Agreement on Maintaining Security with Indonesia in 1995. Australia had long courted Indonesia for two basic reasons: Indonesia was a major regional power, and good relations with it were seen as necessary to advance Australia's own regional interests and engagements. Moreover, Indonesia will be crucial in any scenario in which a hostile power militarily advances towards Australia. The significance of the relationship is evident in successive Australian governments' recognition of Indonesia's annexation of the former Portuguese colony of East Timor in 1975, despite obvious and ongoing human rights atrocities and questionable claims to sovereignty. The successful conclusion of the bilateral security agreement between Australia and Indonesia in 1995 was seen as a culmination of the fundamental shift towards Asia.

Even if the US alliance remained central to Australian security perceptions in this period of Asian engagement, it is not hard to conclude that in the early 1990s Australian policy elites were laying the basis for a move beyond alliance diplomacy that had marked preceding decades. By laying the foundations of multilateralism and by reconceptualizing the region as a place of enmeshment, the underlying rationale for the alliance (security) was indirectly challenged. While the government believed that the US was central to the security architecture of the Asia-Pacific, middle power diplomacy pushed at the limits of the bilateral hub-and-spokes arrangement that could not yet countenance the transformation of regional security along multilateral lines. Australia at this point in its foreign policy was clearly seeking to direct the terms of the alliance in the direction of regionalization, to envelop or surround the hub-and-spokes arrangement with emergent structures of security multilateralism. The difficulty of achieving this end was clearly evident to all concerned, hence the continuing centrality of the alliance.

As it happened, in the mid-1990s a new conservative government led by John Howard took power and shifted the emphasis of Australian foreign policy to alliance diplomacy (see below), an orientation that lasted into the mid-2000s and which was reprised in the 2010s. When the Labor Party returned to office in 2007 the underlying security concerns that were putting pressure on middle power diplomacy in the early period were more keenly felt. The emergence of new security dilemmas in this period revealed that middle power diplomacy was not so much an alternative to alliance diplomacy as a supplementary activity premised on the foundational alliance.

In late 2007 a new centrist Labor government led by Kevin Rudd came to power. A former diplomat and a fluent Mandarin speaker, Prime Minister Rudd starkly contrasted to the Anglophile John Howard. His rise was welcomed in the op-ed pages of Asia's dailies. US policy-makers, however, were cautious about Rudd's foreign policy orientations. Indeed, Rudd's political rise is reputed to have spurred a late push in the Howard period, by then Deputy Secretary of State Richard Armitage, for a firming of security relations between Japan and Australia that resulted in the 2007 Japan–Australia Joint Declaration on Security Cooperation. It was thought that bringing Australia closer to Japan would offset Rudd's expected pro-China orientation (Mulgan 2009) and also edge Japan closer to security activism.

Rudd seemingly confirmed such suspicions when in 2007 he wrote against deepening bilateral security relations with Japan:

> given our current strategic circumstances, it would be premature to embark upon a full, formal bilateral defence pact with Japan containing formal mutual security obligations. To do so at this early stage may tie our security interests to the vicissitudes of an unknown security policy future in North-East Asia.
> (Rudd 2007)

Instead, he argued that Australia should work with Japan and others to ensure that China 'takes its proper place as an essential stakeholder in the future regional and global order' (ibid.).

Early in Rudd's term, policy reversals antagonistic to the Bush administration were enacted, including the ratification of the Kyoto Protocol and the drawdown of Australian commitments to the war in Iraq. However, such reversals were not the harbinger of a pro-China foreign policy. Immediately on assuming office Rudd made clear that the US was Australia's central alliance partner. His 2008 speech in Beijing to students raised the difficult question of human rights, demonstrating distance from the Chinese government (see Barme 2008). Speaking in Mandarin Rudd used the language of American diplomacy, saying that China fell short in its international role and that it should join the international community as a 'responsible stakeholder' (cited in Tubilewicz 2010: 151).

The expected pro-China shift did not eventuate. The 2009 Defence White Paper put China at the heart of Australia's military-strategic calculations, and endorsed nuclear deterrence as a cornerstone of its global approach. Envisioning a China that in 2030 would be capable of extended military reach, well beyond that needed to deal with any Taiwan crisis or border problems, the White Paper recommended extensive military upgrades for the purposes of continental defence.

It is true that the Rudd government reprised the theme of middle power diplomacy, while adding the word 'creative' perhaps in a bid for a foreign policy legacy. However, as in the past, the US alliance was positioned as the ballast of such diplomacy. There was in fact much continuity between Howard and Rudd. Journalist Graeme Dobbell summed up the continuous underlying framework:

> The previous [Howard] Coalition Government was at times scornful about multilateral approaches and the effectiveness of the United Nations. By contrast, the new Labor Government is using old Labor language about Australia's abiding interest in a robust, international rules-based order to underpin security and economic interests…. In laying out Australia's middle power diplomacy, though, Mr Rudd's hierarchy starts with the alliance with the United States before reaching towards the region – an order that the Howard Government also adopted.
>
> (Dobbell 2008)

The 2009 Defence White Paper similarly put the US alliance at the heart of Australia's engagement with the work and the region: 'The Government's judgement is that strategic stability in the region is best underpinned by the continued presence of the United States through its network of alliances and security partnership' (Department of Defence 2009: 43).

Continuity was also evident in a range of free trade agreements negotiated by the Rudd government. In opposition, the Labor Party had called for multilateral negotiations but went on to negotiate bilateral deals with China, Malaysia, South Korea and Japan. It is also possible to speak of continuity in another respect – Australia's difficult quest to position itself in the region. In its early years, the government earned rebuke for unilaterally proposing that in 2020 a new Asia-Pacific Community be formed to deal collectively with issues of security, politics and society. The proposal, injected into a region already possessing a dense network of competing regional projects with deep histories and interests, seemed premature and even hubristic. Despite being stillborn, Australian scholars consider the proposal to reflect a fundamental commitment to middle power diplomacy on the part of Rudd and more broadly the Australian Labor Party (see Wilkins 2016a). Indeed, when Rudd was removed from the prime-ministership by a party vote in 2010, his successor Julia Gillard who governed through to 2013, with Rudd as foreign minister, was quick to reaffirm the government's middle power posture, even as she committed to strengthening ties with the United States of America. Gillard dramatically expanded alliance activities including laying the basis for US troop rotation in Northern Australia. These developments reflected concern about

China's rise, leading also to proposed expansion of Australia's maritime defence capacity. The 2009 White Paper (Department of Defence 2009: 49) laid bare these concerns, noting that unprecedented stability had been 'underwritten by US strategic primacy' and fearfully recognized that change was possible:

> As other powers rise, and the primacy of the United States is increasingly tested, power relations will inevitably change. When this happens there will be the possibility of miscalculation. There is a small but still concerning possibility of growing confrontation between some of these powers.
>
> (Department of Defence 2009: 33)

While Labor had to filter this realist security dilemma through its public rhetoric of middle power diplomacy, and accept the limits it placed on its middle power ambitions, no such challenge faced the conservative forces. For them alliance diplomacy and its realist logic was the bedrock of policy.

Alliance diplomacy

When a new conservative government took office in 1996 it set to work revitalizing the alliance, believing it to have been diminished by its predecessor's decade-long middle power distractions. Australia's new defence minister in 1996 extolled the alliance's merit thus:

> America's security commitment to the region is essential to ensure strategic stability into the long term. Continued US involvement in regional security is critical for the region to realize its full economic potential. While Australia's interests will not always be identical with those of the United States, there is much common ground. Australia's long-term interests in the Asia-Pacific largely converge with those of the United States. Our alliance with the US is a unique asset, enabling us to influence US policies in this part of the world.
>
> (*The Australian* 26 July 1996: 34)

In 1996, the US and Australian governments issued a Joint Security Declaration announcing greater security co-operation, new joint exercises and extension of the lease on the Pine Gap intelligence base. Prime Minister John Howard declared that, 'The ANZUS Pact between Australia and the United States has done more to deliver security of the Australian nation in the years that have gone by since WWII than any other international agreement' (Howard 2001).

Effectively, Howard was claiming that Australia's security has been best served by the US alliance and not by international regimes regulated by the United Nations, or by regional groupings. Renewed alliance diplomacy with the US reflected realist pessimism on the nature of the security environment. The language of 'regional community' and 'co-operative security' that had characterized the earlier response to the post-Cold War environment was displaced by concerns relating to emergent security dilemmas in the region. The government's foreign affairs White Paper, *In the National Interest* (1997) firmly described Australia's national interests as tied up with doing what it could to mitigate strategic competition between regional powers, to thwart the emergence of a regionally dominant hostile power, to work towards a benign security environment in Southeast Asia and to block the proliferation of weapons of mass destruction (Department of Foreign Affairs and Trade 1997: 8). Such objectives easily twinned with those of the US in the region, particularly the US desire to thwart the emergence of a regional hegemon and to maintain its status as a nuclear oligarch.

The government also rejected the implicit idealism of the previous administration, and opted for a firm statement of naked national interest:

> Preparing for the future is not a matter of grand constructs. It is about the hard-headed pursuit of the interests which lie at the core of foreign and trade policy: the security of the Australian nation and the jobs and standard of living of the Australian people. In all that it does in the field of foreign and trade policy, the Government will apply this basic test of national interest.
>
> (Department of Foreign Affairs and Trade 1997: 2)

In keeping with this definition of national interest, the government outlined the strength of bilateral approaches to international politics, viewing multilateral institutions as too sluggish to develop relevant and sustained approaches to various problems. Of course, this did not entail withdrawal from international or regional organizations, but it did mean a greater resource commitment, at the expense of multilateralism, to pursuing bilateral relations in order to advance the national interest. It was felt better to engage in manageable transactional bilateral agreements of mutual benefit than to pursue multilateral pie in the sky ideas. This was most evident in the government's enthusiastic pursuit of bilateral trade agreements, which critics argued undermined multilateral negotiations in the World Trade Organization and elsewhere. The new approach also entailed criticism of the instruments of internationalism, such as the United Nations, seeing these in realist terms as beholden to the states that compose them rather than encompassing an emerging liberal logic that transcends state sovereignty:

> Australia must be realistic about what multilateral institutions such as the United Nations system can deliver. International organisations can only accomplish what their member states enable them to accomplish. If the reach of the UN system is not to exceed its grasp, it must focus on practical outcomes which match its aspirations with its capability.
>
> (Department of Foreign Affairs and Trade 1997: Overview 6)

After the invasion of Iraq (2003) Australia's foreign minister, Alexander Downer, spoke about the increasing impotence of the UN and the need for Australia to participate in security actions with other 'coalitions of the willing' (Downer 2003). In its 'Pacific backyard', the government moved towards 'humanitarian interventions' in the Solomon Islands without a prior United Nations mandate.

At a regional level the conservative government eschewed the previous administration's rhetorical hug and kiss relationship with the region. Howard had distinguished himself a decade earlier by expressing concern about Asian immigration into Australia; in office he distinguished himself by rejecting Australia's emerging multicultural identity in favour of returning to its European roots. In diplomatic terms this meant rejecting ASEAN norms (non-confrontation, consensus, etc.). Rather, Howard's proposed 'practical regionalism' meant openly pursuing relations for the sake of pure national interest. He dispensed with the rhetoric of Special Relations with Asian countries. For several years Australia refused, for example, to sign the ASEAN Treaty of Amity and Cooperation, a condition for its admittance into the East Asia Summit. Similarly, the new government earned the disfavour of Beijing for its support of US naval deployments into the Taiwan Strait in 1996. Even so, the government quickly distanced itself from Sino–US tensions by highlighting economic aspects of the relationship with China. In 1997 the government proposed to develop further economic linkages with China and to channel discussion on human rights into a private bilateral dialogue between the two states. The then Chinese Premier Li Peng asked John Howard that Australia withdraw from an annual UN human rights resolution criticizing China. Australia complied (Kelly 1997: 21). A veteran Australian journalist aptly captured the early thrust of national interest diplomacy in relation to China:

> How does Howard define the national interest with China? First, economic results trade, investment, jobs. Second, a personal relationship with China's leadership. Third, a political relationship that minimises the disruption caused by different values. Fourth, formal but somewhat ritualistic support for China's engagement…
>
> (Kelly 1997: 21)

The government saw itself as advancing Australian national interests through practical, bilateral relationships based on acquirable objectives, eschewing the 'big picture' approach of the previous administration. Three events during the tenure of the Howard government intensified this commitment to national interest diplomacy and the centrality of the US alliance.

First, the Asian Economic Crisis of 1997 brought into question the extent to which Australia's economic future lay with the region. It hardly seemed prudent to hitch Australia's economic future to a region that was demonstrably failing. Such factors fuelled the government's new orientation towards centre-staging links with the US and more practical and goal-based engagement with Asia. Australia contributed to the 1997 IMF rescue packages, and was also reputedly responsible for mitigating some of the harsher demands of the IMF in relation to Indonesia (*Australian Financial Review* 22 September 1998: p. 4). Nevertheless, the economic crisis was used by the government to extol the virtues of Western-style capitalism. Within the affected countries there was a feeling that strict loan conditionality and economic restructuring were nothing less than an attempt to break Asia from its own historic forms of capitalism. In response, there was a growing resentment of the IMF and the 'globalization project' of deregulation, privatization and good governance (Higgott 1999, So 2001), with which Australia publicly identified (Downer 1999).

Second, Australia's response to an emerging crisis in East Timor coloured Australia's relations with the region in the early years of the 2000s. In 1999, as a result of a UN-brokered agreement between Portugal and Indonesia, East Timorese were given an opportunity to vote on autonomy within Indonesia. A negative vote would lead to independence. Close to 80 per cent rejected autonomy in August 1999, setting the scene for independence. Facing loss, forces close to the occupying Indonesian military destroyed infrastructure and killed hundreds of people. As the crisis unfolded on Australian television the government faced pressure to intervene. In this context, and with permission from a reluctant and internationally pressured Indonesia, Australia led a UN-mandated peace-keeping force. Although 'invited' by Indonesia, that country's displeasure was evident when it abrogated the 1995 security agreement with Australia. Howard made it clear that as far as he was concerned this was a cost Australia could bear: 'It has been left to a Coalition government to reverse 25 years of over-accommodation to Indonesia' (*Weekend Australian* 11 December 1999: 25).

While Australia's intervention was widely praised, the image management of its role led to criticism of it as an overbearing and aggressive country. For example, the intervention was publicly discussed in the Australian media as an opportunity for Australia to extend its leadership in the region. Moreover, Howard invested the intervention with a presumed moral superiority, in defiance of his own dictum of practicality: 'We were defending the values we hold as Australians. We were willing to be in dispute with our nearest neighbour, to defend those values' (cited in Brenchley 1999: 22). In words reminiscent of the 'civilizing mission' of an earlier time he explained that Australia had a duty 'above and beyond' to the region:

> We have been seen by countries, not only in the region but around the world, as being able to do something that probably no other country could do, because of the special characteristics we have; because we occupy that special place—we are a European, Western civilisation with strong links with North America, but here we are in Asia.
>
> (Brenchley 1999: 23)

Compounding this, in a much publicized interview Howard did not shirk from suggestions that Australia was acting as the regional deputy sheriff of the United States (Leaver 2001). It took over a week for the government to formally reject the idea, by which time predictably severe criticisms had been aired. Malaysian Prime Minister Mahathir Mohammad fulminated: 'Australia is talking about becoming the deputy to the United States in policing Asia. This is unmitigated arrogance' (*Sydney Morning Herald* 26 October 1999: 13). The notion of the region being policed by two Western powers went stridently against the region's own sense of an emerging security community that was taking shape through ASEAN.

Third, the impact of the 2001 terrorist attacks on the World Trade Centre in New York, and then the terrorist bombings in Bali in October 2002, further strained relations with the region and intensified Australian strategic proximity to the US. In response to the World Trade Centre attack Australia formally invoked the ANZUS alliance. It thus became a partner in the US 'War on Terror', supporting wars in Afghanistan and Iraq while countries with large Muslim populations such as Indonesia and Malaysia were highly critical. Furthermore, Australian defence policy, which is closely watched in Asia, moved from notions of continental defence towards greater integration with US operations, and strategic deployments abroad (Monk 2003).

The Howard government was judged by many commentators to have vandalized Australia's regional relationships. As Michael Wesley (2007: 19) observed: 'A reading of the op-ed pages of Australia's national newspapers for the decade after 1996 would leave one with the impression that Australia was sinking deeper and deeper towards pariah status in its region'. Yet, notwithstanding Australia's battered image, the Howard government's 'hard-headed pursuit of the interests' resulted in significant achievements.

The government signed free trade agreements with Thailand and Singapore and commenced negotiations with other states. It reversed deteriorating relations with Indonesia, first in counterterrorism co-operation, and in 2006 co-signed the Lombok Treaty, which enshrines Australian support for Indonesian sovereignty, thus addressing that country's resentment regarding Australia's intervention in East Timor. The treaty mandates joint military exercises between the two countries. In a similar fashion, the 2007 Japan–Australia Joint Declaration on Security Cooperation (JASC) provides, among other things, for joint military exercises and training, and extensive co-operation on security matters between the two countries (Bisley 2008). Finally, despite diplomatic spats and challenges (especially from China), Australia secured membership of the East Asia Summit in 2005, thereby demonstrating the compelling logic of the Howard approach. Nearing the end of its tenure in 2007, the Howard government could point to an impressive and unexpected deepening of 'practical' engagement with the Asia-Pacific, bereft of sentimental posturing on Australia's cultural relationship to the region.

That a seemingly alienating and 'rhetorically uncompromising' figure such as Howard could build 'such strong links with Asian countries' provides the title for Michael Wesley's book *The Howard Paradox*. Wesley concludes the paradox to be 'more apparent than real' (2007: 24). He argues that Australian policy-makers had over preceding decades developed an approach to the 'Asia game' that took it as axiomatic that regional diplomacy had to be co-operative, multilateral and culturally sensitive (ibid.: 214–26). Howard, in blasting away these norms, revealed that at the heart of transactional international relations lay tangible co-operation based on conjunctural mutual interest, not identity, and in the process rewrote the rules of Australian engagement in Asia with a decidedly realist flourish.

When a new conservative government led by Tony Abbott took office in 2013 it largely returned to this approach, if with less flair and focus. As McDonald describes it, Abbott wanted to develop the alliance further and to be 'more protective of immediate Australian national interests and national security relative to a global sensibility; and concerned with developing key bilateral relations in the immediate region.... The central mantra of the Coalition [government] in this context was that it would be "more Jakarta, less Geneva"' (McDonald 2015: 658). Abbott declared in a speech in Washington that Australia was 'strong enough to be useful but pragmatic enough to know our limits. Australia can't change the world singlehandedly, and we shouldn't try' (*The Diplomat* 14 December 2014). In echoes of Howard's practical regionalism, and continuing work done by the previous government, the Abbott government secured bilateral free trade agreements with China (2015) and Japan (2014), Australia's first and second largest trading partners respectively, in addition to a 2014 agreement with South Korea. At the same time it was a strong supporter of the now ditched Trans-Pacific Partnership free trade agreement that was key to re-energizing the liberal market order under US leadership in the region in an attempt to both thwart China's economic leadership ambitions and to bring it into the fold (see Chapter 10).

In security matters the Abbott government recommitted to implementing the Lombok Treaty by signing a code of conduct in 2014 that provided for the operationalization of the 2006 treaty. This followed a period in which relations had been suspended due to Indonesian anger at Australian intelligence spying activities. Under Abbott, Japan and Australia proved that in diplomacy an adjective goes a long way when they elevated their relationship from a 'strategic partnership' (2005) to a 'special strategic partnership' (2014) that involved greater defence force interoperability and a deepening trilateral complex combining the US, Japan and Australia. The latter occurred despite critics' view that further deepening of that relationship would entrap Australia in Japan's struggles with China in the East China Sea (see Wilkins 2016b). Indeed, in the context of Japan's remilitarization, the move to strengthen the security relationship reflected a strategically realist approach by which two allies are structurally compelled to extend their joint use to the United States. Moreover, the good international citizenship that was part of the hallmark of middle power diplomacy was dealt a significant blow with major cuts to international aid. Relatedly, the government made a habit of attacking the UN for its criticisms of Australia's detention of asylum seekers.

A leadership change in the Coalition government brought Malcolm Turnbull to office in 2015, but that did not stop alliance deepening premised on realist thinking. The 2016 Defence White Paper outlined commitments to major military procurement, and the setting of a five-year deadline to reach a target of 2% of GDP for defence spending (Department of Defence 2016: 9). Underlying these objectives was a sober assessment of the strategic environment. While assuming US pre-eminence for a further two decades the White Paper argued that China was emerging as a competitor, and that the rules-based order was under challenge. It noted an emerging arms race in the region (under the euphemism of 'military modernization'), and committed to using Australian resources to maintain the rules-based order that had underlined generations of relative peace and prosperity.

In such a starkly drawn landscape, middle power diplomacy concerns seemed platitudinous, and in facing the coming storms of uncertain and potential power transition, Australia was placing its money on the alliance.

Australia and the US: cat's paw?

Some years ago when the Australian government indicated support for National and Theatre Missile Defence systems proposed by the US, the Chinese official organ *Renmin Ribao* offered the following advice: 'The Australian government should take a lesson from the past and not act as a cat's paw anymore' (cited in Malik 2001: 124). More recently, an editorial in the Chinese government-sponsored *Global Times* (30 July 2016) in response to speculation of Australia co-operating with the US on surveillance missions in the South China Sea, had this to say: 'If Australia steps into the South China Sea waters, it will be an ideal target for China to warn and strike'. The two statements have resonance in foreign policy debates in Australia. First, some Australians believe the alliance ties Australia into a logic of dependent followership. Second, that dependence is said to endanger Australia as a consequence of being overly identified with and facilitating US interests.

In popular Australian nationalist discourse, Australia's close relationship with the United States is viewed as embroiling it in distant adventurist campaigns linked to US objectives (see, for example, Broinowski 2003, Watson 2001). The fear is that Australia's endless quest for great and powerful friends has robbed it of the means to pursue its own ends. However, there is an argument to be made that Australia has with an independent mind participated in US military campaigns as a kind of insurance policy payment for the alliance, rather than acting as a mere cat's paw.

Historically, during the early years of the Cold War, a key component of strategic independence was the deliberate amplification of the communist threat in Southeast Asia as a means of ensuring continuing US engagement. After 1954 when President Eisenhower first enunciated the domino theory – the idea that if Vietnam went 'communist', others would follow suit like 'falling dominos' – the Australian government regularly invoked the threat of communism in the region. But Australia's rhetoric was hardly matched with physical force and resource commitment throughout its various troop deployments. As one war historian notes:

> Less than one-tenth of the total Australian forces (86,000 personnel) were in Vietnam at the period of maximum commitment. During the war the Australian armed forces constituted about 0.7 per cent of the Australian population, and Australian defence expenditure averaged between 4 and 4.5 per cent of Gross National Product. By way of comparison, the American armed forces constituted 1.6 per cent of the total population and American defence expenditure averaged 9 per cent of Gross National Product during the same period.
>
> (Ekins 2003)

The same kind of disproportionality, between stated threat and actual troop commitment, may be observed in minimal Australian deployments in Afghanistan and Iraq in recent times where it appears engagement in those conflicts was motivated by servicing the alliance rather than providing any substantive military support (see Wroe 2017). Explaining this apparent paradox takes us to the question of Australia's independence in the alliance relationship. While there are many commentators who argue that Australia effectively surrendered its capacity for making independent foreign policy by coat-tailing the US, others argued that Australia managed the alliance to suit its needs. Spender, Australia's external affairs minister at the outbreak of the Korean War, in very telling terms hinted at Australia's strategic interests in following the US:

> from Australia's long-term point of view any additional aid we can give to the United States, now, small though it may be, will repay us in the future one hundred fold.... Time in Korea is rapidly running out and if we refrain from giving any further aid we may lose an opportunity of cementing friendship with the United States which may not easily present itself again...
>
> (cited in Firth 1999: 15)

Regarding Australia's commitment in Vietnam, commentators note Australia was hardly a puppet of American foreign policy, although this is a popular perception. Australia's support for the war in Vietnam was largely related to its perception of the war as Chinese-communist inspired and its generalized fear of China (see Camilleri 1979: 23–4, 49–57). Fearing the long-term dominance of that country in its immediate Southeast Asian neighbourhood, the Australian government campaigned for strengthening the American commitment in Vietnam. As one commentator observes of the escalating conflict in Vietnam:

> beyond doubt the real initiative did not come from the Americans, but from the Australians.... What a study of the available documents from that period reveals is that the relevant parts of the Australian government desired an increased American involvement in the Vietnam conflict at every level...
>
> (Sexton 1981: 1)

What we have here is a picture of a regional power in the context of the Cold War seeking to engage a global power in its immediate neighbourhood. Its leverage is to share in the same threat perception of communism, and to highlight the existence of this threat in the region surrounding Australia. As T. B. Millar (1978: 216) explains:

> The main purpose was to show the United States that Australia was a willing ally, one that stood up to be counted and thus deserved to be stood up *for* if necessary, as well as to encourage the United States to remain committed to the defence of Australia's South East Asian neighbourhood against militant communist action...

Even during the 1980s when there was a discernible divergence of threat perception between the two states, Australia clung firmly to the US alliance despite a number of reservations about trade, nuclear weapons and the half-hearted US approach to multilateralism in the Asia-Pacific. With the return of a conservative government in 1996 Australia moved once again towards viewing the world in a manner congruent with US strategy and more stridently embraced the alliance. In the 2000s, this position has been further strengthened as policy elites have grown uneasy at the prospect of a China-centric regional order.

Richard Leaver has discerned a particular pattern in Australia's relationship with the United States, traced from the 1950s to the present day, which he describes as 'counter-cyclical'. The latter term indicates a constant pattern of divergence between the US and Australia on policy and perception (within the terms of the alliance). Australian policy-makers have attempted to steer a course that avoids entrapment by complete subsumption into US policy, and abandonment, or a condition of irrelevance to US strategic thinking (Leaver 1997: 89). In pursuit of this objective Australia has found itself at odds with the United States on a number of issues; it has not always merely toed the line. Australia had differences regarding the prosecution of the Korean War. It was opposed to the Indonesian takeover of Irian Jaya, which the United States endorsed, expressed doubt about Australian involvement in a war over Taiwan and it has been more supportive in a long-term perspective of multilateral institutions. The thrust of Leaver's critique is to argue against the dominant theme of dependency that is often read into Australian foreign policy. Why, Leaver (1997: 89) asks, is there a stronger narrative of dependence in discussions of Australian foreign policy when a different interpretation might paint Australia's role as that of loyal opposition? Furthermore, Leaver's approach illuminates the very real space in which Australian governments can manoeuvre within the alliance. Thinking in terms of 'counter-cyclical' aspects of the relationship allows an interpretation of the emphatic shifting between middle power and alliance diplomacy as functional avoidance of the dangers of respective entrapment or abandonment by its powerful ally. The approach also allows observers to situate Australia as an active and self-aggrandizing participant in a foreign policy. By extension, it may be argued that Australia has actively benefitted from its relationship with the US because it shares the same global and regional interests.

From a Marxist perspective, that Australia shares a fundamental strategic interest with the United States, as a Western capitalist state, dependent on the maintenance of international order, is not surprising. In a point that could be taken in a Marxist direction, writing of the 1960s, Pemberton (1987: 333) argues that 'Australia's strategic and economic interests demanded that Western hegemony be maintained in that region [Southeast Asia]'. In a realist manner, Coral Bell (1988) makes the point that Australia's relationship to the US was structured by its own interests in the maintenance of existing international order through the system of alliances.

More recently, the post-Cold War era has seen Australia align itself with the globalization project, most associated with the American state and its aligned multilateral institutions such as the World Bank and the IMF. Australia has also associated itself with both US regional strategy in the Asia-Pacific and its more global strategy of hegemonic dominance. These developments are differently explained by realist, liberal and Marxist understandings of politics.

In a realist and Marxist frame, Australia as a significant regional ally of the US can be seen as hitching itself to the fortunes of the major world economy and the institutions that serve those purposes in order to advance its own perceived national interests. In both perspectives Australia is seen as a supporter of the maintenance of international order by a hegemonic power. The Howard government's White Paper *Advancing the National Interest* (2003) would seem to corroborate this point:

> The depth of security, economic and political ties that we have with the United States makes this a vital relationship. No other country can match the United States' global reach in international affairs.... Further strengthening Australia's ability to influence and work with the United States is essential for advancing our national interests.
>
> (Department of Foreign Affairs and Trade 2003)

The difference between the two frames, realist and Marxist, is of course that one supports the alliance, while the other critiques it. From a broadly neoliberal frame it could be argued that Australian foreign policy has largely sought to advance the cause of interdependence through its support for the globalization project, but that it realistically recognizes this project is far from easily pursued via multilateral institutions. It thus chooses to pursue its interests via bilateralism as well as supporting multilateral institutions. Furthermore, until security dilemmas in the region are diminished, it necessarily orients itself decisively in the direction of the US. Historically, Australia has not so much been a pawn of its great and powerful friends, but rather an active participant in the various economic and security mechanisms through which it pursues its national interests.

An inconclusive interregnum

Well before the paradigm-busting Trump administration took office in January 2017, sections of Australia's foreign policy community were arguing that the rise of China was so transformational as to require a re-orientation of Australian foreign policy given that it was unlikely the US could maintain global primacy. Most prominently, Hugh White has in realist vein argued that Australia should use its alliance with the United States to convince its ally of the wisdom of giving up its primacy in the Asia-Pacific and accept the rise of China and the gradual emergence of a concert of powers (White 2011).

Ridiculed at the time, White's arguments have, not necessarily by design, a certain prophetic quality, and it may also be noted that the notion of a concert of powers is not necessarily antithetical to Russian and Chinese-declared objectives of creating a multipolar world. White's model is of course the conservative concert of powers that emerged from the Congress of Vienna (1814–15) which heralded a century-long system of great power co-operation and relative peace to fix European borders and to withstand the revolutionary and nationalist fervour that had been partly unleashed by the Napoleonic Wars (1803–15). As White (2011: 86) describes it: 'The heart of a concert of power is an understanding among all the great powers in a system that if any of them tries to exert hegemony over the rest, the others will fight to prevent or oppose it…'. The logic of a concert was that great powers would respect each other's 'legitimate international interests'. White presents an alarming example of how a concert may have functioned to prevent the Second World War. Had the great powers of the time, he argues, allowed Hitler's expansion into Czechoslovakia, following the annexation of Austria, on the express understanding that any further move into Poland would lead to all-out war, war may have been avoided. It is not necessary to extrapolate what a gruesome example this is, based on mechanical realist logic. What, one wonders, are the legitimate international interests of China, India, Japan, Russia and the United States that must be respected? What would a Concert of Asia mean for the region and its subjects who would become prisoners to a logic of legitimate spheres of influence?

The argument for a concert of powers and its ability to hold great powers to an equilibrium is a direct challenge to the liberal order, backed by military might, that emerged in the mid-20th century and expanded after the end of the Cold War. This giving up on the liberal order is from a realist perspective seen as a structurally determined outcome of a power transition that is bringing into being a new balance of power system. Australian foreign policy in this perspective is based on a fading logic of US supremacy.

If a new form of power politics does indeed erode international institutions the polite dance between middle power and alliance diplomacy that has marked Australian foreign policy may well spin out of control, and the policy choices will be more substantive. This is evident in the Labor foreign affairs spokesperson Penny Wong's (2016) response to the challenges of the Trump presidency:

> The alliance also must continue to be defined by the principles that have always underpinned it – the same principles and shared values that have shaped our postwar world order – democracy, freedom and human rights. Our common interests with the US include support for a strong alliance system in Asia; a liberal, open, global trading system; and a commitment to deal collectively with global threats and challenges.

But now that world order is being challenged by its very centre. The Trump administration's withdrawal from the Trans-Pacific Partnership, its attacks on the UN and the European Union, its dramatically increased arms spending and its pressure on allies to do likewise, its disavowal of liberal institutions and globalization, and its embrace of outwardly authoritarian leaders such as Russia's Putin, dramatically recasts the Australia–US alliance. If the premise of that relationship has been to largely support, under US leadership, a rules-based liberal order, then the relationship has been able to weather various tensions. But what happens if Australia's senior alliance partner departs from a shared worldview?

In the context of a transition to a post-unipolar moment and a US presidency bent on recalibrating the alliance system in a way that primes directly to American interests, Australian foreign policy may well have to reinvent itself. In the early Trump period, Australian fear of abandonment if it does not yield to US demands on increased spending and greater military commitments to operations, may lead to hyper-alliance clinging no matter where it leads. But that would only be a starting point for substantive debate.

Finally, and in recognition of the unpredictable nature of the Trump administration, even if a policy retreat occurs and the administration conforms to a more realist US hegemonic position, a potential future has now been glimpsed and the fragile nature of US strategic posture revealed. Expectations of US primacy lasting for a further generation are likely to be reviewed and foreign policies recalibrated. For Australia's foreign policy establishment that means examining the conflation of eternal interests with the United States that has occurred under ANZUS.

References

Ball, D. (2001) 'The strategic essence', *Australian Journal of International Affairs*, 55 (2): 235–48.

Barme, G. (2008) 'Rudd rewrites the rules of engagement', *Sydney Morning Herald*, 12 April.

Beeson, M. (2003) 'American hegemony: the view from Australia', *SAIS Review*, 23 (2): 113–31.

Beeson, M. and R. Higgott (2014) 'The changing architecture of politics in the Asia-Pacific: Australia's middle power moment?' *International Relations of the Asia Pacific*, 14 (2): 215–37.

Bell, C. (1988) *Dependent Ally: A Study of Australian Foreign Policy*, Oxford: Oxford University Press.

Bell, R. (1997) 'Anticipating the Pacific century? Australian responses to re-alignments in the AsiaPacific' in M. T. Berger and D. A. Borer (eds), *The Rise of East Asia*, London: Routledge.

Bisley, N. (2008) 'The Japan–Australia Security Declaration and the changing regional setting: wheels, webs and beyond?' *Australian Journal of International Affairs*, 62 (1): 38–52.

Bisley, N. (2013) '"An ally for all the years to come": why Australia is not a conflicted US ally', *Australian Journal of International Affairs*, 67 (4): 403–18.

Brenchley, F. (1999) 'The Howard defence doctrine', *The Bulletin*, 28 September, 22–4.

Broinowski, A. (2003) *Howard's War*, Carlton North, VIC: Scribe Publications.

Brown, G. and L. Rayner (2001) *Upside, Downside: ANZUS After Fifty Years*, Current Issues Brief No. 3 2001–02, Canberra: Department of the Parliamentary Library.

Camilleri, J. A. (1979) *An Introduction to Australian Foreign Policy*, South Melbourne: Jacaranda Press.

Catalinac, A. (2010) 'Why New Zealand took itself out of ANZUS', *Foreign Policy Analysis*, 6: 317–38.

Chapnick, A. (1999) 'The middle power', *Canadian Foreign Policy*, 7: 73–82.

Cheeseman, G. (1999) 'Australia: white experience of fear and dependence' in K. Booth and R. Trood (eds), *Strategic Cultures in the Asia-Pacific Region*, Basingstoke: Macmillan.

Cooper, A., R. Higgott and K. Nossal (1993) *Relocating Middle Powers: Australia and Canada in a Changing World Order*, Vancouver: University of British Columbia Press.

Curtin, J. (1941) 'The Task Ahead', *The Herald* (Melbourne), 27 December, http://john.curtin.edu.au/pmportal/text/00468.html.

Dalby, S. (1996) 'Security discourse, the ANZUS alliance and Australian identity' in G. Cheeseman and R. Bruce (eds), *Discourses of Danger and Dread Frontiers: Australian Defence and Security Thinking after the Cold War*, St Leonards: Allen & Unwin.

Department of Defence (1993) *Strategic Review*, Canberra: Commonwealth of Australia.

Department of Defence (1994) *Defending Australia*, Canberra: Commonwealth of Australia.

Department of Defence (2009) *Defending Australia in the Asia Pacific*, Canberra: Commonwealth of Australia.

Department of Defence (2016) *2016 Defence White Paper*, Canberra: Commonwealth of Australia.

Department of Foreign Affairs and Trade (1997) *In the National Interest: Australia's Foreign and Trade Policy: White Paper*, Canberra: Commonwealth of Australia.

Department of Foreign Affairs and Trade (2003) *Advancing the National Interest: Australia's Foreign and Trade Policy White Paper*, Canberra: Commonwealth of Australia.

Dibb, P. (1997) 'Australia's defence policies in the post-Cold War era' in J. Cotton and J. Ravenhill (eds), *Seeking Asian Engagement: Australia in World Affairs, 1991–1995*, Oxford: Oxford University Press.

Dobbell, G. (2008) 'Australia's PM sets out foreign policy agenda', transcript of Connect Asia radio programme, broadcast 27 March, www.abc.net.au/ra/programguide/stories/200803/s2200672.htm.

Downer, A. (1999) 'Australia and Asia—traders and partners', speech given at Perth, 19 August, www.dfat.gov.au/media/speeches/foreign/1999/990819_asia_society.html.

Downer, A. (2003) 'Security in an unstable world', speech given at the National Press Club, 26 June, www.foreignminister.gov.au/speeches/2003/030626_unstableworld.html.

Ekins, A. (2003) 'Impressions: Australians in Vietnam', Official History Unit, Australian War Memorial Online, www.awm.gov.au/events/travelling/impressions/overview.htm.

Evans, G. (1994) 'Cooperative security and intrastate conflict', *Foreign Policy*, 96: 3–20.

Evans, G. and B. Grant (1995) *Australia's Foreign Relations in the World of the 1990s*, 2nd edn, Carlton: Melbourne University Press.

Farrall, J. and J. Prantl (2016) 'Leveraging diplomatic power and influence on the UN Security Council: the case of Australia', *Australian Journal of International Affairs*, 70 (6): 601–12.

Firth, S. (1999) *Australia in International Politics: An Introduction to Australian Foreign Policy*, St Leonards: Allen & Unwin.

Garnaut, R. (1989) *Australia and the Northeast Asian Ascendancy*, Canberra: Australian Government Publishing Service.

Gilley, B. and A. O'Neil (2014) 'China's rise through the prism of middle powers' in B. Gilley and A. O'Neil (eds), *Middle Powers and the Rise of China*, Washington, DC: Georgetown University Press.

Gurry, M. (1995) 'Identifying Australia's "region": from Evatt to Evans', *Australian Journal of International Affairs*, 49 (1): 17–31.

Higgott, R. (1999) 'The international relations of the Asian Economic Crisis: a study in the politics of resentment' in R. Robison, M. Beeson, K. Jayasuriya and H.-R. Sim (eds), *Politics and Markets in the Wake of the Asian Crisis*, London: Routledge.

Howard, J. (2001) 'Transcript of the Prime Minister the Hon MP address at Federation Frontline Centrepiece Event, Darwin', 19 February, www.pm.gov.au/news/speeches/2001/speech760.htm.

Kelly, P. (1997) 'Marriage of convenience', *Weekend Australian*, 5 April, 21.

Leaver, R. (1997) 'Patterns of dependence in post-war Australian foreign policy' in R. Leaver and D. Cox (eds), *Middling, Meddling, Muddling: Issues in Australian Foreign Policy*, St Leonards: Allen & Unwin.

Leaver, R. (2001) 'The meanings, origins and implications of "the Howard Doctrine"', *The Pacific Review*, 14: 15–34.

Mackerras, C. (ed.) (1996) *Australia and China: Partners in Asia*, South Melbourne: Macmillan Education Australia.

Malik, M. (2001) 'Australia and China: divergence or convergence of interests?' in J. Cotton and J. Ravenhill (eds), *The National Interest in a Global Era: Australia in World Affairs, 1996–2000*, Melbourne: Oxford University Press.

McDonald, M. (2015) 'Australian foreign policy under the Abbott government: foreign policy as domestic politics?' *Australian Journal of International Affairs*, 69 (6): 651–69.

McDougall, D. (2001) 'Australia and Asia-Pacific security regionalism: from Hawke and Keating to Howard', *Contemporary Southeast Asia*, 23 (1): 81–100.

Meaney, N. (1995) 'The end of "White Australia" and Australia's changing perceptions of Asia, 1945–1990', *Australian Journal of International Affairs*, 49 (2): 171–89.

Millar, T. B. (1978) *Australia in Peace and War: External Relations, 1788–1977*, Canberra: Australian National University Press.

Monk, P. A. (2003) 'Strategic changing of the guard', *Australian Financial Review*, 6 June, 6.

Mulgan, A. G. (2009) 'Japan is at ease in the house of the risen Rudd-san', *East Asia Forum* 29 March, www.eastasiaforum.org/2009/03/30/japan-is-at-ease-in-the-house-of-the-risen-rudd-san/.

Park, J. (2013) 'The persistence of the US-led alliances in the Asia-Pacific: an order insurance explanation', *International Relations of the Asia-Pacific*, 13 (3): 352–7.

Pemberton, G. (1987) *All the Way: Australia's Road to Vietnam*, Sydney: Allen & Unwin.

Ravenhill, J. (2001) 'Allies but not friends: the economic relationship', *Australian Journal of International Affairs*, 55 (2): 249–59.

Rudd, K. (2007) 'Don't lock China out', *The Age*, 14 March.

Sexton, M. (1981) *War for the Asking: Australia's Vietnam Secrets*, Ringwood: Penguin Books.

So, A. Y. (2001) 'The "globalization project" and East Asia: an opportunity or a trap?' in J. C. Hsiung (ed.), *Twenty First Century World Order and the Asia-Pacific*, New York: Palgrave.

Tavan, G. (2005) *The Long, Slow Death of White Australia*, Carlton North, Victoria: Scribe.

Tereda, T. (2000) 'The Australia–Japan partnership in the Asia-Pacific', *Contemporary Southeast Asia*, 22: 175–98.

Tubilewicz, C. (2010) 'The 2009 Defence White Paper and the Rudd government's response to China's rise', *Australian Journal of Political Science*, 45 (1): 149–57.

Watson, D. (2001) 'Rabbit syndrome: Australia and America', *Quarterly Essay*, 4: 1–59.

Wesley, M. (2007) *The Howard Paradox: Australian Diplomacy in Asia 1996–2006*, Sydney: ABC Books.

White, H. (2011) 'Power shift: rethinking Australia's place in the Asian century', *Australian Journal of International Affairs*, 65 (1): 81–93.

Wilkins, T. (2016a) 'Australia and middle power approaches to Asia-Pacific regionalism', *Australian Journal of Political Science*, 52 (1): 110–25.

Wilkins, T. (2016b). 'The Japan choice: reconsidering the risks and opportunities of the "Special Relationship" for Australia', *International Relations of the Asia-Pacific*, 16 (3): 477–520.

Wong, P. (2016) 'Trump's election is a turning point for Australian foreign policy', *Sydney Morning Herald*, 15 November.

Wroe, D. (2017) 'The Secret Iraq Dossier', *Sydney Morning Herald*, 27 February, www.smh.com.au/interactive/2017/iraq-dossier/

7 Southeast Asia

ASEAN and the challenge of regionalism in the Asia-Pacific

Jörn Dosch

What is ASEAN?

What is ASEAN? An international organization? An economic community? A forum for co-operation and policy co-ordination among governments in Southeast Asia? Something like the European Union? Integration in Southeast Asia has many facets but is strikingly different from the European experience.

ASEAN came into existence in 1967 as a child of the Cold War which had just reached a new peak as the result of the Vietnam War. Although never officially stated, we know today that ASEAN's founding fathers saw intensified regional co-operation as a means of strengthening Southeast Asia's position in the Asia-Pacific area and thereby reducing the risk of becoming a victim of great power rivalry. Over the following three decades the association successfully institutionalized a network of regular meetings among the member states that enabled the governments of Southeast Asia to liaise on problems or challenges the region faced. ASEAN has gained a reputation for having orchestrated Vietnam's withdrawal from Cambodia and the subsequent Paris Peace Agreements of 1991 that ended the Indochina conflict. One of the most remarkable successes of ASEAN has been the ability of its member states to (seemingly) harmonize their foreign policies and often speak with one voice in international affairs. This in turn allowed ASEAN to establish formal relations with the leading regional and global powers such as the United States, the European Union, China and Japan within the framework of annual conference series and fora such as the ASEAN Post-Ministerial Conferences (PMCs) and the ASEAN Regional Forum (ARF).

After the outbreak of the Asian Financial Crisis in 1997, an economic meltdown triggered by a series of currency devaluations and other factors, some observers became rather sceptical and even suggested that ASEAN might dissolve. Subsequently the organization was criticized for holding on to what seem to be decades-old, outdated concepts, such as the strict adherence to the principle of non-interference and the necessity of reaching consensus on every single issue, no matter how marginal it may be. Partly in response to these critical voices that could be heard both within and outside the region, in December 2005 in Kuala Lumpur, the leaders of ASEAN's member states committed themselves to establishing an ASEAN Charter that would serve as the organization's legal and institutional framework. After two years of deliberations the Charter was adopted at ASEAN's 40th-anniversary summit in Singapore in November 2007 (see ASEAN 2007). On paper the ASEAN Charter commits Southeast Asia to liberal norms and values – such as democracy, human rights and the rule of law – that go significantly beyond anything that would have been possible in the preceding decades. The establishment of the ASEAN Intergovernmental Commission on Human Rights (AICHR) and the unveiling of the ASEAN Charter on Human Rights in 2012 provide further evidence of this shift. At the same time the organization has not departed from its traditional rejection of European-style integration where decision-making authority rests with central institutions (most importantly the European Commission) and citizens have their say in politics (for example via casting their vote in elections to the European Parliament). ASEAN on the contrary is still a government-centred entity where national sovereignty rules. As Katja Freistein aptly summarizes,

> The context of ASEAN's institutional discourse is one of politics between heterogeneous states. In their tradition of regional politics, member states of ASEAN have mostly stressed the importance of unanimous agreements, and the association has been censured for its agreements based often on a minimal consensus and for the merely declaratory character of each document produced in ASEAN.
>
> (Freistein 2013: 411)

Then again, few deny that ASEAN has prominently contributed to the management of regional order: after all, war among member states has been absent for five decades, if one discounts occasional skirmishes such as the territorial dispute between Thailand and Cambodia (2008–11) over the area surrounding the 11th-century border temple of Preah Vihear. Moreover, after many unsuccessful and half-hearted attempts at regional trade liberalization, ASEAN finally committed itself to economic integration: the ASEAN Free Trade Agreement, signed in 1992 and gradually implemented in the following years, paved the way for the ASEAN Economic Community which formally came into existence on 31 December 2015.

This chapter will, first, address the issue of regionalism and regionalization in general terms; second, shed some light on the structural framework for community-building in Southeast Asia; third, describe the development of ASEAN over the past fifty years; and fourth, discuss the organization's achievements; before turning to a concluding critical evaluation of co-operation in the region based on a discussion of the comparative strengths and weaknesses of neorealism, liberal institutionalism and social constructivism in the analysis of Southeast Asian regionalism.

Regionalism in international relations

The idea of the regionalization of international relations refers to the underlying, often undirected, processes bringing adjoining states, societies, and economies into intensified interaction. Through this interaction, members of a particular cluster of states may be said to have a distinctive orientation to each other and to constitute a region. The term regionalism is more complex. According to Joseph Nye, 'in the descriptive sense [it means]...the formation of interstate associations or groupings on the basis of regions; and in the doctrinal sense, the advocacy of such formations' (1968: vii). Thus, while regionalization is what happens, regionalism can be understood as a conscious orientation by actors to bring about specific forms of regionalization. In other words, 'we may refer to regionalism as the structures, processes and arrangements that are working towards greater coherence within a specific international region in terms of economic, political, security, socio-cultural and other kinds of linkages' (Dent 2008: 7).

In the debate on regionalism, it has become commonplace to distinguish between an older generation of regionalism (under the label of 'regional integration' these were studies that mainly focused on the process of European integration) in the 1950s and 1960s and a more recent wave of regionalism (the 'new regionalism') which started in the late 1980s. Traditional theories of regionalism (or 'old regionalism') are closely associated with the scholarly works of the 1950s and 1960s, with Europe being the principal base for empirical studies. David Mitrany (1943) and Jacob Viner (1950) are acknowledged as two of the most influential pioneers in this area. While Mitrany is considered the father of functionalism – which focuses on the common interests and needs shared by states and postulates a gradual transfer of authority and sovereignty from the state to a supranational level (that is, new regional agencies at a level above traditional nation states) in functional, technical, and economic areas – Viner made groundbreaking contributions to the analysis of international trade. His work was later refined and built on by many other scholars like Béla Balassa, who described regional economic integration as a linear process occurring in five different stages: a free trade area; a customs union; a common market; an economic union; and complete economic integration (Balassa 1961: 174). No regional group in modern times has reached the ultimate stage of regionalism, a fully integrated economic and political union, although the EU has come close to achieving this goal. Yet the European integration process has never been linear and straightforward and has had to deal with several crises and overcome many hurdles along the way. Examples include the period of stagnation and spill-backs to European regionalism (often referred to as 'Eurosclerosis') in the 1970s and most recently the British decision to exit the EU (Brexit).

Apart from their strong focus on Europe, 'old' theories of regionalism assumed that along the path of gradually intensifying co-operation, nation states would eventually 'pool their sovereignty' (Moravcsik 1993) and create a new supranational level of decision-making situated above the authority or scope of national governments. In the case of the EU the European Commission, which operates as a cabinet government, embodies this idea of supranationality. This perspective on regionalism is best summarized by Ernst Haas who defined regional integration as:

> the process whereby political actors in several distinct national settings are persuaded to shift their loyalties, expectations and political activities to a new

centre, whose institutions possess or demand jurisdiction over pre-existing national states. The end result is a new political community, superimposed over the pre-existing ones.

(Haas 1958: 16)

Trigged by the rapid emergence and expansion of regional organizations and co-operation schemes around the globe in the 1990s, the 'new regionalism' approach follows a much broader understanding of regional integration and acknowledges the existence of alternative pathways to regional community-building which neither aspire nor inevitably lead to the formation of supranational institutions. This latest wave in the study of regionalism discusses regionalism in the context of globalization and is often linked to aspects of economic governance (Hettne 2005). As Harrison contended, 'New regionalists go so far as to claim that contemporary capitalism and its territorial configuration are best regulated and governed in and through the decentralization of socio-economic decision-making and associated policy implementation to sub-national institutional frameworks and supports' (2006: 22). According to Hettne, one of the main proponents of new regionalism, 'the two processes of globalisation and regionalisation are articulated within the same larger process of global structural change' (1999: 2). Väyrynen further adds that 'national actors may…perceive regionalism as a defence mechanism against the competitive pressures arising from the globalization process' (2003: 32). Meanwhile, the Inter-American Development Bank (2002: 24) has observed that 'an increasing number of countries are relying on formal regional integration to mediate the forces of globalization'. Most regional organizations outside Europe share the preference for lean organizational structures to avoid a *Brusselsization*, shorthand for over-bureaucratization and supranationality (Dosch 2003: 38), and opt instead for 'institutional minimalism' (Grimmel and Rüland 2015: 29). ASEAN is no exception. Although being one of the oldest, largest and most important regional organizations, its small secretariat in Jakarta employs just 330 officials and support staff.

In addition to the strong linkages between the 'new regionalism' debate and discourses in international political economy, social constructivists have also discovered regionalism as a preferred empirical focus. There can be little doubt that a sense of regional consciousness has emerged in many world regions and that states have actively promoted the idea of mutual co-operation. Regardless of whether regions need to be defined in geographical terms or can also be thought of as socially constructed 'imagined or cognitive regions' (Väyrynen 2003: 37), identity is one of the most important and solid pillars of regionalism, whether this pillar is based on geographical concepts or has a foundation underpinned by norms and values. This is where ASEAN comes into play as one of the most important empirical case studies of a process of regional integration based on shared norms and a – at least emerging – common regional identity (for one of the most prominent contributions on this, see Acharya 2000, 2001 and 2014). This also applies to Europe, but while European regionalism is characterized by treaties and legally binding commitments, Southeast Asia has followed a non-legalistic approach to intergovernmental co-operation based on the so-called ASEAN way of soft institutions, open regionalism, co-operative security, non-binding decision-making, convention and consensus-building. The ASEAN way is based on the premise that the moral power of informal procedures can determine relations between actors as effectively as legally binding rules. The former – so the argument goes – has allowed for more flexibility in dealing with the specific policy challenges of regional governance than the latter.

Box 7.1 ASEAN at a glance

Founded in August 1967 in Bangkok by Indonesia, Malaysia, the Philippines, Singapore and Thailand.

Later joined by Brunei (1984), Vietnam (1995), Laos and Myanmar (1997) and Cambodia (1999).

Organizational structure

- Meetings of the heads of government (formally every three years supplemented by 'informal meetings').
- Annual Ministerial Meeting (AMM) of the Foreign Ministers (annually): de facto the most important ASEAN meeting.
- Frequent meetings of other ministers, senior officials (1000+ meetings per year).
- ASEAN Secretariat in Jakarta (founded 1976); can advise the ASEAN governments but does not have any decision-making power.

Foreign relations

Annual meetings:

- ASEAN Post-Ministerial Meetings (PMCs), gradually developed since the early 1970s → ASEAN + Dialogue Partners: Australia, Canada, China, EU, India, Japan, New Zealand, Pakistan, Russia, South Korea, United States.
- ASEAN Regional Forum (ARF), founded 1993 (first official meeting 1994) → ASEAN + Dialogue Partners + Mongolia, North Korea.
- ASEAN Plus Three, founded 1999 → ASEAN + China, Japan, South Korea.
- East Asian Summit, founded 2005 → ASEAN + Australia, China, India, Japan, New Zealand, the United States, South Korea and Russia.
- Frequent inter-regional meetings with EU and Latin American states etc.

Milestones of co-operation and important agreements

1967 Bangkok Declaration: Founding Document, stresses the need for economic, political and cultural co-operation and exchange.

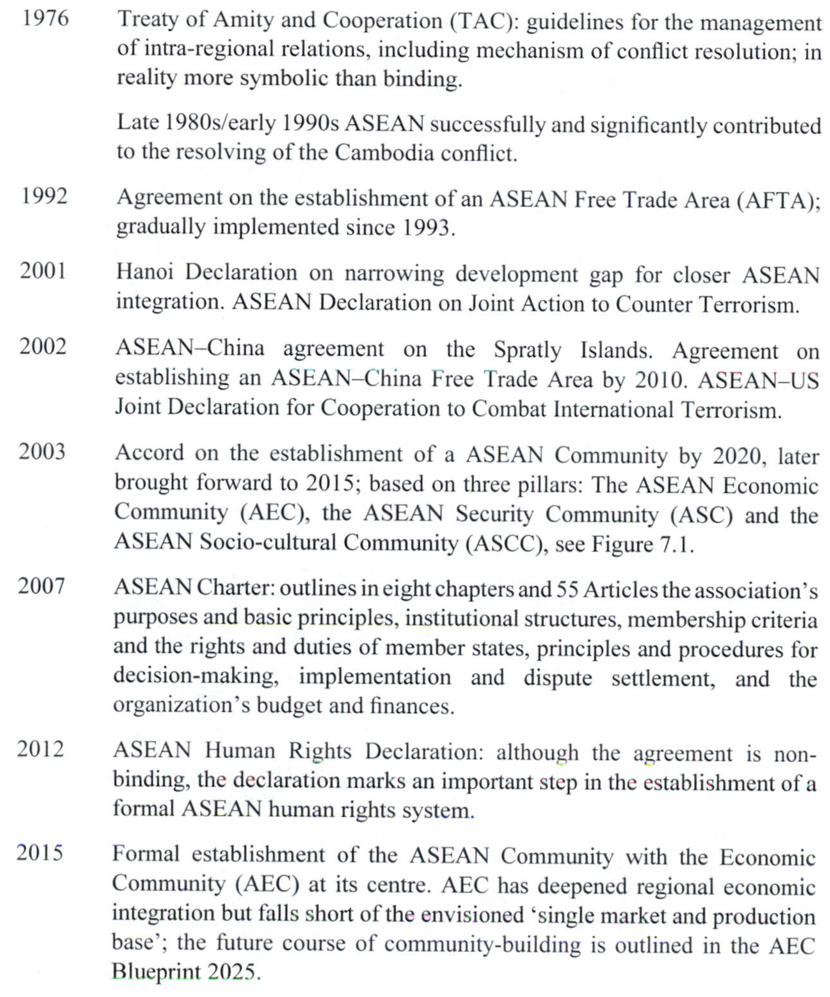

1976	Treaty of Amity and Cooperation (TAC): guidelines for the management of intra-regional relations, including mechanism of conflict resolution; in reality more symbolic than binding.
	Late 1980s/early 1990s ASEAN successfully and significantly contributed to the resolving of the Cambodia conflict.
1992	Agreement on the establishment of an ASEAN Free Trade Area (AFTA); gradually implemented since 1993.
2001	Hanoi Declaration on narrowing development gap for closer ASEAN integration. ASEAN Declaration on Joint Action to Counter Terrorism.
2002	ASEAN–China agreement on the Spratly Islands. Agreement on establishing an ASEAN–China Free Trade Area by 2010. ASEAN–US Joint Declaration for Cooperation to Combat International Terrorism.
2003	Accord on the establishment of a ASEAN Community by 2020, later brought forward to 2015; based on three pillars: The ASEAN Economic Community (AEC), the ASEAN Security Community (ASC) and the ASEAN Socio-cultural Community (ASCC), see Figure 7.1.
2007	ASEAN Charter: outlines in eight chapters and 55 Articles the association's purposes and basic principles, institutional structures, membership criteria and the rights and duties of member states, principles and procedures for decision-making, implementation and dispute settlement, and the organization's budget and finances.
2012	ASEAN Human Rights Declaration: although the agreement is non-binding, the declaration marks an important step in the establishment of a formal ASEAN human rights system.
2015	Formal establishment of the ASEAN Community with the Economic Community (AEC) at its centre. AEC has deepened regional economic integration but falls short of the envisioned 'single market and production base'; the future course of community-building is outlined in the AEC Blueprint 2025.

The structural setting

When the foreign ministers of Indonesia, Malaysia, the Philippines, Singapore and Thailand established the Association of Southeast Asian Nations (ASEAN) in August 1967, they presented very different descriptions of what they had launched. 'A structure for peace and progress', was what the then Philippines Foreign Minister Narciso Ramos called it. Thailand's Thanat Khoman described it as 'a new society'. Singapore's Sinnathamby Rajaratnam declared 'that we have now erected the skeleton and must give flesh and blood to it', and the next moment he referred to it as 'a child sired up by five fathers' (*Philippine Herald* 15 August 1967). However, there is reason to believe that their different sobriquets reflected a difference in form, not substance. For, to be precise, they were all agreed on the idea of establishing a new operational regional organization, one initiated and run by Asians themselves.

Looking back, today's analyst can even go one step further: Although the Bangkok Declaration, ASEAN's founding document, stressed the importance of regional economic co-operation and cultural exchange among the young nations of Southeast Asia, the main objective was security. ASEAN was born at a time when the region's political leaders had strong reasons to believe that their countries could get prominently involved in the global game of East–West confrontation in general and the Vietnam War in particular. The US had just revived President Eisenhower's Domino Theory of 1954, making Southeast Asian leaders aware of world communism's aggressive expansionism. The states, which had achieved independence from colonialism for only a short while, wanted to avoid a situation of new dependence at all costs. They did not want to see the emergence of repeated great power rivalry on their doorstep.

ASEAN leaders have generally shared the view that their national development required a regional international order in which the balance of power would operate, and alternations in the distribution of power would occur peacefully and within an international context of negotiated neutrality. In real terms there can be no doubt that the governments demonstrated a favourable disposition towards an American predominance of power in the region and a suspicion of Soviet motives and activities. Although the ASEAN members never made any comments of anti-communism in their official declarations and documents, nevertheless it was anti-communism that served as an effective common bond. Between official neutrality and sub-official commitment, ASEAN as an organization had managed to stay formally neutral during the Cold War, despite the virulent anti-communism of its members and their engagement in US-assisted counter-insurgency operations. By remaining neutral, ASEAN was able to negotiate its position in respect of possible hegemony, even though Southeast Asia was one of the 'hottest' regions in geopolitical and geostrategic terms. In other words, ASEAN has successfully played the big powers off against each other. This point is best summarized by former Malaysian Foreign Minister Ghazali Shafie: 'The past [decades] had shown the resilience of ASEAN in manoeuvring the turbulences of Cold War and intense East–West rivalries, despite the varied affiliations or non-alignment of its members' (*Jakarta Post* 17 October 1992).

In general, the clear structure of bipolarity and East–West confrontation served ASEAN well. It kept the US engaged in the region as a guaranteed power for a secure geopolitical environment. At the same time the Cold War contained the power projection interests of all three major actors, i.e., the US, the Soviet Union and China. Not surprisingly, uncertainties concerning the new regional political security architecture arose in the wake of the Cold War, including:

- shifting power relativities between the major states;
- the gradual rise of a multipolar security environment with the major Asian powers playing a larger role;

- significant increases in military capabilities and local defence industries;
- the possibility of ethnic and national tensions, economic rivalry, disappointing aspirations for prosperity, and religious or racial conflict.

The profound changes at the system level of international relations in the early 1990s, the alternations to the overall distribution of power and capabilities after the Cold War, first seemed to result in a power vacuum in the Asia-Pacific. Unlike Europe there was no 'iron curtain' in the Asia-Pacific that separated the American and Soviet zones of hegemonic influence and no 'wall' that came down to symbolize the beginning of a new international era. The end of the Cold War left the Asia-Pacific with many question marks. Would the US remain as a regional balancer? Would China try to seize the opportunity and aggressively pursue an alleged national interest of becoming the region's next pre-eminent power? Would Japan change the pacifist nature of its foreign and defence policies? ASEAN actively participated in the emerging debate on multilateral institution-building as an alternative to the hegemonic settings of the Cold War days. Among other ideas, in 1993 ASEAN initiated a regional dialogue scheme on security matters called the ASEAN Regional Forum. Among the members are the United States, the European Union, China and Japan.

At first glance ASEAN seems to prove neorealist thinking in international relations. According to the realist view, the founding of the organization in 1967 and its evolution during the Cold War can be explained as the product of balance-of-power considerations. ASEAN's strong anti-communist posture and the fact that the organization was set up by states that already had strong linkages with the US (first and foremost the Philippines and Thailand), could be interpreted as a typical power-balancing behaviour of small and medium states, namely to jump on the bandwagon of a superpower (the US in this case) in order not to be absorbed by the other (the Soviet Union). It is not surprising that for realists, 'Southeast Asia's turbulent post-war history was proof that under the conditions of anarchy survival constitutes the overriding interests of states in the region. Foreign policy was thus described in terms of self-help and military power' (Rüland 2000: 422). Now if that was the case during the Cold War, it has remained relevant in the post-Cold War era. As Sorpong Peou noted (2002: 121): 'Realism continues to be a key conceptual approach in Southeast Asian Studies.... There is no "peace divided" in Southeast Asia after the Soviet collapse; [and some scholars] see the region as one rife with growing bilateral tensions after the Cold War'. Furthermore, the economic realities of Southeast Asia's dependence on external economic powers such as the US, Japan, the EU and China for trade and investment seem to underpin the neorealist view of regional order and stability as a function of great power strategic dominance.

There is some truth in the neorealist perspective on ASEAN. However, it fails to address the impact of institution-building in Southeast Asia on regional peace and stability. Liberal institutionalists challenge the neorealist standpoint by arguing that co-operation among the states of Southeast Asia has generated a set of agreed principles and rules, which have increased transparency and trust and reduced uncertainties and hostilities in intra-regional relations. According to this perspective it has been primarily a process of institution-building – rather than, for instance, US-bandwagoning – that facilitated security and welfare in Southeast Asia. Looking at the following achievements of ASEAN-driven regionalism, liberal institutionalism does indeed seem to offer a suitable explanation.

Achievements of Southeast Asian regionalism

On 31 December 2015, the association reinvented itself as the ASEAN Community based on three pillars: the Political Security Community, the Economic Community and the Socio-Cultural Community, which were defined and specified in three blueprints unveiled between 2007 and 2009. While the Community is the result of an institutional evolution and reflects the collective will to strengthen the relevance and cohesiveness of ASEAN, it has not altered the main objectives and direction of regionalism in Southeast Asia. Thus, the analysis of ASEAN's general achievements can be based on five broad arguments which have remained valid since the end of the Cold War.

ASEAN is a successful collective actor on the international stage

The strong links that ASEAN members have forged amongst themselves enable them to negotiate and bargain with third-party countries with greater confidence and success. Like no other group of non-Western countries, ASEAN as a collective actor has managed to gain the industrial nations' attention through its well established dialogue mechanisms, which belong to the most recognized

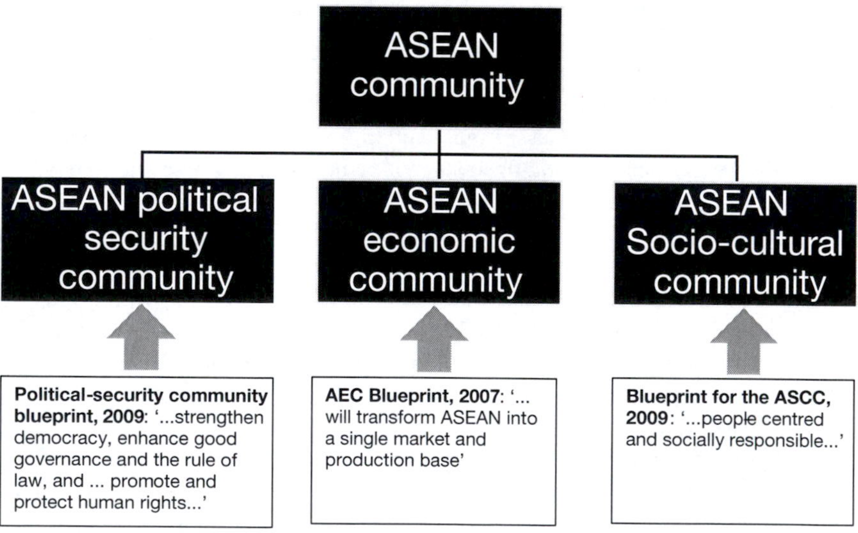

Figure 7.1 The ASEAN Community
Source: the author

international fora in the world. Given this, ASEAN has been described as a 'politico-diplomatic coalition vis-à-vis the outside world' (Sopiee 1991: 320). Since 1972, when ASEAN took the initiative to conduct an institutionalized dialogue with the European Community, ASEAN has developed a network of regional and global meetings that today involve more than a dozen global players such as the United States, the European Union, Japan and China. At the core of these activities are annual conferences on economic and political issues that affect the region. By setting up the ASEAN Regional Forum (ARF) in 1993 – a framework for the discussion of developments related to regional security – the association prominently contributed to shaping a new security order in the Asia-Pacific. ASEAN has also played a central role in the establishment of APEC. ASEAN's successful strategy of 'networking the region' is remarkable because the existing dialogue fora enable the Southeast Asian heads of state, ministers (especially foreign ministers) and senior officials to regularly meet with their counterparts from Washington, Beijing, Tokyo, Brussels and so on. Taking advantage of these extensive dialogue networks, even small powers like Cambodia or Laos are in the position to have at least an annual exchange with the US secretary of state or even the US president, for instance. No other groups of nations outside Europe have ever created for themselves such a favourable position within the international system. A significant international achievement in this respect is the institutionalization of co-operation within the broader East Asian region. ASEAN's initiative to foster relations with China, Japan and South Korea started with an informal gathering in 1997, which was soon formalized and named the 'ASEAN Plus Three Meeting (APT)'. The APT takes place annually, involving the member states' heads of government, with frequent meetings of ministers and senior officials in between summits, and addresses economic and security issues of regional importance, such as closer trade and investment relations, transnational crime and terrorism. In particular, APT is associated with the creation of financial instruments to strengthen the region's defences against future economic turbulences. The most important of these new mechanisms is the Chiang Mai Initiative Multilateralization (CMIM), a series of regional currency swap arrangements meant to promote financial stability in times of economic crisis (Loewen 2014). Some believe that APT is a step closer towards a loose East Asian alliance. The most recent addition to the network of regional organizations centred on ASEAN is the East Asian Summit, an annual meeting of the heads of state and government of the ten ASEAN members, Australia, China, India, Japan, New Zealand, the US, South Korea and Russia. The inaugural summit meeting took place in Kuala Lumpur in December 2005.

ASEAN as a regional conflict mediator

ASEAN has demonstrated its willingness to find regional solutions for regional problems. Most importantly, in the late 1980s, ASEAN contributed to the political solution of the Cambodian conflict as a major player in the peace negotiation process. Furthermore, in 1992, ASEAN adopted the 'Declaration on the South

China Sea', which was regarded as a first step towards a peaceful settlement of the Spratly Islands dispute. The Spratlys are a collection of mostly barren coral reefs, atolls and sand bars – many of which disappear at high tide – which covers an area of some 70,000 square miles. This area is claimed, in whole or in part, by China, Taiwan, Vietnam, Malaysia, Brunei and the Philippines. With the exception of Brunei, all of the disputants maintain a military presence on some of the islands. Since the late 1970s there have been intermittent incidents involving the various claimants, ranging from complaints about the construction of buildings on islands and the arrest or detention of fishermen, to violent clashes between the armies and navies of claimants. For example, in early 2012, China and the Philippines engaged in a lengthy maritime stand-off, accusing each other of intrusions in the Scarborough Shoal which is claimed by both states. In July 2012, China elevated the status of the contested islands to become part of a Chinese prefecture. Bilateral relations between China and Vietnam reached crisis point in early May 2014 when China dispatched an oil rig to waters claimed by Vietnam in the South China Sea. The oil rig was placed some 120 nautical miles (222 km) inside Vietnam's exclusive economic zone, which extends 200 nautical miles (370 km) from the Vietnamese coast, under the 1982 UN Convention on the Law of the Sea (UNCLOS). However, China does not recognize Vietnam's claim based on international law. In July 2016, the Permanent Court of Arbitration in The Hague ruled that China had violated maritime law with its activities in the South China Sea. While the ruling was naturally welcomed in the Philippines (which had brought the case against China to the Permanent Court under the arbitration provisions of UNCLOS) and Vietnam, it was unequivocally rejected by Beijing which dismissed the legitimacy of The Hague arbitration proceedings. Although the ruling is widely considered unenforceable, it has morally strengthened the position of the Southeast Asian claimants.

As early as 2002, at an ASEAN–China Summit, the heads of government of the ASEAN members and the Chinese premier Zhu Rongji signed a so-called declaration of conduct, agreeing not to attempt to occupy the Spratlys. Sometimes referred to as the 'Spratly Islands Pact', the agreement aims at avoiding conflict by means of 'confidence-building activities between ASEAN and China' (ASEAN 2002: para. 28). Although the agreement is not binding and depends on the goodwill of the signatory states, senior officials from ASEAN and China believe the 'pact' will eventually help ensure regional security, although the recent series of bilateral disputes suggests otherwise.

In 1995 the ASEAN states also signed a treaty which – on paper – bans the development, acquisition, use, testing and stationing of nuclear arms in Southeast Asia. Since the ASEAN states do not possess nuclear weapons themselves and the nuclear powers, particularly the US and China, have so far objected to an accession to the Southeast Asian Nuclear Weapons-Free Zone (SEANWFZ), the agreement is of more symbolic than practical value. However, in 2009 the US signed an agreement to accede to the ASEAN Treaty of Amity and Cooperation (TAC; see Box 7.1) after 17 years of consideration, in an attempt to boost multilateral approaches to regional security. A total of 26 states have now signed the 1976 regional code of conduct, making the TAC one of ASEAN's most significant international successes.

ASEAN as a security community

ASEAN is not a military alliance but a security community in the sense that probably no member would seriously consider going to war with a fellow ASEAN state as a means of problem solving in inter-member relations. ASEAN has successfully managed to keep the residual conflicts between the members – especially territorial disputes – on a low-key level. War has never erupted between individual Southeast Asian states once they had become ASEAN members, despite the existence of more than a dozen territorial conflicts among them, regular rows over migration issues (especially between Malaysia and Indonesia) and heated discussion on the distribution of resources (for example, between Singapore and Malaysia about water supply and Indonesia and Singapore about trade in sand). Furthermore, in 2001 ASEAN adopted a Declaration on Terrorism which aims to prevent, counter and suppress terrorist activities in the region. However, the region has not been completely free of armed confrontation or other kinds of threatening behaviour. The spilling over of Burmese ethnic conflicts into Thai territory has occasionally (particularly in 2001) resulted in encounters between the troops of Thailand and Myanmar along their joint border. Between 2008 and 2011 Thailand and Cambodia clashed several times over a disputed border area, a 4.6-square-kilometre spot around Preah Vihear Temple. In 2013, the 'Lahad Datu stand-off', a conflict between 235 Philippine militants and the Malaysian security forces, reignited the lingering Philippine–Malaysian dispute over Sabah, the former North Borneo, which dates back to colonial times.

Yet in these and other cases the existence of – mainly informal – mechanisms of conflict management in Southeast Asia helped to contain bilateral problems from destabilizing the region, and prevented an escalation of disputes into full-scale military battle. An essential element of the ASEAN security community is its inward-looking nature. Rather than concentrating on external military threats, ASEAN members have favoured a comprehensive security agenda. The member states have worked towards enhancing their security through domestic socio-economic development. This approach has strengthened their respective national resilience – which is the term used in the ASEAN rhetoric – and, in turn, has led to reduced intra-regional tensions and regional vulnerabilities and thus regional resilience (Emmers 2016).

ASEAN as an inter-personal network

High-ranking bureaucrats, government officials, scholars and representatives of the private sector within the ASEAN framework have forged a close network of personal links. In this way border-crossing communications and activities have increased and interactions have become much easier. If one takes into consideration that well into the 1950s the various national elites in Southeast Asia were practically not talking to each other, this network building within ASEAN (with its 1000-plus annual meetings) is one major achievement of Southeast Asian regionalism. It has resulted in transparency and confidence-building. However, for many decades inter-personal network building was mainly restricted to state actors. The ASEAN Charter of 2007 in conjunction with the ASEAN Community Blueprints prescribes a development towards a people-oriented integration process that prominently involves the region's civil societies. In fact, some large regional NGOs played an important part in the deliberations that led to the inclusion of liberal and people-centred norms in the Charter (Dosch 2008a, 2008b). The establishment of the 'ASEAN Intergovernmental Commission of Human Rights' (AICHR) in 2009 as prescribed by the Charter and related initiatives such as the 'ASEAN Commission on the Promotion and Protection of the Rights of Women and Children (ACWC)', inaugurated in 2010, are important accomplishments in the process of refocusing the regional integration to the interests and needs of non-state actors.

ASEAN as a framework for economic development

Taking the aforementioned four aspects together, ASEAN has created for itself a peaceful and stable regional situation. This situation in turn has contributed to a conducive climate for ASEAN countries to pursue their national economic development. The Bangkok Declaration, ASEAN's founding document, does not include any firm commitment to regional economic integration. The declaration simply stresses the desirability of collaboration and mutual assistance on matters of common interest in the economic field among other areas of potential co-operation. It was only a decade later, in 1977, that the ASEAN member states signed a Preferential Trading Arrangement (PTA) as a first serious effort to strengthen regional economic relations.

By the early 1990s, tariffs on some 16,000 goods within the PTA framework had been reduced. While this figure looked impressive on paper, it amounted to only about five per cent of total intra-ASEAN trade. Excluded were the main export and import products, which remained protected by high tariff barriers. The member states also demonstrated some creativity in listing products under the PTA with little or no relevance for intra-regional trade – snow ploughs and nuclear reactors are oft-noted examples.

The PTA nevertheless signified an important milestone as it marked the end of some member states' – especially Indonesia's – categorical resistance to trade liberalization. After several subsequent and mostly failed strategies in support of economic integration, a major breakthrough was achieved when, in 1992, the member states agreed on the gradual implementation of an ASEAN Free Trade Area (AFTA). In this regard, AFTA was very clearly a reaction and response to globalization and, thus, a child of the 'new regionalism'. The year 1992 saw the signing of the NAFTA agreement, final preparations for the full implementation of the European Single Market, and US President Bill Clinton setting his sights on economic integration in the Asia-Pacific region. The seeming international move towards economic regionalism happened against the backdrop of the GATT Uruguay Round, which entered troubled waters and finally foundered in December 1990 in Brussels. Although the GATT negotiations were later revived and eventually successfully concluded, in the early 1990s, regionalism emerged forcefully as a way of mitigating the challenges of post-Cold War globalization, if not as an alternative to it. ASEAN did not want to be left out.

The Asian Financial Crisis of 1997–98 interrupted the process of realizing the AFTA vision. However, the ASEAN heads of states and governments provided a fresh impetus to realizing it at their summit meeting in Bali in 2003. The Declaration of ASEAN Concord II envisioned building an ASEAN economic community to 'establish ASEAN as a single market and production base' by 2020 (ASEAN 2003). In 2007, the ASEAN Economic Community (AEC) Blueprint set out a framework and roadmap for implementation and shortened the deadline to 2015. In theory, the establishment of AEC has produced association-wide economic integration centred on a 'single market and production base' characterized by a free flow of goods, free flow of services, free flow of investment, freer flow of capital, and free flow of skilled labour. The ASEAN Secretariat praised the AEC as 'a major milestone in the regional economic integration agenda in ASEAN, offering opportunities in the form of a huge market of US$2.6 trillion and over 622 million people' and pointed to the fact that 'in 2014, AEC was collectively the third largest economy in Asia and the seventh largest in the world' (ASEAN 2016). However, for the foreseeable future, ASEAN member states will continue to have significantly less than full regional economic integration. While progress has been made in reducing or eliminating intra-ASEAN trade tariffs, substantial non-tariff barriers to trade persist. For 99 per cent of goods traded among founding members of ASEAN (ASEAN-6) under the ASEAN Trade in Goods Agreement (ATIGA), a main element of the AEC, import duties have been eliminated. This figure looks impressive but it should not be misread for the total trade volume. The remaining one per cent of goods accounts for a sizable share of regional trade flows. The majority of ASEAN member states have made use of an extensive and ever-expanding exclusion system and placed products on the Temporary Exclusion List, the Sensitive and Highly Sensitive List, or the General Exclusion List. For example, rice – one of the most important commodities in regional trade – is excluded from ATIGA. Intra-regional trade as a percentage of the ASEAN members' overall trade has stagnated at around 25 per cent since the early 2000s. At the same time, ASEAN has advanced in harmonizing customs procedures which have become more efficient and transparent and as a result, the cost of importing and exporting has been reduced. Furthermore, some common technical standards for electronic and electrical products among others have been developed and implemented. AEC also comprises provisions for labour mobility in high skills sectors (engineering, nursing, architecture, medicine, dentistry, tourism, surveying and accountancy). However, implementation has been slow due to restrictive labour policies held by several member states.

The relatively small size of the ASEAN market and the outward-orientation of the member states are other important factors standing in the way of deeper economic integration. Overall, the national economies are more competitive than complementary in structure. They produce a narrow range of similar primary products and labour-intensive manufactured goods for export mainly to the US, the EU, China and Japan. Although there have been some recent improvements, intra-industry specialization and the regional division of labour based on comparative advantage are not yet well developed. The main hurdle in the process of implementing the AEC is the mismatch between political ambitions and the capabilities and, often, the political will – or, maybe, the political autonomy – of several member states to walk the walk. One of the striking characteristics of the regional integration process in Southeast Asia is the gap between ambitious political goals (the vision for economic integration as spelled out in the ASEAN Charter and the AEC Blueprints) and the realities of substantial development gaps, nationalism, and the prevalence of vested interests, or what Lee Jones (2015) calls the 'socio-political contestation over the distribution of economic power and resources'. The argument is between the sizable number of pro-liberalization technocrats and international proponents of deeper integration, on the one hand, and, on the other, a broad range of political, bureaucratic and economic actors who, for various reasons, prefer the status quo (Jones 2015). Such a setting is not uncommon for processes of regional integration. In ASEAN, it is intensified by considerable disparities in technical and institutional capacities, economic development and political priorities. Thus, the basic conditions for creating common regimes or even for harmonizing national legislative frameworks and enforcement practices among the members are not yet in place. Southeast Asia includes some of the richest, but also some of the poorest, states in the world. Singapore's per capita GDP is approximately 60 times greater than Cambodia's. By comparison, the ratio between the largest and smallest per capita GDP in the EU is only roughly fifteen to one (between Luxembourg and Bulgaria).

While economic and also political diversity is a crucial factor, it is difficult to see how economic integration could be deepened on the basis of non-binding agreements. If member states are allowed to opt-out at any time, or to choose not to implement agreed actions, integration is hardly achievable. Yet, this is exactly what happens under the 'ASEAN minus-X' formula that guides almost every aspect of liberalization and integration. This formula allows member states to jump on the bandwagon in their own time. ASEAN members are trying to achieve far-reaching visions of economic community-building without the necessary modifications to the traditional approach to co-operation. The institutions (norms, principles, rules, decision-making procedures) that do exist within ASEAN are 'soft institutions', which are not legally binding because they are based on convention and informal agreement rather than formal treaties. The pillar of ASEAN is voluntarism not legalism. The ASEAN Charter has provided the group with a new identity and legal personality but overall confirmed the traditional 'soft approach' to intergovernmental co-operation. The Southeast Asian type of regional co-operation consists of half a dozen socio-cultural norms, which are derived from Malay cultural practices, and collectively describe the 'ASEAN way', which is based on the following six norms:

1 sovereign equality;
2 the non-recourse to use of force and the peaceful settlement of conflict;
3 non-interference and non-intervention;
4 the non-involvement of ASEAN to address unresolved bilateral conflict between members;
5 quiet diplomacy;
6 mutual respect and tolerance.

(Haacke 2003: 1)

A critical evaluation of Southeast Asian regionalism

Why does ASEAN cling to soft co-operation and not attempt deeper integration? In one of the earliest theoretical contributions to the study of Southeast Asian regionalism, Estrella D. Solidum (1974) of the Philippines observed that co-operation among ASEAN nations was more realistic and successful the more it dealt with 'safe' or non-sensitive issues. Matters of high politics, such as the creation of defence alliances or common markets, were not susceptible to the early stages of co-operation among heterogeneous polities. Malaysian political scientist Pushpa Thambipillai (1980) primarily employed Karl W. Deutsch's hypothesis on community-building. She concluded that ASEAN differed from the process of community-building described by Deutsch. Contrary to his assumption that adjoining states and societies strove for political community-building ('amalgamation' in Deutsch's terminology), within Southeast Asia the idea not to unite politically but to preserve autonomy had prevailed. Accordingly, although interdependence (as conceptualized by Joseph Nye and Robert Keohane) among ASEAN members had been growing, the states of Southeast Asia were still concerned with maintaining and entrenching their respective national identities by subscribing to the principle of non-interference in neighbouring countries' affairs.

Although the studies mentioned here were published many years ago, most of their findings remain resilient. Today, and in spite of the 2007 Charter and the inauguration of the ASEAN Economic Community 2015, national sovereignty rules. Five decades of regional co-operation have not generated any kind of supra-nationality. The ASEAN Secretariat, which was established in 1976, mainly contributes to the co-ordination of the organization's day-to-day business and, to a degree, works as the organization's internal think-tank, but does not have authority to make decisions for or on behalf of the member states. Any centralized decision-making is difficult to achieve and rejected by most actors, because practically all member states are still preoccupied with the process of nation-building; any transfer of national sovereignty to a supranational level is thus out of the question.

Until the late 1990s, analyses of Southeast and East Asia tended to be mainly realist and neorealist in nature (Leifer 1999, Friedberg 2000). In realist tradition, both the idea of an institutionalized community of states in general and ASEAN as an organization in particular are at best regarded as secondary to balance of power considerations in the Asia-Pacific. Stability and security hinge on the crucial great power relationships for which Asia has always been a central stage. Realist assessments tend to focus on the national interest of the member states and the ineffectuality of the ASEAN way, resulting in ASEAN often being seen as no more than a 'talk shop'. Initially, there was great credence to neorealist approaches. Ever since its founding, ASEAN was essentially the institutional response to regional balance of power dynamics and traditional security threats. Self-help dynamics and security consideration were what motivated the original member states to co-operate (see Kliem 2017 for a comprehensive discussion). Liberal institutionalists, by contrast, stress the process-oriented concept of Southeast Asian integration and a firm belief in the learning effects of co-operation which is believed to create mutual benefits as the result of positive sum games. According to this view, the relatively peaceful and co-operative international relations within Southeast Asia 'can be explained by the institution-building efforts of ASEAN, which play a decisive role in reducing uncertainty, binding states' behaviours, and creating norms and principles' (He 2006: 192). Following this line of argument the Treaty of Amity and Cooperation (1975) cultivated a norm of peaceful resolution in dealing with intra-ASEAN conflicts while the founding of multilateral co-operation schemes and fora such as AFTA, ARF, ASEAN Plus Three and so on facilitated a framework for enhancing regional stability and order.

Although both neorealism and liberal institutionalism contribute to our understanding of ASEAN as they provide complementary rather than mutually exclusive approaches to the study of Southeast Asian regionalism, few scholars have applied these theoretical perspectives in recent years. Instead, since the early 2000s, social constructivism has evolved as the mainstream approach in explaining ASEAN regionalism.

> Where neo-realists see an absence of the means of exercising power and a lack of internal cohesion that, in turn, negates the possibility of external efficacy, constructivists see a relatively cohesive group that has managed to project an influence in wider East Asian security affairs that is quite out of proportion to the economic and military capabilities of its Southeast Asian membership.
>
> (Eaton and Stubbs 2006: 139)

According to the social constructivist perspective on international relations regional identities, norms and social learning play a crucial part in the process of community-building. One of the main proponents of the constructivist approach, Amitav Acharya (2001, 2014), argues that the Southeast Asian states have forged a strong collective identity among themselves as the result of political, strategic and functional interactions and interdependencies. Drawing on Benedict Anderson's classic concept of the nation state, Acharya describes ASEAN as an 'imagined community' (Acharya 2001: 2). Constructivists have noted that the organization's durability is attributable to the fact that it is the embodiment of a collective Southeast Asian identity that finds its strongest expression in the 'ASEAN way'. However, as Narine (2006) correctly observes, ASEAN's collective identity is not strong enough to sustain the organization. While constructivists are correct in asserting that an ASEAN identity exists in Southeast Asia, this identity does not explain ASEAN's durability. Social constructivism's main shortcoming is the insistence on the local origins of regional norms or what Acharya (2009) has labelled 'constitutive localization'. Such a distinct 'localized normative order' (ibid.) might have existed in the early days of ASEAN but in today's globalized world any differentiation between regional and universal ('Western') norms has become fuzzy. As confirmed by the Charter and the agreements which form the basis of the ASEAN Community, ASEAN has long abandoned its earlier approach of promoting a Southeast Asian brand of human rights or democracy and adapted to a universal understanding of these concepts. The main reason for the ongoing convergence of regional and universal norms – and ultimately ASEAN's durability – is the organization's increasing interaction with external powers that takes place outside ASEAN's well reported high-level diplomacy with, for example, the US, EU, Japan and so on.

In sum:

> ASEAN behaviour and outcomes cannot be fitted into neat theoretical categories that emphasize either material or ideational variables in explanation. Instead, ASEAN displays complexities in behaviour that are the product of the contingent interaction between the material (power, territory, wealth) and the ideational (norms, ideas, identity) as member states actively seek to manage domestic or intra-state order as well as regional order within and beyond ASEAN. Regional governance, thus, involves a complex balancing act to take account of a range of contending goals and interests as member states respond to shared problems and threats.
>
> (Nesadurai 2009: 94–5)

To conclude, we may argue that ASEAN, or the process of integration in Southeast Asia in general, has advanced as a combination of three factors: a balancing act between coalition-building vis-à-vis common threat perceptions and extra-regional powers, and increasing co-operation with these powers whose support is needed in the community-building process; soft institution-building; and an emerging regional identity.

References

Acharya, A. (2000) 'Developing Countries and the Emerging World Order: Security and Institutions' in L. Fawcett and Y. Sayigh (eds), *The Third World Beyond the Cold War: Continuity and Change*, Oxford: Oxford University Press.

Acharya, A. (2001) *Constructing a Security Community in Southeast Asia: ASEAN and the Problem of Regional Order*, London: Routledge.

Acharya, A. (2009) *Whose Ideas Matter? Agency and Power in Asian Regionalism*, Ithaca, NY: Cornell University Press.

Acharya, A. (2014) *Constructing a Security Community in Southeast Asia: ASEAN and the Problem of Regional Order*, 3rd edn, London: Routledge.

ASEAN (2002) *Press Statement by the Chairman of the 8th ASEAN Summit, the 6th ASEAN+3 Summit and the ASEAN–China Summit*, Phnom Penh, Cambodia, 4 November, http://asean.org/?static_post=press-statement-by-the-chairman-of-the-8th-asean-summit-the-6th-asean-3-summit-and-the-asean-china-summit-phnom-penh-cambodia-4-november-2002-3.

ASEAN (2003) *Declaration of ASEAN Concord II (Bali Concord II)*, http://asean.org/?static_post=declaration-of-asean-concord-ii-bali-concord-ii.

ASEAN (2007) *The ASEAN Charter*, www.asean.org/wp-content/uploads/images/archive/publications/ASEAN-Charter.pdf.

ASEAN (2009) *Roadmap for an ASEAN Community 2009–2015*, www.asean.org/wp-content/uploads/images/ASEAN_RTK_2014/2_Roadmap_for_ASEAN_Community_20092015.pdf.

ASEAN (2016) *ASEAN Economic Community*, www.asean.org/asean-economic community/ (accessed 28 April 2017).

Balassa, B. (1961) *The Theory of Economic Integration*, Homewood, IL: Richard D. Irwin.

Dent, C. M. (2008) *East Asian Regionalism*, Routledge: London.

Dosch, J. (2003) 'The post-Cold War development of regionalism in East Asia', in Fu-kuo Liu and Philippe Regnier (ed.), *Regionalism in East Asia: Paradigm Shifting?* London: RoutledgeCurzon.

Dosch, J. (2008a) 'ASEAN's reluctant liberal turn and the thorny road to democracy promotion', *The Pacific Review*, 21 (4): 527–45.

Dosch, J. (2008b) 'Sovereignty rules: human security, civil society, and the limits of liberal reform' in Donald K. Emmerson (ed.), *Hard Choices. Security, Democracy, and Regionalism in Southeast Asia*, Stanford, CA: Walter H. Shorenstein Asia-Pacific Research Center Books (also published by ISEAS Singapore).

Eaton, S. and R. Stubbs (2006) 'Is ASEAN powerful? Neo-realist versus constructivist approaches to power in Southeast Asia', *The Pacific Review*, 19 (2): 135–55.

Emmers, R. (2016) 'Securitization' in A. Collins (ed.), *Contemporary Security Studies*, 4th edn, Oxford: Oxford University Press.

Freistein, K. (2013) '"A living document": promises of the ASEAN Charter', *The Pacific Review*, 26 (4): 407–29.

Friedberg, A. (2000) 'Will Europe's past be Asia's future?' *Survival*, 42 (3): 147–60.

Grimmel, A. and J. Rüland (2015) 'Regionale Integration als Gegenstand politikwissenschaftlicher Theorien und Erklärungsansätze' in A. Grimmel and C. Jakobeit (eds), *Regionale Integration*, Baden-Baden: Nomos.

Haacke, J. (2003) *ASEAN's Diplomatic and Security Culture. Origins, Development and Prospects*, London: RoutledgeCurzon.

Haas, E. (1958) *The Uniting of Europe: Political, Social and Economic Forces, 1950–1957*, Notre Dame: University of Notre Dame Press.

Harrison, J. (2006) 'Re-reading the new regionalism – a sympathetic critique'. *Space and Polity*, 10 (1): 21–46.

He, K. (2006) 'Does ASEAN matter? International relations theories, institutional realism, and ASEAN', *Asian Security*, 2 (3): 189–214.

Hettne, B. (1999) 'Globalization and the new regionalism: the second great transformation' in B. Hettne, A. Inotai and O. Sunkel (eds), *Globalism and the New Regionalism*, London: Macmillan/New York: St Martin's Press.

Hettne, B. (2005) 'Beyond the "new" regionalism', *New Political Economy*, 10 (4): 543–71.

Inter-American Development Bank (IDB) (2002) *Beyond Borders: The New Regionalism in Latin America: Economic and Social Progress in Latin America*, Washington, DC: IDB.

Jones, L. (2015) 'Explaining the failure of the ASEAN Economic Community: the primacy of domestic political economy', *The Pacific Review*, 29 (5): 647–70.

Kliem, F. (2017) *The Perpetual Promise of ASEAN: A Supply and Demand Analysis of the ASEAN Political Security Community*, PhD Thesis, Institute of Political and Administrative Sciences, University of Rostock.

Leifer, M. (1999) 'The ASEAN peace process: a category mistake', *The Pacific Review*, 12 (1): 25–38.

Loewen, H. (2014) 'Institutional Interplay between the Chian Mai Initiative and the International Monetary Fund', *European Journal of East Asian Studies*, 13 (1): 50–67.

Mitrany, D. (1943) *A Working Peace System*, London: Royal Institute of International Affairs.

Moravcsik, A. (1993) 'Preferences and power in the European Community: a liberal intergovernmentalist approach', *Journal of Common Market Studies*, 31 (4): 473–524.

Narine, S. (2006) 'The English School and ASEAN', *The Pacific Review*, 19 (2): 199–218.

Nesadurai, H. E. S. (2009) 'ASEAN and regional governance after the Cold War: from regional order to regional community?' *The Pacific Review*, 22 (1): 91–118.

Nye, J. S. (ed.) (1968) *International Regionalism: Readings*, Boston, MA: Little Brown.

Peou, S. (2002) 'Realism and constructivism in Southeast Asian security studies today: a review essay', *The Pacific Review*, 15: 119–38.

Rüland, J. (2000) 'ASEAN and the Asian crisis: theoretical implications and practical consequences for Southeast Asian regionalism', *The Pacific Review*, 13: 421–51.

Solidum, E. D. (1974) *Towards a Southeast Asian Community*, Quezon City: University of the Philippines Press.

Sopiee, N. (1991) 'ASEAN and Indo-China after a Cambodian settlement' in D. Alves (ed.), *Change, Interdependence and Security in the Pacific Basin. The 19th Pacific Symposium*, Washington, DC: National Defense University Press.

Thambipillai, P. (1980) *Regional Cooperation and Development: The Case of ASEAN and Its External Relations*, unpublished thesis, University of Hawaii.

Väyrynen, R. (2003) 'Regionalism: old and new', *International Studies Review*, 5 (1): 25–51.

Viner, J. (1950) *The Customs Union Issue*, New York: Carnegie Endowment for International Peace.

8 The EU and the Asia-Pacific

A source of soft power?

Jörn Dosch

As elsewhere in the world after the fall of the Berlin Wall and the end of the Cold War, academic and public discussion in Europe focused on whether the so-called new world order would be dominated by the US or would develop into a multipolar system with the US, East Asia and the European Union as its principal centres. In 1992 when ASEAN announced the gradual implementation of a Southeast Asian Free Trade Area (AFTA) and in 1993 when the APEC countries' heads of state met for the first time in Seattle, European newspapers published scenarios presenting AFTA and APEC as emerging trading blocs and direct competitors of the European Common Market. Although it soon became clear that economic co-operation in the Asia-Pacific will not lead in the foreseeable future to a level of integration comparable to Europe's, many in Bonn, Paris, Rome and other capitals worried that a 'Pacific Century' could leave Europe as the odd person out in the new international order. Special attention was given to the role of the US. It was believed that Washington would shift its main foreign policy focus from trans-Atlantic to trans-Pacific relations (although the US was a Pacific power long before it became an Atlantic one).

Unlike the United States, the EU and its individual member states cannot traditionally be viewed as major players in Asia. However, the role of European actors in the Asia-Pacific region is important in that they are said to exert a decisive influence on a wide range of politically relevant – and often controversial – activities and issues. These include trade and investment, democracy and human rights, migration, the environment, food and energy security, to name but a few. According to this line of argument the EU spreads its normative and soft power throughout Asia. Soft power describes the normative influence projected by states or groups of states in the international system by non-military means (Nye 2004). As far as the EU is concerned, soft power rests on two main pillars. First, Brussels has the benefit of its largely positive experience of European integration. There may have been periodic crises, such as the Greek financial turmoil and Brexit, but these have not had a permanent effect on this overall positive perception. Therefore the EU is in a position to make use of this experience and actively contribute to deepening integration processes in other regions. By promoting regional co-operation, the EU hopes to achieve a prosperity dividend for the countries involved through increased regional trade, but above all it aims to have a positive effect on their peace and stability. And second, the EU is keen to contribute to the global spread of democracy, the rule of law, human rights and other liberal values. In this process of providing and implementing ideas, the EU leans heavily on development co-operation and traditional diplomacy, which in the case of Asia involves a multilayered and complex dialogue.

This chapter begins with a brief overview of the sources of European soft power and explains the concept of inter-regionalism before discussing the empirical examples of the EU's influence (and its limits) on regionalism and normative discourses in Asia respectively. The key argument is that the EU has gained importance as an accepted source of ideas in the sense that central elements of ASEAN as well as wider Asian debates on human rights, democracy and governance bear a European imprint.[1]

The shaping of European soft power

Consideration of the extent to which the EU can generally exert soft power in international relations is largely based on discourses that have been ongoing since the 1970s about the EU's characterization as a civilian power (Duchêne 1972, Kirste and Maull 1996). In contrast to traditional powers, the EU has relied on the primacy of diplomatic co-operation as a solution to global problems. From this, we can deduce that the EU is a normative power (Manners 2002). Richard Rosecrance (1998: 22) described this very succinctly when he wrote: 'It is perhaps a paradox to note that the continent which once ruled the world through the physical impositions of imperialism is now coming to set world standards in normative terms'. Before the concept of soft power found its way into debates on international relations, Johan Galtung had already approximated it with his phrase 'the power of ideas' (1973: 33).

Why is the EU unique in being so strongly focused on pursuing an explicitly normative direction when establishing external relations with Asia and other regions of the world?[2] The answer is that, firstly, the EU has drawn up a number of treaties that officially oblige it to follow this course. The normative power of the EU as a source of ideas is strengthened by the fact that, in its case, constitutive and regulative norms have a mutually reinforcing effect. Constitutive norms, for example international law, create actors and contribute to their identity – this applies to sovereign states and international organizations alike. Regulative norms determine the behaviour of actors in specific situations. As far as the EU is concerned, the normative foundations of European integration also serve to define expectations and perceptions of the EU's actions in its external relations. The Treaty of Lisbon exemplifies this point. The treaty stipulates that the EU's international relations should be governed by the following basic principles (or constitutive norms): democracy, human rights, fundamental freedoms and the rule of law. At the same time, the EU must make every effort to propagate and implement these basic principles (now as regulative norms) around the globe.[3]

In December 2012, the European Union was awarded the Nobel Peace Prize – for its contribution to peace, reconciliation, democracy and human rights. As a collective actor the EU endeavours to promote and to implement these values as regulatory standards internationally. It seems likely that the idea of Europe's normative influence and soft power in Asia will resonate particularly clearly in places with similar institutional structures. In other words, the EU is more likely to have an effect as a provider of ideas when it works with other regional organizations. Here the focus particularly turns to the Association of Southeast Asian Nations (ASEAN), which was founded in 1967. But this is not a matter of course. As briefly outlined above, in the early 1990s European actors reacted nervously to predictions of an imminent 'Pacific century', in which relations between the USA and the Asia-Pacific region would become the main axis of global power. This scenario left little room for Europe to play a prominent and proactive role in 21st-century international relations, and meant that Europeans had to accept responsibility for their difficult situation. It suggested that Europe was to blame for failing to place its relations with Asia on a solid institutional basis. The idea of a Europe in decline was far removed from reality, but the ensuing intensive debate about the post-bipolar world order certainly had an effect. Since the mid-1990s, the EU and leading Asian actors, including ASEAN, have made major quantitative and qualitative improvements to their relations by setting up new mechanisms for co-operation.

In the international relations literature, the term *inter-regionalism* has been coined for such a process that links up entire geographical regions or even continents in an attempt to increase the level of institutionalization in relations between them. The inter-regionalism discourse emerged and differentiated itself from regional integration theory when scholars started to understand that regions were becoming actors in their own right. Regions such as Western Europe and Southeast Asia exercised this status by developing their own external relations. Most studies have focused on the reasons for the emergence, development and maintenance of inter-regional dialogues and relations, including neorealist, institutional and social constructivist arguments (Abad 2010). Depending on the respective theoretical perspective, inter-regionalism serves as a political vehicle for the deepening of interdependence, the mutual increase of material and nonmaterial resources, and the resolution of conflicts through the use of accompanying measures and additional co-operation between governmental and non-governmental actors. It performs certain balancing functions, and contributes to multilateral institution and identity building in international relations (Hänggi *et al.* 2006, Doidge 2007, Robles 2008). All these objectives and functions can be identified in relations between Europe and East Asia, particularly with regard to EU–ASEAN relations and the Asia–Europe Meeting (ASEM).

The origins of inter-regionalism between Europe and Asia date back to 1977 when the European Economic Community (EEC) and ASEAN formalized relations and went on to sign a widely acclaimed Cooperation Agreement in 1980. This was the first international agreement that the EEC had negotiated with another regional organization. It included the important statement that the co-operation was between 'equal partners' (ASEAN 1980). The resulting co-operation was expanded and enhanced in 1996 with the establishment of the

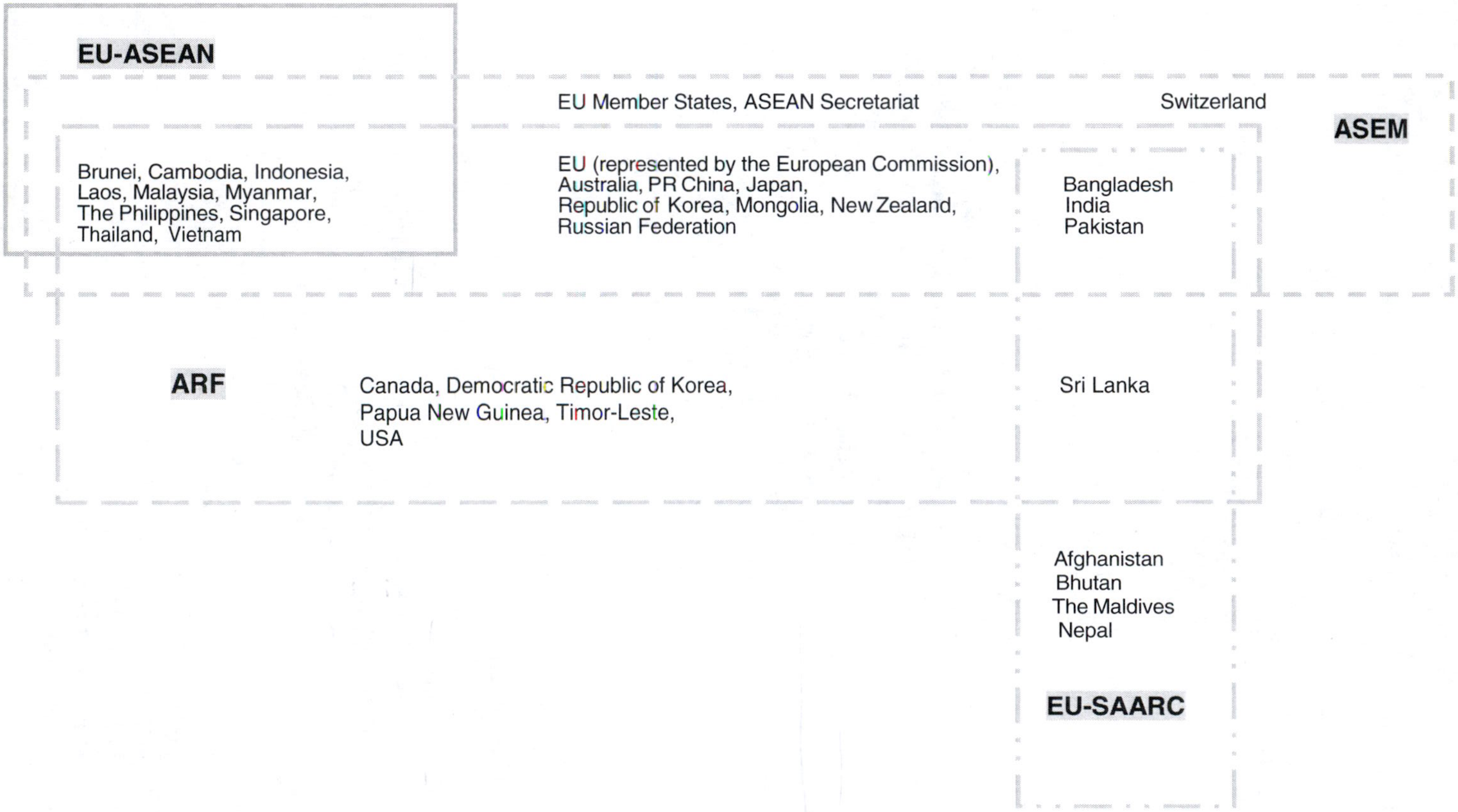

EU-ASEAN

EU Member States, ASEAN Secretariat

Switzerland

ASEM

Brunei, Cambodia, Indonesia,
Laos, Malaysia, Myanmar,
The Philippines, Singapore,
Thailand, Vietnam

EU (represented by the European Commission),
Australia, PR China, Japan,
Republic of Korea, Mongolia, New Zealand,
Russian Federation

Bangladesh
India
Pakistan

ARF

Canada, Democratic Republic of Korea,
Papua New Guinea, Timor-Leste,
USA

Sri Lanka

Afghanistan
Bhutan
The Maldives
Nepal

EU-SAARC

Figure 8.1 EU-supported regional and inter-regional organizations and dialogue mechanisms in Asia

ASEAN–Europe Meeting (ASEM). Closely connected with – but formally independent from – the EU–ASEAN dialogue is the Asia–Europe Meeting (ASEM). Singapore was ASEM's main initiator, strongly supported by France. The first meeting was held in Bangkok in March 1996, followed by regular summit meetings which have taken place every two years and alternate between European and Asian cities. According to the official political statements, ASEM 'is an intergovernmental forum for dialogue and cooperation which fosters political dialogue, reinforces economic cooperation, and promotes collaboration in other areas of mutual interest' (Asia–Europe Meeting 2017). Initially consisting of 26 members, in 2017 ASEM comprised 53 partners: 30 European and 21 Asian countries, the European Union and the ASEAN Secretariat. In the mid-1990s the founding of ASEM was the joint European–East Asian answer to the seeming strengthening of trans-Pacific co-operation as materialized in APEC and other organizations. The most obvious rationale for the existence of ASEM lies in the simple fact that the forum provides the structure for a regular policy dialogue among a highly diverse group of governments that do not necessarily share the same interests, strategies and priorities in international relations. Although ASEM has not fully lived up to initial expectations as an institutionalized approach to the effective management of Europe–Asia relations, it still offers its members the opportunity of carefully testing the waters for new initiatives that can later be followed up in smaller and more formalized diplomatic settings either within the context of bilateral relations or less diverse multilateral groupings. The EU is also a member of the ASEAN Regional Forum (ARF), founded in 1994, which meets on an annual basis to discuss security issues in the Asia-Pacific region. Furthermore, the EU enjoys observer status in the South Asian Association for Regional Cooperation (SAARC).

The EU as a normative reference point for ASEAN

Ever since the early days of Southeast Asian regionalism, there has been a strong belief that ASEAN does not view the European integration process and the EU as an organization as a model that it wishes to emulate. This belief has become so entrenched that the region's politicians almost ritualistically refute any comparisons with the EU, as they do not want to allow the impression to arise that ASEAN could develop into a supranational organization. Most of the relatively young nation states in Southeast Asia are not keen to see ASEAN evolve in this way. Indeed, the huge differences in the economic growth and political systems of the various nations mean that such a development is unrealistic at the present time. But the picture is very different when we leave the sphere of political rhetoric and look at ASEAN's everyday activities. Today, the EU is viewed by the ASEAN Secretariat in Jakarta and many of the foreign and trade ministries of its member states as being an important source of experience on specific integration issues – not in the sense of a blueprint but as a point of reference. A high-ranking official at the Secretariat simply states: 'We are trying to follow what the EU does and also what the EU's member states do' (personal interview, Jakarta, September

2012). A number of high-level ASEAN decision-makers, including two former Deputy Secretary Generals, have also confirmed that ASEAN could not exist without the substantial financial support provided by international donors and above all the EU (personal interviews, Kuala Lumpur, May 2013, and Manila, December 2015).

Between 1996 and 2013 the European Commission provided the ASEAN nations with almost € 200 million as part of its development assistance programme. This funding was used to support a range of integration projects, particularly in the economic sphere, but also latterly in a number of other areas. For 2014 to 2020, Brussels has budgeted € 320 million for the promotion of regional integration in Asia. Of this, € 170 million is destined for ASEAN, an average of € 24 million per year (Vanoverbeke and Reiterer 2014: 186, EU 2014: 8). The relevance and scale of this financial support is made particularly apparent when we realize that ASEAN's annual budget is just US $ 16.2 million (as at 2013). This sum is made up of ten equal contributions by the ASEAN member states and basically only covers the Secretariat's operating and staff costs. Without outside assistance, ASEAN would not be in a position to finance the implementation of the majority of projects under the ASEAN Economic Community (AEC), which formally came into existence on 31 December 2015. The funding for amending the legal and regulative frameworks, training the officials involved, creating the necessary physical infrastructure and other key measures has been almost totally provided by international donors and particularly the EU.

A number of large projects funded by the European Commission are of special significance here: the multi-million ASEAN Programme for Regional Integration Support (APRIS, 2003 to 2010) and its successor ASEAN Regional Integration Support from the EU (ARISE, 2013 to 2016); the EU–ASEAN Project on the Protection of Intellectual Property Rights (ECAP), which has been running since 1993; and the Regional EU–ASEAN Dialogue Instrument (READI), which has been ongoing since 2011 and addresses non-economic issues such as disaster preparedness and management, energy security and human rights. The current initiatives form part of the Bandar Seri Begawan Plan of Action to Strengthen the EU–ASEAN Enhanced Partnership (2013 to 2017), adopted in April 2012. This broad agreement aims to intensify co-operation in the areas of policy and security policy (including human rights), business and trade, socio-cultural and civil society issues and institutional co-operation (European Union 2012).

EU-funded projects have played a crucial role in the establishment of new standards by the ASEAN member countries in fields such as cross-border transport of goods and customs. Development agencies of other countries, such as the US, Australia and Japan, have also supported ASEAN in institutional terms, but there are a number of areas where central new norms have clearly emerged as a result of EU projects. For example, the ASEAN member states went against the US by adopting the EU norm of geographical indications in the protection of intellectual property (i.e., the protection of trade names used in relation to food products identified with a particular region such as Champagne, Serrano ham, Scotch whisky, etc.). The US does not recognize geographical indications in patent law and relies exclusively on trademarks in this respect. In addition, almost all ASEAN states have adapted the legal foundations of their patent laws and the administration of their patent approvals and processes in line with the EU model and have introduced the same software as that used by the European Patent Office. A number of other norms have been adopted as a result of EU projects. These include standards for electronic and cosmetic products and foodstuffs and the harmonization of customs norms and procedures, such as certificates of origin. The ARISE Project, which has received € 15 million in funding, has a vital role to play in the gradual implementation of the AEC. EU support is particularly important in the gradual creation of a single goods market, the ongoing harmonization of technical standards, the improvement of cross-border goods transportation and improved co-operation on customs matters. A pilot project funded by ARISE lies at the heart of the process of implementing the ASEAN Customs Transit System (ACTS). More specifically, it involves the creation of a North–South corridor from Thailand through Malaysia to Singapore, including harmonized export and import procedures for greater efficiency and effectiveness. In the second phase, an East–West corridor is planned to run through Cambodia, Laos, Myanmar and Vietnam. The projects that receive funding from the EU budget are supplemented by initiatives on the part of individual EU member states. Germany is prominent in this respect, with the country's principal aid agency, German International Cooperation (GIZ) running several of its own ASEAN-wide programs in the region. GIZ even maintains an office presence at the ASEAN Secretariat.[4]

Normative influence on the human rights discourse in Asia

The EU not only exerts soft power with regard to trade policies and the institutional framework for regional integration; EU actors also clearly have a normative influence – above and beyond ASEAN – on the human rights discourse in Asia. This first became evident in 2000 during the ASEM summit in Seoul, when the majority of participating Asian nations moved away from the previously postulated approach of localized Asian human rights and began to accept and agree on a European understanding of human rights. In her detailed analysis of the European–Asian human rights discourse, Maria-Gabriela Manea (2008: 380) points out how the dialogue that the EU and ASEAN had been conducting for so many years at so many levels finally led to a radical rethinking. This process concluded with the codification of human rights norms in Southeast Asia, firstly in the form of the ASEAN Charter of 2007 and later and most importantly culminating in the ASEAN Human Rights Declaration of 2012. It is true that the EU did not directly influence the creation of these two documents, but an attendee at the AICHR meetings reports that the ASEAN Intergovernmental Commission on Human Rights (AICHR), which was responsible for formulating the Declaration, used the European Convention on Human Rights as a model during certain difficult situations that arose during the negotiations. As the world's most comprehensive mechanism for protecting human rights, the European approach provides 'a reference point and source of inspiration for ASEAN in the gradual process of constructing its own system' (Vanoverbeke and Reiterer 2014: 195). However, the normative power of the EU rests not only in its role as a model (to a certain extent at least), but is also the result of its active promotion of human rights.

In 1991 the European Commission decreed that all new international agreements should include a human rights clause as an indispensable component. In 1992 the Treaty on European Union (known as the Maastricht Treaty) stated that the spread of democracy, human rights and basic freedoms was a key goal of development co-operation and created an appropriate legal framework in this respect. In 1994 the European Initiative for Democracy and Human Rights (EIDHR) was set up as a funding instrument for the worldwide advancement of participatory and representative democracy, political pluralism, the rule of law, human rights and fundamental freedoms. The EIDHR's budget has grown steadily and is now in the region of € 1.3 billion for 2014 to 2020 (since 2006 the I has stood for Instrument). Also in 1994, the EU announced its first Asia Strategy, stating that its aim was to work on 'the development and consolidation of democracy and the rule of law and respect for human rights and fundamental freedoms' as a direct contribution towards security and stability in Asia (European Commission 1994). Since then, this approach has been steadily intensified and differentiated. The establishment of the Development Cooperation Instrument (DCI) in 2006 provided its chief impetus. It replaced all the EU's previous geographical and thematic approaches to development co-operation and brought them together in a single funding instrument. Under the DCI, the EU agrees to promote good governance, democracy, human rights and institutional reforms. The target countries in this respect are those listed by the Organisation for Economic Cooperation and Development's (OECD's) Development Assistance Committee (DAC).

The EU set out its co-operation with developing nations in Asia for the period from 2007 to 2013 in 18 national strategies and one regional strategy for the whole continent (excluding Central Asia, which has its own strategy) and made available funding to the tune of € 5.2 billion. As part of the regional strategy, which received € 618 million over the same period, a particular focus was placed on providing support for uprooted population groups and demobilized former fighters (Aid to Uprooted People, AUP). One-third of the funding was earmarked for this area. AUP is closely linked to human and civil rights in that the programme aims to achieve the integration and reintegration of uprooted people in order to strengthen their basic rights and provide an opportunity to curtail forced labour and human trafficking. An independent evaluation of the 2007 to 2013 regional strategy concluded that – despite the enormous challenges it faced and the fact that it was not always able to achieve its goals – the AUP had made an effective contribution to improving the lives of uprooted people and former fighters, particularly in Afghanistan, Pakistan, Iran, Myanmar, Thailand, Bangladesh, Nepal, India, the Philippines and Sri Lanka. In Myanmar the EU is the largest source of aid for uprooted people such as the Muslim Rohingya (European Commission 2014: 52–8).

Equally, the (also independent and publicly accessible) evaluations of the co-operation with individual Asian countries provide further evidence of the EU's soft power. By combining diplomacy with targeted support for Philippine human rights organizations (within the EIDHR framework), in 2006 the EU made a major contribution to the abolition of the death penalty in the Philippines (European Commission 2011: 218). In Nepal the EU 'has directly contributed to expanding the outreach of human rights monitoring in the country and, to some extent, to the reduction of human rights violations and discrimination against women and vulnerable people' (European Commission 2012: 20). In Vietnam the situation of ethnic minorities was improved by a number of EU-funded projects, particularly those which provided access to education and health services in highland regions. However, the poorest and most disadvantaged population groups often still gained little or no benefit from the projects (European Commission 2009). In India the government worked on joint initiatives with the EU to involve people and institutions at village level in rural development planning. This led to democratic structures being strengthened at local level (European Commission 2007b).

However, these examples of the EU's positive influence on human rights and democracy cannot detract from the fact that its normative power has not led to widespread, comprehensive change. Despite the fact that the EU has conducted a human rights dialogue with almost all its partners in Asia, the Human Rights Risk Index 2016 still rated the risk of human rights abuses in all Asian countries (with the exception of Japan, South Korea and Taiwan) as 'high' or 'extremely high' (Reliefweb 2016). The only two ASEAN countries to have abolished the death penalty are the Philippines and Cambodia.

The limitations of soft power

There is other evidence that the EU's soft power has not met with universal success. Evaluations of the EU's development co-operation with countries such as China and Bangladesh and other regional associations in Asia such as SAARC show that in these cases the EU has played a minor role as a provider of ideas. In the evaluation of co-operation with China that was carried out some years ago, the question posed was, 'To what extent has the EU contributed to promoting transition to an open society based on rule of law, democratic processes, and respect for human rights?' The response was: 'The EU has provided welcome technical advice, capacity-building, best-practice training, awareness raising, etc., but in the end the pace of progress is driven by Chinese policy priorities and politics' (European Commission 2007a: 31). Regarding this point some might argue that any other result would have been unexpected. It goes without saying that the findings of a 100-page report cannot be summarized in a single sentence, but the evaluation still throws doubt on whether the EU is realistic about what it can achieve through soft power. The current strategy document titled 'EU–China 2020 Strategic Agenda for Cooperation' is less ambitious in its aims (unsurprisingly, as it is a joint European–Chinese paper). It simply refers to the desirability of deepening exchange on human rights 'on the basis of equality and mutual respect' (European External Action Service 2013).

Since 1995 the EU has maintained a regular human rights dialogue with China, including discussions on issues such as the death penalty, the rights of ethnic minorities and political and civil freedoms, but there is little evidence that this has had an effect. Indeed, in her comprehensive study, Katrin Kinzelbach (2015) concludes that the EU has failed in its goal of exerting a positive influence on the human rights climate in China. She also believes that the EU has in fact achieved the opposite of what it is seeking. She claims that over the years Chinese government officials have become experts in dealing with the human rights dialogue. Secret talks behind closed doors have become a diplomatic ritual. They have provided Chinese participants with intensive training on how to handle international criticism and recommendations about China's human rights policy and reject this in the most effective way (Kinzelbach 2015). At the same time China is a complex case and cannot necessarily be seen as a representative example of the EU's soft power in Asia on the whole. However, the EU also has to deal with the criticism that it has failed to make the most of existing opportunities, or in fact even knowingly wasted them. The EU's relations with SAARC are a case in point. The EU was granted observer status, which allows the European Commission to take part in SAARC summits. This opened the door to stronger relations between the two organizations, but this potential has not been fully exploited. Unlike other observers, the EU has never sent any high-level representatives, a fact that is a source of some annoyance for SAARC and EU officials. A high-ranking EU official bemoaned the fact that so much time and effort was poured into gaining observer status only to waste it by not sending appropriate delegates to the meetings (personal interview in Kathmandu, August 2013). Similar concerns have been voiced about ASEAN–EU relations and the ASEM summit. In both these cases, the Asian side has tended to send higher level representatives than the EU, a fact that has been viewed with some incomprehension by Asian governments. A good example of this was the ASEAN–EU summit held on 22 November 2007 in Singapore, marking the 30th anniversary of the establishment of official relations. It was planned that the meeting should be attended by heads of state and government, but unlike the ASEAN nations, only a few EU member states sent their heads of government. Today, observers still talk of the EU's embarrassment and the loss of face suffered by Singapore, which had a negative impact on subsequent diplomatic relations (personal interview, Singapore, September 2014).

Conclusion

As far as foreign policy is concerned, the EU's institutional structure means it cannot act in the same way as a nation state. Co-ordination on foreign and security policy issues has increased, but the EU's external relations still represent the sum of the interests and strategies of the European Commission, the European Parliament and the 28 member states. They do not all consider relations with Asia to be one of their top priorities. Although the Treaty of Amsterdam (which entered into force in 1999) established the office of a High Representative for Foreign Affairs and Security Policy to handle the day-to-day conduct of external relations, this has not necessarily increased the effectiveness of European diplomacy vis-à-vis Asia. The visit by former High Representative Catherine Ashton to the ASEAN Secretariat in November 2013 attracted little public attention, whereas Hillary Clinton's visit in September 2012 in her role as US Secretary of State was reported in the media for weeks.

Overall, high-level diplomacy only plays a minor role in building and expanding normative power. It is equally – or perhaps more – important to focus on the everyday reality of the bilateral and multilateral relations that develop as a result of communication and negotiation between the officials of the governments concerned. The EU's apparatus is characterized by multilayered decision-making processes, complex co-ordination procedures and the principle of rotation. This means that it often lacks the flexibility to make compromises during negotiations, and regular personnel changes make it more difficult to build mutual trust and understanding. It is an open secret that the free trade negotiations between the EU and ASEAN which began in 2007 and broke down in 2009 largely failed because the Brussels representatives tried to push through the EU draft without being willing or able to respond to the specific requirements and wishes of ASEAN.

This all may give the impression that the EU has failed in its objective of exercising a normative influence on Asia, or at least that it has been less successful than Brussels would like to suggest. However, such a verdict fails to take into account the fact that diplomacy is only one side of the coin. It is the academic preoccupation with official diplomacy in EU–Asia relations that has resulted in a widespread international perception that inter-regional relations have not achieved much beyond political rhetoric. The main shortcoming of the existing mainstream in the inter-regionalism debate is its analytical one-sidedness: the political realities of co-operation in Europe–Asia relations are reduced to interactions between the two region's foreign policy elites and a strong focus on dialogue fora such as ASEM. The conduct of development co-operation tends not to appear on the radar screen of analysts. Yet, it is mainly within the context of development co-operation in the broadest sense that meaningful normative change takes place in intra-regional relations. The examples mentioned in this chapter show that the EU does indeed play a role as a soft power – in the sense of an accepted source of ideas. There is clearly a European tone to Southeast Asian regionalism with all its technicalities and the Asian discourse on human rights, democracy and governance.

Notes

1 Many of the following findings are based on personal interviews with government officials at a number of foreign ministries across East and Southeast Asia, staff at the European Commission and international and regional organizations in Asia (particularly ASEAN), NGO representatives, academics and journalists conducted between 2010 and 2016.

2 For the discussion of norms in international relations in general terms see Jepperson *et al.* 1996: 54.

3 See Article III-193(1), Article I-2 and I-3.

4 For the most comprehensive discussion of the EU's role as a normative power in relations with ASEAN see Allison 2015.

References

Abad, G. (2010) 'Non-triadic interregionalism: the case of FEALAC' in J. Dosch and O. Jacob (eds), *Asia and Latin America: Political, Economic and Multilateral Relations*, London: Routledge.

Allison, L. (2015) *The EU, ASEAN and Interregionalism: Regionalism Support and Norm Diffusion between the EU and ASEAN*, Houndsmill: Macmillan.

ASEAN (1980) 'Cooperation Agreement between Member Countries of ASEAN and European Community', 7 March, http://asean.org/?static_post=external-relations-european-union-nuremberg-declaration-on-an-eu-asean-enhanced-partnership-nuremberg-germany-15-march-2007.

Asia–Europe Meeting (2017) *About the Asia–Europe Meeting (ASEM)*, www.aseminfoboard.org/about.

Doidge, M. (2007) 'Joined at the hip: regionalism and interregionalism', *Journal of European Integration*, 29 (2): 229–48.

Duchêne, F. (1972) 'Europe's role in world peace' in R. Mayne (ed.), *Europe Tomorrow: Sixteen Europeans Look Ahead*, London: Fontana.

EU (1994) *Towards a New Asia Strategy*, COM(94) 314 final, Brussels, 13 July, http://aei.pitt.edu/2949/1/2949.pdf.

European Commission (2007a) *Evaluation of the European Commission's Co-operation and Partnership with the People's Republic of China*, Final Synthesis Report, April, http://ec.europa.eu/europeaid/how/evaluation/evaluation_reports/reports/2007/1077_vol1_en.pdf.

European Commission (2007b) *Evaluation of the European Commission's Support to the Republic of India*, Final Report, August, https://ec.europa.eu/europeaid/sites/devco/files/evaluation-cooperation-ec-india-1091-main-report-200708_en_0.pdf.

European Commission (2009) *Evaluation of the European Commission's Cooperation with Vietnam*, Final Report, Vol. 1, October, https://www.oecd.org/countries/vietnam/44652744.pdf.

European Commission (2011) *Evaluation of the European Commission's Cooperation with the Philippines*, Final Report, Vol. 2, June, http://ec.europa.eu/europeaid/how/evaluation/evaluation_reports/reports/2011/1299_vol2_en.pdf.

European Commission (2012) *Evaluation of the European Union's Co-operation with Nepal Country Level Evaluation*, Final Report, Vol. 1 – Main Report, March, http://ec.europa.eu/europeaid/how/evaluation/evaluation_reports/reports/2012/1302_vol1_en.pdf.

European Commission (2014) *Evaluation of the European Union's Regional Co-operation with Asia*, Final Report, Vol. 1, March, http://ec.europa.eu/europeaid/how/evaluation/evaluation_reports/reports/2014/1326_vol1_en.pdf.

European External Action Service (2013) *EU–China 2020 Strategic Agenda for Cooperation*, http://eeas.europa.eu/archives/docs/china/docs/eu-china_2020_strategic_agenda_en.pdf.

European Union (2012) *Bandar Seri Begawan Plan of Action to Strengthen the ASEAN–EU Enhanced Partnership (2013–2017)*, www.consilium.europa.eu/uedocs/cms_Data/docs/pressdata/EN/foraff/129884.pdf.

Galtung, J. (1973) *The European Community: A Superpower in the Making*, London: Verso.

Hänggi, H., R. Roloff and J. Rüland (2006) 'Interregionalism: a new phenomenon in international relations' in H. Hänggi, R. Roloff and J. Rüland (eds), *Interregionalism and International Relations*, London: Routledge.

Jepperson, R., A. Wendt and P. Katzenstein (1996) 'Norms, identity, and culture in national security' in P. Katzenstein (ed.), *The Culture of National Security: Norms and Identity in World Politics*, New York: Columbia University Press.

Kinzelbach, K. (2015) *The EU's Human Rights Dialogue with China: Quiet Diplomacy and Its Limits*, London: Routledge.

Kirste, K. and H.-W. Maull (1996) 'Zivilmacht und Rollentheorie', *Zeitschrift für Internationale Beziehungen*, 3 (2): 283–312.

Manea, M.-G. (2008) 'Human rights and the interregional dialogue between Asia and Europe: ASEAN–EU relations and ASEM', *The Pacific Review*, 21 (3): 369–96.

Manners, I. (2002) 'Normative power Europe: a contradiction in terms?' *Journal of Common Market Studies*, 20 (2): 235–58.

Nye, J. (2004) *Soft Power: The Means to Success in World Politics*, New York: Public Affairs.

Reliefweb (2016) *Human Rights Risk Index 2016, Q4*, http://reliefweb.int/sites/reliefweb.int/files/resources/2016_ITF_Human_Rights_Index_2016-01.pdf.

Robles, A. C. (2008) *The Asia–Europe Meeting – The Theory and Practice of Interregionalism*, London: Routledge.

Rosecrance, R. (1998) 'The European Union: a new type of international actor', in Jan Zielonka (ed.), *Paradoxes of European Foreign Policy*, Den Haag: Kluwer Law International.

Vanoverbeke, D. and M. Reiterer (2014) 'ASEAN's regional approach to human rights: the limits of the European model?' in W. Benedek *et al.* (eds), *European Yearbook on Human Rights 2014*, Antwerp *et al.*: NWV.

9 Regional security

Legacies and new challenges

Jörn Dosch and Frederick Kliem

Introduction: the changing concept of security

In absence of a universal definition, security is a fiercely debated term in International Relations. Complicating matters is that most would certainly agree that establishing and safeguarding security is the top priority of international co-operation and the archetypal responsibility of all international actors, whether those be nation states or non-state actors. Like most concepts, the understanding of security depends on the theoretical starting point. Compare for instance Lippmann's (1943: 51) assertion that 'a nation has security when it does not have to sacrifice its legitimate interests to avoid war, and is able, if challenged, to maintain them by war' to Samuel Makinda's (1998: 282) definition of security as 'the preservation of the norms, rules, institutions and values of society' which must be protected from 'military and non-military threats'. Estrella Solidum equally emphasizes norms and values, but does also move away from the focus on threats per se. Solidum (1991: 26) instead concentrates on security as the satisfaction of values, arguing that security 'consists of the feeling that accompanies actual, perceived, or sustained satisfaction of values and/or reasonable and stable expectation of their realization'. A nation state's values rather than its survival become the main parameters of its core interest of security.

Traditionally, in the realist reading security has been discussed in terms of territory and threats. The nation state is the quintessential actor and, threatened by extra-national actors by military means, its survival is the most rudimental component of having security. Accordingly, threats can be alleviated by increasing power and defence capabilities of the state by enhancing military and economic power, engaging in pre-emptive military action, building and enhancing alliances etc. Some institutional realists also account for the possibility of some form of limited, rational-oriented institutional integration and confidence-building measures (CBMs) among a group of competing states. The above definitions carry a more or less overt theoretical connotation and prescribe a theoretical perspective (see Leffler 2004 for a holistic concept of security). As security studies evolved, non-traditional security (NTS) threats were added and widened the understanding of what constitutes security and, thus, what poses a threat. NTS can be broadly categorized as all non-state challenges to survival and wellbeing of the state and its people. NTS threats include internal threats in the form of, inter alia, subversion by extremist groups, migration, economic hardship, human rights abuses, famines, pandemics and environmental disasters, all of which pose a direct threat to the welfare of state and people (Booth 2005). The traditional realist view is broadened in two ways. First, security is no longer seen as being state-centric. Second, the welfare of society as a whole and the security of the individual is included. Last, in the wake of the Cold War, the security discourse expanded from the nation state as the principle object of security and the understanding of security in exclusively military terms. The emerging notion of human security included food-, economic-, political-, and increasingly environmental challenges (UNDP 1994).

Regional problems show the importance of NTS. A good example is the re-occurring haze problem which is created by illegal hazardous agricultural fires due to industrial-scale slash-and-burn practices in Indonesia that have resulted in almost annual diplomatic quarrels between Indonesia, Singapore and Malaysia since the first major crisis of 1997–98. In China the debate dates even farther back. The 1970s, when Chinese intellectuals responded to the Japanese idea of comprehensive security, may be considered the first serious conceptual attempt at redefining security in international relations since the Second World War (Wang 2005: 2). The significance of NTS was officially recognized in the China National Defence White Paper of December 2004. The paper stresses that 'traditional and nontraditional security issues are intertwined with the latter posing a growing threat' (State Council Information Office 2004).

A rapidly growing number of non-traditional security complexes have appeared on the radar screen of policy-makers in ASEAN, China and Japan, and have started to have an impact on regional security. The agenda includes environmental deterioration; growing pressures on natural resources; developmental policies; the broad field of democracy and human rights; legal and illegal migration and resulting ethnic tensions; increasingly violent criminal acts, prostitution and people smuggling; drug trafficking; piracy; increasing gaps in wealth and income within and between neighbouring regions in part due to international and transnational economic exchanges; mismanagement of national economies and their vulnerability to the intensifying forces of globalization; and separatism, insurgencies and terrorism (see Hoadley and Rüland 2006 for a comprehensive analysis of many of these NTS issues). Human security has become a focal point of critical security studies that rejects the 'unacceptable normative implications of traditional security approaches' (i.e., structural realism) and re-orientates the attention to the individual (Burke and McDonald 2007: 5).

Despite justified warnings that the concept of human security is too vague to serve as a sound analytical framework (Paris 2001: 96), there is now all but universal consensus that exclusively state-centric, military security is no longer sufficient to account for global stability. Buzan *et al.* (1998) highlight the problem that security is by no means an objective measurement. Quite the opposite, securitization of issues often follows normative-ideological elite preferences and therefore, almost any issue can be securitized. Definitions can be endless and their ideological origins almost diametrically opposed (Buzan *et al.* 1998: 24). In particular, Makinda's and Solidum's definitions are prone to the problem of diverse issue securitization. Norms and values of society can be subject to fluctuating and even capricious reinterpretations, depending on elite preferences, and even Lippman's assertion of a state's 'legitimate interest' is contingent on potentially inconsistent elitist understanding. At the same time, traditional security remains as important as it has always been and NTS supplements, rather than replaces, traditional notions. For the purpose of this chapter it suffices to deem security as whatever the relevant actors believe it consists of.

This chapter focuses on the three most decisive conflicts – relations between the People's Republic of China (PRC) and the Republic of China or Taiwan (ROC); tensions on the Korean Peninsula; and the disputes in the South China Sea – which pose the greatest risk to security in the Asia-Pacific. Although NTS comes into play – particularly in the case of the South China Sea – the three cases mainly fit the definition of traditional security conflicts. The case studies are embedded in a general discussion about the structures and actors of the Asia-Pacific security architecture and bilateral versus multilateral approaches to problem solving.

The Asia-Pacific security architecture

Apart from a largely self-sufficient China and the unique case of North Korea, there are three pivotal pillars supporting the East Asian security architecture. First and foremost, there is the US-led largely bilateral 'hub-and-spokes' system. Washington is the principal regional security guarantor, the hub of a complex arrangement of mostly bilateral security relationships (spokes). In this arrangement the Pentagon is primarily responsible for the greater security of the region. Its allies and partners contribute within their often limited means. In East Asia (Tow and Limaye 2016), this is operationalized via a complex web of formal alliances with traditional allies including Japan and South Korea as well as informal, often intentionally ambiguous agreements and security guarantees, in particular but not exclusively with partners where ambiguity serves a wider strategic goal, such as Taiwan. This is supplemented by several treaties, short of formal alliances, supporting US efforts by granting access to military bases, offering logistic support, conducting joint exercises, etc. In recent years, US defence policy-makers have increasingly come to appreciate the importance of strategic partnerships short of formal alliances (Philippines, Indonesia, Vietnam, etc.). There has been a particular surge in such arrangements under the Obama administration as part of a strategy for navigating a more complex security situation in Asia (Parameswaran 2014).

Second, there are significant bilateral co-operative networks among individual East- and Southeast Asian countries such as closer Philippine–Vietnam relations, in particular in reaction to the South China Sea threat originating in China. There are also more or less close military-to-military contacts and joint exercises among most ASEAN member states. Last but not least, a central pillar of Asia-Pacific security is based on ASEAN's centrality, the notion that ASEAN is and ought to be the fulcrum of regional order. And major destabilization of this order is likely to stem from tensions in PRC–ROC relations, on the Korean Peninsula and in the South China Sea.

China and Taiwan

Since 1949, the governments of the PRC and ROC have both claimed to be the only legitimate governments of the whole of China. Until 1972, Taiwan's claim was fully endorsed by the US, and the ROC was a key factor in Washington's anti-communist containment strategy. The serious nature of the US commitment became evident in 1954–55. In July 1954 the Chinese media began to proclaim the intention to 'liberate' Taiwan, and kept up heavy artillery bombardment of Taiwanese offshore islands through the winter, while the US dispatched a naval task force to the area. In 1955, the US threatened explicitly to use tactical nuclear weapons in the event of a Chinese assault on Taiwan, after which the PRC government defused the situation. Chinese bombardment was resumed in 1958, and again was met by a very determined US response. This crisis is thought to have been one of the catalysts for the Sino–Soviet split: the Chinese leadership were deeply angered that Khrushchev would not risk confrontation with the US in support of Beijing's claim to Taiwan.

However, after the Nixon–Mao agreements of the early 1970s, the US recognized the government in Beijing, which led to a rapid deterioration in Taiwan's international position as it removed itself from the UN (to avoid being ejected), and almost all foreign governments withdrew diplomatic recognition. Its isolation was intensified because both Taiwan and Beijing refused to have diplomatic relations with any state that recognized its rival. Many nations followed the US in handling this problem: from 1972 to 1979, they maintained formal diplomatic ties with Taiwan, and quasi-diplomatic ones with Beijing; from 1979 until now, the formal ties are with Beijing, and relations with Taiwan are conducted through a number of semi-official offices, institutes, councils, delegations, etc., which in effect conduct diplomatic business.

In the 1980s, relations between the two states appeared to be improving. Neither government relented on its basic policy, but economic contacts increased dramatically, mainly through indirect trade and investment from Taiwan into South China, filtered through Hong Kong. During the relatively calm period of the 1980s and early 1990s, Taiwan also sought to improve its international position. Its principal resource was its enormously successful economy, which to some extent could compensate for its political weakness. It began to upgrade its commercial, quasi-governmental offices in many countries, especially the US. Another tactic was to join international organizations, from which the PRC had previously excluded it at all costs (for example the Asian Development Bank and Asia-Pacific Economic Cooperation or APEC). It is a very high priority for Taiwan to continue its search for at least some form of diplomatic recognition and international protection. It is extremely keen to develop its role in organizations such as APEC, and would like to enhance relations with ASEAN. A major step towards the goal of a more prominent international role was Taiwan's admission into the WTO (under the name of Chinese Taipei), which came into effect on 1 January 2002 following China's accession a few weeks earlier. Overall, Taipei's foreign policy has been based on a strong national defence against invasion by the PRC, and on flexible, informal and difficult attempts to upgrade its diplomatic status.

The US and other Western countries have continued to sell military equipment to Taiwan, whose booming economy allowed it to become one of the most powerful states in East Asia; despite improving relations with the PRC, and an apparently peaceful international environment, Taipei insisted on maintaining a very high level of military preparedness. This proved to be a wise precaution, because between the mid-1990s and about 2007, Beijing had become increasingly vocal and aggressive towards the ROC, in contrast to its conciliatory behaviour of the late 1980s. There were several reasons for this. Partly, the old generation of CCP leaders was retiring from politics, and they felt deeply frustrated at their lack of success over Taiwan, which in many respects had outdone China itself. They felt that the much higher standard of living on Taiwan, coupled with a reasonably democratic polity, reflected poorly on the achievements of the PRC. But most important, they were alarmed by the growth of a strong independence movement on Taiwan, which asserted itself in various ways: increasing assertion of Taiwanese relations around the world and demands for complete secession from China and the formation of a new nation state.

Consequently, in March 1996, Beijing authorized highly provocative and aggressive military exercises just outside Taiwanese waters, with warnings that any further moves towards independence would be met with an invasion. Since then the warning has been repeated on various occasions. Most people viewed this threat relatively seriously, even believing that China would destroy its own economic development to prevent Taiwanese independence, although this scenario has become less likely in recent years. In 2005, the Third Session of the 10th National People's Congress reaffirmed the tough policy vis-à-vis Taiwan by rubber stamping a government-proposed 'anti-secession' law, authorizing the use of military force to bar any attempt by Taiwan to gain independence. According to Article 8 of the law:

> In the event that the 'Taiwan independence' secessionist forces should act under any name or by any means to cause the fact of Taiwan's secession from China, or that major incidents entailing Taiwan's secession from China should occur, or that possibilities for a peaceful reunification should be completely exhausted, the state shall employ non-peaceful means and other necessary measures to protect China's sovereignty and territorial integrity.
>
> (cited in *People's Daily* 14 March 2005)

The main worry for Taiwan is whether the US will remain as committed to its security in the 21st century as it was in the previous one. For this reason, one can anticipate that Taiwan will, for the medium term, continue to support one of the largest, most modern and best equipped armed forces in Asia. As well as its overseas purchases, it has developed a major national defence industry, capable of building missiles and guided missile frigates that are at least a generation ahead of the PRC's. In early 2010, the Obama administration announced a plan to sell US$ 6.4 billion worth of anti-missile systems, helicopters and other military hardware to Taiwan. Beijing reacted immediately and suspended exchanges between the armed forces of the US and the PRC in retribution for Washington's move (Shanker 2010).

Generally, however, during the term of Ma Ying-jeou (Kuomintang) who served as Taiwanese president from 2008 to 2016, cross-Strait relations improved significantly. The past decade has been characterized by substantial change in bilateral relations and in fact 'a reversal of the political interactions across the Strait' (Beckershoff 2014: 214) mainly due to Ma's accommodative policies and a series of substantial agreements in a variety of sectors.

> While the state of affairs is still far from 'normal' day-to-day politics between governments, a feasible and productive working relationship has developed. The most striking element of this development, however, is the form these interactions have taken: Rather than eroding the condition of political non-recognition, both sides have devised an array of channels and practices that circumvent the persisting ideological obstacles that have complicated cross-Strait relations ever since the end of the Chinese Civil War in 1949.
>
> (ibid.)

These recent developments have pointed towards an optimistic scenario in the long term, which might lead to a de-securitization of bilateral relations or a situation in which Taipei and Beijing no longer considers the other a threat to their own security. It is not unthinkable that the PRC and ROC could produce some kind of agreement along the 'one country two systems' model that was in fact developed by Beijing with reference to Taiwan before being applied to Hong Kong. The Taipei government at various times responded with counter-suggestions, such as 'one country two governments' or 'one country two areas', and with the suggestion that the state of civil war should be formally ended. The Chinese government and many neutral observers are optimistic that the ever-increasing economic co-operation between China and Taiwan will inevitably lead to a political reconciliation, presumably one that would allow both sides to retain face and dignity and postponing the most difficult decisions until a very distant future. The PRC is Taiwan's most important trade partner, top destination for FDI and the most important source of Taiwan's trade surplus. A landmark economic treaty between China and Taiwan was signed in June 2010 to establish a systematic mechanism to enhance cross-Straits economic co-operation. The Economic Cooperation Framework Agreement (ECFA) is seen as the most important agreement between the PRC and ROC to deepen co-operation between financial organizations and to reduce tariffs and commercial barriers (*China Daily* 13 September 2010).

The Taiwan Straits conflict is not primarily based on power considerations anymore, but rather separate political identities. Following the tremendous political and social changes in the PRC and ROC under the influence of economic globalization and political democratization during the past decades, the most prominent source of tension and potential conflict between China and Taiwan is no longer the competition over power within an agreed 'one China'. The source now is the hardening of distinctly separate political identities. In Taiwan, loyalties focus on a new democracy; in China, on a sense of special national destiny. This is paralleled by a shift from how to reunify to whether there should be reunification or independence. Mainland China, Taiwan and the US, however, have failed to respond to these changes with policies. There have been many small adjustments, but the policy frameworks of the three players remain basically unchanged. Mainland China's approach to Taiwan is still the so-called 'two hands policy'. One hand is a hard hand, threatening military coercion and diplomatic blockade. The other hand is 'soft', offering inducements to increase commercial trade and investment, as well as cultural exchanges. Beijing hopes that growing economic and cultural integration will eventually absorb Taiwan as it has Hong Kong and Macao.

For the time being, however, such a scenario has become highly unlikely. In January 2016, when Tsai Ing-wen of the pro-independence Democratic Progressive Party (DPP) was elected president of Taiwan, cross-Strait relations almost immediately worsened. Although her agenda does not include the search for formal independence, Tsai's reluctance to endorse the idea of a single nation (according to the so-called '1992 consensus') was enough for PRC diplomats to suspend communication channels with their Taiwanese counterparts. The '1992 consensus', a term invented and promoted by the Kuomintang and supported by the PRC stipulates that while Beijing and Taipei recognize that mainland China and Taiwan belong to the same China, both sides agree to interpret the meaning of that one China according to their own definition (see Wei 2016 for a detailed discussion). The DPP government denies the existence of this informal agreement and, in reaction to predicted re-emerging frictions with the PRC, has tried to move closer to the US for support. During its first months the Trump administration has sent mixed signals to Taiwan. On the one hand President Donald Trump has indicated plans to authorize substantial arms sales to Taiwan, which will almost inevitably generate tensions with the PRC. On the other hand Washington needs the PRC's co-operation to ease tensions on the Korean Peninsula. 'This has reignited the structural fear in Taiwan that the island could be used as a bargaining chip in a greater US–China game' (Duchâtel 2017: 2). While cross-Strait relations looked stable only a couple of years ago, volatility has increased and the outcome of the long-term conflict between the PRC and the ROC remains as unpredictable as it has always been.

The Korean Peninsula

By the 7th century, Korea had evolved into a unified state that persisted until the end of the Second World War. Because of this history and ethnic unity, the division of Korea along the 38th parallel in 1945 represents a traumatic separation. There is no historical justification for the division of Korea and it is not based on language, culture, ethnicity or natural geography. The decision to divide the country along the 38th parallel was arbitrary, if not absurd. Following Japan's surrender on 15 August 1945, John J. McCloy of the State–War–Navy Coordinating Committee (SWNCC) directed two young colonels, Dean Rusk and Charles H. Bonesteel, to withdraw to an adjoining room and find a place to divide Korea in 30 minutes. Despite the fact that two distinct states have emerged (Republic of Korea/ROK in the south and the Democratic People's Republic/DPRK in the north) and the death of 4 million Koreans during the war (1950–53), Koreans on either side of the demilitarized zone still identify the country as one nation. Roland Bleiker, however, takes a more critical view:

> In contrast to this mythical homogeneity we find the reality of half a century of political division, during which the two Koreas have developed identities that are not only distinct, but also articulated in direct and stark opposition against each other. Over the years these antagonistic forms of identity have become so deeply entrenched in societal consciousness that the current politics of insecurity appears virtually inevitable. It is the tension between these two contradictory aspects of Korea politics – the strong myth of homogeneity and the actual reality of oppositional identity practices – that contains the key to understanding both the sources of the existing conflict and the potential for a more peaceful peninsula.
>
> (Bleiker 2001: 121)

Like Taiwan, the ROK has to take account of an ever-present military threat, invasion from the North. Following the Korean War, the US signed an ROK–US Mutual Defense Treaty, according to which US troops would be stationed in South Korea (they currently number around 30,000), for which Seoul would make a substantial payment. While many Koreans accept the need for this, it has also been unpopular. A US commander is, in effect, in charge of ROK forces, and the South Korean courts have only limited jurisdiction over the US military. Many Koreans would prefer to see the US forces downgraded if not withdrawn.

Among the most decisive problems in North–South relations are the bankruptcy and unpredictable state of the North Korean regime. Reports suggest that the economy is so weak that there are serious food shortages, and that it may be almost impossible to continue as a viable unit for much longer. Although in July 2002 the DPRK introduced a number of important economic changes, including first steps towards the decentralization of economic planning, the scope and impact of the reform programme are as difficult to determine as the overall policy goals and intentions of the ruling elite. One scenario put forward is that in desperation North Korea may launch an attack on South Korea, something that has been threatened for many years. Another issue that may provoke international conflict is North Korean failure to adhere to international norms, and respond to international pressure, concerning the production of nuclear weapons: a nuclear stand-off brought the peninsula to the brink of war in 1994. However, the crisis was resolved following a series of meetings between the US and DPRK, which resulted in the Geneva Agreed Framework (1994). Under this non-proliferation agreement North Korea promised to freeze its nuclear programme. In return the US agreed to develop North Korea's civilian nuclear power capabilities by providing two 1,000-megawatt light water reactors (LWR). Furthermore, Washington gave formal assurances against the use of threat of nuclear weapons against North Korea, and agreed to take steps to lift economic sanctions and to improve political relations. The Korean Peninsula Energy Development Organization (KEDO) was founded to co-ordinate and implement the provisions of the Agreed Framework. KEDO comprised 13 member states with South Korea, Japan, the US and the European Union at the core. However, a new crisis began in October 2002 when North Korea acknowledged its secret nuclear weapons programme and restarted its nuclear reactor in February 2003. The Executive Board of KEDO decided in May 2006 to terminate the LWR project. 'This decision was taken based on the continued and extended failure of the…DPRK to perform the steps that were required in the KEDO-DPRK Supply Agreement for the provision of the LWR project' (KEDO n.d.).

One aspect of the Korean situation is that it gives some leverage to China as Beijing appears to be the only state with some influence in Pyongyang, which is otherwise almost completely isolated diplomatically. China's role was instrumental in organizing the 'Six-Party Talks' between 2003 and 2007. The first talks took place in Beijing in August 2003 with the participation of North and South Korea, the US, China, Japan and Russia. Although no agreement was reached initially, the Six-Party Talks continued as they were widely seen as the most promising route to a peaceful solution to the nuclear stand-off. In February 2005 North Korea suspended talks over its nuclear programme, but in September of the same year North Korea was back at the negotiating table. The meeting concluded with a joint statement, committing Pyongyang to dismantling its nuclear weapons programme. To achieve this breakthrough, the Bush administration agreed to transfer back to North Korea approximately US$ 25 million in funds that had since 2005 been frozen in a Macau bank for reported money laundering. Despite North Korea's testing a nuclear weapon in October 2006 – much to the shock of the global public and in violation of the 2005 agreement in which North Korea had consented to only use nuclear energy for peaceful means – the Six-Party Talks were resurrected as a potential negotiation mechanism. A new agreement was reached during the fifth round of talks held in February 2007. North Korea promised to shut down and seal its nuclear facilities at Yongbyon in a deal that was supposed to implement the joint statement (Grzelczyk 2009, Gross 2007). However, in April 2009 North Korea declared that it would terminate its participation in the Six-Party Talks and resume its nuclear enrichment programme in order to boost its nuclear deterrent. This decision was preceded by international condemnation of North Korea in the same month. While Pyongyang claimed to have launched a communications satellite, the international community accused North Korea of testing long-range missile technology. Pyongyang subsequently carried out an underground nuclear test a month later. Nuclear tension has gradually risen, particularly since 2011 when Kim Jong-Un succeeded his father Kim Jong-Il to become supreme leader of North Korea. North Korea says it has conducted five successful nuclear tests so far: in 2006, 2009, 2013 and two in 2016. Tension reached new heights in April 2017 when Kim Jong-Un's regime threatened to conduct a sixth nuclear weapons test and the Trump administration moved an anti-missile system, submarines and aircraft carriers into the region and hinted at the possibility of a military action.

> During the U.S. presidential transition, Barack Obama had warned Donald Trump that North Korea would be the most pressing foreign policy problem the new commander in chief would face.... And Trump, by all accounts, got the message. What he doesn't have – because no one does – is an attractive option to avoid the disaster that may soon unfold on the Korean Peninsula.
>
> (Powell 2017)

To this day the Korean Peninsula represents the Cold War's final frontier, with a total of two million troops on either side of the DMZ. In neither the case of the Korean Peninsula nor with regard to China–Taiwan relations has a clear and irrevocable peace-building strategy emerged yet. All actors involved have followed policies that oscillate between containment and engagement in response to changing structural framework conditions. At the same time there has been a clear tendency – in China–Taiwan relations particularly between 2008 and 2016 and concerning the Korean Peninsula mainly between 2000 and 2008 – to de-securitize the respective bilateral relations. At the core of this strategy lies the attempt of shifting the policy agenda from confrontation based on military threat perceptions to a political rhetoric that stresses the importance of economic co-operation and other forms of transactions. However, as we have seen, in neither case has this strategy prevailed, ultimately always returning to more confrontational approaches. While both conflicts are best subsumed under the concept of traditional security, in the case of the South China Sea traditional and non-traditional security mix.

The South China Sea

The interconnected maritime disputes in the South China Sea (SCS) revolve around both territory and resources in the Spratly and Paracel Islands and adjacent waters, including features such as the Scarborough Shoal, as well as, owing to recent developments, the Natuna Islands.[1] All official SCS claimants (China, Taiwan,[2] Vietnam, Philippines, Malaysia, Brunei) have multiple overlapping claims in the SCS. Additionally there are what shall henceforth be called the 'interested parties', particularly Indonesia and Singapore. Territorial disputes in Southeast Asia are not limited to the SCS and there is also the very significant, mostly non-ASEAN, geopolitical element of a wider great power struggle currently unfolding between Washington and Beijing. However, as arguably the greatest traditional security concern of contemporary Southeast Asia, largely determining Sino–ASEAN relations, the SCS represents a great test for ASEAN's claims to be in the 'driver's seat' of multilateral regional security, i.e., its centrality.

The importance of the SCS can barely be overestimated for three reasons: resources, trade, and geopolitical posturing. First, the US believes the SCS holds about 15.6 billion barrels of petroleum, while Chinese estimates are as high as 213 billion barrels, in addition to high volumes of natural gas (Rogers 2012: 87). It is also one of the most biologically diverse marine areas and home to some of the world's richest fishing grounds, contributing a minimum of 12 per cent of the global catch (Sumalia and Cheung 2015: 3). Second, some 30 per cent of all global trade passes through the vicinity of the SCS, including US$ 1.2 trillion worth of US trade (De Luce and McLeary 2015). Since it connects the Western Pacific to the Indian Ocean and thence the Middle East, most of the East Asian global goods and resource trade passes through the SCS, most of it via the Strait of Malacca. In the opposite direction, almost all East Asia-bound crude oil transports cross these waters, almost five times more than through the Suez Canal, with China being the world's largest net oil importer. Currently 80 per cent of all Chinese imports pass through the Strait of Malacca, which is controlled and patrolled by mostly US and Singaporean forces. This has come to be known as China's 'Malacca Dilemma' (Davies 2014), meaning that China has only limited control over its most crucial sea lines of communication (SLOC). With this in mind, imagining the wider geostrategic and political consequences is not a tough ask. Maritime domain control in the SCS is of utmost importance to all relevant states including the US and strategic positioning has become a principle task of all navies involved. What is more, to a greater or lesser extent all claimant states are guilty of playing domestic politics with their respective claims and tough approaches occasionally serve to please domestic audiences. Hence, claimant or not, most Asian states and the US have significant interests in the SCS, including territorial and exclusive economic zone (EEZ) control, safeguarding SLOC, and general freedom of navigation (FON). Only with this in mind is one able to appreciate the significance of the contest unfolding in the SCS among a multitude of claimant states.

The situation is further complicated by Southeast Asia's uniquely dense maritime geography, resulting in the entire SCS being a claimed maritime zone of some kind. The UN umbrella agreement regulating the maritime domain, the United Nations Convention on the Law of the Sea (UNCLOS), divides seas into two basic categories endowed with respective jurisdiction and rights; territorial seas stretch 12 nautical miles (nm) off a state's coastline and constitute sovereign territory, while the high seas are essentially the global commons and thus, theoretically open to unrestricted navigation for all. UNCLOS also provides for EEZs extending 200 nm from a state's coastline into the high seas, or more if coastal states can claim a continental shelf extension within which it possesses sovereign rights to all natural resources. All claims must be derived from sovereign land-territory or archipelagic baselines, although a median line may apply should legal zones overlap. UNCLOS effectively leaves it to international courts and arbitration tribunals, such as the International Court of Justice (ICJ), to interpret maritime law if no bilateral agreement can be reached (UNCLOS 1982: Art 15, 30). All parties to UNCLOS, including China and the ASEAN member states, have committed themselves to abide by such rules. One of the main problems with

UNCLOS as far as the SCS is concerned is the regime's ambiguity as to what exactly counts as an island. To be considered capable of generating maritime zones, the land must be above water at high tide and capable of sustaining human or economic life. Artificially created islands do not count (UNCLOS 1982: Art 121).

All littoral states claim an EEZ, but all officially disputing parties have directly competing, partially overlapping claims in the SCS. While Vietnam and China have solved their disputes in the Gulf of Tonkin, both claim all of the Paracel Islands. The Philippines, Vietnam and Malaysia have overlapping claims to either some or all of the Spratly Islands. The most low-key claimant and the only one to not have established military outposts is Brunei. Although not official claimants, countries such as Indonesia and Singapore shall be considered interested parties. Indonesia is an archipelagic state and values a rules-based maritime order while the Singaporean economy depends on the uninterrupted flow of goods transported via the Strait of Malacca and regards stability here as a top security priority (Ho 2012: 129). Jakarta has also had EEZ problems with China around the Natunas of late.

However, the most important factor in this dispute is China's nine-dash line (9DL). This imprecise and ambiguous demarcation line expresses Beijing's claim on the outer limits of its maritime territory, enclosing almost 90 per cent of the entire SCS. Although party to UNCLOS, Beijing implicitly rejects, or at least violates UNCLOS principles by insisting on the 9DL, extending far beyond any reasonable maritime zone and cutting deep into the EEZ of other littoral states (Jayakumar, Koh and Beckman 2014). With some exceptions in the Paracels, under Beijing's control since 1974, China's legal EEZ gives it not much but deep blue water. Beijing has for instance no UNCLOS-based right to the very distant Spratlys (*Nansha*) but claims some unspecified 'historic rights' (Ministry of Foreign Affairs of the PRC 2016). In a note verbale to the UN in 2009, Beijing argued that 'China has indisputable sovereignty over the islands in the South China Sea and the adjacent waters, and enjoys sovereign rights and jurisdiction over the relevant waters' (Note verbale 2009). Similarly, Xi Jinping stated that 'the South China Sea islands have been Chinese territory since ancient times. It is the bounded duty of the Chinese government to uphold China's territorial sovereignty and legitimate maritime rights and interests' (*New York Times* 10 December 2015).

Over recent years China has become increasingly assertive over what it claims to be its rights within the legally unsubstantiated 9DL. Whilst the Deng Xiaoping policy was to 'keep a low profile' and subsequent leadership generations had exercised some restraint true to the narrative of 'China's peaceful rise', foreign policy assertiveness has increased significantly under Xi Jinping. With a strong sense of nationalism, Xi advocated his very own narrative of the 'Chinese Dream' (*Zhongguo meng*), or 'the great rejuvenation of the Chinese nation' after a century of humiliation in order to restore what he regards as China's rightful place in Asia (Brown 2016, Johnson 2016, Blackwill and Campbell 2016, Wacker 2015). The

Table 9.1 Conflict parties and their claims in the South China Sea

Claimant	*Selected important SCS claims*	*Problem with China*	*Occupation*
Brunei (insignificant claimant)	Claims UNCLOS-based EEZ; overlaps with Malaysia's EEZ; also, 2 Spratly Island features within EEZ (Louisa Reef, Rifleman Bank, both low-tide elevations, not generating further extensions).	Potential dispute; 9DL cuts into Brunei's EEZ.	None occupied; no military presence.
China (crucial claimant)	Largest claimant (80–90% of entire SCS); keeps claim basis ambiguous; claims undefined 'historic rights' to all islands in Paracel and Spratlys and surrounding grounds; Natuna Islands only surroundings, not islands themselves.	–	Significant military presence; occupies several islands in Spratlys (incl. 7 artificial) and all Paracel Islands, incl. artificial islands.
Indonesia (unofficial claimant)	UNCLOS EEZ and continental shelf extensions off coastline and Natuna Islands; owns Natuna Islands (undisputed).	9DL overlaps with Natuna-generated EEZ; important fisheries affected; significant ongoing conflict.	Significant military presence on Natunas and in surrounding waters.
Malaysia (claimant)	EEZ and continental shelf extension; at least 3 islands in the Spratlys.	9DL extends into EEZ; important fisheries; dispute over some Spratly islands.	Military and coast guard presence on several islands and features; 5 outposts in the Spratlys.
Philippines (claimant)	Significant parts of SCS, EEZ and continental shelf generated by archipelagic baseline; 8 islands in the Spratlys, Scarborough Shoal.	Most significant conflict in 2012; ongoing.	Military presence on 8 outposts in Spratlys.
Vietnam (claimant)	Significant parts of the SCS; EEZ and continental shelf extensions.	Overlapping EEZs; competing claims to entire Paracels and some Spratly features; significant ongoing conflicts.	Occupies 48 outposts in Spratlys with military presence on some.

Source: The authors

SCS is the maritime realm of this 'rightful place', since 2010 considered one of China's non-negotiable 'core interests' (Yoshihara and Holmes 2011), putting the SCS on an equal footing with interests such as the 'One China' policy and Tibet and to be militarily defended (Zhang 2015). In rather peculiar fashion China demonstrated that it has no intention of backing down from its SCS position by including the 9DL on maps printed inside new Chinese passports. By now, Chinese elites have managed to generate near popular domestic consensus within China that they possess sovereign rights in the SCS and any disagreement with this is an offensive act carried out by a hostile foreign coalition ganging up against China (Wang 2015: 520). At the same time Chinese delegations continue to refuse all SCS references in any multilateral channel, including specific security fora in which China participates. According to Chinese Foreign Minister Wang Yi, the SCS disputes are 'not an issue between China and the ASEAN, and many ASEAN countries do not wish to see specific forces expanding specific matters' (*ABS-CBN News* 1 March 2016). At the ASEAN Plus Three Foreign Ministers' Meeting in 2014, Wang Yi for instance proposed his 'dual-track approach' to the SCS. According to him, all ASEAN member states and China should jointly maintain peace and stability in the region, but all disputes must be addressed through bilateral negotiations between directly concerned countries (Embassy of the PRC in the UK 2014). However, ever since the Gulf of Tonkin agreement in 2000, no serious bilateral settlements have occurred.

One prominent example is Manila's 2013 initiation of international arbitration proceedings. Following several incidents, Manila initiated proceedings against Beijing at the International Court of Justice (ICJ) and the Permanent Court of Arbitration (PCA). China reacted furiously, rejected the submission and refused outright to participate. The Foreign Ministry argued that the PCA had no jurisdiction in what was a strictly regional matter and that Manila had in fact dishonoured the consensus outlined in the 2002 ASEAN Declaration on the Conduct of Parties in the South China Sea (DoC) to resolve disputes through negotiations between directly concerned sovereign states. China has also signed the DoC. When in 2015 the PCA (ITLOS) announced that it would indeed exercise jurisdiction in this case and initiate due procedure, and in July 2016 decided in Manila's favour, Beijing's response was more of the same, rejecting any jurisdiction of the tribunal and refusing to participate, much less comply.

On the hard, material side, Xi Jinping's China is more willing to use the PLA as well as a set of paramilitary forces mostly coming in the form of the Chinese Coast Guard (CCG) (Bitzinger 2015), and increasingly (sometimes armed) militia style civilians, in particular fishermen, in order to realize goals in the SCS. Beijing allows, and most likely even actively dispatches means of resource exploitation such as fishing fleets or oil rigs into disputed waters and ensures 'protection' by either paramilitary CCG forces or even PLA-N warships (Dupont and Baker 2014). This is supposed to signal dominance and control over disputed waters, to block vessels of other claimants and to protect Chinese fishermen from being detained by foreign navies and coast guards when fishing in disputed areas. Beijing is using its fishing and paramilitary fleets for geopolitical purposes, designed to reinforce its sovereignty and resource claims in disputed waters and coerce other claimants into acceptance. It acquires domain control and often follows up with land reclamations and construction of military fortifications. Dupont and Baker (2014: 80) call this the 'fish, protect, contest, and occupy' strategy.

In 2012, for the first time since the 1995 Mischief Reef (Philippines) incident, China grabbed an uninhabited island, Scarborough Shoal, approximately 120 nm west of Luzon, claimed by both the Philippines and China. Following a more than two-month-long confrontation between the prime vessel of the Philippine Navy and several paramilitary CCG ships over the use of local fishing grounds, Manila had to give in and forfeit the shoal to China, which established de facto administrative control (*Sansha*). Occupation and control is not limited to land features, though. The past five years have seen an increase in instances of Chinese state-owned companies placing movable oil rigs in disputed waters or inviting foreign companies to tender for such rights. In May 2014 for instance, China moved the oil rig Haiyang Shiyou 981 (HY-981) close to the Paracels where China's and Vietnam's EEZ overlap. The ensuing stand-off between Chinese and Vietnamese coast guard and navy vessels marked perhaps the worst Sino–Vietnamese row since the Sino–Vietnamese War in 1979 and triggered anti-China protests and even riots in Vietnam that left several people dead and prompted China to evacuate citizens from Vietnam.

Malaysia reported some 100 intrusions by CCG vessels as well as at least two PLA-N exercises around the disputed James Shoal in 2013. Back then Kuala Lumpur (KL) had remained largely quiet in line with its overall China policy. In late 2015 though, the tone began to change following a series of events that suggested Beijing was upping the ante vis-à-vis KL. Malay fishermen have reported that the CCG frequently intimidates Malaysian fishing vessels and actively prevents fishing around Luconia Shoals, 84 nm off the Malay coast and within China's 9DL. Malaysian fishermen claimed that they were chased from the shoals by PLA-N boats and would not dare to return to their usual fishing grounds (*The Borneo Post* 31 October 2015). The Philippines have reported many similar cases in the Spratlys. Lastly, China is engaging in significant land reclamation and militarization projects in the SCS as well as establishing administrative control on occupied islands. Often, construction efforts turn initially uninhabitable features into actual islands that either can or already do host military facilities. Although China is not the only claimant to have unilaterally occupied disputed features, the extent dwarfs all others in comparison and increasingly alarms non-Chinese stakeholders. For example, in less than two years China has built outposts on top of seven reefs in the Spratlys, covering more than 12 km^2 of new land, 8 km^2 in the first half of 2015 alone (De Luce and McLeary 2015). Satellite images evidence at least three airstrips on these outposts, including a 3-km long runway on Fiery Cross reef, which China successfully tested in December 2015, prompting severe protest by other claimants. Additionally, there are aircraft aprons, helicopter pads, deep ports to accommodate large warships, and satellite facilities (*Jane's Defence Weekly* 2015). In the wake of the US–ASEAN summit in January 2016, the deployment of an advanced Chinese ground-to-air missile system on Woody Island in the Paracels was reported, followed by the deployment of at least 16 Shenyang J-11 fourth-generation fighter jets. Since 2012, when Beijing established control over Scarborough Shoal, administrative quasi-governmental structures have been set up and despite agreements to the contrary, the PLA-N maintains a military presence. Construction of significant further military facilities are likely and observers have warned that China intends to establish an air defence identification zone (ADIZ) in the SCS. In sum, by basing significant military assets on Hainan and subsequently expanding further southwards into the SCS, Beijing gains an island chain from where it can more effectively enforce its authority within the 9DL. China has already established point defence capabilities on its outposts and has created the necessary military infrastructure for future area-denial capabilities.

Attempts at dispute management: how feasible are multilateral approaches?

The SCS can reasonably be called the most significant traditional security threat ASEAN has faced in decades. In spite of stark power asymmetries, ASEAN member states as a collective as well as individually still try to be masters of their own fate. In terms of ASEAN's desire to create a rules-based order based on its own norms, it is useful to begin with the laudable efforts to codify specific rules of behaviour in the SCS. The need for regional conflict resolution measures was realized early on when ASEAN adopted the ASEAN Declaration on the South China Sea in 1992. In line with the ASEAN way, it was an informal code geared towards conflict management and avoidance. In 2003, China signed up to the ASEAN-initiated TAC, becoming the first non-Southeast Asian country to do so. This would be the first point of call for a legal settlement. All parties have committed themselves to the 'renunciation of the threat or use of force', 'respect for the independence, sovereignty, equality, territorial integrity' of states, and the 'settlement of differences or disputes by peaceful means' (Art. 2). Accordingly, in the SCS all claimants would have to honour the primary obligation to maintain peace. If adhered to, the TAC could de-escalate the SCS into an ordinary legal dispute over sovereignty.

More specific than the TAC, Chinese ratification of the DoC in 2002, including promises to work towards a binding code of conduct in the South China Sea (CoC), raised hopes that disputes were manageable despite China's continuous rise. Based on more general TAC principles, the DoC commits signatories to a more specific rules-based order in the SCS, such as respect of FON and to exercise self-restraint so as not to complicate or escalate disputes. Crucially, signatories also agreed not to inhabit non-occupied features and to work towards a binding Code of Conduct (Art. 4, 5, 10).

In more general terms and beyond the specific case of the SCS the establishment of the ASEAN Regional Forum (ARF) in 1994 was an ASEAN effort to control a stable regional security architecture under native regional leadership to minimize outside interference while keeping all regional powers engaged. Most of all, to support the establishment of the rules-based system required for ASEAN to be central in the light of deficient material might. China joined immediately and became a regular participant in a number of additional subsequent security fora where the SCS could be addressed (e.g., East Asian Summit or EAS; ASEAN Plus Three and the ASEAN Defence Ministers Meeting Plus or ADMM-Plus). This was perceived to encourage China to become a responsible stakeholder with a good sense of international citizenship, to be constrained through participation based on norms and principles (Emmers 2003: 117). It seemed as if China was indeed turning towards norm acceptance in an ASEAN-led security environment (Acharya 2014: 257).

However, as many critics rightly argued, regional co-operative security mechanisms in Southeast Asia tend to prefer soft-security issues and eschew discussion of territorial disputes. Based on the ASEAN way, conflicts are at best multilaterally managed, not solved, since individual parties are able to keep certain contentious issues off the official agenda. For that reason, as Juergen Haacke has shown, even less sensitive security co-operation, such as combating piracy where all participants have a more or less common interest, takes place on bi- or trilateral agreements among ARF members outside the ARF avenue (Haacke 2009: 434). Each participant is able to more or less effectively block any multilateral discussions within ARF, ASEAN Plus Three or ADMM-Plus channels. Institutional effectiveness is therefore limited and being held hostage to great power rivalry. This could lead to a situation where ASEAN meetings become ineffective. This was exemplified at the November 2015 ADMM-Plus meeting in Malaysia where Defence Ministers could not agree on the usual end of summit joint statement. Allegedly, China would not allow any mention of the SCS, while the US could not countenance a declaration that did not touch on this, the greatest security issue (*The Strait Times* 4 November 2015).

The above is indicative of ASEAN's multilateral dilemma. Existing security fora and regimes including all relevant actors ought to result in the ability to effectively deal with SCS and other pressing security agenda via multilateral channels. Yet, since all ASEAN-spawned initiatives have inherited the ASEAN way, while they allow for maximum flexibility, their inconclusive non-binding outcomes and consensus requirements more often than not cause inefficacy. As Nicholas Khoo (2015: 194) recently put it: '[once] the meetings end and the real international politics begins, an alarming and unimpressive record has been recorded on an issue that is critical to [ASEAN] members' security'. Those ASEAN-based vehicles of alleged norm projection, a few confidence-building measures notwithstanding, have not yet managed to move beyond dialogue.

Conclusions

In spite of its obvious limits, ARF and other ASEAN-centred institutionalized dialogue mechanisms have gained importance as the first serious post-Cold War approach which mediated the former reliance on bilateralism and enhanced the debate about the role and impact of multilateralism on security. Although ARF is still generally understood as a 'process' rather than an institution, security dialogue and co-operation pursued under its auspices have assumed a clearly identifiable pattern. The ARF's aim of emphasizing a gradualist, consensual approach over a legalistic, functional approach demanding legally binding treaties and agreements gains the support of most East Asian governments and means that more countries are at least willing to engage in dialogue than would otherwise be the case. At the same time this means, as explained, that existing agreements rely essentially on the goodwill of member states who are under no legally binding obligation to, for example, produce defence papers or make their processes more transparent. Furthermore, unresolved territorial disputes, deep historical suspicions, longstanding rivalries and nationalistic tendencies all undermine the process of socialization on which ASEAN-centred multilateralism is based. Perhaps one of the major achievements of the group is to have engaged China within some multilateral structure, and gained its agreement to discuss contentious issues (such as the Spratly Islands) with all ASEAN members, rather than at a strictly bilateral level, although tangible achievements are still lacking.

Most importantly, the limits of the multilateral management of security are clearly evident in the case of Northeast Asia. There had been widespread hope for the Six-Party Talks 'to constitute the starting point for future institutional development' (Haggard and Noland 2009). Ever since the end of the Cold War scholars have been discussing the possible emergence of a concert of power in Northeast Asia that would eventually replace the existing bilateral alliance systems or at least mediate the power-balancing behaviour of the sub-region's largest nations (for example Shirk 1997). However, the most likely scenario for the regional order is a continuation of the bilateral alliance system centred on US primacy in the region (see Chapter 2). The US–Japan military alliance is based on agreements reached in the 1950s and 1960s, whereby the US is essentially responsible for security in Northeast Asia, and has large numbers of troops based there (approximately 100,000 troops, 330 warplanes and 60 warships). For the time being, this gives the alliance a clear superiority in the region.

For the present, security in Northeast Asia and indeed the wider Asia-Pacific area is likely to be dominated by a 'strategic triangle' comprising the US, China and Japan. Of these, the US–Japan and US–South Korea relations will attempt to maintain the status quo, while China will try to maximize its benefits from the situation to become even more powerful, until such a time as it may become a challenger, or at least able to carve out a satisfactory sphere of influence for itself. For the time being at least, China should, logically, maintain good relations with both Japan and the US. The PRC's leadership knows it must continue its modernization programme for several decades more, during which time it will need technology, capital investment and access to markets in the West. It will therefore also be likely to be reluctant to escalate any conflict. The dynamics of this new strategic triangle are being closely observed by academics and policy-makers alike, since the way the three powers interact with each other and react to regional stimuli will to a large extent determine the stability of the region as a whole. In particular, their handling of the Taiwan issue and the North Korea problem will be crucial to the peace of the Asia-Pacific.

In sum and from the perspective of IR theory, liberal institutionalists and social constructivists are optimistic that despite the current limitations, multilateral co-operation in the Asia-Pacific will eventually contribute to the gradual emergence of a stable security order in the region. 'They believe that strong feelings of trust and community can be generated over time, thereby allowing states to avoid conflicts of interest or settle them without resorting to violence' (Garofano 2002: 503). Neorealists, however, are less optimistic. In their view, most multilateral organizations such as the ARF or frameworks like the Six-Party Talks do not possess the hard power capabilities to deal with order-building in the Asia-Pacific and are largely irrelevant. According to the neorealist perception, the management of regional order is determined by zero-sum games and the states' overriding concerns for their own security.

Notes

1 Reefs, islands and the sea itself will be referred to by common, internationally recognized, not country-specific names. Usage does not imply any political statement.
2 Taiwanese claims correspond to those of the PRC.

References

Acharya, A. (2014) *Constructing a Security Community in Southeast Asia: ASEAN and the Problem of Regional Order*, 3rd edn, London and New York: Routledge.

Beckershoff, A. (2014) 'The KMT–CCP forum: securing consent for cross-Strait rapprochement', *Journal of Current Chinese Affairs*, 43 (1): 213–41.

Bitzinger, R. (2015) *IMDEX Asia 2015. Coast Guards in the South China Sea: Proxy Fighters?* RSIS Commentary No. 121, Singapore: RSIS.

Blackwill, R. and K. Campbell (2016) *Xi Jinping on the Global Stage. Chinese Foreign Policy under a Powerful but Exposed Leader*, Special Report No. 74, New York Council on Foreign Relations.

Bleiker, R. (2001) 'Identity and security in Korea', *The Pacific Review*, 14 (1): 121–48.

Booth, K. (2005) *Critical Security Studies and World Politics*, Boulder, CO: Lynne Rienner.

Brown, K. (2016) 'Foreign policy making under Xi Jinping: the case of the South China Sea', *Journal of Political Risk*, 4 (2), February, www.jpolrisk.com/foreign-policy-making-under-xi-jinping-the-case-of-the-south-china-sea/.

Burke, A. and M. McDonald (2007) 'Introduction: Asia-Pacific security legacies and futures' in A. Burke and M. McDonald (eds), *Critical Security in the Asia-Pacific*, Manchester: Manchester University Press.

Buzan, B., O. Waever and J. de Wilde (1998) *Security. A New Framework for Analysis*, Boulder, CO: Lynne Rienner Publishers.

Davies, M. (2014) 'An agreement to disagree: the ASEAN Human Rights Declaration and the absence of regional identity in Southeast Asia', *Journal of Current Southeast Asian Affairs*, 33 (3): 107–29.

De Luce, D. and P. McLeary (2015) 'In South China Sea, a tougher US stance', *Foreign Policy*, 2 October, foreignpolicy.com/2015/10/02/in-south-china-sea-a-tougher-u-s-stance/.

Duchâtel, M. (2017) *Taiwan between Xi and Trump*, London: European Council on Foreign Relations, April, www.ecfr.eu/page/-/China_Analysis_Taiwan_Between_Xi_and_Trump.pdf.

Dupont, A. and C. Baker (2014) 'East Asia's maritime disputes: fishing in troubled waters', *The Washington Quarterly*, 37 (1): 79–98.

Embassy of the PRC in the UK (2014) *Wang Yi: Handle the South China Sea Issue through the 'Dual-Track' Approach*, 9 August.

Emmers, R. (2003) *Cooperative Security and the Balance of Power in ASEAN and the ARF*, Routledge: London.

Garofano, J. (2002) 'A security community for Asia? Power, institutions and the ASEAN Regional Forum', *Asian Survey*, (42): 502–21.

Gross, D. G. (2007) 'U.S.–Korea relations: unexpected progress on all fronts', *Comparative Connections: A Quarterly E-Journal on East Asian Bilateral Relations*, April.

Grzelczyk, V. (2009) 'Six-Party Talks and negotiation strategy: when do we get there?' *International Negotiation*, 14: 95–119.

Haacke, J. (2009) 'The ASEAN Regional Forum: from dialogue to practical security cooperation?' *Cambridge Review of International Affairs*, 22 (3): 427–49.

Haggard, S. and M. Noland (2009) 'A security and peace mechanism for Northeast Asia: the economic dimension', *The Pacific Review*, 22 (2): 119–37.

Ho, J. H. (2012) 'Singapore's maritime interests' in J. H. Ho and S. Bateman (eds), *Maritime Challenges and Priorities in Asia: Implications for Regional Security*, London and New York: Routledge.

Hoadley, S. and J. Rüland (eds) (2006) *Asian Security Reassessed*, Singapore: ISEAS.

Jane's Defence Weekly (2015) China completes runway on Fiery Cross Reef, 24 September.

Jayakumar, S., T. Koh and R. C. Beckman (eds) (2014) *The South China Sea Disputes and Law of the Sea*, Cheltenham: Edward Elgar Publishing.

Johnson, C. (2016) 'President Xi Jinping's "Belt and Road" initiative: a practical assessment of the Chinese Communist Party's roadmap for China's global resurgence', *CSIS Report*, Washington, DC.

KEDO (n.d.) About us, www.kedo.org/au_history.asp.

Khoo, N. (2015) 'The ASEAN Security Community: a misplaced consensus', *Journal of Asian Security and International Affairs*, 2 (2): 180–99.

Leffler, M. (2004) 'National security' in M. J. Hogan and T. G. Paterson (eds), *Explaining the History of American Foreign Relations*, 2nd edn, Cambridge: Cambridge University Press.

Lippmann, W. (1943) *U.S. Foreign Policy: Shield of the Republic*, Boston: Little, Brown and Co.

Makinda, S. (1998) 'Sovereignty and global security', *Security Dialogue*, 29 (3): 281–92.

Ministry of Foreign Affairs of the PRC (2016) *Foreign Ministry Spokesperson Hua Chunying's Regular Press Conference*, 21 March.

Note verbale (2009) 7 May, www.un.org/depts/los/clcs_new/submissions_files/mysvnm33_09/chn_2009re_mys_vnm_e.pdf.

Parameswaran, P. (2014) 'Explaining US strategic partnerships in the Asia-Pacific region: origins, developments and prospects', *Contemporary Southeast Asia*, 36 (2): 262–89.

Paris, R. (2001) 'Human security: paradigm shift or hot air?' *International Security*, 26 (2): 87–102.

Powell, B. (2017) 'Donald Trump and the looming nuclear crisis in North Korea', *Newsweek*, 7 March, www.newsweek.com/2017/03/17/kim-jong-un-north-korea-nuclear-crisis-ballistic-missiles-564433.html.

Rogers, W. (2012) 'The role of natural resources in the South China Sea' in P. Cronin, *Cooperation from Strength: The U.S., China and the South China Sea*, Washington, DC: Centre for a New American Security.

Shanker, T. (2010) 'U.S. pushes to resurrect military ties with Beijing; Defense secretary meets with counterpart amid tension on Taiwan arms', *The International Herald Tribune*, 12 October.

Shirk, S. (1997) 'Asia-Pacific regional security: balance of power or concert of powers?' in David A. Lake and Patrick M. Morgan (eds), *Regional Orders: Building Security in a New World*, University Park, PA: Pennsylvania State University Press.

Solidum, E. (1991) *The Small State: Security and World Peace*, Manila: Kalikasan.

State Council Information Office (2004) *China's National Defense in 2004*, Beijing: State Council Information Office. www.fas.org/nuke/guide/china/doctrine/natdef2004.html.

Sumalia, R. and W. Cheung (2015) *Boom or Bust: The Future of Fish in the South China Sea*, Vancouver: University of British Columbia.

Tow, W. and S. Limaye (2016) 'What's China got to do with it? U.S. alliances, partnerships in the Asia-Pacific', *Asian Politics & Policy*, 8 (1): 7–26.

UNCLOS (1982) 'United Nations Convention on the Law of the Sea', www.un.org/depts/los/convention_agreements/texts/unclos/unclos_e.pdf.

UNDP (1994) *UN Human Development Report*, New York: Oxford University Press.

Wacker, G. (2015) 'The irreversible rise: a new foreign policy for a stronger China' in A. Amighini and A. Berkofsky (eds), *Xi's Policy Gambles: The Bumpy Road Ahead*, Milan: ISPI.

Wang, Y. (2005) *Defining Non-Traditional Security and Its Implications for China*, Working Paper, Institute of World Economics and Politics, Chinese Academy of Social Sciences.

Wang, Z. (2015) 'Chinese discourse on the "nine-dashed line"', *Asian Survey,* 55 (3): 502–24.

Wei, C.-H. (2016) 'China–Taiwan relations and the 1992 consensus, 2000–2008', *International Relations of the Asia Pacific*, 16 (1): 67–95.

Yoshihara, T. and J. Holmes (2011) 'Can China defend a "core interest" in the South China Sea?' *The Washington Quarterly*, 34 (2): 45–59.

Zhang, J. (2015) 'China's new foreign policy under Xi Jinping: towards "Peaceful Rise 2.0"?' *Global Change, Peace & Security*, 27 (1): 5–19.

10 Building blocs

Regionalism and globalization in the Asia-Pacific

Rémy Davison

Introduction: one globalization or many?

The emergence of Asia as the epicentre of the global supply chain is owed entirely to the globalization of production. This chapter examines the impact of globalization and regionalism on the global economic and political order, as well as the role that regionalism now plays in the strategies of individual states to maintain or strengthen their positions in the global political economy. The first part examines how Asia-Pacific states have responded to the challenge of globalization, and discusses the growth and development of a number of regional initiatives. The second part considers the links between economic globalization and the growth of regionalism, particularly regional organizations. Both trends may reinforce each other: the spread of globalization can inhibit the ability of the state to implement national policy preferences and, as a result, globalization may encourage the state into closer regional co-operation. In summary, the thrust of this chapter is that globalization and regionalism are integrally interdependent and mutually reinforcing.

Globalization is a relatively new term, popularized by the mass media during the 1990s. In this chapter, we focus on the political economy of globalization, and discuss how states have reacted to, and attempted to accommodate, globalization. To accomplish this, we examine the realist, liberal and neo-Marxist perspectives and also evaluate some of the more sceptical views of globalization. An important theme in this chapter is the centrality of the state: how important is the state as a political and economic actor in an era of globalization? Proponents of globalization argue that global integration has developed to such an extent that it is no longer sufficient to speak of merely 'China' or 'Indonesia' in territorial terms. For example, 'hyperglobalists', such as Keiichi Ohmae (1995: xiv) argue that one can no longer equate territoriality with the traditional Westphalian view of state authority; globalization has become so intensive and extensive that the state cannot reassert itself as a central actor. Even realist political economists, such as Susan Strange (1996), argue that financial and economic globalization have produced world markets that are independent of the state.

The rise of globalization

The study of globalization has become the major focus of international relations and political science research in recent years. The development of globalization presents international relations with complex and difficult issues that have an impact on a range of theoretical and conceptual concerns. One of the most fundamental of these is the shift from internationalization to globalization, what drives it and how it affects the nation state. A key concern is conceptualizing globalization as both a political and economic development, and how states respond to, and manage, the demands created by the forces of globalization. These are crucial issues in the study of international relations.

First, it is important to distinguish between *global*, *international* and *transnational* processes. *International* transactions take place *between nations*, such as international relations, international economics and international trade. Conversely, *transnational* relations take place *across* nations. The international and the transnational appear to be almost interchangeable terms, and often they are used in this way; many commentators use the transnational corporation (TNC) or multinational corporation (MNC) to mean one and the same thing: a corporation operating in two or more states. However, the transnational and international have at least one thing in common: they contain the word *nation*, which suggests that transactions take place at the level of the state, or *between* or *across nations*. Generally speaking, most authors understand the international to refer to interactions between states. On the other hand, transnational processes may take place at the *sub-national* level, between non-governmental organizations (NGOs), such as business networks, or human rights groups. Conversely, the *global* refers to actors (states, firms, networks, organizations) conceiving of the world in spatially and geographically planetary proportions.

Globalization is difficult to define; when we speak of 'globalization', what do we mean? Are we referring to the globalization of international finance, of production, of trade? Do we mean technology, communications and transport? Or perhaps we can speak of the globalization of culture and language? Arguably, the international environmental agenda, such as air and ocean pollution, as well as access to critical resources like water and fishing grounds, has also become not merely regional, but global in its implications. According to Keohane and Nye (2001: 2), 'For a network of relationships to be considered "global," it must include multi-continental distances, not simply regional networks'.

The problems inherent in the concept of globalization are compounded by the enormous range of definitions available (Scholte 1997). Globalization has been referred to as universalization, internationalization, Westernization, Americanization or liberalization. More radical perspectives argue that globalization represents the development of a 'borderless' world (Ohmae 1990, 1996). Irrespective of definitional difficulties, globalization represents a challenge to the traditional idea of sovereignty and its notion of exclusive jurisdiction within a state's territorial borders. However, due to a combination of forces (international capital, non-state actors, global communications, technology), the state has arguably become more porous, less autonomous, and more susceptible to infiltration by non-state actors. Consequently, the state has increasingly been compelled to accommodate the forces of globalization, to the detriment of its own policy-making autonomy. In some instances, the state has beaten a 'strategic retreat' to the relative safety of regionalism, which we discuss in the second part of this chapter. In many respects, regionalism represents a halfway house, which states employ in an attempt to control, or at least ameliorate, some of the negative effects of globalization.

Globalization: realist perspectives

Perspectives on globalization differ markedly. In previous chapters, we have discussed three key theoretical perspectives, which may be classed broadly as realist, liberal and neo-Marxist. These three paradigms not only contest the significance of globalization, but whether it is accurate to describe the breakdown of traditional national borders as globalization at all. Realists assert that liberal claims of the increased levels of interconnectedness and interaction wrought by globalization are exaggerated, and that most international transactions still involve the state. Realists also argue that the management of global finance, trade and debt by intergovernmental organizations (such as the G20, WTO and IMF) remains largely dominated by the most powerful states in the system.

Realists argue that what we are experiencing is not globalization, but the 'Americanization' of national economies and culture. For realists, this has occurred because of the US's clear military dominance since 1945 which, in turn, has fuelled the expansion of American finance, firms and culture. Realist perspectives, emphasizing US dominance, are reflected by policy-makers, such as US trade representative (USTR) and, later, president of the World Bank, Robert Zoellick (2002):

> We will promote free trade globally, regionally and bilaterally.... By moving forward on multiple fronts, the United States can exert its leverage for openness, create a new competition in liberalization, target the needs of developing countries, and create a fresh political dynamic by putting free trade on to the offensive. America's trade policies are connected to our broader economic, political, and security aims.

In many respects, the realist view overlaps with Kindleberger's hegemonic stability theory, which argues that a hegemonic state is required to provide international public goods. These include an international monetary system, central banking, an open trade regime and military security. The US provided these goods in the form of the gold-dollar standard and the GATT regime, while also delivering military security to its allies throughout the Cold War. As a consequence, the US exported its financial and, to a lesser extent, liberal democracy and free-market capitalism to many parts of East Asia. While China, the USSR, North Korea and Vietnam experienced virtual isolation from international capitalism and experimented seriously with centrally planned economies, South Korea, Japan, Taiwan, Hong Kong and the ASEAN countries were the recipients of American technology and, with the exception of Japan, significant US direct investment and loans from the American-dominated IMF and World Bank. The difference here is that hegemonic stability theorists adopt a hybrid realist–liberal model, which argues that hegemony combines military power with elements of economic liberalism and international economic management. Conversely, realists assert that the projection of financial and ideological power flows from a state's military capabilities. With the Soviet Union's collapse in 1991, the restrictions on US influence were far fewer and, as a result, American military and economic power expanded to global proportions during the 1990s. According to some commentators, the 1990s were characterized not by globalization, but by the emergence of the US as a *hyper-power* (Gordon 2002). The post-Cold War emergence of the US as the sole superpower gave rise to a number of influential perspectives arising out of America's global preponderance. These included Fukuyama's (1992) liberal 'end of history' thesis, and, from a conservative perspective, Huntington's (1996) warning of a 'clash of civilizations'. In many respects, these two concepts reflected different sides of the globalization coin.

Globalization: liberal perspectives

Economic globalization largely reflects the dominant neoliberal paradigm. Liberal analyses view political and economic liberalism as interlocking, complementary forces that have expanded beyond the Western world, served to democratize societies, and raised living standards throughout the world. However, liberals differ markedly in their interpretations of globalization. Keohane and Nye (1977: 13) argue that states' relative insularity from globalization is governed by the complexity of their interdependence. In times of crisis, states are either 'sensitive' or 'vulnerable' to the activities of other actors in the system. For example, sensitivity interdependence 'involves degrees of responsiveness within a policy framework – how quickly do changes in one country bring costly changes in another, and how great are the costly effects', whereas vulnerability interdependence refers to 'the relative availability and costliness of the alternatives that various actors face'; i.e., states that possess few policy tools are forced to make costly adjustments to exogenous shocks. Arguably, the extent of East Asian states' vulnerability to the 1997 Asian Financial Crisis (AFC) was exacerbated by conditions of complex economic interdependence and the deregulated nature of global financial markets. However, whereas *economic interdependence* generally denotes mutual dependence between states, *economic globalization* reduces governments' influence to the extent that they are unlikely to be able to assert control over capital flows. Keohane and Nye (2001) view the development of globalization as an opportunity to determine how the new world order might be governed. The current institutional framework, they argue, has traditionally been dominated by the US, Japan and the EU, leading to heavy-handed policy-making, such as IMF conditionality imposed on East Asian states in the wake of the AFC.

However, the importance of Asia, and the centrality of China, India, Russia and South Korea to the world economy was exemplified by the replacement of the G8 by the G20 group of major economies in 2009 in the wake of the Global Financial Crisis (GFC) in an attempt to multilateralize the management of the 21st-century global economy. In 2016, the IMF's reformed quota system gave China the third largest number of votes, behind the US and Japan (IMF 2016).

Political liberals emphasize the centrality of co-operation and consensus-building. The most influential recent analysis of capitalism, by Thomas Piketty (2014), supports 'reconcil[ing] globalization and global economic competition with global justice…globalization is a positive-sum game that serves all our interests' (*The European* 28 December 2014). By contrast, economic liberals or, more commonly, 'neoliberals' largely dominate national government departments and international organizations, such as the World Bank, IMF and OECD. Neoliberals, such as Zoellick, advocate zero tariffs and deep cuts to agricultural subsidies to promote free trade which, economic liberals argue, results in significant welfare gains for all countries engaging in free trade. This sits uneasily with the traditional disposition of East Asian governments to protect key industry sectors, to subsidize development, and to engage in political cronyism to the detriment of economic welfare. Michel Camdessus, IMF managing director during the AFC, said that the collapse was in reality a 'blessing in disguise', as it would force closed markets open and ensure both governments and the private sector developed more prudential lending practices. East Asian states, as a result of the crisis, were compelled to accept the liberal prescriptions of the IMF. Economic liberals argue that this represents the homogenizing power of globalization, in that it sweeps away state intervention and regulation, resulting in a more 'level playing field'. Conversely, governments in the East Asian NICs saw the IMF's intervention as promoting a culture of economic dependency on the major powers. Krugman refers to post-crisis 'fire-sale FDI', pointing to the FDI boom in affected East Asian economies, which itself was sparked by the relaxation of foreign ownership controls demanded by the IMF. Consequently, US, European and Japanese firms acquired significant assets at nominal prices, such as GM's acquisition of Daewoo, Ford's stake in Kia, and the sell-offs of Seoul Bank and Korea First Bank (Krugman 1998).

Economic globalization transformed national economies in the 1990s. The collapse of Soviet–Indian trade saw New Delhi abandon semi-autarkic economic policies as the Rao government from 1991 restructured the Indian economy on the basis of IMF technical advice. Finance minister (and future prime minister) Manmohan Singh was instrumental in the restructuring process. State assets were sold off, and foreign investment in the nationalized banking sector was permitted, together with the establishment of private banks and foreign financial institutions. The Reserve Bank of India is now relatively independent of government and the rupee is not a pegged currency. Although New Delhi has managed FDI, foreign ownership and exchange rates cautiously, it has increasingly reduced state intervention in the economy in order to accommodate the demands of globalization. Throughout the same period, Russia has also experienced the shock of economic globalization, manifested in the 'shock therapy' administered by the Yeltsin administration during Russia's rapid transition to a market economy in the 1990s, a process which left a small number of oligarchs in control of most of Russia's most valuable resources, such as oil and gas. In 1998, the contagion of the 1997 Asian Financial Crisis reached Russia, decimating the rouble, leaving the state effectively bankrupt and dependent on US$ 24 billion in IMF financial assistance, the majority of which simply disappeared as a result of corruption (see Stiglitz 2002: 133–65). However, Russia under the Putin and Medvedev presidencies has reversed privatization and reasserted the state's role in the national economy, the most prominent example of which has been the Russian government's acquisition of a majority stake in Gazprom, the world's biggest natural gas producer. Through its subsidiaries, Gazprom has also acquired a substantial holding in the assets of former oil giant Yukos.

In many respects, China, India and Russia have attempted to resist Western neoliberal, free-market ideology, viewing globalization essentially as an extension of American capitalism, exemplified by the omnipresence of US multinational firms in world markets. In part, Beijing, New Delhi and Moscow have been undeniably influenced by the success of the Japanese capitalist developmental state (CDS) in the post-1945 period, which discouraged foreign investment and import dependence in favour of closed domestic markets and export-oriented industrialization (see Chapter 11). Nevertheless, the demands of world markets have compelled China, India and Russia to make considerable concessions to global capitalism; these include IMF membership; adherence to the rules-based WTO multilateral system; and permitting increasingly large volumes of FDI, despite the considerable restrictions all three countries continue to impose in this area.

Globalization: neo-Marxist perspectives

The global reach of capital, in combination with the 1997 East Asian Economic Crisis, prompted some analysts to rearticulate theories of dependency to accommodate the phenomenon of globalization. Wallerstein's (1979) world-systems theory predicted many aspects of the development of globalization; Wallerstein argued that there was a single world system, a single world economy: the capitalist world economy. The uneven distribution of benefits of globalization also reignited the North/South debate. Yoshihara (1988) argues that the type of growth experienced in Southeast Asia is 'technologyless growth'; that is, growth *without development.* Yoshihara points to trends in investment and technology flows which suggest that the bulk of these move primarily from North to South, while high value-added trade remains largely between developed market economies. Yoshihara argues that the consequence is that globalization embeds inequalities in the world system, and global wealth may be rearranged to some extent, but not redistributed. After the AFC, Yoshihara (1999) criticized the IMF's prescriptions, arguing that states should retain a role in national economies by fixing exchange rates and improving domestic economic regulation, although he endorsed the role played by free trade and open markets in lifting people out of poverty. However, by default, Yoshihara implicitly acknowledges that states cannot insulate themselves from the forces of economic globalization.

Wallerstein's (2013) prognosis of globalization since the 2008 GFC is more dire. He argues that the modern world system is undergoing a structural crisis. He divides the modern world system into two eras: 1945–70 and 1970–2010. The 1945–70 era was a period of unprecedented growth and economic expansion, and it was the height of quasi-monopoly or oligopolistic capitalism. The 1945–70 era saw US hegemony go unchallenged. However, the 1970–2010 period saw a decisive shift away from the productive phase to a focus on financial speculation. This produced not only speculative growth bubbles, but also exceptionally high levels of private and public indebtedness. For example, US public debt by the end of 2016 was slightly less than US$ 20 trillion (US Treasury 2017). Wallerstein further argues that US hegemonic decline will be swift and total. He asserts that the 1997 AFC and the 2008 GFC are among the last bubbles in a series of crises since the 1970s, including the Latin America (1978–82), Mexico (1994–95), Russia (1998), Argentina (1998–2002), the dot-com Nasdaq crash (2001) and the Eurozone crisis (2009–2012). Wallerstein posits that this structural crisis will persist until around 2050 and, until then, global conditions will be chaotic. 'Chaos' in this context means rapid and constant fluctuations brought about by economic dislocation, climate change, geopolitical crises and ideological conflicts. Producers will face uncertainty and high risk, due to rapid shifts in national, regional and global economic conditions. Conversely, states and firms that control resources, such as energy and minerals, will find it profitable to speculate.

Cox (1996) and Gill (1990) adopt alternative neo-Marxist perspectives, arguing that international capitalism produces a transnational capitalist class. Global elites identify similar interests (liberal capitalist ideology; the importance of coopetition as well as competition in international business) and achieve domination through consensual bargaining (effective use of military power to ensure international stability). For Cox, this results in the development of an 'historic bloc', a coalition of like interests which govern international public and private policy, via a network of state, intergovernmental and corporate actors. Gill argues that organizations such as the WTO, IMF and World Bank have successfully globalized liberal capitalism, building a historic bloc, consolidating US global hegemony.

Globalization moves beyond both the international and the transnational to describe a range of interactions that are truly global in nature. For example, free trade may be limited to a few states; this was the case after the Second World War, when membership of the GATT predominantly comprised the advanced industrial states, such as the US, Japan and Western European countries. However, in 1994, the GATT was replaced by the WTO, which reflected its increasingly global membership. Irrespective of whether we are referring to the globalization of trade or culture, globalization suggests, implicitly, a 'borderless' world, where there is a relatively unfettered flow of goods, services, capital, labour, ideas, culture and language. Whereas international transactions may affect only a few states, the impact of globalization affects *all* states to some extent or another. In summary, then, globalization refers to the intensification of interconnectedness between a vast array of human activities; no longer are states and citizens affected only by what governments may do.

Globalization: critical perspectives

Hirst and Thompson (1996: 2) provide one of the most forceful critiques of globalization, arguing that its effects have been uneven, rather than diffuse. They critique globalization on three grounds: first, that the 'new' global economy differs little from the 'previous' model; second, that the internationalization of production does not automatically suggest that global market forces have gained some form of autonomy; and, third, that globalization itself represents a break in a historical continuum, a unique development which will persist well into the future. Hirst and Thompson contend that globalization's impact has been restricted largely to the industrial 'North', with only some aspects penetrating East Asia and South America, and that it has not infiltrated Central Asia and Africa to any significant extent. Hirst and Thompson also assert that it has been firms predominantly from the industrialized North, such as the US, Japan and Western Europe (the 'G3'), which have traditionally dominated the internationalization of finance and production. But the rise of industrializing Asia has transformed this picture in the last two decades. For example, 33 Chinese firms appeared on the Fortune 500 list of the world's biggest corporations in 2015, second only to the US, with three of the world's ten largest firms (*Fortune* 31 July 2016).

Hirst and Thompson assert that the state has not surrendered key areas of sovereignty to the forces of globalization; rather, they argue that the state can still assert its power in areas such as preventing or restricting population flows. While states have encouraged some trends, such as increased flows of foreign investment and trade, they also preserve their ability to impose restrictions on these flows. For example, during the 1997 crisis, the Malaysian government placed restrictions on short-term speculative investments that had wrought severe damage to the economy. During the 2010 Bangkok 'Red Shirt' protests, the government switched off a critical communication satellite's transmissions and kept journalists away from the fray; consequently, pictures of clashes between protestors and police could not be transmitted to television networks. In this context, Hirst and Thompson argue that the internationalization of capital and communications opens up a new type of space that exists *alongside*, but does not *displace* the sovereign state. For Hirst and Thompson (2006), although globalization has challenged governments, the state has transformed itself into an entity distributing and rendering accountable forms of governance.

A number of liberal commentators are sceptical about some of the more radical claims made about globalization, such as homogenization, universality, equality or global integration. As Keohane and Nye (2001: 2) argue, '[Globalization] does not imply either homogenization or equity…an integrated world market would mean free flows of goods, people and capital, and convergence in interest rates. That is far from the facts'. Keohane and Nye even eschew the term 'globalization', arguing that 'globalization' and 'deglobalization' merely represent an increase or decline in 'globalism'.

A number of theorists also argue that the negative impact of globalization has been restricted largely to the Global South, and that 'globalization correlates negatively with absolute poverty' (Bergh and Nilsson 2014: 56). Critics of globalization contend that liberalizing reforms associated with globalization benefit the already powerful, widening disparities between North and South. Although Northern economies have experienced some negative effects, such as manufacturing unemployment as industrial production has shifted to the South, this has been offset to a large degree by the development of new manufacturing or services industries in the North that have created new forms of employment. As Chapter 3 suggests, the 'Beijing Consensus' may represent a new, state-led development model that challenges the neoliberal orthodoxy on the benefits of economic globalization.

The diffuse impact of globalization

A key characteristic of globalization is its centripetal force that appears to draw states inexorably into a web of economic and financial interconnectedness. Major powers are not immune; although they may have the option of remaining outside a system, their capacity to do so indefinitely may be limited, and the transaction costs may be high. An example of this was China's quest to obtain permanent MFN status in the WTO in 2001. To some extent, this represents the centripetal force of the global trading system; it was too costly for China to remain outside the WTO, and to isolate itself from the rules-based international trade regime, as it sought to deploy an export-oriented industrialization strategy to ensure high rates of growth, as well as economic development. This demonstrates, realists argue, American dominance of the global trade regime, as well as the ability of the US Congress to accord or deny China MFN status. Although realists claim this gives US administrations a strategic advantage over China, liberals would reply that China's importance to global manufacturing and trade is such that the US has been locked into China's economic success; American firms have developed a significant dependence on unrestricted access to the huge variety of cheap consumer goods and manufacturing components exported from China. As a result, the US has been drawn into the web of globalization, and this led the Trump administration in 2017 to state it would renegotiate trade deals with Canada, Mexico and South Korea (Noland *et al.* 2016: 22–5, CNBC 28 April 2017). Globalization has not resulted in a 'borderless world'; however, restrictions on states' domestic and foreign policy autonomy are heavily influenced by exogenous events beyond their capacity to predict or control. Woods (2001) argues that this means that, 'The loss of autonomy associated with globalization falls unevenly with powerful states better able to insulate themselves.... Those states that are able to resist "internationalization" will emerge far more powerful than those that fail to do so'.

Almost US$ 5 trillion in foreign exchange is traded daily, which exceeds the total capital (US$ 1.4 trillion) in the IMF's accounts (Reuters 25 October 2016). Bank computers operate 24/7, monitoring market trends, while trades in foreign currencies, shares, bonds and derivatives have long been automated. The 'herd mentality' of trading and financial speculation will become even more globalized and consumer-oriented, as phone- and tablet-based applications deliver financial trading to individual hand-held devices. As Mahathir (2001) noted,

> [Speculators] do not work in concert of course. Nor do they enter a conspiracy. But they do behave like herds. Thus when one of the more important members swing in one direction, the others will follow. The effect is not unlike acting in concert…

Programmed to follow market trends, computerized trading employs algorithms that respond to panic selling or trends in the market, without human intervention, which can lead to an electronic frenzy of activity across the globe. Automated trading is merely one technological advance, which was certainly not available to financial institutions prior to the 1980s. Consequently, the revolution in information technology from the 1990s made an overwhelming contribution to the globalization of the world's communications infrastructure.

Debate also surrounds the impact of economic globalization on inequality, although the general consensus is that its effects vary considerably according to the level of national development. In 2002, the *Financial Times* argued that, 'Evidence suggests the 1980s and 1990s were decades of declining global inequality and reductions in the proportion of the world's population in extreme poverty' (Wolf 2002). However, the difficulty is *how* to measure the negative and/or positive aspects of globalization. A number of economists have used the level of openness of economies to determine the extent to which larger trade and investment flows have raised living standards and increased purchasing power. Lutz (2001) argues that the outcomes are complex, and that the empirical evidence, based on factors such as firm productivity or national economic growth, is ambiguous. Piketty (2014) argues that returns on capital investments have always outperformed wages growth, but that this divergence became even more accentuated between 1977 and 2010.

Nevertheless, Asia as a whole (including Central Asian states, such as India) continues to display considerable regional variations in terms of the impact of economic globalization. Nor is globalization and the economic growth it tends to encourage necessarily a panacea to income inequality. For example, although China has made significant gains in terms of growth and income since 1978, its GDP per capita position *relative* to the US, Japan and Germany has not changed a great deal; in 2009, China's GDP per capita ranking among world nations was only 99 or 84 at best (IMF 2010, World Bank 2010). Globalization means the PRC is no less vulnerable to a 'middle income trap' than any other developing economy, where economic globalization has lifted Chinese incomes over the medium term, but the PRC's rate of development starts to atrophy (Cai 2012,

Zhang *et al.* 2013). Globalization can only deliver exogenously a certain amount of financial restructuring, industrial optimization and technological innovation. Governments must still develop national educational, financial and industrial structures that deliver high-income jobs, a transition that Singapore made successfully. However, China's growth rate fell from over 14 per cent in 2007 to under 7 per cent in 2015–16 (*Trading Economics* 29 April 2017). Lutz (2001: 27) argues in his analysis of globalization and open markets, 'We are thus left with the conclusion that the potential benefits of greater openness and, by implication, increased globalization for developing countries have been significantly overstated. There simply is [not] the empirical evidence to substantiate the claims'.

Globalization has forced most East Asian states into trade and economic alliances, primarily due to individual weakness, and the state remains a key actor in this regionalization process. However, globalization has also compelled East Asian states to retreat from their role in the market, particularly since the 1997 crisis. States are unwilling to surrender large portions of their economic sovereignty to the forces of globalization or regional institutions, but they are nevertheless obliged to cede an increasing number of policy areas to transnational actors. In summary, globalization is a process which is far from complete; indeed, we may be witnessing only its embryotic stages; and, in that context, it is probably far too early to assess or predict what its ultimate outcomes might be. As Rodrik (1998: 156) puts it, 'it is not *whether* you globalize that matters, it is *how* you globalize'. One clear consequence of globalization is the emergence of regionalism, which we examine in the next section.

Regionalism in the Asia-Pacific

In this section, we examine various forms of regionalism found in East Asia. We also discuss the various East Asian regional fora which have emerged over the last four decades, such as the AFTA, APEC and APT. According to Nye, regions consist of 'a limited number of states linked by a geographical relationship and by a degree of mutual interdependence' and can be differentiated according to the level and scope of exchange, formal organizations and political interdependence (cited in Butler 1997: 410). Between 1990 and 2014, ASEAN intra-regional trade increased from 16.9 per cent to 24 per cent of the group's total world trade. Over the same period, ASEAN Plus Three trade grew from 28.6 per cent to 37 per cent (OECD 2016: graph 42). Clearly, the trade integration effects of closer intra-regional production networks are irrefutable.

The growth of regionalism

Regionalism and globalization are integrally connected; arguably, regionalism is in many ways a *response* to globalization, in that the state is experiencing a significant decline in its capability to control, regulate and develop its own territorial space. While military security has had a regional dimension for some decades (for example, NATO, SEATO, ASEAN and the Warsaw Pact), it was only during the 1980s that economic regionalism markedly intensified, with 41 GATT notifications of regional trade agreements (RTAs) in 1990–94 alone. More than 400 regional goods and services arrangements have been notified to the WTO since 1995 (WTO 2017).

The rise of regionalism is at least partly attributable to the economic insecurity of the 1970s and 1980s, as both states and firms faced significant global shocks (oil crises, financial and monetary instability), as well as intense competition for world market shares. The decreasing capacity of states to compete individually in a world of proliferative non-trade barriers (NTBs) and other trade barriers led even the strongest economies such as Japan (APEC), the US (NAFTA) and Germany (EU) to develop closer regional links with their trade and investment partners.

During the 1970s, the global economy experienced severe instability, caused by a number of international shocks, the effects of which extended well into the 1980s. The 1971 collapse of Bretton Woods, and the 1973 and 1979 oil crises, exposed states to the ravages of intense competition for world market shares in a recessionary global economy. Increasingly, individual states were unable to deal with the demands of inflation, debt, current account deficits and state-led investment. This was demonstrated by the IMF rescue packages of the ASEAN economies of the 1970s and early 1980s.

The first significant regional response to economic uncertainty was the EU's establishment of its Single European Market (SEM) programme in 1986. Effectively, this amounted to a single EU internal market comprising 12 (currently 28) European states. The SEM would have a market of over 400 million consumers, and it would also be the largest internal market in the world (Davison 2011: 35). The importance of the EU's regional integration project was that it prompted similar responses in North America and East Asia. In 1989, the US responded with the Canada–US Free Trade Agreement (CUSTA), which became NAFTA in 1994 with the inclusion of Mexico. Although East Asian responses to the challenge of trade blocs emerged quickly, the inequality of the players in the region, and their disparate interests, meant there was a lack of coherence and co-ordination in the various initiatives.

Prior to the 1980s, East Asian regional agreements had been largely restricted to security arrangements, such as SEATO (1954), the Five-Power Defence Arrangements (1971) and ASEAN (1967). While closer economic co-operation had been suggested for some time, it was not until the SEM and CUSTA initiatives that East Asian states began to take the threat of 'closed' or discriminatory regionalism seriously. Although EU and North American diplomats argued that the 'new regionalism' did not mean closure of these key markets to third countries, states outside trade blocs feared both discriminatory or 'closed' regionalism, allied with substantial trade and investment diversion within the new regional blocs.

Table 10.1 Membership of Asia-Pacific regional organizations

Association of Southeast Asian Nations (ASEAN) (established 1967)	*Shanghai Cooperation Organization (SCO) (established 2001)*	*South Asian Association for Regional Cooperation (SAARC) (established 1985)*	*ASEAN Regional Forum (ARF) (established 1993)*	*East Asia Summit (EAS) (established 2005)*
Brunei	China	Afghanistan	Australia	Australia
Indonesia	India	Bangladesh	Bangladesh	Brunei
Malaysia	Russia	Bhutan	Canada	China
Myanmar	Kazakhstan	India	China	Cambodia
Philippines	Kyrgyzstan	Maldives	East Timor	India
Singapore	Pakistan	Nepal	{European Union}	Indonesia
Thailand	Tajikistan	Pakistan	{EU-28 countries}	Japan
Vietnam	Uzbekistan	Sri Lanka	India	Laos
Cambodia			Japan	Malaysia
Laos	***Observers*:**		North Korea	Myanmar
	Iran		South Korea	New Zealand
	Mongolia		Mongolia	Philippines
			New Zealand	Russia
			Pakistan	Singapore
			Papua New Guinea	South Korea
			Russia	Thailand
			Sri Lanka	Vietnam
			United States	

	***Dialogue Partners*:**	***Observers*:**
	Belarus Sri Lanka	Australia China European Union Iran Japan Mauritius Myanmar South Korea United States
	Attendees:	*Attendees:*
	Afghanistan ASEAN Commonwealth of Independent States Turkmenistan	South Africa

Asian regionalism

By the mid-1990s, East Asian economies had grown so rapidly that they collectively accounted for the largest proportion of global GDP. In 1995, East Asia produced 31 per cent of the world's output, compared with the EU's 30 per cent and NAFTA's 24 per cent. Admittedly, the largest proportion of East Asian GDP was produced by Japan, the world's second largest economic power, but this was not to deny the phenomenal growth and output figures of China and the first-tier NICs. Even the Philippines, the 'laggard' economy of the second-tier NICs, produced growth rates of over 5 per cent between 1985 and 1995. The tremendous spurt of growth experienced by East Asia from the mid-1980s until 1997 demonstrated the region's importance as the engine of growth for the world economy. This performance was all the more impressive given the bursting of the Japanese economic bubble after 1990.

Although analysts frequently distinguish between political and economic development in Northeast and Southeast Asia, one can identify five main groupings within the region. These are the first-tier NICs (South Korea, Taiwan, Hong Kong and Singapore); the second-tier NICs (Thailand, Indonesia, the Philippines and Malaysia); developing countries (Bangladesh, Bhutan, Cambodia, Laos, Maldives, Myanmar, Nepal, New Guinea, East Timor, Sri Lanka); socialist/post-socialist states (Vietnam and North Korea); and core economies (Japan, China and India). Until the early 21st century, Japan was not only the dominant regional player, but also a global economic power. However, China's extraordinary growth since 1990 saw the PRC become the world's second largest economy by 2010. India's emergence as an Asian regional economic power from the 1990s was also impressive as New Delhi adopted wide-ranging domestic reforms that produced a world-class information technology sector. Over the same period, India saw the development of a burgeoning middle class; by 2016, one study argued that rising disposable incomes meant 50 per cent of Indians were middle class and that India's population would outstrip China's by 2022 (World Economic Forum 2016). As these export-geared economies expanded dramatically, it was only natural that Asian business would seek to expand its market shares through regional economic integration.

The new regionalism

Analyses generally draw a sharp distinction between the 'old regionalism' of the 1950s and 1960s, and the 'new regionalism' of the 1980s. 'Old regionalism' was characterized by minimalist customs union models, exemplified by the EC (now the EU), and the Caribbean Common Market, which emphasized formal agreements and institution-building. Conversely, the 'new regionalism' is principally market-led, an outgrowth of complex economic interdependence driving firms, markets and states closer together, which Hurrell (1995) characterizes as 'regionalization' (Box 10.1). Regional economic linkages spill over into regional agreements, which have served to deepen the process of integration. Examples of market-led regional integration include Hong Kong's and Taiwan's outgrowth into extensive production networks and labour forces within mainland China, a development which received little or no state assistance. What is distinctive about the new regionalism is that politics tends to *follow* markets: AFTA and NAFTA, for example, placed institutional and legal frameworks on regional markets that were already a *fait accompli.* However, regional agreements, such as APEC, have a tendency to steer states and markets in directions they do not necessarily wish to go, as evidenced by APEC's debate on tariff elimination and the development of 'open' versus 'closed' regionalism.

Competing regionalisms: open versus closed

Open regionalism

The concept of 'open regionalism' first found expression in APEC's Bogor Declaration of 1994. Wei and Frankel (1998: 441) define open regionalism as 'external liberalization by trade blocs'. Concrete proposals for open regionalism were delivered by APEC's Eminent Persons' Group (EPG) in their 1994 report, which argued for the adoption of a quadripartite approach:

- the highest possible levels of unilateral liberalization;
- unilateral extension liberalization by individual APEC members to non-members on a conditional or non-conditional basis;
- the extension of regional liberalization to third countries on a reciprocal basis;
- member commitments to reduce internal barriers within APEC, while also reducing barriers to non-member countries.

(APEC 1995)

On the basis of these proposals, issues arise concerning the costs and benefits of membership under conditions of open regionalism. Why pay the transaction costs arising out of membership (e.g., tariff reductions) when non-members accrue the same benefits? Clearly the temptation would be for third countries to 'free ride', enjoying the benefits of open regionalism, while paying none of the costs. The answer is two-fold. First, blocs adopting open regionalism will tend to have high tariff barriers to begin with, which is certainly the case in much of East Asia. Second, the concept of reciprocity is critical; if, for example, APEC countries were to reduce market entry barriers to the EU, this would be conditional on the EU granting similar tariff concessions to either individual APEC countries, or to APEC members as a whole.

Box 10.1 *Regionalism: five different forms*

Hurrell (1995) identifies five core explanatory variables of regionalism which are summarized briefly below. These are regionalization; regional awareness and identity; inter-state regional co-operation; state-prompted regional integration; and regional cohesion.

- Regionalization: flows of goods, services, capital and technology across state boundaries, driven largely by networks of private-sector actors (MNCs, markets, business groups). Firm-led M&A, FDIs and the internationalization of production are the key elements of the regionalization process, although there are inter-societal interactions which develop without the necessity of state intervention.
- Regional awareness and identity: the extent to which regional social networks have developed, and the level of social and cultural cohesion within a region.
- Inter-state regional co-operation: the building of institutions, frameworks, treaties, agreements and fora for the development and implementation of intra-regional agendas. The state is a key actor in this context, as regional co-operation may be bilateral or multilateral, and takes place at the levels of both high and low politics.
- State-prompted regional integration: regional integration refers to specific government policy decisions designed to increase levels of economic integration in order to reduce barriers on the flow of goods, services, labour and capital.
- Regional cohesion: the extent to which the regional links alluded to in the first four categories have deepened to the point where the regional becomes the organizational base for multilevel (regional, national, local) policy development. Regional cohesion also refers to the role the region may perform in determining relations between member states.

In forming regional trade blocs, states reduce their internal barriers (technical, physical and financial barriers to trade) to promote market growth. This may take the form of a customs union or preferential trade agreement, where members of the bloc receive benefits unavailable to outsiders. For example, the EU has removed tariff barriers between its 15 members, but retains a Common External Tariff on imports from third countries. Nevertheless, since 1958, the EU has effectively abrogated Article XXIV of the GATT, which dealt with regional associations. The GATT attempted to ensure that regional groupings would be open, rather than closed, by stating that:

> Duties and other regulations of commerce imposed at the institution of any such union …shall not on the whole be higher or more restrictive than the general incidence of duties…prior to the formation of such union.
>
> (GATT Secretariat 1947: Art. XXIV (5))

The EU never received a waiver of this condition, and the GATT never ruled on the legality of the EU's interpretation of Article XXIV. Consequently, discriminatory regionalism has persisted in the EU, while the GATT pursued a free trade agenda. The number of RTAs grew to the extent that GATT could identify at least 69 by 1994. Of these, only six were found to comply with GATT rules, although none was found to be in breach of GATT regulations; GATT compliance by most RTAs surveyed was found to be inconclusive.

Closed regionalism

Closed regionalism extends preferential trade only to members of a bloc. While internal liberalization takes place, third countries face external tariffs and, possibly, quantitative restrictions. Examples include the EU and NAFTA, although AFTA falls into this category to some extent. Closed regionalism means producers and consumers enjoy the benefits of liberalization, lower prices and reduced market entry costs. Conversely, non-members face restrictions and more barriers to market access.

Proponents of closed regionalism argue that international competitiveness does not automatically arise from liberalization and deregulation. Instead, states must act to protect strategic industry sectors until they become sufficiently competitive. By participating in closed regionalism, firms gain access to larger markets, without being forced to pay the full costs of competition. As recently as 1991, the EU negotiated a ten-year Voluntary Export Restraint (VER) with Japan, limiting Japanese auto firms to 15 per cent of the EU market, until EU auto-makers could become competitive.

Closed regionalism versus open regionalism closely approximates older debates between developmental and *laissez-faire* capitalism. A key feature of East Asian development has been the capitalist developmental state, exemplified by MITI and the MoF's roles in Japan's industrial restructuring, as well as South Korea under the Park regime. While market deregulation and liberalization increased markedly in East Asia from the 1980s, the history of economic development in the region is such that it is likely to prove difficult to extricate the state from the economy. The 1997 crisis, as well as the stalled APEC and AFTA processes, suggest that the state in East Asia is not quite through as an economic unit.

Expansionist regionalism

Certain regions have also engaged in overt expansionism in recent years, while others have widened their membership considerably. The EU's absorption of a number of Eastern European countries is one example of an expansionist regional strategy. As Chapter 5 noted, SAARC has produced SAFTA, which aims to integrate all of the South Asian economies, while BIMSTEC's objective is to link South Asia with Southeast Asian economies. Conversely, APEC has attempted to integrate various Asia-Pacific groupings and states into a single trading zone, with its members drawn from four continents. The Bush II administration also initiated attempts to create a multicontinental North and South American trade bloc in the form of the Free Trade Area of the Americas (FTAA), with the aim of linking 34 countries in a single free trade agreement. However, opposition from Argentina, Brazil, Paraguay, Uruguay and Venezuela saw the proposal defeated in 2005. Nevertheless, in 2003 Washington signed the Central American Free Trade Agreement (CAFTA), which expanded to encompass the Dominican Republic (2006) and Costa Rica (2009). The lesson of expansionist regionalism is that, as WTO multilateral negotiations are increasingly fraught with difficulties, states turn to RTAs that, in turn, produce a trade-bloc mentality amongst members.

Blocism

A number of analysts in the 1980s and early 1990s conjectured that the international trading system would fragment into three major trade blocs: NAFTA, the EU and an East Asian 'yen bloc' dominated by Japan. Blocism was seen as both a response to globalization, as well as the fear of discriminatory or 'closed' regionalism in other parts of the world. However, Nye predicted correctly that states in the post-Cold War order would be increasingly preoccupied with internal affairs, as the security threat was removed (Nye *et al.* 1991). However, the 'three-bloc' thesis, which gained some currency during the early 1990s, was undermined by the fact that the US remained heavily enmeshed in European and Asia-Pacific security.

Nevertheless, the threat of blocism remains in the forefront of the mind of many policy-makers in East Asia, and can prompt states to undertake regional or bilateral initiatives in order to counter possible market access discrimination or trade diversionary measures taken in NAFTA or the EU. Following the Japan–South Korea agreement to boost co-operation in the IT and investment sectors, a MITI official was quoted as saying, 'With economic blocism expanding in Europe and in the United States, Korea and Japan must take the initiative in setting up a co-operative economic entity in these parts of Asia' (*Korea Times* 3 November 2000). Although North American and European officials argue that their regional blocs do not discriminate against outsiders, the perception remains that NAFTA and the EU are relatively closed to non-members which, in turn, affects and conditions the international public policy responses of East Asian states.

Regional trade, financial and dialogue fora

ASEAN (1967)

As we noted in Chapters 7 and 9, ASEAN has developed into the linchpin of Southeast Asian co-operation, encompassing a wide range of security, trade and investment agreements, including the ARF, AFTA, ASEM (see Chapter 8) and the APT. The growth in the importance of the Southeast Asian region has been such that ASEAN has developed into one of the main drivers of regional co-operation in the East Asian region as a whole. ASEAN has a number of framework agreements designed to encourage trade and investment within the

Box 10.2 *Trade agreements, open regionalism and closed regionalism compared*

Model	*Characteristics*	*Examples*
Multilateral trade	• Free trade based on national treatment • Application of most-favoured nation (MFN) principle • Virtually global membership	• GATT • WTO
Preferential trade agreements	• Free trade agreements between two or more member states • Include bilateral (two states), plurilateral (three or more states) and regional trade agreements • Only members are bound by trade agreement • Involve specific liberalization commitments and market protections • May include services, agriculture, intellectual property, pharmaceutical trade, investor–state dispute resolution; liberalization of foreign investment	*Plurilateral:* • TPP • RCEP • TTIP *Bilateral*: • EU–ROK • Australia–US • India–Thailand *Regional*: • ASEAN FTA • SAFTA • BIMSTEC
Closed regionalism	• Preferential trade area or customs union • Elimination or substantial reduction of internal barriers to free movement of goods, services, capital within the bloc • Restrictions on free movement of labour may or may not be included in regional agreement • Significant external barriers to non-members • Discrimination against countries via tariff barriers, quantitative restrictions or non-tariff technical barriers	• EU • NAFTA • CERTA • EFTA • CARICOM • MERCOSUR • Free Trade Area of the Americas (FTAA) [2005] • SAARC (South Asian Council for Regional Co-operation)
Open regionalism	• Preferential trade area • Elimination or substantial reduction of internal barriers to free movement of goods, services, capital within the bloc • Restrictions on free movement of labour may or may not be included in regional agreement • Few restrictions on third-country trade and investment Principle of non-discrimination based on MFN principle applied	• APEC • AFTA

region. These include the Framework Agreement on the ASEAN Investment Area (AIA), the ASEAN Framework Agreement on Services (AFAS), and the Framework Agreement on Intellectual Property Rights (Thanadsillapakul 2001: 14).

Asia-Pacific Economic Cooperation (APEC) (1989)

APEC was chiefly an Australian–Japanese trade initiative (Cooper *et al.* 1993: 92), and now comprises members from four continents. APEC links a number of free trade areas together, including AFTA, NAFTA and the Australia–New Zealand Closer Economic Relations (CERTA) customs union. APEC's membership extends to Latin America (Chile and Peru), as well as the former Cold War 'socialist bloc' of Russia, China and Vietnam. Taiwan and Papua New Guinea are also included.

A key feature of the APEC agenda is 'open regionalism'. In stating this, APEC members commit themselves to non-discriminatory trade and investment policies in accordance with the WTO's MFN principle. As such, APEC differs considerably from PTAs such as NAFTA and the EU. Unlike many of the East Asian intra-regional dialogues, APEC has the rudiments of an institutional structure, with a secretariat based in Singapore and annual meetings. In this respect, it has developed consistency as an international forum. Keohane and Nye (2001: 2) describe APEC as 'multi-continental interdependence'.

The high-water mark of APEC was the Bogor Declaration (1994), which committed member states to the elimination of trade barriers by 2010 for developed economies and 2020 for developing countries. Following the summit, President Clinton described the declaration as an exemplar of 'open regionalism'. However, it was clear by the 1996 Manila APEC summit that the 1995 Kyoto Action Plan targets would not be met, and Japan, China and South Korea openly declared that agriculture would not be on the free trade agenda. Trade tensions between APEC partners were worsened by the US's policy of 'aggressive unilateralism', which saw the USTR target Japan, South Korea and Taiwan for alleged use of non-tariff barriers (NTBs) in traded goods sectors, such as automotive parts, imaging products and agriculture, as well as intellectual property (product patent piracy). While US demands were largely met in the face of trade retaliation threats, the APEC process was disrupted to the extent that its agenda became derailed. Moreover, APEC's in-principle commitment to external liberalization through open regionalism obscured the fact that APEC itself was dealing with complex regional liberalization issues of its own. This was demonstrated by APEC's decision at the 1997 Vancouver summit to abandon consensus decision-making and to focus on individual action plans (IAPs) to achieve Bogor's goals. Effectively, this means APEC members may offer unilateral trade concessions; however, there is no commitment to reciprocity, which means there are few incentives for members to grant concessions when there are no guarantees of reciprocity. The 1997 Asian Financial Crisis derailed any prospect of ASEAN or South Korea implementing IAPs, beyond insignificant tariff concessions. From 1997, ASEAN became less enthusiastic about open regionalism, evidenced by its

Box 10.3 Membership of Asian regional trade organizations

ASEAN Free Trade Agreement (1992)	*APEC (1989)*	*EAEC Proposal (1990)*	*ARF (1994)*	*BIMSTEC (1997)*	*ASEAN Plus Three (1997)*	*SAFTA (2005)*	*AANZFTA (2008)*
Brunei	Australia	ASEAN	ASEAN	Bangladesh	ASEAN	Afghanistan	ASEAN-10 member countries
Indonesia	Brunei Darussalam	China	Australia	Bhutan	China	Bangladesh	Australia
Malaysia	Canada	Taiwan	China	India	Japan	Bhutan	New Zealand
Myanmar	Chile	Japan	Canada	Myanmar	South Korea	India	
Philippines	China	South Korea	European Union	Nepal		Maldives	
Singapore	Hong Kong (China)	Vietnam	Japan	Sri Lanka		Nepal	
Thailand	Indonesia	Hong Kong	New Zealand	Thailand		Pakistan	
Vietnam	Japan		South Korea			Sri Lanka	
Cambodia	South Korea		Russia				
Laos	Malaysia Mexico New Zealand Papua New Guinea Peru Philippines Russia Singapore Taiwan Thailand United States Vietnam		North Korea India Papua New Guinea United States Mongolia				

cautiousness in pursuing the radical liberalization agendas of APEC and AFTA. Moreover, as APEC's rejection of Indian membership in 2007 demonstrated, ASEAN members were largely concerned about the impact of Indian trade competition on the Southeast Asian economies; India had originally applied for APEC membership in 1991. By imposing a 10-year enlargement ban, APEC introduced a measure of membership exclusivity. In 2009, President Obama made his first visit to Asia, attending the Singapore APEC summit. But the single underwhelming achievement of the leaders' meeting was to announce there would be no APEC climate change deal prior to the December 2009 Copenhagen climate conference.

The ASEAN Free Trade Agreement (AFTA) (1992) and the ASEAN–Australia–New Zealand Free Trade Agreement (AANZFTA)

In 1992, AFTA envisaged a functional ASEAN free trade area by 2002 for the original ASEAN six, with the FTA schedules to be incorporated by Vietnam in 2006, Laos and Myanmar by 2008, and Cambodia by 2010. AFTA itself was a reaction to the development of APEC's open regionalism, in the absence of which, Bello (2000) argues, AFTA's preferential trade agreements would have been 'irrelevant'. While ASEAN states feared the development of 'closed regionalism' in NAFTA and the EU, they nevertheless opted to give preferential tariffs to ASEAN members, under the Common Effective Preferential Tariff (CEPT). This encourages intra-ASEAN trade, as members gradually reduce their tariffs on an MFN basis. As this results in a larger regional market for third-country investors and traders, AFTA subscribes to the principle of 'open regionalism'. This encourages intra-ASEAN trade on a WTO-MFN basis. AFTA's removal of tariff barriers proved critical to ASEAN's and, more broadly, Asia's growth. It is impossible for a regional supply chain to function efficiently without cross-border, tariff-free access.

AFTA has broadly supported the principle of open regionalism, although there are exceptions. Despite moves by individual AFTA members, such as Indonesia and the Philippines, to unilaterally extend market access to all of their trading partners on an MFN basis in 1996, unilateral liberalization was unlikely to cover key sectors, such as TFC and agriculture (Bergsten 1997). The 1997 Financial Crisis meant that the incentives for further unilateral liberalization were few. AFTA missed its 2002 deadline for the implementation of the FTA, with outstanding issues including Malaysian auto tariffs (extended to 2005) which, in turn, encouraged other members to extend the deadline for the implementation schedule. In 2000, Bello argued that creeping protectionism made it increasingly likely that AFTA would postpone its deadline until 2010; his prediction was mostly accurate: the 2008 ASEAN summit saw the deferment of AFTA targets for the ASEAN-4 until 2015–18. However, since 2007, AFTA's objectives have been subsumed within the broader agenda of the ASEAN Community (see Chapter 8).

Arguably, AFTA has imposed fewer restrictions on trade and investment since the external imposition of the IMF structural adjustment programmes (SAPs). The withdrawal of government support from some public enterprises, increased regional investment co-operation, and reduced influence from 'crony capitalists' and presidential families in the assignation of contracts has been at least an indirect consequence of IMF conditionality. This was evidenced by post-currency crisis initiatives, such as the ASEAN Investment Area (AIA) (1998). However, FDI *outflows* from ASEAN to China were more conspicuous, increasing to over US$ 5 billion in 2008, a position that was only marginally affected in 2009 following the GFC (UNCTAD 2010: 10). Given global investment scarcity in the wake of the GFC, it is noteworthy that ASEAN firms were investing in Chinese assets, rather than domestic ASEAN production. Moreover, since the GFC, ASEAN outward FDI has continued to increase rapidly (Lee and Sermcheep 2017: 3–6). This was mostly from Singapore, which is ASEAN's only significant investor in China (Salidjanova and Koch-Wesser 2015: 7). Despite the AIA, intra-ASEAN FDI remains persistently weak; ASEAN-sourced FDI in 2015 accounted for only 18.5 per cent (US$ 19.5 billion) of ASEAN inward investment, although this was an improvement since 2005 (ASEAN 2016a: Table 25). Indonesia benefits from intra-ASEAN FDI (US$ 18.4 billion), but more than half of non-ASEAN inward FDI in 2015 was hosted by Singapore (US$ 55.8 billion). The US was the only source country that increased its FDI position substantially in ASEAN throughout 2013–15, while the EU and Japanese positions declined, and China's increased incrementally to 7 per cent of total FDI. The evidence shows that AFTA integration has had comparatively little impact on both intra- and extra-ASEAN inward FDI flows (ASEAN 2016a: Table 25).

The most significant expansion of AFTA's Pacific trade linkages emerged with the 2008 AANZFTA. Australia and New Zealand had promulgated a bilateral customs union as early as 1984, but the AANZFTA represented the first plurilateral agreement entered into by Australia. However, the AANZFTA demonstrated the caution exercised by some ASEAN countries in relation to FTAs, particularly when brokering deals with major agricultural exporters, such as Australia and New Zealand. Although the AANZFTA was promulgated in January 2010, only Singapore, Myanmar, Brunei, Malaysia and Vietnam had ratified the agreement. However, by 2015, the AANZFTA First Protocol entered into force.

ASEAN Plus Three (APT) (1997)

Although the EAEC proposal had failed to gain significant support in the region, the 1999 initiative to form APT represented a major turning point in intra-regional relations between Northeast and Southeast Asia. APT comprises ASEAN, plus the three largest East Asian economies: Japan, China and South Korea. Again, this involves a case of soft regionalism, in the form of dialogue, rather than 'hard' institution-building. While significant in terms of the new linkages it brings to Northeast/Southeast Asian relations, the APT's only major initiative, the AMF, has not been pursued since its proposal in 2000. The APT's importance to Northeast Asian dialogue should not be understated, however, given the traditional economic rivalry which underpins relations between Japan, South Korea and China.

China's growing centrality to the region was demonstrated by the considerable leverage Beijing exercised in negotiating the FTA it signed with ASEAN. In 2015, the ASEAN–China FTA encompassed 2 billion persons, with two-way merchandise trade totalling US$ 345 billion (ASEAN 2016b: Table 20). The agreement set a target of 2010 for the completion of a free trade area between China and the original ASEAN six, and 2015 for Cambodia, Laos, Myanmar and Vietnam. However, the FTA has also given Chinese exports a considerable presence in a part of Asia traditionally dominated by Japanese firms and investment. By 2015, ASEAN imported US$ 211.5 billion worth of goods from China, 1.5 times ASEAN exports to the PRC (ASEAN 2016b: Table 20).

Intra-regional FTAs such as ASEAN–China demonstrate the importance of the regional balance of economic and political power within the East Asian region. Buffered by a considerable trade surplus in the region, Japanese governments did not pursue regional agreements seriously during the 1990s, preferring to free ride on APEC's promise of open regionalism. In marked contrast with the progressive 2001 ASEAN–China bilaterals, Japan spent the year engaged in a tit-for-tat protectionist dispute with China; refused to include agriculture in a Japan–Singapore bilateral FTA; and damaged relations with its neighbours by backing away from its AMF proposal, opting instead for an IMF fallback position (i.e., that no funds would be disbursed to Asian countries in difficulty without seeking IMF approval). Slow to react to the ASEAN–China FTA, Japan finally responded in 2002 with Prime Minister Koizumi's Initiative for Japan–ASEAN Comprehensive Economic Partnership. Labelled 'ASEAN Plus Five', Koizumi's cabinet made an abortive attempt to block Beijing's establishment of an ASEAN–China trade area by provocatively including Taiwan, as well as Hong Kong. The Japanese government stated that, 'In the future, the area could be extended to Australia and New Zealand, as well as the United States' (*Japan Times* 14 April 2002). As a counter to the ASEAN–China FTA, Japan initiated the Japan–ASEAN Comprehensive Economic Partnership Agreement, which entered into force in December 2008.

Despite APT, intra-regional disagreements suggest that great power rivalry – principally between Japan and China – can play a major role in determining the shape and outcomes of regional policy; in other words, not only globalization but *inter-state rivalry within the region* has also been responsible for prompting the growth of regional co-operation. Japan's traditional regional economic hegemony faces the dual challenges of rising China, and Japan's domestic economic difficulties. The result has been an enhanced role for second-order, but influential organizations, such as ASEAN, to play a brokering role. Individual ASEAN countries' markets on their own are too insignificant to exert bargaining leverage on Beijing or Tokyo.

The Asian Monetary Fund proposal and the Chiang Mai initiative

In the wake of the 1997 currency crisis, Japan proposed an Asian Monetary Fund (AMF), which received some support within ASEAN. The AMF proposal, with initial capitalization of US$ 17 billion, emerged from the Chiang Mai initiative (CMI), a multilateral currency swap arrangement, backed by APT in 2000. The AMF was clearly the result of ASEAN members' dissatisfaction with the SAPs demanded by the IMF following the AFC, which involved large-scale structural and institutional reforms. The AMF initiative envisaged an East Asian system of central banks monitoring and co-ordinating speculative banking activities, such as debt-for-equity swaps. The reasoning was that AMF co-ordination would limit the degree of speculation by international markets and, therefore, serve to stabilize East Asian currency markets. Although the AMF was a Japanese proposal, the US Treasury's strong opposition to its formation, together with China's refusal to support the proposal, resulted in Japan's abandonment of the concept. There were clear reasons for Japanese support for, and US opposition to, the AMF. First, Japanese financial institutions made credit widely available to East Asian countries affected by the 1997 crisis, giving Japanese lenders a distinct competitive advantage over US and European capital in East Asian markets. Japanese banks also held almost 50 per cent of Thai foreign debt and 40 per cent of Indonesia's, suggesting protection of the Japanese banking sector was, in reality, the key objective (Higgott 1999: 268–9). Second, Japanese financial institutions made loans available without imposing the harsh conditionality inherent in the IMF's SAPs. Third, the Japanese government argued that any AMF role would be subordinate to that of the IMF, which meant that, in effect, the IMF remained the 'lender of last resort', and would, therefore, carry the largest part of the risk.

The proposal revealed a serious deterioration in relations between APT members and the IMF. However, some parts of the AMF agenda have been implemented in a number of bilateral agreements within the APT, which exemplifies the importance of 'soft' regionalism in East Asia, particularly when dealing with sensitive areas of national economic sovereignty such as central bank independence. However, the CMI did lead to concrete developments, such as the 1997 ASEAN Swap Arrangement (ASA), a currency stabilization programme formed following the AFC. The Clinton and Bush administrations accepted the CMI and also engaged in a number of modest IMF reforms in response to the AFC, under the rubric of the 'post-Washington Consensus'. However, despite lying dormant for a more than a decade, two initiatives revived the AMF and CMI. In February 2009, the 13 APT states increased CMI reserves from US$ 80 billion to $ 120 billion, with Japan and China contributing US$ 34 billion each to the fund. In December 2009, the APT announced the CMI Multilateralization (CMIM), a lightly veiled attempt to re-introduce the AMF by institutionalizing the CMI. As Beeson (2003) argues, APT may well exemplify 'reactionary regionalism' to the extent that it corresponds with an economic and cultural rejection of US-led market liberalism.

The CMIM exemplified the growing dependence of the ASEAN states' financial systems on their Northeast Asian partners, exemplified by China's two bilateral currency swap agreements with Malaysia and Thailand. The CMIM was also viewed by some analysts as the prelude to the establishment of an Asian currency union by stealth, potentially duplicating the World Bank's Special Drawing Rights

(SDR) facility, established in 1969. Moreover, it was not coincidental that the chairman of the PRC central bank, Zhou Xiaochuan, called for the US dollar's replacement as the global reserve currency in May 2009, a position reinforced by other BRICS members Russia, India and Brazil. A UN Conference on Trade and Development (UNCTAD) panel, dominated by members of the G77 developing countries, reinforced this message by echoing the BRICS in its September 2009 report (UN 2009). The reactivation of the AMF in the form of the CMIM implies that Asian states are still wary of the US Treasury–IMF nexus, and APT countries are making a concerted attempt to undermine Washington's traditional dominance of international monetary relations. In 2012, the CMIM fund was doubled to US$ 240 billion, with ASEAN-4 countries able to draw up to 500 per cent of their financial commitment, while ASEAN-6 states may draw up to 250 per cent. However, CMIM members cannot access any more finance, unless they subject themselves to an IMF programme; the Initiative remains linked to IMF conditionality.

The Asian Infrastructure Investment Bank

The original development bank for the region was the Asian Development Bank (ADB), a regional subsidiary of the World Bank, founded in 1966. Although the ADB was an important vehicle for Japanese economic strategies, the ADB is dwarfed by the financial depth of the IMF and World Bank. ADB lending in 2016 totalled US$ 31 billion, while the IMF's outstanding credit exceeded US$ 95 billion during the peak of the Eurozone financial crisis in 2012 (ADB 2017, IMF 2017). In 2009, the ADB estimated that US$ 8 trillion in infrastructure spending and investment within Asia was required throughout 2010–20, to update existing infrastructure and develop new capacity (ADB 2009). Of the US$8 trillion, 51 per cent was needed for electricity, 29 per cent for road construction and 13 per cent for telecommunications (*The Economist* 21 March 2015). Existing multilateral lenders, such as the Asian Development Bank and the World Bank, lack the funds to address and overcome this infrastructure shortfall, resulting in a lack of development and sustained poverty, as well as weak job and growth prospects for many poor parts of Asia (Bhattacharyay 2010). According to the ADB, a lack of basic infrastructure means 1.8 billion people in the region are not connected to basic sanitation services, 0.8 billion lack electricity, and 0.6 billion do not have access to safe water' (ADB 2012: iii). Given the private sector's unpreparedness to invest in developing Asia, owing to risk, President Xi Jinping initially proposed an Asian Infrastructure Investment Bank (AIIB) in Indonesia ahead of the annual APEC forum in October 2013 (ADB 2012: 60).

Headquartered in Beijing, China is the AIIB's largest shareholder, with 26 per cent of the voting rights, with Beijing's nominee, Jin Liqun, as the AIIB's first president (Dreyer 2015, *South China Morning Post* 30 June 2015). Illustrating the regional makeup and orientation of the AIIB, 75 per cent of the AIIB's share votes are held by Asia-Pacific members and India is the second largest shareholder, thus granting developing Asian countries a much greater voice than they receive in any of the other multilateral lenders (Dreyer 2015, *Times of India* 24 May 2015). The bank commenced operations in January 2016 with 57 prospective foundation members and US$ 100 billion in authorized capital stock, with China contributing one-third of the total, giving Beijing approximately a third of the bank's total shares (*New York Times* 2015). The AIIB extended loans of US$ 1.7 billion in 2016, including a US$ 300 million hydropower plant in Pakistan, US$ 301 million in port and railway infrastructure in Oman, and a US$ 600 million loan to construct the Trans-Anatolian gas pipeline, linking Azerbaijan to Europe (AIIB 2016, *Forbes* 14 January 2017). The objectives of the AIIB are clear: China and its partners are building commercial infrastructure AIIB members can utilize. Although other multilateral lenders, such as the ADB and World Bank are involved in many projects, it is clear Beijing can exercise a great deal of soft power via the AIIB, as well as using its presidency to approve or veto projects that are useful to Beijing. Jin Liqun also announced in 2016 that the bank would lend exclusively in US dollars, and not the yuan renminbi, allaying Western concerns that the AIIB would be a vehicle through which Beijing could promote the renminbi as a competitor to the US dollar (*Financial Times* 8 May 2016). It also obviates the need for China to liberalize its capital account and float the renminbi, which could make Chinese markets unpredictable. The AIIB also represents Beijing's strategy to dilute the power of the US-dominated World Bank and the Japanese-controlled ABD. Washington is a noteworthy absentee from the AIIB membership group, although key US allies, such as Britain, France, Germany and Australia, all have substantial subscriptions.

The Trans-Pacific Partnership

The Bush administration initiated the Trans-Pacific Partnership (TPP), but President Obama endorsed the concept of a multicontinental trade bloc in the Asia-Pacific, noting that, 'If we don't write the rules, China will write the rules out in that region' (*Wall Street Journal* 27 April 2015). The TPP had its origins within APEC when Brunei, Chile, New Zealand and Singapore established a 'Pacific-4' (P4) agreement in 2004–05. In 2008, the US Trade Representative (USTR) announced it would negotiate entry into the P4. Other APEC members, including Australia, Peru and Vietnam, quickly followed, announcing their intention to negotiate a wider Pacific partnership. The USTR lobbied South Korea to enter the negotiations, but Seoul declined. By 2012, the TPP-11 had commenced negotiations, with Japan joining the group in 2013. The potential for the TPP is vast. Its members have a combined GDP of US$ 30 trillion, total annual trade of US$ 5 trillion, and account for 30 per cent of global agricultural exports and 20 per cent of food imports.

The TPP is known as a 'WTO-plus' agreement, meaning it exceeds the minimum standards set under existing WTO rules and further liberalizes trade, investment and harmonizes regulations between members. The TPP set out comprehensive market access, removing restrictions on services trade. It has a 'fully regional' framework, with a single tariff schedule and a single rules of origin (RoO) agreement. It also focuses on green jobs, renewable energy trade and digital economy. Unlike most FTAs, the TPP is not static; it is a 'living agreement', which is open to further modification, continual reform and liberalization measures, and is reviewable every 3–5 years (DFAT 2015).

In April 2015, South Korea sought to join the bloc, but Seoul was told it would need to wait for the second wave of membership applications. In June 2015, President Obama gained fast-track Trade Promotion Authority (TPA) from Congress. Japan originally refused to remove tariffs on agricultural imports, but caved. All of TPP-12 have committed to elimination or phased removal of food tariffs. By October 2015, the TPP-12 had an agreed draft comprising 30 chapters. Five chapters deal with trade. Its most controversial chapters included intellectual property, pharmaceuticals and investor–state dispute settlement (ISDS) provisions. ISDS allows corporations to litigate against governments, utilizing external judicial panels. ISDS has been controversial, not least because some critics argue that it prevents governments from legislating in areas such as public health and pharmaceutical drugs (Davison and Canny 2015). Australia specifically ruled out the applicability of ISDS for tobacco products, as Philip Morris had previously employed an ISDS provision in the Australia–Hong Kong bilateral investment treaty (BIT) in a failed attempt to sue the Australian government. In developing Asia, ISDS is increasingly viewed with suspicion; for example, the Indonesian government has reviewed all BITs and terminated 20 investment treaties with ISDS provisions (*Jakarta Post* 27 June 2016).

The overarching objective of the TPP is a FTA of the Asia-Pacific. However, in January 2017, President Trump formally withdrew the US from the TPP. However, other members can ratify the TPP, with a view to American readmission under a future administration. The remaining TPP-11 is not likely to abandon the long-negotiated agreement, and Washington's role as an international trade 'rule-maker' could be threatened by Beijing if China is permitted to establish the rules for its own regional trade initiative, the Regional Comprehensive Economic Partnership (RCEP).

The Regional Comprehensive Economic Partnership

Launched in 2013, the RCEP involves ASEAN, China, Japan, Korea, Australia, New Zealand and India. As with the TPP and other FTAs, the RCEP represents a comprehensive agreement, although it will be limited to goods and services trade, as well as investment; like the TPP, it will also include ISDS provisions.

For many years, both Australia and Japan had sought a region-wide FTA that went beyond APEC. However, both Canberra and Tokyo sought to integrate Beijing into a plurilateral RTA which complemented, rather than competed with, the Washington-led TPP. Australia had achieved its bilateral objectives by signing FTAs with South Korea, Japan and China in 2014–15. However, Australia and Japan's bilateral FTAs were fragmented, with a host of different rules and regulations unique to each agreement. Notably, the US has no FTA with ASEAN, as ASEAN states would not agree to meet the high-standard disciplines of the

TPP. However, India's and China's existing FTAs with ASEAN, together with the AANZFTA, simplify the process of extending the RCEP process to include Japan and South Korea. From Tokyo's and Seoul's points of view, an FTA with China is the chief incentive. For India, RCEP provides the opportunity to be fully integrated into East Asia's production networks and the regional supply chain, as New Delhi lacks FTA links with South Korea, Japan and China. In this respect, RCEP helps fulfil Narendra Modi's 'Act East' agenda. Through their FTA linkages with the EU, India and South Korea have effectively globalized Asia's trade networks.

The ultimate aim is to integrate TPP and RCEP into a single, multicontinental agreement. With Washington's withdrawal from the TPP, Latin America is making its own pivot to Asia, not only through Brazil's membership of the BRICS, but also as a result of Chile's, Mexico's and Peru's memberships of both APEC and the TPP. In 2015, Chinese Premier Li Keqiang, stated that, 'TPP and RCEP can…contribute to the joint goal of establishing an Asia-Pacific free trade zone' (*The Diplomat* 17 March 2016). If promulgated, RCEP would comprise the largest trading bloc in the world, with a GDP of over US$ 20 trillion.

Conclusion: the state in retreat?

A major theme in this chapter is that accelerating globalization has served to prompt increased regionalization, as individual states demonstrate a decreasing ability to deal with the diverse range of problems presented by globalization by implementing state-centric policies. In this respect, intra-regional and inter-regional initiatives, such as AFTA, APEC, APT and ASEM, are responses to complex policy issues that states are unable to resolve individually. Regional initiatives also 'bring the state back in' by giving national governments a key role in regional agenda-setting and policy-making. Globalization may force states to confront new and difficult challenges to their policy-making autonomy; however, as Hirst and Thompson (1996) argue, the state has been far from passive or defenceless in the face of globalization.

References

Asia-Pacific Economic Cooperation (APEC) (1995) *Achieving the APEC Vision: Free and Open Trade in the Asia-Pacific*, Second Report of the Eminent Persons' Group, Singapore: APEC Secretariat.

Asian Development Bank (2009) *Infrastructure for a Seamless Asia*, Tokyo: ADB and ADB Institute.

Asian Development Bank (ADB) (2012), *Infrastructure for Supporting Inclusive Growth and Poverty Reduction in Asia*, Manila: ADB.

Asian Development Bank (ADB) (2017) 'ADB – Our work', https://www.adb.org/about/our-work.

Asian Infrastructure Investment Bank (2016) 'Articles of Agreement', https://www.aiib.org/en/about-aiib/basic-documents/_download/articles-of-agreement/basic_document_english-bank_articles_of_agreement.pdf.

Association of South-East Asian Nations (ASEAN) (2016a) 'Foreign Direct Investment Statistics', 30 June, http://asean.org/?static_post=foreign-direct-investment-statistics.

Association of South-East Asian Nations (ASEAN) (2016b) 'External Trade Statistics', 30 August, http://asean.org/?static_post=external-trade-statistics-3.

Beeson, M. (2003) 'ASEAN Plus Three and the rise of reactionary regionalism', *Contemporary Southeast Asia*, 25: 251–68.

Bello, W. (2000) 'The Association of Southeast Asian Nations: a preliminary autopsy', www.focusweb.org/publications/2000/The_Association_of_Southeast_Asian_Nations.htm.

Bergh, A. and T. Nilsson (2014) 'Is globalization reducing absolute poverty?' *World Development*, 62: 42–61.

Bergsten, C. F. (1997) 'Open regionalism', Institute for International Economics Working Paper No. 97–3, Washington, DC: IIE.

Bhattacharyay, B (2010), 'Financing Asia's infrastructure', *Asian Development Bank Institute*, no. 229, July, www.adb.org/sites/default/files/publication/156084/adbi-wp229.pdf.

Butler, F. (1997) 'Regionalism and integration' in J. Baylis and S. Smith (eds), *The Globalization of World Politics*, Oxford: Oxford University Press.

Cai, F. (2012) 'Is there a "middle-income trap"? Theories, experiences and relevance to China', *China and World Economy*, 20: 49–61.

Cooper, A., R. Higgott and K. Nossal (1993) *Relocating Middle Powers*, Vancouver: University of British Columbia Press.

Cox, R. W. (1996) 'A perspective on globalization' in J. H. Mittelman (ed.), *Globalization: Critical Reflections*, Boulder, CO: Lynne Rienner.

Davison, R. (2011) *The Political Economy of Single Market Europe: The State, European Integration and the Challenge of Neorealism*, Saarbrücken: Lambert Academic Publishing.

Davison, R. and J. Canny (2015) 'Debunking the TPP myths', *The Australian*, 8 October, www.theaustralian.com.au/business/business-spectator/debunking-the-tpp-myths/news-story/ebe741172e87dbcf63a9a63415891cd5.

Department of Foreign Affairs and Trade, Australia (DFAT) (2015) 'Trans-Pacific Partnership – background document: free trade agreements as living agreements', 8 October, http://dfat.gov.au/trade/agreements/tpp/Documents/background-papers-ftas-living-agreements.pdf.

Dreyer, J. (2015) 'The Asian Infrastructure Investment Bank: who will benefit?' Foreign Policy Research Institute, 6 April, www.fpri.org/article/2015/04/the-asian-infrastructure-investment-bank-who-will-benefit/.

Fukuyama, F. (1992) *The End of History and the Last Man*, New York: The Free Press.

GATT Secretariat (1947) *General Agreement on Tariffs and Trade*, Geneva: GATT Secretariat.

Gill, S. (1990) *American Hegemony and the Trilateral Commission*, Cambridge: Cambridge University Press.

Gordon, P. H. (2002) 'It's time for a trans-Atlantic summit', *International Herald Tribune*, 13 March.

Higgott, R. (1999) 'The international relations of the Asian Economic Crisis: a study in the politics of resentment' in R. Robison, M. Beeson, K. Jayasuriya and H.-R. Sim (eds), *Politics and Markets in the Wake of the Asian Crisis*, London: Routledge.

Hirst, P. and G. Thompson (1996) *Globalization in Question*, Cambridge: Cambridge University Press.

Hirst, P. and G. Thompson (2006) 'Globalization and the future of the nation state', *Economy and Society*, 24 (3): 408–42.

Huntington, S. P. (1996) *The Clash of Civilizations*, New York: Simon & Schuster.

Hurrell, A. (1995) *Regionalism in World Politics: Regional Organization and International Order*, Oxford: Oxford University Press.

International Monetary Fund (2010) 'World Economic Outlook Database', April 2010, www.imf.org/external/pubs/ft/weo/2010/01/weodata/index.aspx.

International Monetary Fund (2016) 'IMF Survey: Historic Reforms Double Quota Resources and Enhance Voice of Emerging and Developing Economies', January, www.imf.org/external/pubs/ft/survey/so/2016/POL012716B.htm.

International Monetary Fund (2017) 'Total IMF Credit Outstanding for all members from 1984 – 2017', 31 March, https://www.imf.org/external/np/fin/tad/extcred1.aspx.

Keohane, R. and J. Nye (1977) *Power and Interdependence: World Politics in Transition*, Boston, MA: Little, Brown.

Keohane, R. and J. Nye (2001) 'Introduction' in J. Nye and J. D. Donahue (eds), *Governance in a Globalizing World*, Washington, DC: Brookings Institution Press.

Krugman, P. (1998) 'Fire-sale FDI', http://web.mit.edu/krugman/www/FIRESALE.htm.

Lee, C. and S. Sermcheep (eds) (2017) *Outward Foreign Direct Investment in ASEAN*, Singapore: ISEAS.

Lutz, M. (2001) 'Globalization, convergence and the case for openness in developing countries: what do we learn from open economy growth theory and empirics?' CSGR Working Paper No. 72/01, May.

Mahathir, M. (2001) 'The future of Asia in a globalized and deregulated world', speech delivered at The Future of Asia conference, Tokyo, 8 June.

Noland, M., G. Hufbauer, T. Moran and S. Robinson (2016) 'Assessing trade agendas in the US presidential campaign', Policy Brief, Peterson Institute for International Economics, no. 6–16.

Nye, J., B. Biedenkopf and M. Shiina (1991) *Global Co-operation after the Cold War: A Reassessment of Trilateralism*, New York: Trilateral Commission.

Ohmae, K. (1990) *The Borderless World: Power and Strategy in the Interlinked Economy*, London: Fontana.

Ohmae, K. (1995) *The Evolving Global Economy: Making Sense of the New World Order*, Boston, MA: Harvard Business School Press.

Ohmae, K. (1996) *The End of the Nation State: The Rise of Regional Economies*, New York: The Free Press.

Organisation for Economic Co-operation and Development (OECD) (2016) *Economic Outlook for Southeast Asia, China and India 2016: Enhancing Regional Ties*, Paris: OECD.

Piketty, T. (2014) *Capital in the 21st Century*, Cambridge, MA: Belknap Press.

Rodrik, A. (1998) 'Globalization, social conflict and economic growth', *The World Economy*, 21: 143–58.

Salidjanova, N. and I. Koch-Wesser (2015) 'China's economic ties with ASEAN: a country-by-country analysis', US–China Economic and Security Review Commission, staff research report, 17 March, https://www.uscc.gov/sites/default/files/Research/China%27s%20Economic%20Ties%20with%20ASEAN.pdf.

Scholte, J. A. (1997) 'Global capitalism and the state', *International Affairs*, 73: 427–52.

Stiglitz, J. (2002) *Globalization and Its Discontents*, New York: W. W. Norton.

Strange, S. (1996) *The Retreat of the State: The Diffusion of Power in the World Economy*, Cambridge: Cambridge University Press.

Thanadsillapakul, L. (2001) 'Open regionalism and deeper integration: the implementation of ASEAN Investment Area (AIA) and ASEAN Free Trade Area (AFTA)', *CEPMLP On-line Journal*, 6 (16), www.dundee.ac.uk/cepmlp/journal/vol6–16.html.

United Nations (UN) (2009) 'UN panel calls for new global reserve, credit systems to avert future crises', 10 September, www.un.org/apps/news/story.asp?NewsID=32020.

United Nations Conference on Trade and Development (UNCTAD) (2010) *World Investment Report*, UNCTAD: Geneva, 22 July, www.adb.org/Documents/Fact_Sheets/KIR.pdf.

US Treasury (2017) 'The daily history of the debt results', Treasury Direct, 29 April, https://treasurydirect.gov/NP/debt/search?startMonth=01&startDay=01&startYear=2016&endMonth=12&endDay=31&endYear=2016.

Wallerstein, I. (1979) *The Capitalist World Economy*, Cambridge: Cambridge University Press.

Wallerstein, I. (2013) 'Structural crisis, or why capitalists may no longer find capitalism rewarding' in I. Wallerstein, R. Collins, M. Mann, G. Derlugan and C. Calhoun, *Does Capitalism have a Future?* New York: Oxford University Press.

Wei, S. and J. A. Frankel (1998) 'Open regionalism in a world of continental trade blocs', *IMF Staff Papers*, 45: 440–53.

Wolf, M. (2002) 'Doing more harm than good', *Financial Times*, 8 May.

Woods, N. (2001) 'Prague – a failed opportunity', *Prospect*, December.

World Bank (2010) 'World Development Indicators database', April, http://siteresources.worldbank.org/DATASTATISTICS/Resources/GDP_PPP.pdf.

World Economic Forum (2016) '6 surprising facts about India's exploding middle class', 7 November, https://www.weforum.org/agenda/2016/11/6-surprising-facts-about-india-s-exploding-middle-class/.

World Trade Organization (WTO) (2017) 'Regional Trade Agreements: facts and figures', https://www.wto.org/english/tratop_e/region_e/regfac_e.htm.

Yoshihara, K. (1988) *The Rise of Ersatz Capitalism in Southeast Asia*, Oxford: Oxford University Press.

Yoshihara, K. (1999) *Building a Prosperous Southeast Asia: From Ersatz to Echt Capitalism*, New York: Routledge.

Zhang, L., H. Yi, R. Luo, C. Liu and S. Rozelle (2013) 'The human capital roots of the middle income trap: the case of China', *Agricultural Economics*, 44: 151–62.

Zoellick, R. (2002) 'Unleashing the trade winds', *The Economist*, 7 December.

11 State and markets

Political economy explanations of East Asia's economic miracle

Michael K. Connors

In the last third of the 20th century a number of Asian states, following Japan's example, underwent enormous economic growth. A rash of books on the 'Asian miracle' appeared which sang the praises of Japanese industrialization and its governing capacity, praised Confucian culture, lauded the role of what was called a 'developmental state', and identified the region's export-oriented industrialization strategy and integration into the international economy as reasons for success. Many commentators predicted spiralling economic growth. The 'Asian century' was approaching, the 'American century' was receding. In the 1990s the miracle turned sour. First Japan entered its 'lost decade' after a dramatic stock market crash led to stagnant growth, falling wages and declining property prices. Then more widely, in 1997 the region's growth nose-dived, as a currency crisis hit South Korea and Southeast Asia, with trigger effects globally. Books such as *The Tigers Tamed* (Garran 1998) or *The Asian Eclipse: Exposing the Dark Side of Business in Asia* (Backman 1999) typified much popular writing on Asia's economic malaise. Asia's strengths were now viewed as liabilities: Asian states were said to be too interventionist, Asian culture was endemically corrupt, and Asian education failed to spark entrepreneurship. Help was needed. And as capital dried up, currencies depreciated and thousands of companies went bankrupt, the World Bank, the International Monetary Fund and others provided bail-outs to Indonesia, South Korea and Thailand conditional on governments following a programme of financial austerity and economic liberalization. From the perspective of the financial heartlands of the world – the US Treasury and the international financial institutions – the Asian crisis confirmed the virtue of Western capitalist market models towards which they assumed the rest of the world would converge.

The so-called Global Financial Crisis (GFC) of 2007–08, which was really a Western financial crisis with global implications, ended such heady triumphalism. While impacted by the GFC because of falling exports, many Asian economies returned to pre-crisis growth levels, while Western economies continue to experience stagnant or minor growth late into the second decade of the 2000s. Although the causes of the GFC are debated, its impact and consequences are clear to see: robust economies lay comatose, requiring massive state intervention. Once derided Keynesian pump-priming measures such as pouring money, printed on demand, into projects or the pockets of consumers to stimulate demand were widely used.

Wholesale nationalization of private bank debt occurred. The GFC demonstrated that not only were the West's most significant economies vulnerable to seizure, but in bailing out financial institutions Western governments and international organizations were willing to engage in rescue measures that they had prohibited in favour of austerity during the Asian Economic Crisis (Pempel and Tsunekawa 2015). Such double standards are not surprising, for privilege lies where power resides. What is surprising is how quickly the demoted economies of Asia were once again accorded global salience following the GFC. It is developments such as these that make international political economy (IPE) fascinating.

For many students of international relations, opening a textbook on IPE may come as a shock. Beyond the strangely comforting – because constantly familiar – notions of security dilemmas, balance of power, international regimes, the Westphalian system and nuclear deterrence, and the easy chronology of foreign policies, the table of contents of a typical IPE book reveals an unsettling world of exchange rates, financial crises, the gold standard, national systems of political economy, international trade and fortified acronyms. But unlike the mystical models of economics, political economy directs attention to explicable human decisions and actions structured in a world of available resources that are unevenly distributed. Power is central to the analysis.

This chapter focuses on a key theme in IPE literature: the question of how to interpret the role of the state in Asia's remarkable economic growth. This topic has endured for over a generation. Walden Bello, a leading scholar in IPE, has noted, 'if there is one theory or approach that might be said to be uniquely associated with the region [East Asia], it is the theory of the developmental state' (Bello 2009: 180). The question of what the developmental state is and how it functions has led to a deeply political debate that encompasses the legitimate role of state power in the construction of national capacity and extends to matters of geopolitical consequence. In exploring the developmental state literature, this chapter attempts to equip students with a basic orientation to different approaches to political economy.

The Asian economic 'miracle'

As economists surveyed the wastelands of East Asia after the Second World War, few expected an economic miracle. South Korea was plunged into a war with North Korea, Taiwan was in the hands of the unproven Kuomintang, Hong Kong was a centre for fleeing Chinese refugees, Indonesia was in the grips of Sukarnoism, and in China the dogma-driven catastrophes of the Great Leap Forward and the Cultural Revolution led to the loss of millions of lives (Rowen 1998: 1–2). By the 1980s the region was described as having performed an economic miracle. Pempel (1999: 147) notes that 'The various macroeconomic statistics on Japan, Taiwan, and Korea have become boringly familiar even to those who are not specialists on the region'.

The 'miracle' was that a number of countries in East and Southeast Asia achieved rapid economic growth. In its famous report *The East Asian Miracle: Economic Growth and Public Policy* (1993), the World Bank listed Japan as leading the high performing Asian economies (HPAEs) of Hong Kong, Singapore, South Korea (the four tigers, or the first-tier newly industrializing countries, or NICs) and Indonesia, Malaysia and Thailand (the second tier of the newly industrializing countries). These countries taken together experienced higher growth rates than anywhere else in the world between 1965 and 1990, averaging 4.6 per cent per annum. This compared with 0.2 per cent for sub-Saharan Africa, 1.8 per cent for the Middle East and Latin America, 1.9 per cent for South Asia and 2.4 per cent for the high-income economies of the West. The HPAEs experienced growing equal distribution of income relative to other economies. In 1960 life expectancy in the eight HPAEs was 56 years. By 1990 it was 71. Each country experienced dramatic declines in the levels of absolute poverty (World Bank 1993). If China is included a striking picture emerges:

> Prior to the Asian Financial Crisis in 1997, [the] East Asian region as a whole exported $1,392 billion to rest of the world, accounting for 25.6% of the total world export. Compared to the 14.29% share of total world export in 1978, the relative importance of the East Asian region in the world economy has increased substantially.
>
> (Bark 2000: 1–2)

Let us look more specifically at a few countries. Japan stands in the vanguard. There are many facts about Japan's rebound after its surrender to the Allied Powers in 1945, perhaps none as astonishing than that between 1948 and 1960 Japanese industrial production increased eight-fold (Garran 1998: 24). The pace of gains barely halted until the 1990s:

> Between 1965 and 1990 Japan's industrial production increased fivefold whereas it only doubled in the United States and leading economies of Western Europe. By 1980, the Japanese economy represented 44% of the US economy; by 1990 the proportion had risen to 62%.
>
> (Camilleri 2000: 68)

Although experiencing fluctuating trade patterns, by the 1980s Japan was enjoying sustained trade surpluses with its major trading partners – oil-producing states being the exception. Japan had by the mid-1980s become the world's largest creditor nation and provider of foreign aid; it was also the largest exporter of foreign direct investment. Japan was clearly a leader of the industrialized world. Its success was often attributed to the 'iron triangle', a pattern of close and vested relations between business, politicians and bureaucrats, who worked closely to plan economic development.

No less spectacular was the growth of other East Asian economies, especially the 'tigers' South Korea, Taiwan, Hong Kong and Singapore, described at the time as newly industrializing economies (NIEs). The Organisation for Economic Co-operation and Development (OECD) defined newly industrializing economies as having:

1 fast growth in both the absolute level of industrial employment and the share of industrial employment in total employment;
2 a rising share of the world exports of manufactures;
3 fast growth in real per capita GDP such that the country was successful in narrowing the gap with the advanced industrialized countries.

(Chowdhury and Islam 1993: 3)

All the tigers possessed these three attributes in the 1960s and 1970s, while the second-tier NIEs underwent similar processes in the following two decades. It was assumed by many that the 'miracle' flowed from an emulation of Japanese-style development by the NIEs, which Japan had assisted with aid and technical assistance. Strong states with the ability to implement plans seemed to be the key to the miracle and this assumption led to the idea of a generic form of 'Asian capitalism'. Yet these countries had state and society structures sufficiently different to bring into question the idea of an 'Asian form of capitalism'. Speaking of economic governance in East Asia for instance, Kim (1999: 99) noted that it was possible to distinguish between *chaebol* capitalism in South Korea, where large-scale conglomerates dominated with a high degree of concentration and vertical integration, family capitalism in Taiwan, characterized by small-to-medium enterprises' reliance on patrimonial networks, and alliance capitalism in Japan, where small and large businesses formed networks and institutional linkages through subcontracting.

If the dominant economic actors varied in each country, so too were the institutional arrangements for economic governance. Pempel (1999) differentiated countries in terms of four factors: politics, financial and business structures, and state strategy. Politically, Japan had sustained a form of democracy for all of the post-war period, while power in Taiwan and South Korea, until the late 1980s, was held by militaristic cliques or autocrats. On finance structure, in Japan most banks were private and linked to industrial groups, but the keystone of the system, the Bank of Japan, was controlled by the government's Ministry of Finance, while the public postal saving system was a key component of the entire system. In South Korea, foreign capital inflows were limited, but considerable capital was raised abroad. Most banking was privatized, yet government oversight was critical in directing capital to desired sectors. In Taiwan, the ruling nationalist KMT favoured the interests of immigrant capitalists from the mainland of China, and kept finance and industry as largely separate spheres. What becomes clear from this analysis is that the idea of a development state or a generic form of Asian capitalism was far too general inasmuch as it suggested identity between states, when substantial difference was evident (Pempel 1999). Furthermore, the experience of the second tier of NIEs differed from the first. These economies were less likely to have strong states with the capacity to implement plans. They were also more open than Japan and the first-tier NIEs to high levels of FDI. It was clear that the HPAEs did not display commensurable structure or experience. Indeed, as MacIntyre (1994: 16) noted, there were significant difficulties in any attempt to generalize East Asian development because the 'differences in the patterns of business–government interaction among the Southeast Asian countries or the Northeast Asian countries are as notable as the differences between the two sub regions'.

Relatedly, Evans (1995) invited a further aspect of differentiation in his study of the 'embedded autonomy' of the developmental state. He posited that those states which were both possessed of functioning state bureaucracy and which were embedded with strategically relevant social forces, were best able to steer development. Using this approach, scholars saw South Korea, Japan and Taiwan as such states. In each of these states the bureaucracy of the developmental state existed in productive relation to other actors; the administrative guardians were not the sole variable accounting for success. Evans' work advised against reifying the state from its relevant social entanglements. It invited empirical enquiry as to the concrete nature of those relations rather than the template application of models which assumed state centrality. Such observations as these have since fed into a growing literature on the varieties of capitalism in the region (see Carney 2016).

Nonetheless, the idea of a specifically Asian form of developmental state has persisted, and remains an area of research and argument. Most famously, Chalmers Johnson (1985, 1999) proposed that Japan, rather than exemplifying good market policies, was in fact a capitalist development state (CDS). The CDS, as Johnson described it in relation to Japan, encompassed a number of features including a state bureaucracy closely associated with economic planning, a state role in the allocation of credit, state-led industrial policy specifically planned for growth outcomes rather than laying the ground rules for universal competition. The state's various machinations induced Japanese business to take a particular course of action that conformed not only to business profit requirements, but also to national objectives set down by the state in the name of the 'national interest'. This, Johnson described as a plan-rational political economy, in contrast to the regulatory state of Western capitalism and the centralist state of communism. Johnson (1985) argued that in some senses the key economies of the region (Japan, Taiwan and South Korea) could be identified as capitalist development states.

Thus far the discussion indicates that the HPAEs benefitted from a particular form of state that could steer capital through direct bureaucratic intervention for national purposes. In the following, how different political approaches address the relation of markets, states and society is addressed.

Approaches to political economy

The different schools of thought in international political economy may be broadly classed as realist, liberal and radical, or neo-Marxist. While political economy studies the relationship between economic and political processes, each school differs on the nature of this relationship. For liberals, economic activity should be largely free of political interference. Political institutions need to be constrained so as not to interfere in the market. A state should provide no more than the necessary legal regulatory framework for capitalism and the basic infrastructure such as education and roads (although there are economic libertarians who believe all public goods should be privatized). Benefitting from a regulatory state, the operations of the market can lead to economic growth that benefits all, liberals believe. For realists, the anarchy of the international system drives the prevalence of politics over economics. In the rush to self-reliance, and facing ever diversifying security dilemmas, the state must ensure the economic underpinnings of military capacity. Not for realists is the idealized 'stand-offish' state of liberalism. For realists, economic developments are related to national power and interest. For radicals, the fundamental division seen by liberals between economics and politics is an illusion. Political institutions are understood as serving the interests of the dominant social classes that prevail at any one moment, not the national interest as posited by realists, or the private interest of citizens as liberals believe. Economic developments are not neutral, from this perspective, but reflect an ongoing struggle between classes, both domestically and transnationally. At the same time, different fractions (conceived by the economic sector and nationally) of the dominant class are recognized as being in contestation, so reference is also made to intra-class conflict in the radical perspective, say between finance capitalists and industrial capitalists, although of course they can pact.

The different perspectives outlined above are not simply neutral but represent different underlying political values about the nature of the good society. By extension, what is at stake in the debate about Asian economic growth and crisis is not just 'facts' – that is, what variables allowed economic growth to proceed at a rate higher than the rest of the world – but normative positions about how states should be structured, how civil society and business should interact with the state, and how countries should relate to the international economy.

Explaining the growth: liberal perspectives

Liberalism, in relation to economics, purports to treat the individual as the key unit of analysis. It claims that individuals, conceived of as maximizers of their own interests, know what they want best, and they will seek this in a freely interacting market place. The market, seemingly responsive to individual demands, best drives growth and is the most efficient allocator of resources. Liberals support the expansion of international trade, arguing that competition will lead to more efficient production. This would be an optimal outcome for all. Liberals perceive the growing international economic interdependencies that result from trade and investment as beneficial to all, or as positive sum. Benefits extend beyond economics. Because trade furthers economic growth, countries have an interest in pursuing international co-operation. The intensification of economic interdependency between economies ties states into co-operative and reciprocal relations, diminishing the prospect of a world of warring states.

In explaining the 'Asian miracle' liberals will point to the general structural factors sustaining Asian economic growth. The first of these is the existence of international trading and monetary regimes, known as the Bretton Woods system, established after the Second World War and composed of institutions such as the

World Bank, the International Monetary Fund, the General Agreement on Tariffs and Trade, and a system of relatively fixed exchange rates. These institutions, sustained by the mutual interdependence of different states and economies, provided the rules, procedures and norms for the conduct of trade and commerce. More specifically, in the early years of East Asia's rapid economic growth, there was a temptation to see the success of the tiger economies, and indeed of Japan, as reflective of a broad embrace of market economics. Some commentators spoke of 'market economy superstars', and as recently as 1998 Palma described Korea as an example of 'virtual free trade' (cited in Raffer and Singer 2001: 139). Liberals also speak of nations possessing a 'comparative advantage', meaning what a country is able to produce more efficiently than another country. Should countries seize their comparative advantage they can compete in the world market and earn foreign exchange with which to purchase goods from other countries and upgrade their own productive capacity. For liberals, the long history of international trade is a positive process entailing liberalization and the breaking down of national borders. The key actors in this are multinational corporations (MNCs), liberally oriented states and international governmental organizations that are charged with regulating the international economy. Liberals note that the East Asian economies were adept at promoting their comparative advantage (cheap labour and an educated workforce) in order to climb up the developmental ladder, at the same time as reducing tariffs and opening up to the world market. Having initially looked towards import-substitution strategies, the HPAEs all turned towards export-oriented industrialization, the first-tier NICs in the 1960s and the second-tier NICs in the 1980s.

As the 1980s progressed it became apparent that the 'market' could not totally account for the growth sustained by the HPAEs. An increasingly frustrated US, facing chronic balance of payments deficits and high levels of foreign debt, began to criticize the trade practices and state interventions in East Asia, especially Japan and South Korea, as market deforming. This led to the revisionist attack on Japan (see Chapter 4). However, liberals were capable of countenancing a role for the state in economic development. Indeed, throughout the 1990s there emerged a greater appreciation of the state. While liberals give priority to market freedom, the state is recognized as providing the regulatory framework necessary for the operation of a free market. It provides guarantees for property, it provides the policy framework for economic matters, and it enforces rules and laws and deals with market failures. It guarantees the predictability of contract which is necessary for sustained investment and growth. Liberals could see well enough that if markets were to function, institutions were required. This 'institutional political economy' became increasingly influential, and from the early 1990s onwards the World Bank and the International Monetary Fund began to call for 'good governance' (transparency, participation and efficiency) as part of the necessary institutional ingredients of sustainable economic growth in East Asia.

This shift from market fundamentalism to recognition of the role of institutions was reflected in the World Bank's attempt to explain the East Asian miracle in its 1993 report *The East Asian Miracle: Economic Growth and Public Policy* (World

Bank 1993, Rodan *et al*. 2001: 17–20). The report's appraisal of the role of the state in the HPAEs was ambiguous. It praised the market-facilitating behaviour of states, such as the provision of the regulatory framework for markets in commodities and labour, and sound macroeconomic management of the economy. However, it also warned against practices that varied from free-market ideas such as excessive subsidies to infant industries, excessive protection and strict management of resources by the state. The report argued that in the era of the global economy such interventions should be avoided (World Bank 1993), suggesting that countries should conform more to market-facilitating strategies. Eager to attribute East Asia's success to market-oriented economies, liberals tended to gloss over the role played by the state.

Explaining the growth: realist perspectives

In the economic arena, realist perspectives are often described as realist-mercantilist. This approach to international political economy focuses on the state and its role in advancing the interests of a national economy against other states. Seeing interaction in the international economy as zero-sum, realists recommend the pursuit of economic strategies that maximize national interests at the expense of rival states. For realists, the interdependency valued by liberals invites danger, particularly if there is asymmetrical interdependency on another state for key factors of production. The state should therefore attempt to establish and maintain strategic industries that provide the national economy with a degree of self-sufficiency, and to manage international economic relations in a manner that does not augment the power of rival states. As Gill and Law (1988: 28) explain, the concept of 'strategic industries' relates to

> the constellation of industries which can create the optimum conditions for a high degree of national autonomy and economic sovereignty.... This also entails the ability to exert power within the inter-state system.... Such strategic industries might therefore include arms and related industries, capital goods more generally, and sometimes agriculture.

More specifically related to East Asia, we have already noted the importance of 'developmental states'. A realist would argue that the East Asian states pursued a strategy of neo-mercantilism in a quest for security, national power and prestige. At a concrete level mercantilism describes a political economy of national growth based on limiting imports and encouraging exports, while maintaining a positive balance of payments. Japanese economic planners were greatly influenced by European mercantilist thought that had informed Bismarck's strategy of industrialization in late 19th-century Germany (Deans 1999: 78). Unlike the liberal approach, which posits mutual benefit from growth in trade, mercantilism entails opportunistic behaviour at the expense of rivals. This approach suggests that fundamentally, no matter how many international engagements are pursued, or international regimes and treaties entered into, the state stands perennially poised against other states; it remains concerned with relative gain over absolute gain (Gilpin 2001: 43). The developmental states of East Asia in this perspective may be seen as having taken advantage of the international trading regime, built largely by the US as a hegemon (ibid.: 94) to bolster their own national wealth, not that of the global community at large. Japan is often described as having a contemporary mercantilist orientation. Japan during its rise resisted import penetration by the major industrialized nations, securing for itself massive trade surpluses (Heginbotham and Samuels 1998). And in classic mercantilist fashion, it has limited foreign investment, despite liberalizing FDI regulations in the late 1970s. Speaking of the early 2000s, the Japan External Trade Organization (2002: 22) reports that, 'FDI inflow is equivalent to 1.2% of GDP, far less than the near 20% averaged in other major industrialized countries'. A decade later liberalization policies had produced some growth of inward FDI stock to 3.5 per cent of GDP but as Urata (2015) observes Japan remains significantly behind the global average of 34.1 per cent, as of 2013.

In summary, in the realist-mercantilist approach the state is a central actor. Further, there is an implicit assumption that this actor is unified and rational in pursuit of its mercantilist objectives defined as national interest. Clearly the stress on the centrality of the state is a far cry from the World Bank's notion of a market-enhancing regulatory role for the state.

Before moving to the third perspective it is worth noting that an attempt was made to synthesize liberal and realist approaches to explain the international economic order after the Second World War. Both realists and liberals observed that the Bretton Woods system, which provided the international context for export-led growth for East Asia, was secured by the continuing leadership and dominance of the US, which had an interest in maintaining and leading the system for its own economic benefit. This explanation of US leadership has become known as the 'hegemonic stability thesis', an approach that combines liberal and realist premises. It consists of a number of propositions. Given the premise of fundamental anarchy that realists invoke as an attribute of the international system, it follows that authority is required to bring some semblance of order to militate against the pull of anarchy. A dominant power is viewed as the only entity able to establish order and enforce relevant rules. By leading and sustaining the system of liberal trade and stable currency exchange rates, and by the provision of international security through military projection and threat, the US effectively functioned as a hegemonic power that stabilized the international system. As Gilpin noted, being a hegemon was not merely about providing so-called public goods (security, trade regime), there was a good deal of self-interest going on: 'The United States has assumed leadership responsibilities because it has been in its economic, political and even ideological interests to do so, or at least it has believed this to be the case' (Gilpin 1987: 88). Whilst realists would expect a hegemonic power's interests to prevail in any international order that it controls, liberals see the possibility of that system transforming into an order that benefits an increasingly interdependent world of states.

Explaining the growth: radical perspectives

There are competing radical interpretations of economic growth in East Asia. Here we will look briefly at dependency thought and Marxist thought. The dependency school of thought was concerned with developing a political economy focused on the power asymmetry between the developed and developing countries. The benign interdependency envisioned by liberals was seen as ideological obfuscation by dependency theorists. In short, dependency theorists posited that a fundamental condition of dependence characterized developing countries (the Global South) and tied them to the economic fortunes of the industrialized capitalist countries (the Global North). This relationship entailed the extraction of the South's surplus by the North and the reproduction of exploitative relations between the two. Furthermore, in some instances it was argued that the exploitation of the South by the North led to a condition of systematic underdevelopment (Frank 1967). This suggested that the nature of global trade functioned to actively construct underdevelopment in the Global South.

In the light of East Asian economic growth the merit of these ideas came into question. Observable growth suggested that the premise of dependence and underdevelopment was wrong, such that some speculated on the 'end of the third world' as a system of dependency and as a political project of subaltern solidarity (Harris 1986). However, those sympathetic to dependency currents of thought argue that East Asian growth occurred because the various CDSs acted in a manner that partially broke through power asymmetries, which is to say that growth was a symptom of political resistance by economic policy. Indeed their mercantilist strategies, which were implemented in order to catch up with the industrialized North, were said to have been inspired by Paul Presbisch, an economist who considerably influenced the dependency school (Raffer and Singer 2001: 141). Notwithstanding the relative success of the first tier of NIEs, there were criticisms that Southeast Asian growth was predominantly externally driven, and therefore dependent growth. Kunio Yoshihara (1988), writing in the late 1980s, argued that Southeast Asian capitalism was ersatz capitalism, by which he meant a form of capitalism that was an inferior imitation of developed industrial capitalism. Yoshihara recognized that the role of foreign capital in the ASEAN economies was declining and that some gains in economic development were evident (especially in the tertiary sector). However, the appellation 'ersatz' indicated a level of dependency on foreign capital in relation to large export-oriented industrial enterprises. The result of this dependence was the emergence of 'technologyless capitalism' and the rise of 'technologically dependent capitalists as comprador capitalists…[which has] allowed foreign capital to come in, in order to generate new exports' (Yoshihara 1988: 132). This kind of capitalism was also noted for its lack of a productive domestic and indigenous capitalist class that focused on long-term economic growth and productive investment. Instead the economic arena was said to be animated by all sorts of 'deviant' speculative capitalists focused on short-term gains who pursued market-distorting strategies to enhance their own wealth, including rent-seeking activities such as 'protection from foreign capital…concessions, licences, monopoly rights and government subsidies' (Yoshihara 1988: 3). Yoshihara's solution to these 'intractable' problems and the problem of dependency (1988: 118–20) was to preach a strategy of national economy development that weaned Southeast Asian nations off their need for foreign capital and for the state to take a greater role in research and development. Another feature of critical literature was to look behind the headlines of the Asian economic miracle and identify the environmental and social costs of unequal development (Bello and Rosenfeld 1992) and to seek alternatives. Dependency theory, in its various forms, is often attacked from those on the left who argue that it is too focused on the national issue of dependence, when the defining feature of political economy is not the struggle between nations but between classes in the international political economy (Rodan *et al.* 2001: 23–5). This brings us to Marxist political economy.

If individuals and states are the driving force of economics in the liberal and mercantilist perspective respectively, Marxist political economy focuses on the role of classes in the construction of world order. For Marxists the state system is dominated by capitalist interests, it is a system that expands the capitalist mode of production in the interests of capitalists. To understand this system, influential Marxist political economist Robert Cox (1981) calls for a critical theory that throws light on the way in which the existing structures of power, accumulation of capital and exploitation have emerged and how they are maintained through practices of hegemony. In line with its radical posture, Marxist political economy also attends to the question of which social forces might be in a position to transform existing world orders. Regarding East Asian economic growth, a Marxist perspective would first map out the general system into which East Asia was integrated, which was the world capitalist system, reconstructed after the Second World War and facilitated through the instruments of discipline created by the dominant powers such as the IMF and the World Bank. Yet integration into international capitalism was uneven, and was shaped by historical and political differences.

In order to place East Asian growth into a system level of analysis that relates to class and conflict, Marxists deploy the concept of hegemony. As described by Cox, hegemony:

> means dominance of a particular kind where the dominant state creates an order based ideologically on a broad measure of consent, functioning according to general principles that in fact ensure the continuing supremacy of the leading state or states and leading social classes but at the same time offer some measure or prospect of satisfaction to the less powerful.
>
> (Cox 1986: 7)

For Cox and others, at the end of the Second World War the United States emerged as the hegemonic power and established the *Pax Americana*, through which it regenerated the industrialized states of Europe and Japan, in order to construct an open world economy. Furthermore, it linked developing countries into this project.

These states were not, as a rule, compelled by means of force into a US-led system, but rather elites could see benefits for their own countries by submitting to a US-led order. These benefits included stability and relations with an international trading regime through which economic growth could be pursued. In this new world order, production was to be increasingly linked to the world economy. Cox (1986: 211) argues that to further this liberal order, elites in the hegemonic state had to forge alliances with other states and elites, drawing them into its hegemonic bind, in order to sustain a project of liberal trade and capitalist development. At the core of the world system, Western industrialized states were generally liberal in orientation. At the periphery of the system, in developing countries, the hegemonic power sustained authoritarian developmentalist regimes, even as they eschewed market rationality, in order to achieve the suppression of communism or anti-Western economic nationalism in the periphery and to keep the peripheral economies on the side of the 'free world' (Cox 1986: 231–44). The United States poured aid for economic development into developmentalist regimes, especially Taiwan and South Korea. Such inputs, which were dispersed throughout East and Southeast Asia, assisted in the provision of the necessary capital injection that eventually transformed the region (So and Chiu 1995).

In this approach the intimate connection between economics and politics is paramount: the hegemonic project of the United States to isolate, and indeed aggressively push back, the communist sphere led to a strategy that enhanced the prospects for economic growth. Some scholars highlight how the wars in Korea and Vietnam led to injections of capital into East Asia that provided fuel to the engine of growth (see the discussion in Bello 2009: 183–4).

We have reviewed three competing interpretations of East Asian economic growth. All agree that the existence of an international trading regime was fundamental to Asia's growth and all, significantly, point to the importance of a hegemonic power in at least establishing a world order to which capitalist East Asia, as an economic entity, could direct its productive activities.

The unmaking of the miracle

The Asian Economic Crisis is commonly understood as beginning in 1997 when currency speculators launched an attack on the Thai baht. However, it is probably useful to recognize that before the dramatic events that unfolded in 1997, the Asian economic miracle was under strain in the core economy of Japan.

In 1985, in an agreement known as the Plaza Accord, the central banks of the major industrialized economies moved to depreciate the dollar. This was related to the US's ongoing quest to reassert its economic position that had been eroded by the rise of Japan since the 1970s, whose currency it viewed to be deliberately undervalued. In Japan, the Plaza Accord led to an appreciation of the yen, and resulted in a mild recession. In response the government promoted economic stimulus measures such as loosening monetary policy, which led to a greater supply of credit. In effect the government partially liberalized capital markets, and began to undo the close relationship between banks and industry that had characterized the economy. Furthermore, the Bank of Japan embarked on an expansionary programme to return the economy to growth. With excessive credit in the system, much was lent to various projects, many in real estate, leading to a massive rise in land prices and a property boom. At the height of the boom, for instance, it was said, perhaps with some exaggeration, that the Imperial Palace Grounds alone were of greater market value than Canada (Murphy 2000: 37). On average, commercial properties quadrupled in value between 1985 and 1991, while residential and industrial properties 'were a comparatively modest 250% above their earlier value' (Alexander 1997: 7). Effectively Japan had become a bubble economy in which price rises in assets (such as land and stocks) were unrelated to economic fundamentals (incomes, GDP, productivity), but based on the expectation of rising prices driven by demand.

Several factors led to the bursting of the bubble. The Basel Accord of 1988, which stipulated certain conditions relating to minimal capital requirements for banks, eventually forced Japanese banks to impose stringent criteria on loans, leading to a drying up of credit. The government itself imposed new taxes on retail sales, land and capital gains, in order to slow the bubble (Reynolds 2002). These factors led to a downturn in the economy. Many banks had loaned money based on land as collateral. That land was heavily overpriced, and throughout the 1990s experienced successive annual declines in value. This left banks saddled with non-performing loans running into trillions of dollars. Since the 1990s the country's growth rate has barely jumped above 1 per cent. Although a major creditor to the US, the country is nonetheless in the grip of economic stagnation that throws a shadow across the region. In the West, Japan's economic problems have led to attacks on its unique political economy and calls for profound reform.

If the Plaza Accord of 1985 may be said to have triggered a series of events leading to the bubble and its bursting in Japan, in some senses the same may be said for Southeast Asia. As a result of the revaluation of the yen in the years after the Plaza Accord, the region experienced rising foreign direct investment from Japan. By the late 1980s Japanese FDI began to tail off, but credit was now also readily available from European and United States sources eager to tap into the region's boom and extract quick profits.

The funds that entered Asia, fuelling the bubble, were made possible by significant changes in the world economy. Under the Bretton Woods system it was assumed that capital flows between nations would largely relate to trade matters and investment, and that stable exchange rates would underpin this: capital would be productively invested in order to produce goods or services for the market, or would be transferred in order to pay for imports. It was also expected that capital flows would take the form of loans for productive investment. With the partial collapse of the system in 1971, when the US ended its fixed exchange rate, this expectation proved increasingly irrelevant. Encouraged by new communications technologies, international capital has flowed along largely divergent paths, often disconnected from what actually gets traded or produced in the economy. From the 1960s international finance has largely become more and more 'decoupled' from production and has taken on a life of its own. Vast flows of money are sent in search of profits though short-term portfolio investments, currency speculation, high-risk loans and so on. The scale of financial movement compared to trade is obvious if one considers that in 1990 the value of world trade was estimated at US$ 5.2 trillion while daily foreign exchange transactions stood at US$ 1 trillion (Maswood 2000: 86). This increase in capital mobility was felt in developing countries. Before the end of the 1960s, government loans to developing countries accounted for the bulk of foreign finance. Steadily, the proportion of private capital flowing to developing countries mounted, so that between 1996 and 1997 some US$ 300 billion was invested by private investors; this compared with the US$ 300 billion provided by the World Bank over its 50 years of operation (Winters 1999: 36).

The increasingly deregulated flow of capital placed significant pressure on states. In the Western capitalist countries, the 1980s had been marked by increasing deregulation of all economic sectors, privatization and reduced taxation, as different states competed with each other in order to attract capital. In the developing world, various forms of state intervention related to late industrialization strategies, such as high tariffs, industrial policies, limits to foreign ownership and capital controls, had been retained. Increasingly, economic liberals, both domestically and internationally, were seeking the end of these obstacles to foreign entry. According to Bello, from the early 1990s onwards a number of states, especially South Korea, Thailand and Indonesia, responded in various ways to the demands for liberalization, and devised strategies to attract the much desired foreign capital. This included:

- Financial liberalization: this might involve removal of restrictions on foreign exchange or other capital controls that limit the inflow and outflow of foreign capital; allowing foreign banks and other financial institutions greater entry into domestic markets; opening the stock exchange to foreign portfolio investors;
- The maintenance of high interest rates relative to interest rates in other countries in order to attract foreign capital;
- Providing exchange rate stability, by pegging the currency, in order to provide peace of mind to investors who converted their money into local currency and wanted a guarantee that the local currency would not suddenly devalue.

(Bello 1998: 11)

Once provided with these basic conditions, capital quickly flowed into the countries, fuelling speculation in property and stock markets in the region. Then the crash happened.

In response to fears that the region's growth was not only unsustainable, but that the economies would collapse, there was a massive outward flow of capital, with tens of billions of dollars departing in 1997 (Winters 1999: 38). The impact of capital withdrawal and the drying up of credit for investment was massive. For instance, in 1998 Indonesia, Korea, Malaysia and Thailand experienced a 13.0 per cent, 6.7 per cent, 7.4 per cent and 10.2 per cent decline in real GDP respectively. Evidence of the crisis is nowhere more obvious than in reference to imports, which declined exponentially: Indonesia (36.3 per cent), Korea (38.0 per cent), Malaysia (25.0 per cent) and Thailand (40.4 per cent) (Greene 2002: 4–7).

Faced with the credit tap being turned off, massive depreciation of currencies, contracting markets, and with the bailiff at the door, the afflicted countries turned to the International Monetary Fund in order to seek temporary funds to keep the economies afloat. The IMF injected over US$ 120 billion into Indonesia, South Korea and Thailand. However, in agreeing to render assistance, the IMF imposed a series of conditions on loans, which recipient countries were required to follow. Among these measures were:

- temporary budgetary cuts;
- structural reforms to remove features of the economy that had become impediments to growth (such as monopolies, trade barriers and non-transparent corporate practices) and to improve the efficiency of financial intermediation and the future soundness of financial systems;
- the closure of unviable financial institutions, with the associated write-down of shareholders' capital;
- increased potential for foreign participation in domestic financial systems.

(IMF 1999)

Explaining the crisis

The most pervasive explanation of the Asian Economic Crisis has been developed from a broadly liberal perspective that views the demise of the Asian economies as indicative of the crisis of the development state and, more colloquially, the consequences of 'crony capitalism', a catch-all term that captures the prevalence of corruption and collusion between political, business and bureaucratic elites. Having once hailed the region's HPAEs as exemplars of growth, liberals now turned to attacking the governance structures in each country as either corrupt and/or incapable of proper market regulation.

The leading liberal critique came from the IMF, which argued that:

> the crisis stemmed from weaknesses in financial systems and, to a lesser extent, governance.... Although private sector expenditure and financing decisions led to the crisis, it was made worse by governance issues, notably government involvement in the private sector and lack of transparency in corporate and fiscal accounting and the provision of financial and economic data.
>
> (IMF 1999)

Liberals argued that with high levels of political intervention and corruption in the Asian economies, the market effectively malfunctioned. Robison *et al.* (2002: 18) explain the liberal position succinctly: 'Market discipline...was simply not strong enough in these economies, and the task of recovery had to centre on establishing this discipline'.

From a realist or state-centred perspective, the Asian Economic Crisis proves one of the basic points about the centrality of politics over economics, of the state over markets and the importance of power capability in the international system (see Acharya 1999). Against the idea that globalization is an ineluctable force, realists will likely point to its limits, and the centrality of home-based MNCs and the role of the state in shaping economic institutions both at home and abroad (Waltz 1999). Given the premise of realism, that states pursue their interests defined as power, in the unipolarity then prevailing, the US as the predominant state could be expected to advance its own interests in the crisis. Thus a realist perspective focuses on how the crisis was used to advance US interests in the region, and in particular to push forward its opening of trade and capital markets in the region. The US also opposed Japan's proposed Asian Monetary Fund to ensure its pre-eminence against a potential regional competitor. For decades the United States attempted to open up the region to US corporations. APEC, structural adjustment programmes, the protection of intellectual property and various GATT discussions all indicate the extent of US designs on opening the region. The crisis allowed Western states, led by the US, to dismantle key aspects of mercantilist strategies or political–business relations that advocated nationalist policies. It was just one more episode in the battle of relative benefit. Realists find further vindication of their perspective in the fact that the regional institutions such as ASEAN did little to mitigate the crisis – suggesting that their significance had been overstated by liberal institutionalists.

Neo-dependency observers see the crisis and the intervention of the international financial institutions as evidence of further attempts to downgrade the gains made by the NIEs, leading to new ties of dependency as well as further integration into a Northern-dominated economy. The crisis was viewed as limiting the capacity of Southeast Asian countries to resist fast-track liberalization sought by IFIs and the US (Bello 1998: 12). The crisis is also said to vindicate the dependency thesis, that the South is dependent on Western capital and agencies in the determination of its economic future. The Asian Miracle, especially in Southeast Asia, is retrospectively described as Western capital-driven, having led the region into a debt crisis and further delimiting its capacity to resist Northern penetration. If the IMF intervention is to be understood as anything it is simply a battering ram for advanced capitalist interests in the region. The words of Larry Summers, US Treasury Chair, are often cited as evidence of this. Summers, speaking in 1994 on the structural adjustment programmes in Argentina, crowed about the results:

> Today, fully 50 per cent of the banking sector, 70 per cent of private banks, in Argentina are foreign controlled, up from 30 per cent in 1994. The result is a deeper, more efficient financial market, and external investors with a greater stake in staying put.
>
> (cited in Bello 1999)

From the dependency perspective, there is no reason not to think that the US hopes to make the same gains in Asia through the restructuring forced on the economies as part of their IMF loans.

If the dependency thesis sees the *Pax Americana* alive and well in the events of the Asian economic crisis, the more classically oriented Marxist account suggests that the crisis reflects a new era of capitalism in which transnational classes, through international agencies and through the alliances of various state institutions, work together in order to advance the interests of capitalism in general. According to this perspective, from the 1970s onwards the increasing internationalization of production by MNCs and the creation of global financial markets set the scene for a fundamental shift in the nature of national capitalisms, as states became hostage to market discipline and the structural power of capital, a form of new constitutionalism emerged with new rules and regulations to enforce neoliberal dynamics (Gill 2000). Especially in the 1980s states were required to pursue policies that made them attractive sites for investors, thus creating policy convergence across much of the Western world. The 1990s may be read as the attempt to extend this process to developing countries. Robert Cox (1997: 60) has argued that increasingly there is a loosely ordered global governance centred on what he calls a 'nebuleuse' or 'a loose elite network of influentials and agencies, sharing a common set of ideas that collectively perform the governance function'. Constituting the nebuleuse are organizations such as the World Bank, the OECD, the IMF and the World Economic Forum. These organizations function to bring together global elites who hammer out a consensus on the requirements for a flourishing and viable capitalism. By this process and through these institutions, a common economic ideology emerges and is dispersed through intergovernmental agencies, texts and networks. This leads to national policy that is largely in conformity with the hegemonic ideology of economic liberalism. Related to the Asian Economic Crisis, the IMF's intervention is taken as an example of the advance of 'disciplinary neoliberalism' at the expense of the poor. According to Stephen Gill, the neoliberal perspective as it manifests itself in various international financial institutions (IFIs) privileges 'investors', who possess a structural power that compels states to act in certain ways. States are ever cautious to please investors in order to attract capital; the result is a mindset that believes:

> economic growth depends on the need to maintain investor confidence and thus governments are driven to sustain their credibility in the eyes of investors by attempting to provide an appropriate business environment. This is a form of the structural power of capital.
>
> (Gill 2000: 4)

The crisis is read by radicals as having furthered the cause of market opening in the interests of capital, and as having fundamentally altered the configuration of power in the region. In imposing conditions on IFI loans, largely at the behest of the United States, there was significant progress in bringing the states in the region into line with the dominant neoliberal orthodoxy.

Interestingly, in a multi-country study of the impact of the crisis Robertson (2008) reports a disjuncture between the aims of the regulatory arms of Western states (and their international partners in the international financial institutions) and the activities and objectives of Western firms. The former pursue long-term strategies of economic reform while the latter broadly seek short-term investment strategies to maximize profit. This rather than conformity to IFI reforms is what dictates their investment activities (ibid.: 12). If foreign actors are often uncoordinated and seeking different objectives in moments of crisis and are bereft of common intent, does that mean that the radical critique is misguided? How to explain the disjuncture between state and capitalist actors? Radicals would answer that the state and its agencies do not pursue the needs of particular firms but rather act as a co-ordinating agency seeking to provide the best framework for capital as a whole. This disjuncture then can be read as confirming broadly Marxist insights about the role of the state as the 'collective capital' – able to stand above the interests of particular interests and plan long-term futures.

The crisis in perspective: divergence, convergence and novelty

A decade after the crisis, the World Bank (2007: 3) had this to say about East Asia:

> the region is far wealthier, has fewer poor people and a larger global role than ever before. Led by continued strong growth in China, Emerging East Asia now has an aggregate output of over $5 trillion, double the dollar value just before the crisis. In per-capita terms real incomes are some 75 percent higher.

The extent to which this growth could be accounted for by strict adherence to the aims of the IFIs is debatable. It is true that debt restructuring was shouldered by state agencies through national asset management (Cochrane and Larmer 2003: 28), ensuring that creditors were compensated, creating confidence among future investors. Gains were made for international capital: an important feature of the crisis was the growing levels of foreign ownership of banking and other sectors of the economy. After the crisis, the IMF negotiated lifting the ceiling on foreign ownership in a number of sectors, leading to higher levels of foreign ownership in Asian economies (see Hewison 2001). In South Korea IMF-backed legislation imposed during the crisis opened the economy fully to direct investment and removed restrictions on foreign ownership of land. Some would argue that the market rather than state rationale now drives economic growth and strategy (Bello 2009: 197–8).

But at the same time, when faced with the crisis imperative to reform, countries did so in a manner intended to protect vested interests, respond to domestic pressure and simultaneously address external demands. In South Korea, for example, while the government pressed ahead with massive restructuring in the banking sector and succeeded in lifting foreign ownership provisions, it faced a nationalist push back that limited its ability to restructure the *Chaebol* (see Ha and

Lee 2007: 913–14). South Korea is perhaps illustrative of a broader pattern, where changes were contested and their impact a matter of degree. Adaption does not indicate the death of the development state. Indeed, a study of business–state relations during the painful process of economic liberalization after the crisis demonstrates the continuing presence of the developmentalist ethos, even if in 'degraded' form (Hundt 2014). Despite inroads into the Asian economies there are limits to the neoliberal agenda. In a decadal retrospective on the crisis that remains relevant today, Donald Hellmann (2007: 836) argued that the 'basic market-supporting institutional reforms' desired by the IMF 'remain at best long term goals for all the nations touched by the crisis'.

Since the crisis, scholarly literature has focused on the way in which Asian states have adapted to the pressure of neoliberalism and attempted to protect themselves. Some have noted the persistence of political–business networks that surround the state and make particularistic claims on it (Thirkell-White 2008). These have earned the pejorative label 'crony capitalism'. Joseph Wong (2004), writing on East Asia in the aftermath of the crisis, suggested that while pressure to conform to market principles was strong, states continued to selectively shape patterns of regime–capital relations. He thus spoke of an 'adaptive development state' to indicate that the basic idea of strategic state intervention into the market to push forward economic transformation, industrialization and growth remained in place. Meredith Jung-En Woo (2009) was even more strident, suggesting that the institutional reform agendas of the IFIs were poor attempts to impose ideal-type institutional structures of the regulatory state onto Asian political economy. Such projects were bound to fail because they assumed that there is only one path to capitalist development. Against this Woo persuasively demonstrated the persistence of 'developmentalism', a term she described as 'a shorthand for the seamless web of political, bureaucratic, and moneyed influences that structures economic life in capitalist Northeast Asia' (Woo 2009: 14). The recognition of developmentalism remains important for it suggests that underneath specific state structures, even those that may formally be regulatory, there are broader cultural ideas about state and market relations based on a degree of statism and 'civil service primacy', which will structure capitalist dynamics into the future. Recent studies confirm this relevance, for example showing how developmental approaches are informing various states' activities, including: Japan's export of major infrastructure systems (Yoshimatsu 2017); the structuring of Chinese labour markets (Gore 2014); and undervaluation of exchange rates (Steinberg 2016).

Finally, what to make of China's emergence, which accelerated after the Asian Economic Crisis, and which now is home to the world's second largest economy? China's rise has given succour to developmentalists, those who argue for the beneficial economic consequences of plan-rational capitalism. It is apparent that since the late 1970s the effort to initiate a graduated capitalist revolution, under the auspices of the Chinese Communist Party, has gone from strength to strength. Ordered and relatively conscious policy measures, including opening to FDI, budgetary and tax reforms, corporatization of state enterprises, and constitutional recognition of private ownership and private property have unlocked dynamic capitalist growth in the country (see Wu 2009). Yet if economically China is hurtling towards capitalist economic organization, it will undoubtedly fail to mirror idealized Anglo-American models of market rationality. Moreover, its political structures will reflect the ethos of authoritarian developmentalism rather than the more open developmentalism of Japan, unless a revolutionary transformation occurs. China's rise then as a variant of a developmental capitalist state – with its own unique 'socialist' features – is perhaps the final nail in the coffin of the convergence thesis.

Among the many labels that now attach to the Chinese state is 'socialist developmental state', reflecting the paramount position of the Communist Party which mandates that all major market economic reforms must be channelled through the party and the bureaucracy. Any, yet even a modest, degree of curiosity will raise questions about what the label means. For example, Wing-Chung Ho (2013: 827) reports that by some estimates the children of ranking communist cadre make up the bulk of the country's rich, creating a blurred line between bureaucracy and firm. This has created a class of 'bureaucratic capitalists', whereas the developmental state model assumes functional division.

Others, echoing dependency theorists, doubt the longer-term viability of the Chinese model of economic development. Downes (2009) portrays China, despite having established a niche position within capitalist global production, as having exposed itself to dependency on Western and Japanese capital and technology, making it a semi-peripheral economy (some 50 per cent of its exports being connected to firms with FDI). Others fear China's vulnerability to external shock, suggesting that China's growth is a rollercoaster of mixed fortunes rather than a well thought out strategy. Yuqing Xing and Manisha Pradhananga (2013) note that during the Global Financial Crisis of 2008–09 external demand (net exports and FDI) dramatically declined as a proportion of China's GDP (from 40 to 11 per cent). Also, estimating that at least half of China's GDP growth was dependent on external demand, they viewed the country as vulnerable to external shocks. External dependency also renders vulnerable the capacity of the state to address market inequalities and to lift living standards.

Transitions?

Given the nature of the transitional period of the late 2010s, this chapter can only end on a speculative note, one that steps back from the hyperbole of an imminent collapse of the liberal economic order, and which appraises China from a different perspective. Relevant to the focus of this chapter is the question of how China's state form might impact on the future of the global economy? In response, one productive approach is to follow the provocative arguments of a China scholar, Johan Lagerkvist (2015), who notes that despite the expectations of many scholars China has not moved to challenge the liberal economic order in any substantive manner. Rather it has moved to support it both domestically and internationally. Greatly benefitting from trade and FDI, and the export of its own capital, China in its 16 years of membership of the WTO would seem to have played the vaunted role of responsible stakeholder. Indeed, President Xi's speech at the 2017 World Economic Forum praised globalization as a force for good, and warned of protectionist approaches to economic woes: 'Any attempt to cut off the flow of capital, goods, and people between economies and channel the waters in the ocean back into isolated lakes and creeks is simply not possible' (*Guardian* 17 January 2017). Domestically, the Chinese Party-State is avowedly Maoist-Marxist but explains its economic liberalization and market integration as a necessary strategy during the first stages of socialism so as to drive forward 'productive forces'. In this thinking, it is part of a state plan that China is host to the second largest number (over 300) of the 2,000 billionaires spread across the globe (*Forbes* 20 March 2017).

When Deng Xiaoping, China's 'paramount leader' from 1978 to 1992, advised 'let some people get rich first' he was not speaking as an acolyte of the poet of capitalist selfishness, Ayn Rand, but cajoling the unleashing of productive forces through pragmatic experimentation in the ideological hope that it would take China to the next stage of economic development. Such imaginings remain present. In 2014, the Chinese Communist Party Central Committee explicitly decided to centre 'on the decisive role of the market in allocating resources'. Its rationale is worth reproducing:

> we must bear in mind the fact that China is still in the primary stage of socialism and will remain so for a long time to come. We should adhere to the major strategic judgment that development is still the key to solving all problems in China, take economic construction as our central task...balance the relations of production with the productive forces as well as the superstructure with the economic base, and promote sound, sustainable economic and social development.... The underlying issue is how to strike a balance between the role of the government and that of the market, and let the market play the decisive role in allocating resources and let the government play its functions better. It is a general rule of the market economy that the market decides the allocation of resources. We have to follow this rule when we improve the socialist market economy....
>
> (Central Committee of the Communist Party of China 2014)

Indeed the Communist Party of China declares that the role of the government is to 'maintain market order' and to 'intervene in situations where market failure occurs' (ibid.). Yet this 'market orthodoxy' is not exactly what it seems. The argument is not that the market is the best way to allocate resources for individual wellbeing, as liberals would hold, but rather that a greater national purpose of moving towards communism will be achieved by pragmatically embracing this historical stage. The role of the party-state is to maintain social order and to mitigate against market failure in pursuit of that purpose. The party-state will serve development and will employ market rationality so long as it serves that higher purpose. In this worldview, the socialist developmental and the market rationales will be constantly recalibrated to suit circumstances.

Perplexing as such ideological gymnastics may be, one line may easily be discerned: in the current conjuncture developmental rationalities steer market rationality, and it is an approach that would seem to have served China's economic growth well. This has implications for the liberal trading order, from which China has benefitted. Scholars argue that China has a stake in that order. Rather than challenge, it is more likely to adapt to it and reform from within as a rule-maker. Of course it does not do so as a fully liberal regulatory state in relation to its national economy and it is expected to retain elements of developmental interventionism as it sees fit to mitigate market failures (which may be as broadly defined as politically necessary in an authoritarian state). Here a historical pattern may now be evident. Just as the US liberal hegemony was secured by integration of plan-rational economies into the Western orbit after the Second World War, so now, after the waning hopes of post-Cold War convergence and the damage done by the GFC, that liberal order may be sustained by new modes of integration with emerging forms of plan-rational economies.

China's rise and its strident support for globalization and open trade occurs as the West is experiencing new forms of economic nationalism and growing calls for economic protectionism and the implementation of more strategic economic policies. In his campaign for the presidency of the United States of America Donald Trump singled out China as thieving American jobs and labelled it a currency manipulator (the latter he later retracted). Empirically, there was a political truth to the claim that cheaper Chinese imports were leading to a decline in American manufacturing jobs, with some estimates that 2 million had been lost between 1991 and 2011 (Acemoglu *et al.* 2016). But trade policy was premised on American comparative advantage and the promise of jobs growth in services and technology that would absorb and even exceed such losses. But that was an economist's view. It left a large pool of under- or unemployed unskilled and semi-skilled labour that was not readily reskilled for new positions, leading to strong opposition to the dominant free trade idiom of US economists and politicians – the 'globalists', as the nationalist movement that supported Trump's campaign called liberal elites.

In 2017, the Trump administration turned to a more nationalist, protectionist rhetoric and began to identify countries that it considered to have potentially unfair trading or currency practices, including China, Japan, Malaysia, Thailand, Vietnam and South Korea. These countries enjoyed a trade surplus with the US. Most dramatically, the administration issued an executive order withdrawing from the Trans-Pacific Partnership Agreement, a painstakingly secretly crafted comprehensive free trade agreement between 12 partners that account for 40 per cent of the world's economy and which would have further intensified market liberalization of their respective economies. Trump was signalling the end to free trade orthodoxy and the embrace of a more strategic-based economic policy that may come to be a more coherent form of mercantilism. With nearly ten years of liberal trade and financial policy having failed to revive an indebted American economy, Trump's rise may indicate a broader historic shift in ideological outlook. Although viewed as remarkable and dangerous, Trump's attacks on foreign economies echoed a longstanding concern that while the US was providing the public good of a security guarantee to international order with its global empire of bases, Asian and European states were winning the peace dividend by enjoying persistent trade surpluses with the US, resulting in American decline.

Ironically, one outcome of these stresses may well be a more open embrace of developmentalism in the homelands of the free market. This is not as absurd as it sounds. As the US responds to its declining position, eminent political economists have begun to note aspects of developmental state behaviour there too. Fred Block (2008) has described a 'hidden developmental state' that supports start-ups in emerging technologies. Robert Wade (2014) concurs, arguing that the ideological dominance of economic liberalism means that the long history of developmental interventions by the US state are disguised. Both favour a more interventionist state and the shifting of the terms of debate away from free-market liberalism.

By way of conclusion, it is surely a sign of a changed historical conjuncture, when Lawrence Summers, who so eagerly sought to dismantle Asian forms of capitalism in the late 1990s (see above) should argue that neither job losses to or currency manipulation by the Chinese are the real causes of America's economic malaise. Pointedly, he advised that the US government should respond more assertively, but co-operatively, to China's rhetorical commitment to economic globalization and its significant projection of soft power. For Summers what is necessary is co-operation not confrontation and expansion not retirement of US soft power in the liberal order. And almost echoing the idea of a G2, he calls for a China–US economic dialogue on global co-operation and the two powers' respective roles: 'this move will require the United States to focus less on specific near-term business interests and more on what historians will remember a century from now' (Summers 2017). Although it wasn't said, Summers, like many liberals, wanted the US to maintain its hegemonic leadership by strategically relating to China. A new era of political economy has emerged.

References

Acemoglu, D., D. Autor, D. Dorn, G. Hanson and B. Price (2016) 'Import competition and the great US employment sag of the 2000s', *Journal of Labor Economics*, 34 (S1) (Part 2, January 2016): S141–S198.

Acharya, A. (1999) 'Realism, institutionalism, and the Asian Economic Crisis', *Contemporary Southeast Asia*, 21: 1–17.

Alexander, A. (1997) 'Asset prices in Japan: the bubble and its breaking', *Japan Economic Institute Report*, 36, September.

Backman, M. (1999) *Asian Eclipse: Exposing the Dark Side of Business in Asia*, Singapore: J. Wiley & Sons.

Bark, T. (2000) 'Trade patterns of East Asia: before and after the currency crisis', *Journal of International and Area Studies*, 7: 1–14.

Bello, W. (1998) 'The end of the miracle: speculation, foreign capital domination and the collapse of the Southeast Asian economies', *Multinational Monitor*, 19 (1 & 2).

Bello, W. (1999) 'Deconstructing Harry: what the new man at Treasury has in store for Asia', *The Nation* (Bangkok), 28 July, www.tni.org/archives/bello/larry.htm.

Bello, W. (2009) 'States and markets, markets versus states' in M. Blyth (ed.), *Routledge Handbook of International Political Economy*, London: Routledge.

Bello, W. and S. Rosenfeld (1992) *Dragons in Distress: Asia's Miracle Economies in Crisis*, San Francisco: Food First.

Block, F. (2008) 'Swimming against the current: the rise of a hidden developmental state in the United States', *Politics and Society*, 36 (2): 169–206.

Camilleri, J. A. (2000) *States, Markets and Civil Society in Asia-Pacific*, Cheltenham: Edward Elgar.

Carney, R. (2016) 'Varieties of hierarchical capitalism: family and state market economies in East Asia', *The Pacific Review*, 29 (2): 137–63.

Central Committee of the Communist Party of China (2014) 'Decision of the Central Committee of the Communist Party of China on Some Major Issues Concerning Comprehensively Deepening the Reform', www.china.org.cn/china/third_plenary_session/2014-01/16/content_31212602.htm.

Chowdhury, A. and I. Islam (1993) *The Newly Industrialising Economies of East Asia*, London: Routledge.

Cochrane, J. and B. Larmer (2003) 'The cronies return', *Newsweek*, February, 28.

Cox, R. W. (1981) 'Social forces, states and world orders: beyond international relations theory', *Millennium: Journal of International Studies*, 10: 126–55.

Cox, R. W. (1986) *Production, Power, and World Order*, Vol. 1, New York: Columbia University Press.

Cox, R. W. (1997) 'Democracy in hard times' in A. McGrew (ed.), *The Transformation of Democracy*, Cambridge: Polity Press.

Deans, P. (1999) 'The capitalist developmental state in East Asia' in R. Palan and J. Abbott, with P. Deans (eds), *State Strategies in the Global Political Economy*, rev. edn, London: Pinter.

Downes, G. (2009) 'China and India: the new powerhouses of the semiperiphery?' in O. Worth and P. Moore (eds), *Globalization and the 'New' Semi-Peripheries*, Basingstoke: Palgrave Macmillan.

Evans, P. (1995) *Embedded Autonomy: States and Industrial Transformation*, Princeton, NJ: Princeton University Press.

Frank, A. G. (1967) *Capitalism and Underdevelopment in Latin America: Historical Studies of Chile and Brazil*, New York: Monthly Review Press.

Garran, R. (1998) *Tigers Tamed: The End of the Asian Miracle*, St Leonards: Allen & Unwin.

Gill, S. (2000) 'The constitution of global capitalism', paper presented at International Studies Association Annual Convention, Los Angeles.

Gill, S. and D. Law (1988) *The Global Political Economy: Perspectives, Problems, and Policies*, Baltimore, MD: Johns Hopkins University Press.

Gilpin, R. (1987) *The Political Economy of International Relations*, Princeton, NJ: Princeton University Press.

Gilpin, R. (2001) *Global Political Economy: Understanding the International Economic Order*, Princeton, NJ: Princeton University Press.

Gore, L. (2014) 'Labour management as development of the integrated developmental state in China', *New Political Economy*, 19 (2): 302–27.

Greene, J. E. (2002) 'The output decline in Asian crisis countries: investment aspects', IMF Working Paper No. 02/25.

Ha, Y. and W. Lee (2007) 'The politics of economic reform in South Korea: crony capitalism after ten years', *Asian Survey*, 47 (6): 894–914.

Harris, N. (1986) *The End of the Third World*, London: Tauris.
Heginbotham, E. and R. J. Samuels (1998) 'Mercantile realism and Japanese foreign policy', *International Security*, 22: 171–203.
Hellmann, D. (2007) 'A decade after the Asian Financial Crisis: regionalism and international architecture in a globalized world', *Asian Survey*, 47 (6): 834–49.
Hewison, K. (2001) 'Pathways to recovery: bankers, business and nationalism in Thailand', Working Paper No. 1, Hong Kong: Southeast Asian Research Centre, City University.
Ho, W. (2013) 'The new "comprador class": the re-emergence of bureaucratic capitalists in post-Deng China', *Journal of Contemporary China*, 22 (83): 812–27.
Hundt, D. (2014) 'Economic crisis in Korea and the degraded developmental state', *Australian Journal of International Affairs*, 68 (5): 499–514.
International Monetary Fund (IMF) (1999) 'The IMF's response to the Asian crisis: a factsheet', www.imf.org/external/np/exr/facts/asia.htm.
Japan External Trade Organization (2002) *White Paper on International Trade and Investment*, Summary, www.jetro.go.jp/it/e/pub/whitepaper/2002.pdf.
Johnson, C. (1985) 'Political institutions and economic performance: the government–business relationship in Japan, South Korea and Taiwan' in R. Scalapino, S. Sato and J. Wanandi (eds), *Asian Economic Development: Present and Future*, Berkeley, CA: Institute of East Asian Studies, University of California.
Johnson, C. (1999) 'The development state: odyssey of a concept' in M. Woo-Cumings (ed.), *The Development State*, Ithaca, NY: Cornell University Press.
Kim, H. (1999) 'Fragility or continuity? Economic governance of East Asian capitalism' in R. Robison, K. Jayasuriya, M. Beeson and R. H. Kim (eds), *Politics and Markets in the Wake of the Asian Crisis*, London: Routledge.
Lagerkvist, J. (2015) 'The ordoliberal turn? Getting China and global economic governance right', *Global Affairs*, 1 (4–5): 411–19.
MacIntyre, A. (1994) 'Business, government and development; Northeast and Southeast Asian comparisons' in A. MacIntyre (ed.), *Business and Government in Industrializing Asia*, St Leonards: Allen & Unwin.
Maswood, J. (2000) *International Political Economy and Globalization*, Singapore: World Scientific.
Murphy, R. T. (2000) 'Japan's economic crisis', *New Left Review (New Series)*, 1: 25–53.
Pempel, T. J. (1999) 'The developmental regime in a changing world economy' in M. Woo-Cumings (ed.), *The Development State*, Ithaca, NY: Cornell University Press.
Pempel, T. J. and K. Tsunekawa (eds) (2015) *Two Crises, Different Outcomes: East Asia and Global Finance*, Ithaca, NY: Cornell University Press.
Raffer, K. and H. W. Singer (2001) *The Economic North–South Divide: Six Decades of Unequal Development*, Cheltenham: Edward Elgar.
Reynolds, A. (2002) 'Economic distinction', *The Washington Times*, 13 October.
Robertson, J. (2008) 'Introduction: key theoretical divides and directions' in J. Robertson (ed.), *Power and Politics after Financial Crises*, Basingstoke: Palgrave.
Robison, R., G. Rodan and K. Hewison (2002) 'Transplanting the regulatory state: a pathology of rejection', Working Paper Series No. 33, September, Hong Kong: Southeast Asian Research Centre, City University.
Rodan, G., K. Hewison and R. Robison (2001) *The Political Economy of South-East Asia*, 2nd edn, Melbourne: Oxford University Press.
Rowen, H. S. (ed.) (1998) *Behind East Asian Growth: The Political and Social Foundations of Prosperity*, London: Routledge.

So, A. Y. and S. W. K. Chiu (1995) *East Asia and the World Economy*, Thousand Oaks, CA: Sage.

Steinberg, D. A. (2016) 'Developmental states and undervalued exchange rates in the developing world', *Review of International Political Economy*, 23 (3): 418–49.

Summers, L. (2017) 'The most important economic challenge that China poses', *Washington Post*, 9 April.

Thirkell-White, B. (2008) 'Indonesia and Malaysia: the persistence of a domestic politico-business class' in J. Robertson (ed.), *Power and Politics after Financial Crises*, Basingstoke: Palgrave.

Urata, S. (2015) 'Revitalising sluggish FDI in Japan', *East Asia Forum*, 23 February, www.eastasiaforum.org/2015/02/23/revitalising-sluggish-fdi-in-japan/.

Wade, R. H. (2014) 'The mystery of U.S. industrial policy: the developmental state in disguise' in J. Manuel Salazar-Xirinachs and R. Kozul Wright (eds), *Transforming Economies: Making Industrial Policies Work for Growth, Jobs and Development*, Geneva: ILO-UNCTAD.

Waltz, K. (1999) 'Globalization and governance', PS Online, December, www.mtholyoke.edu/acad/intrel/walglob.htm.

Winters, J. A. (1999) 'The financial crisis in Southeast Asia' in R. Robison, K. Jayasuriya, M. Beeson and R. H. Kim (eds), *Politics and Markets in the Wake of the Asian Crisis*, London: Routledge.

Wong, J. (2004). 'The adaptive developmental state in East Asia', *Journal of East Asian Studies*, 4 (3): 345–62.

Woo, M. J.-E. (2009) 'After the miracle: neoliberalism and institutional reform in East Asia' in M. J.-E. Woo (ed.), *Neoliberalism and Institutional Reform in East Asia: A Comparative Study*, Basingstoke: Palgrave Macmillan.

World Bank (1993) *The East Asian Miracle: Economic Growth and Public Policy*, Washington, DC: World Bank.

World Bank (2007) 'East Asia and Pacific Update', April 2007, http://siteresources.worldbank.org/INTEAPHALFYEARLYUPDATE/Resources/550192-1175629375615/EAP-Update-April2007-fullreport.pdf.

Wu, J. (2009) 'China's transition to a market economy: how far across the river?' in S. Ichimura and T. Sato (eds), *Transition from Socialist to Market Economies*, Basingstoke: Palgrave Macmillan.

Xing, Y. and M. Pradhananga (2013) 'How important is exports and FDI for China's economic growth?' GRIPS *Discussion Paper* 13-04.

Yoshihara, K. (1988) *The Rise of Ersatz Capitalism in South-East Asia*, New York: Oxford University Press.

Yoshimatsu, H. (2017) 'Japan's export of infrastructure systems: pursuing twin goals through developmental means', *The Pacific Review*, Advance online publication. DOI: 10.1080/09512748.2016.1276953

12 The state in retreat?

Transnational actors in the Asia-Pacific

Rémy Davison

Introduction: defining transnational actors

In 1986, the political economist Susan Strange warned presciently in *Casino Capitalism* that international financial markets now resembled a giant casino, replete with 'mad money' that required regulation in order to avert collapse. A decade later, in *The Retreat of the State* (1996), Strange argued that transnational actors, from international crime syndicates to global financial institutions, had effectively taken over the economic and financial space previously occupied by states, compelling governments to beat a 'strategic retreat' as they competed for shares of capital and technology in a world of investment scarcity.

A key issue in this chapter is the extent to which transnational actors (TNAs) have challenged the centrality of the state as the most important actor in international relations. The transnational corporation (TNC), for example, has proven to be a durable instrument of both economic power and financial weakness, as evidenced by the 2008–09 Global Financial Crisis (GFC). Equally, non-government organizations' (NGOs) impact on issue areas as varied as trade, investment, poverty and climate change has, arguably, grown measurably over the last decade. Realists, such as Mearsheimer (1995: 9–11), argue that TNAs and intergovernmental organizations (IGOs) are second-tier actors; they are merely 'intervening variables in their ability to change state behaviour'. Conversely, some liberal and critical perspectives assert that TNAs are an integral part of the structure of international politics, advancing interests as diverse as transnational capital, secessionist movements, women and children's rights, and the environment. According to these analyses, TNAs can redefine the boundaries of political community.

In this chapter, international institutions are largely excluded from the discussion, as they are essentially *intergovernmental* organizations (IGOs) and, thus, state-based actors. Although some non-state actors have representation or observer status at certain IGOs, membership and voting is generally restricted to states. As some TNAs perceive IGOs as fundamentally state-centric, they have frequently directed their discontent at IGOs, such as the IMF, World Bank and WTO. Conversely, other non-state actors, such as TNCs, have strongly supported IGOs dealing with international trade and finance, while often opposing issues on the global agenda raised by environmental NGOs. Nevertheless, non-state actors view the infiltration of IGOs as crucial to the promotion of their policy agendas. Major transnational NGOs are affiliated with the UN's Economic and Social Committee (ECOSOC), which, while it does not give them similar power and influence to states within the UN, does accord them a legitimate place in international diplomacy.

TNAs can play a significant role in international politics, particularly in terms of their influence on negotiations and the policy-making process. TNAs may be defined as contributors to these processes, but they are not parties to actual decisions, which remain in the hands of states or IGOs. Many TNAs, such as TNCs, do not have a local basis in a state; they may merely be 'hosted'. Depending on the issue area and their relative resources, TNAs' influence varies considerably. TNAs can also operate not only across a number of states, but also at the sub-national level in order to promote their agendas and interests. Whereas 'international relations' describes transactions *between* states, 'transnational relations' describes interactions *across* state boundaries.

The term 'transnational actor' describes an exceptionally broad range of activities and organizations including labour unions, industrial groups, the media or environmental lobbyists. TNAs also include non-state actors such as private citizens living in different states connected through private, rather than governmental, channels. Examples include transnational business enterprises, religious groups and terrorist organizations. It is notable that although TNAs may interact frequently with the state, they are not state-based actors. However, Higgott *et al.* (2000) argue that TNAs are increasingly important contributors to the process of globalization, as their networks form important transnational linkages across a range of issue areas. Moravcsik's (1993) two-level analysis asserts that domestic as well as international actors affect and constrain policy-making, although TNAs are largely excluded from the two-level framework. By contrast, Stopford and Strange's (1991) model asserts that state–firm relationships are characterized by 'triangular diplomacy', comprising state–state, firm–firm and state–firm negotiations. According to Stopford and Strange's analysis, TNCs have emerged as important global actors, forming transnational business alliances between traditional industry competitors across national boundaries. Examples of this include Boeing's partnership with Japanese engineering firms to develop the 787, as well as Airbus's multinational consortium; Guangqi Honda, the automotive joint venture between Honda and China's GAC; and the Renault–Nissan merger. The TNC emerged as the route to national economic power in the post-war era. As Strange (1992: 7) notes, 'power, especially military capability, used to be the means to wealth. Now it is the other way around'.

TNAs operate across national borders, rather than globally, although some are global in their composition and reach. Such is the diversity and extent of TNAs that Castells (1999) has argued we live in a 'network society'. Risse-Kappen (1995) defines the transnational as interactions across national borders involving at least one non-state actor. Liberal critiques of TNAs go further, asserting that INGOs are instrumental to the formation of global civil society. However, realists argue that INGOs and other TNAs remain constrained by the state, and that shared norms and values among some TNAs are not sufficient to overcome competition and often differing objectives between actors (Cooley and Ron 2002). Conversely, Bello (2002) takes a more radical perspective, arguing that:

> The days when technocrats, politicians, and industrial elites monopolized decision making when it came to regional coordination are over. Whatever one thinks about civil society groups or NGOs, they are on the rise and they will make tremendous demands for inclusion in decision making in this decade.

TNAs are frequently regionally based, due to their links with a particular geographic part of the world. Only a few, such as the largest corporations, are truly global actors. In this respect, TNAs differ markedly from their state-based counterparts in that they often break down the barriers between countries by establishing sophisticated business, financial or social media networks that transcend national boundaries. A number of TNAs, such as manufacturing or trade organizations, operate in tandem with governments; others, for example environmental groups (Greenpeace), human rights organizations (Amnesty) and wilderness/animal rights groups (the Humane Society), may be at odds with national governments in a wide range of issue areas.

Transnational firms have been arguably the most influential TNAs, although IGOs have also developed critical policy relevance, particularly after the 1997 AFC and the 2008–09 GFC. Organizations such as the IMF and the G20, together with the Asian Development Bank (ADB) and the Asian Infrastructure Investment Bank (AIIB), have gained increasing responsibility for policy formulation and development in the region. For example, the G20 largely subsumed the role of the G8 following the GFC. The G8 had contained only one Asian member: Japan. Conversely, the G20 also includes China, India, Australia, South Korea and Indonesia.

Domestic firms have proven to be powerful locomotives of regional economic integration in the Asia-Pacific, evidenced by the interdependence between Hong Kong, Taiwan and mainland China, as well as Japan's development of intra-firm and intra-industry linkages throughout the ASEAN region. National business associations in certain industry sectors (automotive products; oil; steel) have also expanded within the region, resulting in more cohesive lobbying by industry associations of governments at both the local level, and in various regional and international fora. These transnational networks and linkages at the firm level mean government and business throughout the region have become increasingly interdependent; for example, there are few incentives for Japanese governments to countenance tariffs or taxes on Chinese imports when major Japanese corporations, such as NEC and Sony, are heavily reliant on Chinese manufacturing for their consumer electronics industries.

Transnational activism has also increased exponentially, partly as a result of, and partly as a response to, the accelerating pace of globalization. Social media has transformed the efficiency and communications costs of NGOs and transnational activist groups. Almost 1.9 billion Asians have internet access, a 1500 per cent rise from 2000 (Internet World Statistics 2017). Domestic NGOs frequently develop links with other domestically based NGOs, resulting in regionally based, trans-border networks. For instance, human rights groups have been responsible for monitoring and publicizing human rights violations (Burma; PRC) or development projects which affect traditional inhabitants (Yangtze; Tumen River Delta). Florini and Simmons (2000: vi) argue that 'these border-spanning networks are a real and enduring force in the international relations of the twenty-first century'. NGOs themselves have so proliferated across a range of issue areas that they are given specific acronyms, such as religious international NGOs (RINGOs); business international NGOs (BINGOs); and environmental NGOs (ENGOs) (Stephenson 2000: 270).

Transnational cultural networks are also highly visible within the Asia-Pacific region, and these often extend globally. Connections between individuals, social groups, family members and cultural organizations transcend borders and provide for continuous interaction across an extremely broad range of issue areas. Some contacts may be between business and government elites, such as the Australia–China Business Council; however, groups such as this partly reflect their expatriate Chinese citizenship, and the family, business and regional connections that arise from this. As Chapter 3 notes, the Chinese diaspora represents a significant transnational investor in the PRC, as well as comprising an important entrepreneurial production and distribution network largely centred in Hong Kong, Singapore and Taiwan (Arrighi 2002, Sheng 2006: 192, Smart and Hsu 2004: 545).

Analysts frequently emphasize the role of the capitalist developmental state in promoting not only export-led growth, but also the labour conditions which make the state attractive to transnational capital. According to Deyo *et al.* (1987), the demands of foreign actors (TNCs) and international market pressures condition East Asian domestic labour regimes to some extent. This has meant that NGOs concerned with labour conditions in the region face opposition from both states and firms. Although a UN agency, the ILO has had a limited effect on the development and maintenance of labour standards and working conditions in East Asia. The PRC, for example, has ratified four of the ILO's eight major labour conventions, but Beijing has failed to ratify the ILO convention on forced or compulsory labour, or the convention on freedom of association. Chinese workers are unable to join trade unions, except the state-sanctioned Federation of Trade Unions. Consequently, for PRC workers, although they can earn the minimum wage, and ILO-prescribed minimum working conditions are notionally met, implementation is weak, and sweatshop conditions are the norm. For example, the rate of suicide amongst Chinese technology workers employed by subcontractors for HP, Apple and Dell drew global attention to the plight of employees in the PRC's manufacturing industries in 2010, a problem that persists, despite worldwide media coverage (Bloomberg 2010a, *Forbes* 22 August 2016). In summary, the evidence suggests that, despite widespread labour exploitation,

TNAs such as human rights NGOs have had a nominal impact in redressing such problems.

However, some TNCs, such as Nike and Mattel, have been forced to abide by the ILO Code of Conduct due to pressure from NGOs in their home countries, which had widely publicized these firms' labour exploitation in East Asia (ILO 2003, Lindblom 2016). This is due partly to the fact that the ILO is widely regarded as a 'Western' organization, but also partly because government and international business in the Asia-Pacific view the ILO's role as interventionist, regulatory and likely to impose considerable costs on business. However, this has not prevented human rights NGOs in East Asia from networking and formulating harmonized strategies for dealing with the protection of workers across the region. For example, the Asia-Pacific Centre of Education for International Understanding (ACEIU), which is sponsored by UNESCO, has NGO worker-representatives from Cambodia, India, Indonesia, Japan, Korea, Malaysia, Mongolia, Nepal, Pakistan, Philippines, Singapore, Sri Lanka, Taiwan, Vietnam, the PRC, Bangladesh, Hong Kong, Papua New Guinea and Thailand. Through advertising, research, training and education, NGOs, such as ACEIU, maintain pressure on governments, as well as attempting, where possible, to elicit international support for transnational human rights issues (Human Rights Osaka 2000).

The plethora of TNAs demands a wide-ranging discussion, particularly as TNAs' influence varies considerably in different states and issue areas. The following section considers the issue of the relative autonomy of 'insularity' of 'strong' and 'weak' states in the East Asian region from rent-seeking TNAs. The third section discusses the power and influence of the TNC and transnational capital. The fourth section examines the proliferation of transnational NGOs and assesses their influence on national policy-making.

The influence of TNAs: the 'strong state' versus 'weak state' conundrum

The 'strong state/weak state' thesis argues that the more susceptible states are to infiltration by rent-seekers, such as domestic interests, transnational firms, NGOs and other TNAs, the weaker they are. This hypothesis is particularly applicable to Southeast Asia. The extent to which rent-seekers and transnational actors can gain access to national political systems is often governed by their level of openness. In both democratic and non-democratic political systems, coalitions of domestic and TNAs can frequently influence policy-making. Risse-Kappen argues that differences in domestic structures determine the variation in the policy impact of TNAs (Risse-Kappen 1995, Huang 2001: 141).

In Johnson's (1982) conception of the capitalist developmental state, Japan is characterized as a 'strong state' as it was able to organize and implement its administrative guidance model via the *keiretsu* networks. In China, the CCP under Deng from 1978 radically shifted the economy to export-led growth and market-based capitalism. In South Korea, the Park government from the early 1960s forcibly compelled industrialists to merge firms into giant *chaebols* – massive industrial conglomerates that would drive South Korean export growth. In Taiwan, the governing KMT developed strategies such as 'guerilla capitalism', which encouraged the development of small firms specializing in particular products, such as electronic components. Thus, there is a general consensus that Northeast Asian economic development has been largely based on the existence of the 'strong' state, relatively untainted by excessive business infiltration. China, for example, limits foreign TNC ownership of PRC enterprises across virtually all sectors to 50 per cent, while Japan pursued similar, unofficial policies directed at minimizing inward FDI for decades. However, even the 'strong' Japanese state has become more susceptible to rent-seeking by its own TNCs. There are other exceptions to the 'strong state' rule: pre-1997 Hong Kong was an exceptional economic success that was notable for the *absence* of the strong, guiding (or deadening) hand of the state. However, Hong Kong's system of governance was not heavily affected by rent-seeking or corruption either. In critiquing this 'strong state' hypothesis, Arts (2000: 525) argues that 'any "weak" agent is able to mobilize (at least some) countervailing power vis-à-vis any "strong" agent'. Pei (1994: 92–100) notes that the prevalence of 'neoautocracies' in parts of East Asia, such as China, Vietnam, Suharto's Indonesia and Thailand (under Thaksin Shinawatra, as well as the military junta in 2006–07), have resulted in serious political, social and economic problems, such as official corruption and increased economic inequality. Somewhat counterintuitively, 'spillover' effects arising from a successful economic transition under a 'strong' neoautocratic state can also lead to democratization, as business organizations operate under less strict regulation, while social forces from below challenge the power and legitimacy of the neoautocratic elite. There are several recent examples of emerging challenges to the 'strong' state: the Suharto regime's collapse in Indonesia in the face of economic turmoil following the AFC, which saw the Golkar party lose its ruling party status; the Tiananmen Square revolt, the suppression of Tibetans during the 2008 Beijing Olympics, and the rebellion amongst the large Uighur minority in Xinjiang province in 2009; and the political and constitutional crises in Thailand since 2005, culminating in the 'Red' and 'Yellow Shirt' clashes of 2010. In all of these cases, the decline of neoautocracy in Asia has meant that it has become increasingly difficult for these states to contain challenges to their authority. Moreover, TNAs, such as the Uighur Congress, and over a dozen Tibetan organizations are not only thorns in the side of the Beijing government, but also draw global attention to these issues. Similarly, another NGO, the Nobel Committee, embarrassed the Beijing government profoundly by awarding the 2010 Nobel Peace Prize to human rights campaigner Liu Xiaobo, who had been sentenced to 11 years' imprisonment in 2009.

In marked contrast with the 'strong state' exemplified by the Northeast Asian model, the Southeast Asian state, with the exception of Singapore, has long been penetrated by rent-seekers, and compromised by weak, corrupt or inefficient bureaucracy. In its drive to survive as a small, independent state, Singapore is noteworthy for its commitment to public investment, infrastructure development and compulsory pension fund schemes. Conversely, Indonesia, Malaysia, the

Philippines and Thailand have traditionally been viewed as exponents of 'crony capitalism', exemplified by the influence of 'presidential families' (Indonesia, the Philippines), and party-political cronyism (Malaysia, Thailand). Weak states are also characterized by a 'captive bureaucracy', which is driven by the policy agendas of rent-seekers, rather than efficiency and the implementation of national policy objectives. This has resulted in 'weak' Southeast Asian states, easily permeable by influential non-state actors, such as firms, which limit the state's relative autonomy.

Box 12.1 Strong states v. weak states

1 Extent of financial control over the economy.

2 Extent of control over labour relations.

3 The degree of autonomy of the economic bureaucracy.

4 The degree to which the state has been captured by its main economic clients.

5 The balance between incentive and command in economic guidance.

6 Special private sector organizations (e.g., *chaebols* (ROK) and *caifa* (Taiwan)).

7 The role of foreign capital.

Johnson (1987)

In effect, weak states often provide the antithesis of national policy autonomy; more accurately, policy beneficiaries are rent-seeking firms and individuals (associates of presidential families; members of political parties; interest groups; and domestic and foreign TNCs). The key problem is that 'weak' states are unlikely to achieve optimal policy outcomes in terms of their technical, dynamic or allocative efficiency, due to penetration by both domestic and TNAs, particularly firms. The environment wrought by the Asian Financial Crisis demonstrated the extent to which 'weak' states of Southeast Asia – as well as some 'strong' states, such as South Korea – were susceptible not only to the vagaries of transnational capital, but also to the influence of international institutions (IMF, World Bank). Transnational NGOs also exploited states' relative weakness; the pressure placed on Indonesia to hold an autonomy/independence ballot in East Timor demonstrated how NGOs could affect the national policies of weak states, particularly when supported by other actors, such as the UN, the US and Australia. However, although strong states are less vulnerable to the influence of TNAs than weak states, the diversity, resources and networks developed by TNAs suggest that no state can claim complete autonomy in policy-making. As Acemoglu (2005: 1223) notes, both strong states and weak states have costs and benefits, and excessively strong or weak states are inherently distortional; what is required for the functional efficiency and political stability of the state is a 'balanced distribution of power between state and society'.

Transnational corporations

Also known as international or multinational corporations (MNCs), TNCs have developed considerable politico-economic influence. The TNC dates from at least the 19th century, and possibly even earlier. During the 1970s, TNCs were the subject of widespread criticism for their activities, which some viewed as antithetical to the social, economic and environmental goals of developing countries. Wilson (1990: 163) argues that TNCs may be viewed as 'companies without governments'. Although the OECD has developed a number of guidelines governing the behaviour of TNCs in member countries, most East Asian states are not party to conventions governing workers' conditions, such as the International Labour Organization's (ILO) Fundamental Conventions. Thus, TNCs' behaviour is more likely to be regulated by pressure from either their parent country or transnational NGOs, rather than the host state.

Realists, such as Gilpin (1975), Waltz (1970) and Krasner (1978), argue that TNCs frequently operate as adjuncts of the state, increasing the state's international diplomatic leverage and projecting its economic and market power. It is difficult to dissociate GM, Ford, Google and Apple from the US, just as it is hard to conceive of Toyota, Mitsubishi and Sony as anything but 'Japanese' corporations. For Waltz (1970: 218), TNCs are not international corporations; they are 'national corporations operating abroad'. As Stopford and Strange (1991) note, firms are not autonomous actors; they rely heavily on states to provide public goods, as well as a stable market environment. Both states and firms engage in competition for markets. States' revenues and market power are enhanced by a strong economy, giving them the opportunity to project their power and influence the policies of others. However, Gilpin (2001: 17) argues that 'realism should acknowledge the importance of such non-state actors as transnational firms, international institutions and NGOs in the determination of international affairs'. This point is taken up by Nye, who argues that:

> the realist assumption is that security is the dominant concern, force is the major instrument, and governments more or less maintain their coherence as they interact with each other. In complex interdependence, security is less dominant as a concern, force is less useful as an instrument, you have many TNAs that are going to and fro across borders, making coalitions that are not always well described by national labels…
>
> (Institute of International Studies 1998)

The global business landscape has changed dramatically with the rise of China. In 2003, 90 per cent of the world's 500 biggest TNCs were based in the US, Japan and Western Europe, with just three from China. By 2015, 22 per cent (103) of the Fortune 500 companies were Chinese, with an additional three from Taiwan. US firms formed the largest contingent (134), with 52 from Japan, 29 from France, 28 from Germany and 28 from Britain. Very few of the top 500 are from developing countries, with the noteworthy exception of China. India had seven corporations among the global 500 in 2015, while Malaysia's sole entry was Petronas, ranked 125th (Fortune 2015). Clearly, PRC corporations have made significant gains in less than a decade, largely at the expense of Japanese and European firms. In early 2016 alone, PRC firms bought US$ 68 billion in foreign assets, half of their 2015 total (*Wall Street Journal* 4 February 2016). However, the position of Asia-Pacific TNCs alters markedly when one considers the foreign asset position of the largest financial and non-financial TNCs. Although PRC firms, such as Sinopec, State Grid and China National Petroleum Company (CNPC), rank in the world's top 100 firms in terms of total assets, their foreign asset position is dwarfed by firms such as General Electric (GE) (US), which held over US$ 350 billion in foreign assets in 2015, although this represented a steep fall from 2007, when GE held over US$ 800 billion in assets. In terms of total assets, Chinese banks have overtaken American financial institutions; JP Morgan Chase, the largest US financial institution, had total assets of US$ 2.5 trillion in 2016, while China's biggest bank, Industrial & Commercial Bank of China, had US$ 4.3 trillion in assets in 2015 (JP Morgan Chase 2016, Fortune 2015).

When comparing national tax revenues to corporate revenues, 69 of the world's top 100 entities in 2015 were TNCs (*The Independent* 13 September 2016). Measured by GDP, fewer firms generate higher revenues than states' GDPs, but a number of mega-corporations' revenues exceed the GDPs of some countries. To place this in context, Walmart is 'bigger' than Taiwan, while China National Petroleum's annual sales turnover exceeds the GDP of Malaysia (Fortune 2015). In 1968, there were 7,276 firms operating globally, with the number rising to 35,000 in 1990. By 2000, there were approximately 45,000 global firms operating 280,000 subsidiaries internationally, accounting for one-third of the world's products. UNCTAD (2003) estimated in 2003 that the number of TNCs had increased to 70,000. TNCs are also heavily dependent on revenues from their foreign operations. In 2011, 20 of the world's largest corporations' foreign sales exceeded 52 per cent of their revenues, with some firms realizing more than 80 or 90 per cent of their turnover overseas, including Honda, Toyota and GE (*The Economist* 10 July 2012).

TNCs may often control more assets than a state; however, these assets do not include the state's monopoly on the means of coercion, in the form of police, courts, bureaucracy and the military. Moreover, sales and assets do not necessarily provide an adequate picture of a firm; in the 1990s, Enron was one of the world's largest TNCs; it collapsed in 2001. In 2008, GM was effectively bankrupt, requiring US government intervention, while Amoco, Compaq, Chrysler and DEC have disappeared, having been acquired by, or merged with, larger corporations. During the 2008 GFC, the 150-year-old financial institution, Lehman Brothers, filed for bankruptcy, despite assets of almost US$ 300 billion. In summary, TNCs can wield considerable politico-economic influence; however, like states, they are susceptible to market forces and corruption.

Although Microsoft is the world's largest supplier of PC operating systems, IBM's sales revenues have frequently exceeded Microsoft's (IBM 2017, Microsoft 2016). However, due to Microsoft's overwhelming dominance in PC operating systems and business software markets, it has considerable economic and political leverage both in the US and internationally. In an attempt to reduce its dependence on Western high-technology TNCs and costly licensing, the Chinese government in 2003 announced it would develop its own audiovisual (AV) standards and supercomputers. Ironically, however, the Chinese government was compelled to invite Microsoft, IBM and Philips to form a consortium to help develop the AV standard (c|net Asia 2003). Another example is the Business Software Alliance (BSA), whose members include the world's three largest software publishers – Microsoft, Adobe and Apple – which has successfully lobbied both the US and Asian governments, leading to crackdowns on software piracy in China, Japan, Taiwan, Hong Kong and South Korea. Nevertheless, even Microsoft finds its market influence blunted by state power: in the late 1990s, the US Department of Justice launched anti-trust proceedings against the firm, threatening to break up its monopoly. In 2003–08, Microsoft was compelled by the EU Commission to separate its Windows Media Player software from its operating system, required to hand over software code to its competitors, and was fined US$ 625 million (BBC News 17 September 2007). In 2006, Hu Jintao even declared Microsoft a 'friend of China'; yet, by the end of the decade, the PRC government and Microsoft were embroiled in a bitter dispute over software piracy (*Seattle Post-Intelligencer* 19 April 2006, Bloomberg 2010b). Similarly, Google quit China in 2010, due to censorship, thus giving up access to the enormous Chinese market, but the company looked to return in 2017 (CNBC 2017).

As realists note, the state–firm nexus can provide firms with substantial international influence. In the mid-1990s, GM, Ford and Chrysler charged that Japanese protectionism and dumping were behind US automotive trade deficits, leading to threats of retaliation from the US Trade Representative (USTR). The Clinton administration utilized Section 301 of the US Trade Act, employing 'aggressive unilateralism', by readying punitive tariffs. The Japanese government capitulated, encouraging similar lobbying from Eastman-Kodak against allegedly protectionist Japanese and South Korean trade practices. Again, the USTR intervened, in this case to protect US film and camera makers. In 2017, the Trump administration imposed tariffs of 24 per cent on Canadian lumber, as well as tariffs on dairy. The US administration has also threatened to impose tariffs of up to 45 per cent on China. The response of the administration to perceived 'unfair trade' demonstrates the power of corporate lobbies in Washington (CNN 2017, *Washington Times* 22 January 2017). In summary, the considerable resources available to TNCs, as well as business–government networks, can translate into significant influence on national policy formation.

Commentators frequently compare the revenues and assets of giant TNCs with states' GDPs, but the comparison is not particularly helpful. Although TNCs can exercise considerable policy leverage in states where there is relative investment scarcity (for example, Toyota's FDI in Myanmar, Vietnam and the Philippines), individual firms have little influence in highly competitive investment climates, even in developing countries. The technological prowess and vast capital of Japanese firms such as Toyota and Nissan was not the first consideration of the

Chinese government as it sought to enter the global automotive industry in the early 1990s. Given Japanese dominance of the auto industry at the time, it would have appeared rational for China to adopt the best technology and production processes available. However, three key factors influenced the Chinese government to form joint ventures with European and American firms, such as VW, Daimler-Benz, Fiat, Chrysler and GM. First, anti-Japanese sentiment still runs deep in China; second, Japanese corporate culture is resistant to non-Japanese financial or management control, which posed difficulties, as China generally does not permit more than 49 per cent foreign ownership of joint ventures; and, third, China's model of capitalist economic development was heavily based on Japan's post-war experience, which had largely kept foreign ownership and firms out of the Japanese market. China welcomed TNCs in its initial development phase, providing they delivered technology transfers; however, the government still restricted foreign ownership. Prior to China's WTO accession in 2001, Japanese TNCs struggled to gain a strong investment foothold in China, as the PRC favoured South Korean and Taiwanese investment over Japanese. However, Japanese corporate FDI has penetrated China; in 2015, the net stock of Japanese FDI in China was US$ 1.2 trillion (UNCTAD 2016).

At the height of East Asia's extraordinary growth cycle of the mid-1990s, the number of Asian TNCs among the world's 200 largest grew rapidly. Japan accounted for the largest proportion, while South Korean *chaebols*, such as Samsung, Hyundai and Daewoo, emerged as global corporations of considerable importance. However, the post-1997 period saw GM acquire most of Daewoo's assets, while other South Korean TNCs struggled to accommodate the dual problems of debt and softer global export markets. Even China, which escaped much of the damage wrought by the 1997 crisis, has begun to develop a growing dependence on TNCs for FDI, technology transfer and joint ventures. Two thousand TNCs were operating in Hong Kong before the PRC resumed sovereignty in 1997 (Sheng 1997). Thousands of global TNCs have a presence in China, but by 2015, foreign brands were losing market share in the PRC as their Chinese rivals began taking increased market shares (*The Economist* 30 October 2015).

Japan has not been immune to the growing domestic influence of foreign TNCs either. Japanese firms began to suffer catastrophic liquidity shortages as early as 1990, leading to the *heisei* recession, from which the country only emerged very slowly late in the decade. When in the mid-1990s, Ford acquired 25 per cent of Toyo Kogyo (Mazda) and assumed effective control, one MITI official said in amazement, 'How could an inefficient American corporation take over a Japanese firm?' Similarly, Nissan's failure in 1999 saw it form an 'alliance' with Renault. The French firm took one-quarter of Nissan's shares and fired its Japanese management, installing its own CEO, and ultimately controlling over 44 per cent of Nissan's stock by 2010. In 2016, Renault–Nissan took a majority stake in struggling Mitsubishi Motors (Bloomberg 2016). Toyota, Japan's largest firm, experienced its first loss in 70 years in 2008–09. Japanese corporate failures and collapses persisted throughout the 1990s and 2000s, including Daiwa, the world's third largest bank. In line with new banking policies, Japanese governments began to refuse to guarantee bank deposits or rescue financial institutions from debt, as they had in the past. The impact was regional; as Asian currencies crumbled in 1997, the Japanese government floated the idea of an Asian Monetary Fund (AMF; see Chapter 10), which was conceptually similar to the IMF. Japan was motivated less by altruism than by the need to protect its financial sector, which faced heavy debt exposure in Southeast Asia. Although the AMF concept ultimately failed to gain Japanese government endorsement due to Washington's opposition, it has found contemporary expression in the Asian Infrastructure Investment Bank (AIIB) proposal (see Chapter 10).

Transnational investment in the Asia-Pacific

Foreign investment has two classifications: foreign direct investment (FDI) through direct equity in firms or plants; and foreign portfolio investment (FPI), which denotes private or corporate investment in stocks, bonds or other financial instruments, such as derivatives. During the 1980s, FDI was increasingly directed towards mergers and acquisitions (M&A) as firms sought to buy out competitors or to strategically enhance their ability to compete on global markets. Although during the 1950s and 1960s, MITI had forced firms such as Nissan and Prince to merge in order to *reduce* domestic competition, US firms in Asia, conversely, sought 'greenfields' investment, where they established service sector and manufacturing subsidiaries. These included American Express (region-wide), GM (Philippines) and Ford (Malaysia). By 2008, PRC M&A totalled US$ 130.8 billion, with Chinese outbound M&A increasing to US$ 37.7 billion in 2009 (China Stakes 2010). However, foreign TNCs have also made major investments in the PRC market; for example, China is now Asia's third largest M&A market, with US$ 28.5 billion in transactions in 2005, rising to US$ 362 billion in the first two quarters of 2010 alone. PRC outbound M&A also reached remarkable heights, totalling over US$ 28 billion by May 2010, the highest ever recorded (Mercer 2006: 1, *Financial Times* 23 September 2010, MarketWatch 2010). Nevertheless, despite the softness of the post-GFC global economy, the Chinese financial sector was the main target for FDI by TNCs; the PRC's giant AgBank initial public offering (IPO) in 2010 – the world's largest – accounted for the majority of over US$ 12 billion in FDI in the banking sector, with US TNCs making US$ 3.8 billion in investments (*Financial Times* 23 September 2010). Chinese FDI was particularly active in the energy and resources sectors in 2009–10, with PetroChina's 45.5 per cent stake in Singapore Petroleum, together with China MinMetals' acquisition of US$ 1.4 billion of Australian firm Oz Minerals assets. Nevertheless, US TNCs have maintained their dominance of global assets, with acquisitions valued at over US$51 billion in 2009, followed by France (US$31 billion) (*Financial Times* 14 January 2010).

The key point is that TNCs have driven financial, business and market integration throughout the Asia-Pacific. The extraordinary growth of FDI/FPI flows to the East Asian region from the mid-1980s until 1997 illustrates the importance of the region to TNCs. In the mid-1990s, East Asia was the destination of over half the world's FDI and FPI directed towards developing countries, accounting for some 15 per cent of total investment in the region. In 1993, total global investment in China exceeded foreign investment in the US (World Bank 1999b). As Chapter 11 suggests, a number of the East Asian economies developed a dangerous degree of dependence on, and vulnerability to, shocks in the international financial system. In this context, East Asian governments (Japan excepted), with few policy tools with which to deal with monetary policy changes in the 'big five', were highly susceptible to abrupt changes in the FDI climate.

Liberals argue that all states exhibit vulnerability or sensitivity interdependence when FDI stocks are withdrawn. Intra-Asian FDI more than halved in the second half of 2008, contributing to the sharp downturn in the region as the financial crisis spread from North America to Asia (KPMG 2009: 20–1).

Throughout the 1990s, TNCs demonstrated an increasing preference for subcontracting manufacturing. In sectors such as textiles, footwear and clothing, US retailing giants, such as Walmart and Target, looked to East Asia as their manufacturing base. Similarly, PC manufacturers, including Hewlett-Packard, Dell and Apple, subcontracted the majority of their output to medium-sized Taiwanese firms. By the late 1990s, China and Malaysia developed niches in computer peripherals markets, such as printers and input devices, while South Korean manufacturers, including LG and Samsung, gained strong positions in display technology. However, although Japanese, US and European firms continued to direct their FDI towards East Asian manufacturing investments, they retained the high value-added service-sector positions in their 'home' economies. For example, while large volumes of circuit boards are manufactured in China, processor and circuit board design and technology remain largely in the hands of the transnational parent, such as Intel, Apple or IBM.

Particularly in knowledge-based sectors, TNCs remain powerful and influential actors, as developing countries are keen to obtain not only investment, but also technology transfers. Intellectual property – governed much more stringently by the WTO under the Trade-Related Aspects of Intellectual Property Rights (TRIPS) agreement since 1994 – is frequently a corporation's most valuable asset. Core states' firms invest significant proportions of their revenue in R&D, whereas businesses in the East Asian NICs invest in plants in order to manufacture TNCs' products. Although NICs' firms are eager to obtain technology transfers, TNCs are naturally cautious about product piracy, reverse engineering or design theft.

Core states' TNCs continue to exercise a considerable monopoly over key factors of production in East Asia, such as capital and high technology. Despite the brief success of the first- and second-tier NICs during the 1980s and 1990s, East Asian countries, with the notable exception of Japan, remain 'host' countries to transnational capital, supplying low-cost manufacturing and labour at the expense of their own development. Apart from Japan and, to a lesser extent, Singapore, East Asian states tend to remain FDI recipients, rather than originators, which suggests a considerable degree of dependence on foreign capital. Of more concern to East Asian governments is the fact that their countries are the source of few technological innovations. Even Japan registers fewer industrial designs annually than Italy or Germany. BMW chief Erbhardt von Kuenheim in the late 1980s predicted – accurately – that Japan, despite its economic ascendancy and burgeoning trade surpluses, was vulnerable because its strengths were concentrated in very few products: cars and consumer electronics. However, as Japanese TNCs sought to remain competitive in the 1990s, the strong yen meant Japanese FDI was directed increasingly towards Southeast Asia, and production moved to the second-tier NICs. Although Southeast Asian countries benefitted from FDI, industrial development and a higher rate of employed labour, Japan experienced a phase of deindustrialization, which led not only to the 1990s *heisei* recession, but also to structural unemployment, giving Japan a Western unemployment rate of over 5 per cent, a condition brought about largely by Japan's own TNCs.

By the late 1980s, Japanese TNCs had voted with their feet and moved significant proportions of their capital and production to less costly regions of Asia in order to avoid the high wages and real estate costs associated with manufacturing in Japan. In this respect, TNCs have demonstrated the dependence of the Japanese economy on firms' strategies. Although Japanese governments had exercised considerable control over most domestic firms via *keiretsu* networks, much of this influence disappeared during the 1980s, as corporations began to behave more independently of the 'administrative guidance' model MITI had established in the 1920s. From 1993, Japanese governments were forced into a radical restructuring of the economy, due partly to the policy preferences of their TNCs, and partly to exogenous pressures from the US and the WTO. However, as Chinese labour markets began to undercut their ASEAN competitors, Japanese TNCs increasingly sought to establish themselves in the PRC. In 2015, two-way trade reached US$ 304 billion (JETRO 2016).

Dobson and Yue (1997) argue that East Asian integration has largely been driven by the TNC, particularly as Japanese firms spread their wings across Asia (the 'flying geese' thesis). Dobson and Yue assert that in China, Hong Kong, Indonesia, Malaysia, the Philippines, Singapore, Taiwan and Thailand, intra-firm, inter-firm, inter-industry and intra-industry trade has been largely responsible for economic growth. They also note that foreign firms – especially from Japan, China and the US – are central economic actors in the first- and second-tier NICs. However, they conclude that East Asia's heavy reliance on transnational networks of foreign firms introduces a strong element of risk and weakness (Dobson and Yue 1997). Although this network of TNCs supplies FDI, which acts as an employment multiplier, Dobson (2001: 2) notes that before the AFC, '[t]hese activities increased the openness and integration of economies but also increased vulnerability to external shocks'.

The emergence of the TNC as a transnational actor has profound implications. Economic liberals assert that TNCs can contribute positively to growth, development, employment, infrastructure, technology transfer, trade and training. However, TNCs in East Asia, particularly before the AFC, acted as catalysts of the collapse, engaging in speculative foreign exchange deals and short-term investment. The implications of dependence on FDI are clear enough: decisions made by firms in Tokyo, London and New York have ultimately forced East

Asian governments to engage in serious structural reform, significant micro- and macroeconomic policy change, and increased trade liberalization.

Since the 1997 AFC, the entire Asian economy has undergone a profound structural transformation in order to adjust to Japan's relative decline, while simultaneously accommodating the rise of South Korea, ASEAN, China and India. Japanese TNCs' production networks, clustered largely within ASEAN due to the 'super yen' and Japanese off-shoring during the 1980s, began to switch to the PRC in the 1990s. Rising business costs in ASEAN, combined with a vastly undervalued Chinese yuan and low labour costs, compelled Japanese firms to seek PRC corporate partners. The major difference was that Japan's TNCs were now forced to engage in joint ventures with PRC enterprises, rather than operating wholly owned subsidiaries in Southeast Asia, reducing Japanese firms' exclusive control over production and strategic technologies. In the short term, the clear economic losers from the diversion of Japanese TNCs' FDI to China were the ASEAN countries. Japanese investment in ASEAN fell dramatically after 1997, coupled with a concomitant expansion in Japan's investments in the PRC. Japan remains the second-most important foreign investor in ASEAN, but the European Union was the largest source of ASEAN FDI in 2015 (US$ 20.1 billion), although this was a US$ 4 billion decrease on 2014 (ASEAN 2016). However, some financial analysts view ASEAN as a key hub of Asian investment, as FDI in the bloc was on track to surpass China as an FDI host for the first time in 2017 (*The Star* 16 February 2017). Bangladesh, Cambodia, Indonesia, the Philippines and Pakistan are becoming competitive with Chinese manufacturing, as China's wages rise, and firms migrate mature technologies to lower-cost production centres (*ASEAN Briefing* 26 May 2015, World Bank 2013).

In summary, TNCs have had a significant impact on the relative autonomy, living standards and types of industrial development experienced by East Asian states. The region's NICs are hosts to Western capital and core Asian capital, drawn predominantly from the US, Japan and the EU, while PRC outward investment, if not trade, has yet to reach its full potential throughout the region. In a world of capital scarcity, governments and indigenous firms are forced to compete for FDI. As investment is the engine of growth, East Asian governments are, to some extent, compelled to orient policy to accommodate TNCs. Affected policy areas may include taxation, environmental regulations or labour relations. For example, Indonesia and Vietnam have successfully introduced tax holiday and income tax incentives to compete with China and attract more FDI (*ASEAN Briefing* 7 August 2015, *Thanh Nien News* 1 April 2016). However, labour may be particularly subject to exploitation by TNCs in the absence of strong unions or ILO regulation, as well as the need for employment growth in highly competitive labour markets. In 2000, the Asia-Pacific NGO Symposium attributed the vulnerability of low-paid workers largely to globalization and TNCs:

> This vulnerability stems from the myriad effects of capital mobility, re-structuring of production systems and increased exploitation of labour, including child labour brought about by economic globalization. Some of

> these forms of economic related violence against women include sexual exploitation in prostitution and trafficking, slavery-like labour conditions facing certain migrant workers, trans-border smuggling of humans and human organs, occupation-related accidents and ailments among cheaply paid women workers in overseas factories of transnational corporations.
>
> (Asia-Pacific NGO Symposium 2000)

Almost two decades later, NGOs such as the Asia Floor Wage Alliance argue that the situation has not improved. Its 2016 report 'identifies persistent rights violations' by US clothing retailers Walmart, H&M and Gap in the treatment of supply chain workers in Bangladesh, Cambodia, India and Indonesia (CNN 2016).

If East Asian states remain heavily dependent on TNCs as the major source of capital and technology in the longer term, this may validate some neo-Marxist theories which have long asserted that transnational forces, such as firms, and ownership or control of the means of production, lead, ultimately, to a state of *dependency* (Frank 1975, Yoshihara 1988). Nevertheless, some neo-Marxists, such as Wallerstein, viewed the 1997 economic crisis as temporary, arguing that 'the so-called East Asian financial crisis is a minor, temporary event of limited importance, which will probably change nothing of the underlying rise of Japan or Japan/China or Japan/East Asia' (Wallerstein 1998). Other neo-Marxists, notably Yoshihara (1988), disagree, arguing that the Southeast Asian NICs in particular are structurally dependent on TNCs and transnational capital. In the wake of the AFC, Yoshihara (1999) posited that the state needed to reassert itself as a dynamic, forceful actor in the national economies of Southeast Asia, by building and consolidating institutions to accommodate free trade and investment. Conversely, economic liberals assert that the forces of globalization impose necessary adjustments on East Asian states, compelling them to abandon 'crony capitalism' and state-led economic intervention, resulting in economic stabilization, while Dobson and Yue (1997) argued that Japanese and US firms would remain the key TNAs driving growth within the region. In the case of the AFC, liberal analysts proved correct in many respects, although it is also true that liberalization, competition and regionalization has meant that TNCs have gradually displaced entrenched domestic firms within the region.

Transnational NGOs/civil society actors

The number of non-governmental organizations (NGOs) operating internationally increased from 1,899 in 1968 to 4,646 in 1990. The number doubled between 1990 and 2000. In 1999, there were an estimated 42,100 domestic and transnational NGOs (*Yearbook of International Organizations* 1999: 549). The estimated number of active IGOs and NGOs operating internationally totalled 37,000 by 2016 (UIA 2016). Transnational NGOs may be defined as cross-border interactions between civil society actors, a process Falk (1999: 130) describes as 'globalization from below'. However, the distinction between domestic and transnational activities needs to be explicit; for example, China hosts 662,000 NGOs, but only

516 participate in international affairs (Asia Foundation 2016). Transnational NGOs have almost developed into a distinct field of study, as analysts determine the extent of NGOs' influence and significance in national and transnational policy-making processes.

Keck and Sikkink (1998: 12) describe NGOs operating across borders as 'transnational advocacy networks', arguing that even domestic NGOs 'bypass their state and directly search out international allies to try to bring pressure on their states from outside'. Conversely, some analyses do not characterize NGOs as 'networks'; rather, they categorize NGOs by identifying essential NGO attributes. According to Salamon and Anheier (1994), all NGOs have characteristics in common. These include non-governmental and non-profit-making status; and possessing a solid and continuing form.

The importance of NGOs is exemplified by the fact that the US government now prefers to direct the largest proportion of its aid budget through NGOs, rather than UN agencies. The impact of NGOs on significant areas of national policy can also be critical. For example, the International Committee of the Red Cross (ICRC), in coalition with five other NGOs, launched the International Campaign to Ban Landmines (ICBL) in 1987. More than 1,000 NGOs joined the campaign, which resulted in most states signing the Ottawa Land-mine Convention in 1999 (Vines and Thompson 1999). However, despite a campaign that persuaded many states to ban the production and deployment of landmines, the largest producers and consumers of landmines (China, Russia, India, Pakistan, Iraq and the US) refused to sign the convention.

Transnational NGOs in the Asia-Pacific region

An increasing focus for Asia-Pacific NGOs has been funding enterprise, rather than aid. For example, women's groups across the Asia-Pacific have seed funded entrepreneurial women, particularly in micro-enterprises, in an effort to foster not only independent commercial cultures, but also ethical production. Human Nature, a body products company, was assisted by Gawad Kalinga, a community development foundation NGO based in the Philippines, committed to poverty alleviation and nation-building (Gawad Kalinga 2017). Human Nature now has a plant in the Philippines and sales outlets in the US, Malaysia and Singapore.

Privately raised NGO funds remain a significant proportion of global ODA spending. The OECD's Development Assistance Committee (DAC) estimates that OECD DAC member countries had US$ 30 billion committed in funds, on average, approximately 24 per cent of the OECD's total ODA budget, between 2010 and 2013. The US accounts for 70 per cent of these funds, drawn from NGOs, foundations and philanthropic organizations (OECD 2015: 6). Although many NGOs remain independent of government, they are frequently co-opted by governments as policy operatives. One reason for this is that NGOs can be heavily dependent on government funding. For example, Japan's Ministry of Foreign Affairs (MFA) directly funds a large number of nominally independent NGOs, such as the Overseas Economic Co-operation Fund (OECF). OECF managers evaluate aid projects in Southeast Asia, and report on their feasibility and desirability. In turn, the OECF reports to another NGO, the Overseas Development Agency (ODA), which then determines whether the project will be funded from Japan's aid budget. In this respect, there is a powerful nexus between the Japanese government, business and NGOs, which serves to increase the politico-economic influence of the MFA, as well as Japanese TNCs' leverage in the region. The South Korean government also funds 183 NGOs, devoting seven per cent of its total ODA budget to development NGOs in 2015, while the Australian government channelled 12 per cent of its ODA budget through NGOs in 2014–15 (Asia Foundation 2016).

Despite this, many analysts argue that the government–NGO relationship also works to strengthen global civil society. Both TNCs and NGOs assist governments by relieving them of growing domestic and international welfare demands. States generally do not and cannot use their military forces to distribute aid and run medical facilities. However, UN agencies, such as the World Food Programme (WFP) and the World Health Organization (WHO) depend heavily on NGOs in the South to co-ordinate and distribute food, provide medical treatment and help develop industries, such as agriculture. TNCs are also frequently involved in such programs. Partly because TNCs generally wish to be viewed as 'good international citizens', and partly because work with NGOs can provide practical experience for their professionals, corporations have increasingly sought to co-ordinate their charitable activities with NGOs. There is also a strong commercial incentive; in some emerging national markets, it makes sense for firms, such as McDonald's, Microsoft and Toyota, to develop and promote their brands through good corporate citizenship.

The relative power and influence of TNCs and NGOs governs the extent to which they can influence national decision-making. TNCs' access to capital, and their importance to economic development, assures firms an influential role in the policy-making process. As Risse-Kappen (1995) notes, the governmental structure of the state can be a key factor in determining the level of influence exerted by TNAs. As firms' and NGOs' policy objectives are frequently diametrically opposed (for example, ocean- and land-based mining firms versus Greenpeace), the case for economic development often takes precedence over environmental concerns. However, this is not always the case. In 1993, Greenpeace gained Japanese support against Russian nuclear waste dumping in the Sea of Japan. Japan obtained East Asian and EU support for a UN resolution banning the practice, although China abstained (Ringius 1997: 84).

NGOs and transnational economic policy-making

The restructuring package developed by the IMF and World Bank following the AFC caused protest among a number of transnational NGOs, which viewed the strict conditionality associated with loans as excessively stringent. As a result, the World Bank sought to integrate NGOs into its decision-making processes. As the bank itself acknowledged:

Table 12.1 The diversity of NGOs operating in the Asia-Pacific

Base	*NGO/grouping*	*Issue area*	*Affiliation (if any)*
Cambodia	Women's Media Centre of Cambodia	Development	USAID Office of Women in Development
Cambodia	Women for Prosperity	Development	USAID Office of Women in Development
China	China Youth Development Foundation	Development	
China	Network of Foundations and Non-profit Organizations	Reference	
Hong Kong	Asian Human Rights Commission	Human rights	UNHCR
Hong Kong	Greenpeace: Hong Kong	Environment	
Indonesia	Watch Indonesia	Human rights	
Indonesia/UK	Tapol	Human rights	
Malaysia	Aliran	Human rights	UN ECOSOC
Philippines	Gawad Kalinga	Development	
Philippines	Philippine NGO Beijing Score Board	Human rights	
Singapore	Institute of Southeast Asian Studies	Development	ASEAN
EU-UN	EC/UNFPA Initiative for Reproductive Health in Asia	Women	EU/UNFPA
Transnational	Médecins sans Frontières	Medical health	
Transnational*	Green Empowerment	Environment	
Transnational	Asian and Pacific Development Centre	Development	
Transnational	Southeast Asia Watch	Human rights	

* Involves NGOs based in Malaysia, Indonesia, Nepal, Papua New Guinea, India and the Philippines.

Source: Union of International Associations (UIA) (2001) Yearbook of International Organizations (2001/2002), Edition 38 London: K.G. Saur Verlag; UIA (2016) *Yearbook of International Organizations 2016–2017: Guide to Global Civil Society Networks*, Edition 53. Brussels: Union of International Associations.

> There is widespread scepticism in the NGO community concerning what they call 'the World Bank's development/growth paradigm'. In East Asia, some NGOs felt that the World Bank was part of the problem rather than part of the solution. They felt that the World Bank needed 'to be made accountable for the crisis'...NGOs still need to be convinced that the World Bank talk of participation is more than a 'marketing trick'...
>
> (World Bank 1998: 4)

In order to encourage NGO participation in its Asia programme, the World Bank organized an East Asia-Pacific Regional Working Group. The group's Steering Committee is chaired by, and involves, a number of NGOs, including ANGOC (Indonesia), NGO-Cord (Thailand), Bina Swadaya (Indonesia), NGO Forum of Cambodia, Oxfam UK (Vietnam office), Consortium Laos, and Freedom from Debt Coalition (Philippines). Of the 26 Steering Committee members, ten are drawn from NGOs across the Asian region (World Bank 1999a). The first meeting was held in the Philippines in 1999 and was attended by representatives of five Southeast Asian NGOs from Indonesia, the Philippines, Cambodia, Thailand and Vietnam. The meeting established a secretariat and initiated plans for convening a regional assembly of NGO representatives (World Bank 1998: 4–12).

Similarly, civil society actors were prominent in the protests at the Seattle WTO meeting in 1999, which saw highly organized protests of 40,000 to 60,000 people, initiated largely by transnational and domestic NGOs, mobilizing against the WTO's free trade agenda. Despite US offers to extend bilateral aid to developing countries in an attempt to salvage the Seattle WTO meeting, it was insufficient to prevent a unified effort by African, Caribbean and Latin American countries to abandon the trade talks (Vidal 1999). Although most Southeast Asian governments and South Korea, dependent on the US-controlled IMF and World Bank for assistance, supported the US position, many of their NGOs did not. Protests organized by Asian NGOs persisted well beyond the Seattle WTO meeting, with the Asian Third World Network (Malaysia), Focus on the Global South, the Transnational Institute, and the International Society for Ecology and Culture pledging to continue their opposition to the trade round. NGO anti-WTO activity continued beyond the Doha WTO ministerial, at the April 2000 IMF and World Bank meetings. Digital video, social media and real-time distribution via the internet have transformed the tactical, organizational and communications efficiency of NGOs, allowing them to organize globally at virtually zero cost. Transnational NGOs, far from being mere lobby groups or aid agencies, are arguably part of a broader social movement which seeks to challenge the neoliberal orthodoxy which dominates the global trade system. In this respect, INGOs have allied themselves with, and assisted, LDCs by opposing the policy prescriptions of both IGOs, as well as the 'rich countries' club' (the G8) in fora such as the WTO and IMF. However, it is unlikely that INGOs would have been successful in their opposition to the Doha Round without the emergence of China and India as influential actors in the global trade regime.

The gulf between the policy objectives of intergovernmental organizations, such as the WTO, and transnational NGOs is ironic, given that many IGOs rely heavily on transnational and domestic NGOs' expertise to implement projects, as well as research. Transnational groups, such as Médecins sans Frontières, contribute to the WTO's TRIPS negotiations, particularly in the area of public health. Transnational NGOs, such as Oxfam, represent the interface between UN agencies, such as WHO, and impoverished people in the Global South (WHO 2017).

International investment regulation has been one area where transnational NGOs have had notable success. The OECD's proposed Multilateral Agreement on Investment (MAI) in 1995 was the subject of an exceptionally vigorous campaign that lobbied national governments to refrain from signing the agreement. The MAI was generally viewed by transnational NGOs as particularly disadvantageous to countries of the Global South. States such as Indonesia, the Philippines, Malaysia, Thailand and Vietnam, which compete for a share of global FDI in a world of investment scarcity, would have been forced to accept investment on terms heavily biased in favour of TNCs under the MAI. Similar NGO campaigns have been launched against corporations and governments, particularly in the wake of the 2008 GFC. For example, there was widespread protest against the TPP and FTAs in general. NGOs in South Asia have also developed in opposition to the China-led RCEP; in April 2017, NGOs including Karnataka Rajya Raitha Sangha, La via Campesina, the Asia-Pacific Forum on Women, Law and Development, IT for Change, and Forum against FTAs met in Bangalore. These NGOs represent a diverse set of policy areas, including health, agriculture, labour rights, women's rights and financial and public services. The NGOs questioned the Indian government's commitment to existing FTAs, such as ASEAN–India. They argued that the RCEP would privilege corporate power, damage farmers through intellectual property protection of corporate seeds, and make medicines unaffordable (Bilaterals.org 2017).

NGOs and transnational environmental activism

Environmental NGOs also have a notable presence in the East Asian region. The first conference of Asia-Pacific ENGOs was held in Bangkok in 1991. They developed co-ordinated and influential strategies which gained the support of a number of major powers for the Kyoto Declaration (1994) (Asia-Pacific NGOs' Environmental Conference 1994). The declaration established the Asia-Pacific NGO Environmental Council and Secretariat (based in Seoul), which was instrumental in developing the framework for the UN-sponsored Kyoto Protocol (1996). Asia-Pacific ENGOs have since developed strong links with research centres and development NGOs. The Kyoto Protocol proposals were succeeded by more ambitious Asia-Pacific ENGO plans, detailed in the Singapore (1998), Agra (2000) and Kaohsiung (2002) Declarations (Asia-Pacific NGOs' Environmental Conference 2002). As pollution, climate change and degraded fishing stocks have affected Asia-Pacific countries significantly, regional organizations have operated more collaboratively with ENGOs. Under pressure from ENGOs, the Paris Climate Change Summit produced a Green Climate Fund (GCF) for developing countries that was endorsed by ASEAN (ASEAN 2015). Wapner (1995) argues that ENGOs have been particularly effective as TNAs, especially in Asia where high levels of pollution, generated by 'smoke-stack' industries, have been exported largely from developed Northern economies. Wapner (1995) asserts that ENGOs 'disseminate an ecological sensibility'. However, he also argues that the 'influence' TNAs have on state behaviour is less important than 'manipulating governing structures of global civil society'. Nevertheless, lack of state ratification of the Kyoto Protocol meant it did not enter into international environmental law until 2005, and specifies no enforcement mechanism, which suggests ENGOs have had a relatively limited impact on states' policies, at least in relation to carbon emissions, as the outcomes of the 2009 Copenhagen climate summit suggested.

In 2010, an umbrella group of 60 South Asian NGOs, including Greenpeace and the World Wildlife Foundation, urged India and other South Asian states to withhold their signatures from the 2009 Copenhagen Climate Change Accord (CCCA). The CCCA included no binding commitments and desultory compensation for developing countries reducing emissions. The three largest carbon emitters and coal consumers, China, the US and India, stood to lose a great deal if they agreed to binding targets at Copenhagen. Moreover, the power of coal and oil TNCs in the 'G5' – China, the US, India, South Africa and Brazil – at Copenhagen demonstrated that TNCs exercised more influence over governments than ENGOs. It is noteworthy that these five states consume the majority of the world's coal (IEA 2009: 17). In the wake of the 2008–09 GFC, developed countries were reluctant to make the financial commitments required by the Kyoto Protocol, which would have resulted in billions of dollars in transfers from developed countries to LDCs, as well as carbon-reduction technologies. Consequently, China and India – the world's largest and third largest CO_2 emitters, respectively – employed the developed economies' reluctance as political cover for their refusal to reach a deal at Copenhagen. By 2015, at the Paris climate summit, the leadership and perspective of the PRC government had changed. Major Chinese cities frequently experienced days of choking smog. Xi Jinping's government ratified the Paris agreement in 2016, as did the Obama administration by executive agreement; however, the Trump administration indicated it could withdraw, even as major US oil and coal TNCs urged the government to retain the agreement (Reuters 2017).

The relative influence of transnational NGOs needs to be qualified and contextualized. Although both East Asian and other ENGOs were instrumental in assisting in the establishment of the framework for Kyoto, Copenhagen and Paris, ratification and implementation was left to states. China's, the US's and India's bland statements of principle, rather than adherence to binding commitments at Copenhagen, meant that the world's largest carbon emitters had no obligation to adopt serious pollution reduction targets. In contrast, Beijing, Washington and New Delhi all ratified the Paris agreement in 2015, not only exemplifying the increasing influence of ENGOs, but also demonstrating the growing commercial importance of environmentally sourced products, carbon trading, renewable energy technologies and green jobs.

NGOs and labour conditions

NGO influence in the East Asian region is particularly apparent in the area of labour conditions. The ILO and a number of NGOs were responsible for widely publicizing Nike's use of child labour in Indonesian factories, which drew much media attention. As a result, firms – particularly Western firms operating in Asia – have been forced to adhere more closely to international labour standards, even if the country in which they operate is not a party to the relevant ILO conventions. Most East Asian countries have yet to ratify all eight of the ILO's fundamental conventions, adopted in 1998. These include freedom of association and the right to collective bargaining; the elimination of forced labour; abolition of child labour; and abolition of discrimination at work (ILO 1998). Moreover, the right to strike is not part of the ILO's conventions. Consequently, NGOs' and INGOs' influence on workers' rights in East Asia is generally very limited. One reason for this is that exploitation, such as child labour, is often done behind closed doors, or within the confines of a family enterprise.

In this context, a link can be made between the influence of TNAs, such as TNCs, East Asia's export-oriented industrialization and labour conditions in the region. Park argues that in South Korea, TNCs 'accept traditional attitudes towards women where they justify giving women lower wages…and expect greater deference to authority and conscientiousness at work from them'. A representative of a US TNC has noted, 'It is in our own selfish interest to have a strong government that controls…labour so everything will blossom and we can continue to make profits' (Park 1993).

In Taiwan, girls and boys routinely work in textile and related industries. Despite Taiwanese laws regulating employing of persons under 15 years of age, Taipei has not ratified ILO Conventions 29 and 105 on forced labour. Child exploitation does persist, and workers are often injured when using factory machinery, due to poor occupational safety. Workers are usually fired when injured; as a result, girls who are laid off and unable to work often turn to prostitution. Sex trafficking is also common in Taiwan, along with unskilled work performed by illegal migrant workers (RHSF 2017). Although the ILO requires member states which have not ratified ILO Conventions 138 and 182 to abolish child labour, the ILO and NGOs monitoring abuse are forced to rely heavily on the co-operation of governments and police. In this respect, the East Asian state's emphasis on industrial development means labour standards run a poor second to productivity and economic growth. In 2012, Apple found that 11 of the firms in its supply chain were employing 106 children unlawfully in China. The company was forced to take action eliminating rogue suppliers, as Foxconn, its Taiwanese supplier, experienced a significant number of suicides due to poor working conditions in 2012 (*The Guardian* 25 January 2013). Although China ratified the

ILO's child protection conventions in 1999, it has yet to ratify the ILO conventions on the elimination of forced or compulsory labour. One NGO, the National Labour Committee, has uncovered recent evidence of widespread flouting of ILO and national industrial laws in Chinese factories manufacturing products for firms such as Microsoft, Lenovo, HP and Apple. Investigations found that firms were exceeding ILO overtime rules, as well as underpaying workers (*Sydney Morning Herald* 15 April 2010).

Conclusions

Detailed empirical studies of the level of influence exercised by TNAs are lacking; thus, it is difficult to evaluate the extent of their impact on states' national policy decisions. As Uhlin *et al.* (2002) note, 'The routine work of networking (across geographical and organizational boundaries as well as between issue areas), planning campaigns, seeking funding, collecting information, producing documents and other everyday activities of transnational activists is a highly under-researched topic'. Despite the attention paid to the power and policies of TNCs, the level of influence exercised by firms remains a strongly contested area. Realists assert that the TNC remains a subordinate actor to the state, while non-realists argue that the largest firms have become more significant actors than many states. Equally, proponents of global civil society point to the Kyoto Protocol, East Timorese independence and democracy in the Philippines as evidence of the influence exerted by NGOs on the state. However, Betsill and Corell (2001: 65) point out that 'there is a surprising lack of specification about what is meant by "influence" and how to identify NGO influence in any given arena'.

As the ACEIU reports, divisions between Asia-Pacific NGOs on a wide range of policy issues dilutes their effectiveness as TNAs: 'There are many divisions among them [Asia-Pacific NGOs]. Much of their time is consumed by fighting each other rather than developing a common stand' (Human Rights Osaka 2000). Critics of the liberal view of NGOs also argue that:

> this view [liberalism] does not adequately address the organizational insecurity, competitive pressures, and fiscal uncertainty that characterize the transnational sector. Powerful institutional imperatives can subvert IO and INGO efforts, prolong inappropriate aid projects, or promote destructive competition among well-meaning transnational actors.
>
> (Cooley and Ron 2002: 6)

The disparity in the relative power and resources of TNAs is also demonstrated by the financial dependence many NGOs have on UN agencies or national governments, while TNCs have their own resources and, frequently, privileged access to government. Conversely, NGOs may have limited resources, flexibility or detailed knowledge in given issue areas, which can reduce their effectiveness. For example, NGOs possess no consultative status whatsoever at the WTO (Van den Bossche 2008). Furthermore, as Dür and de Bièvre (2007) argue, NGOs constitute 'inclusion without influence' as other, more powerful, actors limit the ability of NGOs to shift policy outcomes in their favour. As Hanlon (2014: 144) argues, 'local NGOs struggle to hold (T)NCs and government accountable'.

References

Acemoglu, D. (2005) 'Politics and economics in weak and strong states', *Journal of Monetary Economics*, 52: 1199–226.

Arrighi, G. (2002) 'The rise of East Asia and the withering away of the interstate system', Fernand Braudel Research Centre, http://fbc.binghamton.edu/gaasa95.htm.

Arts, B. (2000) 'Regimes, non-state actors and the state system: a "structurational" regime model', *European Journal of International Relations*, 6: 515–44.

Asia Foundation, The (2016) 'Asian NGOs expand global influence', *In Asia*, 4 May, http://asiafoundation.org/2016/05/04/asian-ngos-expand-global-influence/.

Asia-Pacific NGOs' Environmental Conference (1994) 'Kyoto Declaration towards co-operation among environmental NGOs and sharing of its outcomes in the Asia-Pacific region', press release, Kyoto, 19 November.

Asia-Pacific NGOs' Environmental Conference (2002) 'Kaohsiung Declaration', press release, Kaohsiung, 3 November.

Asia-Pacific NGO Symposium (2000) *Final Report of the Asia-Pacific NGO Symposium, Asia-Pacific Women 2000: Gender Equality, Development and Peace*, Part B, www.aworc.org/bpfa/ngo/bangkok99/reports/partb.html.

Association of South-East Asian Nations (ASEAN) (2015) 'ASEAN joint statement on climate change to the 21st session of the Conference of the parties to the United Nations Framework Convention on climate change (COP21)', 30 June, http://environment.asean.org/download/climate-change/agreement/ASEAN-Joint-Statement-on-Climate-Change-Adopted.pdf.

Association of South-East Asian Nations (ASEAN) (2016) 'Foreign Direct Investment Statistics', 30 June, http://asean.org/?static_post=foreign-direct-investment-statistics.

Bello, W. (2002) 'East Asia's future strategic economic co-operation or marginalisation?' Asia Europe Crosspoints, Transnational Institute, September, www.tni.org/reports/asia/crosspoints/paper6.htm.

Betsill, M. and E. Corell (2001) 'NGO influence in international environmental negotiations: a framework for analysis', *Global Environmental Politics*, 1: 65–85.

Bilaterals.org (2017) 'India: people's groups reject RCEP', 4 April, http://bilaterals.org/?india-press-statement-people-s.

Bloomberg (2010a) 'Microsoft's Ballmer says China piracy is a problem', 24 May, www.businessweek.com/news/2010-05-24/microsoft-s-ballmer-says-china-piracy-is-a-problem-update1-.html.

Bloomberg (2010b) 'Suicide tops 2.8 million years' work', 6 June, www.businessweek.com/news/2010-06-06/suicide-tops-2-8-million-years-work-william-pesek-update1-.html.

Bloomberg (2016) 'Nissan seals $2.3 billion Mitsubishi motors stake acquisition', 21 October, https://www.bloomberg.com/news/articles/2016-10-20/nissan-seals-2-3-billion-mitsubishi-motors-stake-acquisition.

Castells, M. (1999) *The Rise of the Network Society*, Cambridge, MA: Blackwell.

c|net Asia (2003) 'China to snub MPEG standard for own format', 1 August, http://asia.cnet.com/newstech/applications/0,39001094,39144293,00.htm.

China Stakes (2010) 'China and HK M&A: Strong 2009, Stronger 2010', 15 January, www.chinastakes.com/2010/1/china-and-hk-ma-strong-2009-stronger-2010.html.
CNBC (2017) 'Is Google another step closer to being unblocked in China?' 12 March, www.cnbc.com/2017/03/12/is-google-another-step-closer-to-being-unblocked-in-china.html.
CNN (2016) 'Report slams Walmart for "exploitative" conditions in Asia factories', 1 June, http://money.cnn.com/2016/05/31/news/companies/walmart-gap-hm-garment-workers-asia/.
CNN (2017) 'Trump slaps first tariffs on Canadian lumber', 25 April, http://money.cnn.com/2017/04/24/investing/canada-lumber-tariff-trump/.
Cooley, A. and J. Ron (2002) 'The NGO scramble: organizational insecurity and the political economy of transnational action', *International Security*, 27: 5–39.
Deyo, F. C., S. Haggard and H. Koo (1987) 'Labour in the political economy of East Asian industrialization', *Bulletin of Concerned Asian Scholars*, April: 42–53.
Dobson, W. (2001) 'Deeper integration in East Asia: implications for the international economic system', ADB Working Papers, Asian Development Bank, Tokyo.
Dobson, W. and C. S. Yue (eds) (1997) *Multinationals and East Asian Integration*, Ottawa: IDRC.
Dür, A. and D. de Bièvre (2007) 'Inclusion without influence? NGOs in European trade policy', *Journal of Public Policy*, 27: 79–101.
Falk, R. (1999) *Predatory Globalization – A Critique*, Cambridge: Polity Press.
Florini, A. and P. Simmons (2000) 'What the world needs now?' in A. Florini (ed.), *The Third Force: The Rise of Transnational Civil Society*, Washington, DC: The Carnegie Endowment.
Fortune (2015) 'Global 500', http://beta.fortune.com/global500/list.
Frank, A. G. (1975) *On Capitalist Underdevelopment*, Oxford: Oxford University Press.
Gawad Kalinga (2017) 'Gawad Kalinga Community Foundation', January, www.gk1world.com/home.
Gilpin, R. (1975) *US Power and the Multinational Corporation*, New York: Basic Books.
Gilpin, R. (2001) *Global Political Economy*, Princeton, NJ: Princeton University Press.
Hanlon, R. J. (2014) *Corporate Social Responsibility and Human Rights in Asia*, Abingdon: Routledge.
Higgott, R., G. Underhill and A. Bieler (eds) (2000) *Non-State Actors and Authority in the Global System*, London: Routledge.
Huang, X. (2001) 'Contested state and competitive state: managing the economy in a democratic Taiwan' in X. Huang (ed.), *The Political and Economic Transition in East Asia: Strong Market, Weakening State*, Abingdon: RoutledgeCurzon.
Human Rights Osaka (2000) 'Human rights NGOs in Asia and the Pacific', *Focus Asia-Pacific News*, 22.
IBM (2017) 'IBM reports 2016 fourth-quarter and full-year results', 19 January, https://www.ibm.com/investor/att/pdf/IBM-4Q16-Earnings-Press-Release.pdf.
Institute of International Studies, University of California, Berkeley (1998) 'Harry Kreisler interviews Joseph S. Nye on theory and practice in international relations', for Conversations with History, http://globetrotter.berkeley.edu/conversations/Nye/1.
International Energy Agency (IEA) (2009) *CO_2 emissions from fuel combustion – highlights*, Paris: IEA, https://www.iea.org/publications/free_new_Desc.asp?PUBS_ID=2143
International Labour Organization (ILO) (1998) *Declaration of the Fundamental Principles and Rights at Work*, New York: ILO.

International Labour Organization (ILO) (2003) *Codes of Conduct for Multinationals*, Bureau for Workers' Activities, www.itcilo.it/english/actrav/telearn/global/ilo/guide/main.htm.

Internet World Statistics (2017) 'World internet users and 2017 population stats', 25 March, www.internetworldstats.com/stats.htm.

Japan External Trade Organization (JETRO) (2016) 'JETRO survey: Analysis of Japan–China Trade in 2015', 17 February, https://www.jetro.go.jp/en/news/releases/2016/c52b1f3efe0aa231.html.

Johnson, C. (1982) *MITI and the Japanese Miracle: The Growth of Industrial Policy, 1925–1975*, Stanford, CA: Stanford University Press.

Johnson, C. (1987) 'Political institutions and economic performance: the government–business relationship in Japan, South Korea and Taiwan' in F. C. Deyo (ed.), *The Political Economy of the New Asian Industrialism*, Ithaca, NY: Cornell University Press.

JP Morgan Chase (2016) 'Financial results – Q3 2016', 14 October, https://www.jpmorganchase.com/corporate/investor-relations/document/3Q16_Earnings_Presentation.pdf.

Keck, M. E. and K. Sikkink (1998) *Activists Beyond Borders: Advocacy Networks in International Politics*, Ithaca, NY: Cornell University Press.

KPMG (2009) *Asia Pacific's New Corporate Landscape: Asian Outbound M&A*, Melbourne: KPMG.

Krasner, S. D. (1978) *Defending the National Interest: Raw Materials Investments and US Foreign Policy*, Princeton, NJ: Princeton University Press.

Lindblom, H. (2016) 'Do code of conduct audits improve chemical safety in garment factories? Lessons on corporate social responsibility in the supply chain from Fair Wear Foundation', *International Journal of Occupational and Environmental Health*, 22 (4): 283–91.

MarketWatch (2010) 'China's M&A activity hits likely record this year', 24 May, www.menafn.com/qn_news_story.asp?StoryId={4927EB83-17A6-4A43-89C1-E17767009A81}.

Mearsheimer, J. (1995) 'The false promise of international institutions', *International Security*, 19: 5–49.

Mercer Human Resource Consulting (2006) 'M&A in emerging markets – a focus on China', www.mmc.com/knowledgecenter/M&A_China_MercerHRC.pdf.

Microsoft (2016) 'Annual Report 2016', 28 July, https://www.microsoft.com/investor/reports/ar16/index.html.

Moravcsik, A. (1993) 'Introduction: integrating international and domestic theories of international bargaining' in P. B. Evans, H. K. Jacobson and R. D. Putnam (eds), *Double-Edged Diplomacy: International Bargaining and Domestic Politics*, Berkeley, CA: University of California Press.

Organization for Economic Cooperation and Development (OECD) (2015) *Aid for CSOs: Statistics Based on DAC Members' Reporting to the Creditor Reporting System Database*, Paris: OECD.

Park, K. A. (1993) 'Women and development: the case of South Korea', *Comparative Politics*, 25: 127–46.

Pei, M. (1994) 'The puzzle of East Asian exceptionalism', *Journal of Democracy*, 5: 90–103.

Resources Humaines San Frontières (RHSF) (2017) 'Forced labour in Taiwan', www.rhsansfrontieres.org/en/183-to-see/281-forced-labor-in-taiwan.

Reuters (2017) 'U.S. coal companies ask Trump to stick with Paris climate deal', 4 April, www.reuters.com/article/us-usa-trump-coal-idUSKBN1762YY.

Ringius, L. (1997) 'Environmental NGOs and regime change: the case of ocean dumping of radioactive waste', *European Journal of International Relations*, 3: 61–104.

Risse-Kappen, T. (1995) 'Bringing transnational relations back in: introduction and structures of governance and transnational relations: what have we learned?' in T. Risse-Kappen (ed.), *Bringing Transnational Relations Back In: Non-State Actors, Domestic Structures, and International Institutions*, Cambridge: Cambridge University Press.

Salamon, L. M. and H. K. Anheier (1994) *Emerging Sector: The Nonprofit Sector in Comparative Perspective – An Overview*, Baltimore, MD: Johns Hopkins University Institute for Policy Studies.

Sheng, A. (1997) 'Hong Kong and Japan in East Asian finance', keynote address delivered to the 'Hong Kong after the handover' seminar, Nikko Research Centre, Hong Kong, 11 April.

Sheng, A. (2006) 'The Asian network economy in the 21st century' in I. Gill, Y. Huang and H. Kharas (eds), *East Asian Visions: Perspectives on Economic Development*, Washington, DC: World Bank.

Smart, A. and J.-Y. Hsu (2004) 'The Chinese diaspora, foreign investment and economic development in China', *Review of International Affairs*, 3: 544–66.

Stephenson, C. M. (2000) 'NGOs and the principal organs of the United Nations' in P. Taylor and R. J. Groom (eds), *The United Nations at the Millennium*, London: Continuum.

Stopford, J. and S. Strange (1991) *Rival States, Rival Firms: Competition for World Market Shares*, Cambridge: Cambridge University Press.

Strange, S. (1992) 'States, firms and diplomacy', *International Affairs*, 68: 1–15.

Strange, S. (1986) *Casino Capitalism*, Oxford: Blackwell.

Strange, S. (1996) *The Retreat of the State: The Diffusion of Power in the World Economy*, Cambridge: Cambridge University Press.

Uhlin, A., N. Piper and J. Lindquist (2002) 'Everyday forms of transnational activism: networks in and beyond Southeast Asia', Department of Sociology, Stockholm University, www.soc.lu.se/soc/distans/global/uhlin.pdf.

Union of International Associations (UIA) (2016) *Yearbook of International Organizations 2016–2017: Guide to global civil society networks*, Edition 53, Brussels: Union of International Associations.

United Nations Conference on Trade and Development (UNCTAD) (2003) *World Investment Report*, Geneva: UNCTAD.

United Nations Conference on Trade and Development (UNCTAD) (2016) *World Investment Report 2016*, 21 June, http://unctad.org/en/Pages/DIAE/World%20 Investment%20Report/Annex-Tables.aspx.

Van den Bossche, P. (2008) 'NGO involvement in the WTO: a comparative perspective', *Journal of International Economic Law*, 11: 717–49.

Vidal, J. (1999) 'The WTO in Seattle: why the talks collapsed', *The Observer*, 5 December.

Vines, A. and H. Thompson (1999) *Beyond the Landmine Ban: Eradicating a Lethal Legacy*, London: Research Institute for the Study of Conflict and Terrorism.

Wallerstein, I. (1998) 'The so-called Asian crisis: geopolitics in the Longue Durée', paper presented at International Studies Association meeting, Minneapolis, 17–21 March.

Waltz, K. (1970) 'The myth of national interdependence' in C. P. Kindleberger (ed.), *The International Corporation*, Cambridge, MA: MIT Press.

Wapner, M. (1995) 'Politics beyond the state: environmental activism and world civic politics', *World Politics*, 47: 311–40.

Wilson, G. K. (1990) *Business and Politics: A Comparative Introduction*, Basingstoke: Macmillan.

World Bank (1998) *Summary of the Fourth Meeting of the World Bank/NGO Asia-Pacific Committee*, Washington, DC: World Bank.

World Bank (1999a) 'East-Asia-Pacific Regional NGO Working Group in the World Bank: a briefer', press release, 29 April.

World Bank (1999b) *Managing Capital Flows in East Asia*, Washington, DC: World Bank.

World Bank (2013) 'Bangladesh: The Next China?' 17 January, http://blogs.worldbank.org/endpovertyinsouthasia/bangladesh-next-china.

World Health Organization (WHO) (2017) 'Oxfam International – member profile', www.who.int/workforcealliance/members_partners/member_list/oxfam/en/.

Yearbook of International Organizations (2001/2002) Edition 38, 4 vols, London: K. G. Saur Verlag.

Yoshihara, K. (1988) *The Rise of Ersatz Capitalism in South-East Asia*, Oxford: Oxford University Press.

Yoshihara, J. (1999) *Building a Prosperous Southeast Asia: Moving from Ersatz to Echt Capitalism*, New York: Routledge.

13 Civilisade

Asian values, democracy promotion and fateful hubris

Michael K. Connors

With the collapse of the Soviet Union in the late 20th century, Western adherents of liberal democracy largely concluded that history was on their side. Like others before them who had experienced giddy historical change, they were as shocked at the ease with which an old order faded as they were certain that a liberal international order would now emerge. As post-communist states underwent fundamental economic and political reform, the Cold War faded from view. Further entrenching this sentiment was the Asian Financial Crisis (AFC) of the late 1990s, when a number of Asian states were subjected to currency declines and negative growth, leading to great hardship (see Chapter 11). Commentators noted that the crisis was 'Asian' and vaunted the coming to Asia of Western market capitalism based on an idealized triad of transparency, good governance and efficiency. In turn, they pejoratively cast Asian regimes as crony-capitalist and either deeply corrupt or suffocating under the dead weight of state developmentalism. And just in case the new era needed a nudge, organizations such as Transparency International, Freedom House, USAid, the World Bank and the IMF enforced or cajoled liberalization in those states that were deemed too authoritarian or too closed.

It was well-understood by its protagonists that the objective of this liberal-democratic project was nothing less than a revolutionary restructuring of the economic and political institutions of foreign states. One may thus, and with only slight exaggeration, name this politics a 'civilisade', rather than a crusade: a form of secular liberal imperialism that attempts to cultivate 'higher' levels of moral, social and political development in other places (see discussion in relation to liberal philosopher J. S. Mill in Ryan 2012: 113). This civilisade unsurprisingly led to arguments over which political regime form best served national and international interests. The stakes were high. To the extent that targeted states edged towards liberal forms of rule, it was hoped that their erstwhile corrupt and authoritarian ruling elites would submit to reform and become stakeholders in a global liberal market order. If not, they would have to give way to new reformist leaders or be subject to sanction. In 2003, Larry Diamond, voicing the new zeitgeist in his manifesto 'Universal Democracy', surveyed a world ripe for political intervention:

> There is a lot of work to be done around the world to build the culture of democracy.... Some of this cultural change happens with economic development, increasing education, and exposure to the global environment. Much of it can and should happen through deliberate programs of civic education and civil society construction.... But the principal obstacle to the expansion of democracy in the world is...the ruling elites who have hijacked the structures of state power and barricaded themselves inside. We must craft a global strategy, asking Lenin's classic question: What is to be done?
>
> (Diamond 2003)

For some years, the organizations of Western market-democracy promotion pushed ahead, fuelled by the hubristic certainties that came with an almost ten-fold increase in financial aid directly spent on democracy promotion between 1989 and 2014 (Carothers 2015: 60). However, even by the mid-2000s it was already becoming clear that the global political trajectory was not aligning with their expectations. Authoritarian leaders, challenged by the aggressive politics of universal democracy, proved more resilient than anticipated. A spokesperson for Freedom House, the agency that rates countries' observance of a range of rights and liberties, noted in its 2015 annual report:

> For the ninth consecutive year... the condition of global political rights and civil liberties, showed an overall decline. Indeed, acceptance of democracy as the world's dominant form of government – and of an international system built on democratic ideals – is under greater threat than at any point in the last 25 years.
>
> (Puddington 2016: 1)

Freedom House's 2016 report reported yet another decline. In East and Southeast Asia, only Taiwan, Mongolia, South Korea and Japan were identified as 'free'. Indonesia, the Philippines, Malaysia, Singapore and Timor-Leste were rated as 'partly free', while China, North Korea, Thailand, Myanmar, Vietnam, Laos, Cambodia, Brunei were rated as 'not free' (Freedom House 2016). Evidently, the project to promote liberal freedoms and liberties and democratic forms of rule had yielded little in a region where both political elites *and* sections of the public advanced different political projects, premised partly on the claim that Asian cultural values were antithetical to liberal democracy.

If the regime contests were conventionally seen as having geographical and civilizational dimensions, behind which lay the moralism of a civilisade, others including liberals within Asia made the point that the contest was as much intra-national as it was international, for liberals, conservatives and authoritarians are not geographically *sui generis*. They pointed out that cultural resources for liberalism within Asia were abundant (see for example Kim 1994, Connors 2003, Thompson 2015). By the mid-2010s, this point was underlined by real-world developments, for just as liberalism could take root in Asia, commentators could detect strong authoritarian winds blowing westwards. Freedom House's 2016 (ibid.) report expressed concerns about the health of the liberal-democratic heartlands of Europe and the Americas where various pressures were said to be leading to populist upsurges that might 'threaten the core values of an open society'. The implications of this development will be addressed at the end of the chapter.

To conclude this introductory section, there is the question of why this topic is within the purview of the discipline of international relations. One response is that a study of how several states ideologically mobilized against Western democracy promotion, by promoting Asian values and Asian forms of democracy, provides an interesting example of strongly realist politics in Asia pushing against the so-called 'liberal Leviathan' of the West (Ikenberry 2012). A second response is that exploring modern history illustrates just how fervently a universally aspirant hegemonic power will seek to sculpt the world in its own image using a combination of soft and hard power. And as that power now declines, and the international order enters a period of power transition, the question of how a new power will act on questions of regime form is highly relevant.

Writing in 2001, scholar Mark Thompson linked these two responses. Thompson viewed the early 1990s Asian values position as highly specific in time and place, taking shape as a response to the promotion of liberalism. But in an interesting observation on the debate's international longevity, Thompson (2001: 163) looked to China as a bellwether: 'Looming over all these considerations is the ideological struggle for China's soul. It is the outcome of this battle that will determine above all the long-term significance of "Asian values"'. The implication was that China's long-term survival as an authoritarian state would provide sustenance for other Asian states to resist liberal democratization and continue to argue for a culturally specific form of democracy, at variance with putatively universal forms of liberal democracy in the West.

In the remaining parts of this chapter we look at the early Asian values debate and its international and domestic context, before moving to consider the emergence of an international human rights regime. Following Thompson's observation on authoritarian endurance in China giving a lifeline to Asian values advocates, the last section considers the status of 'Asian democracy' in the shadow of China's ascendancy, potential 'deconsolidation of democracy' (Foa and Mounk 2017) in the West, and expectations of a geopolitical shift in terms of declining US-led global hegemony.

The context of the Asian values debate

The promotion of Asian values, and the underlying premise of an Asian form of government, reflects a long subscription to the idea that Asian or national specificity supports forms of social and political life that diverge from Western forms (which are relentlessly presented as universal forms). Furthermore, this specificity is said to have contributed to sustaining Asian economic growth and social order. The Japanese had attempted to bring this idea into imperial realization during their efforts to construct an Greater East Asia Co-Prosperity Sphere. After the Second World War, the South Korean military dictatorship (Thompson 1999:

21) emphasized a social order predicated on Confucian values that elevated the collective over the individual, the value of social hierarchy in furthering national objectives, and the right of leaders to rule without participation from subject populations. Confucianism was also influential in the political thought of Lee Kuan Yew in the early years of the Singaporean republic (see Barr 2002: 35–6), and was intermittently propagandized by state-sponsored institutions. Similar positions stressing the guardian role of leaders over subjects, but without the Confucian tag, were developed in the Philippines under President Marcos, Sarit in Thailand and Suharto in Indonesia. What was articulated in each of these instances was a national ideology that stressed national unity and order for the sake of economic development, above the liberal regard for the individual. In contrast to these nationally focused ideologies, the Asian values debate of the 1990s witnessed the re-emergence of a pan-Asian position, one which attempted to articulate cross-national values that could unite non-liberal-democratic countries in Asia, in order to resist the pressure of liberalization that was being felt both domestically and from external forces (Wright-Neville 1995).

In East and Southeast Asia a number of democratic transitions were taking place that, by demonstration effect, undermined the legitimacy of highly restricted 'democracies' in Malaysia and Singapore – where electoral systems were skewed in favour of incumbents. In South Korea, Taiwan, Thailand and the Philippines erstwhile dictatorships had given way to emergent democracies in which political contest was real and conflicted. The causes of these transitions were complex and contradictory. Taiwan, South Korea and Thailand had each undergone substantial economic growth that had spawned a middle class, which some observers see as having democratic consciousness. Others saw democracy as offering these countries the best solution to perennial conflict among political and economic elites. Democracy offered the possibility of turning that destabilizing conflict into regularized and manageable politics mediated through parties and parliaments. Democratic transitions, then, offered political solutions to increasingly modernizing societies in which there was a plurality of power (as opposed to the centralization of power under authoritarianism). Furthermore, the transitions were said to be liberal in that they attempted to entrench a separation between the political and the economic spheres. While political power was now open to contestation, the nature of capitalism and the right to property ownership were untouched.

Such domestic stirrings as described above were facilitated by a more receptive international environment for democratic transition. For example, in the early 1980s the US set up important organizations, especially the National Endowment for Democracy, through which it sponsored democratic education throughout the world and spread technical knowledge about judicial, legislative and party processes. USAID also played a role in sponsoring democratic development (Robinson 1996). Increasingly, liberals in democratizing countries were thus buttressed by both domestic constituencies seeking more open political environments, and the world's hegemonic power supporting reform – as long as it did not threaten US economic interests. Indeed, the new democracies proved themselves to be more liberal in economic policy, opening the borders to foreign capital.

A parallel development was a gradual drift in the 1980s away from US support for anti-communist authoritarian regimes. In part, this drift was driven by the rise of the Asian economies, such as Japan and South Korea, which had sheltered under US military protection only to emerge as economic competitors. This shift has been linked to domestic capitalist lobbies within the West, especially in the US, who wanted to link trade rights to the observance of human and labour rights. It was thought that many Asian countries had a profit and cost advantage because of the poor state of human and labour rights. Better human rights would effectively increase the cost of such countries' exports, making them less competitive vis-à-vis the US. Given that the lobby for linkage of trade with rights threatened the economic gains of East Asia, Malaysian Prime Minister Mohammed Mahathir argued that the West's attack on Asian values was selfishly motivated by 'fear that Asian success might lead to Asian self-assertion' (Mahathir 1996a). To counter-attack an emerging political liberalism within Asia, such leaders claimed that the region's economic growth and relative political stability were due to the specificity of Asian cultural values, which they viewed as a kind of political comparative advantage to be preserved rather than attacked.

The Asian values position that emerged in the face of this liberal critique became identified with two relatively small Southeast Asian states – Singapore and Malaysia – and it was within these states that a new pan-Asian position became most pronounced. As Kenneth Christie writes:

> Both countries share the reputation of being the champions of the 'Asian way'.... Their respective statesmen, Dr Mohammed Mahathir and Lee Kuan Yew...have become self-appointed spokesmen for East Asian values in general, regularly appearing at international conferences, meetings and in the media to denounce Western interference, Western value systems, liberal versions of democracy and human rights...
>
> (Christie and Denny 2001: 31)

In Malaysia and Singapore modernizing elites held state power and were able to rule with relative immunity from popular pressure. While each country's political system resembled democracy, the internal operations of the system reflected tightly controlled politics, in which political opposition was severely restrained, if not punished. It was not hard to see that just as Western arguments for liberal values had a political edge, so too did arguments advanced by authoritarian leaders that highly controlled politics was culturally preferable.

The Asian values position

It is now time to turn to the substance of the Asian values position. It should be noted that variants of the Asian values position, with different ideological overlays, existed and indeed persist in China, Vietnam, Laos, Thailand, Myanmar and elsewhere. But the following discussion will mostly treat exponents of Asian values in Singapore and Malaysia for illustrative purposes. It has been observed that both Mahathir and Lee presided over societies in which there was substantial tension related to order and economic growth and the question of democracy. Each moved towards a system of one-party dominance (in effect), and each justified this as assisting the respective countries to reach new economic goals. In articulating a pan-Asianism, both leaders began to find common cause against Western liberalism and political opposition, despite the tensions between their respective states. They, along with many others, argue for a distinctive notion of Asian values related to the commonality of Asian societies. These values are given prominence in their explanations of Asian economic growth and political stability. Rather than simply arguing that growth flowed from well-thought-out development policies, culture was aggressively invoked by Asian values proponents as a contributing factor. In a sense, this might be understood as expressing no more than a pragmatic need to shroud economic success in cultural terms, to give it a kind of spiritual and nationalist meaning: an ideology for domestic consumption. However, it was also part of the articulation of Asian regionalism – part of the attempt to construct Asian identity. Asian values then are an assertion of confidence that, while modernizing, the newly industrializing countries were not Westernizing, and indeed were resistant to Western culture. In that sense Asian values were a culturalist assertion that stamped economic growth with an endogenous rationale and a programme for the protection and promotion of values that could sustain growth and social order (Kahn 1997). Furthermore, against the West, the Asian values position cohered into a discrete position. Jacobsen and Bruun suggest that four key claims are made concerning Asian values: the cultural specificity of rights; communitarianism; the role of discipline for the common good; and the organic nature of the state (Jacobsen and Bruun 2000: 3).

First, a claim is made that human rights are contextual and culturally specific, emergent in specific historical, political and economic settings. This clearly goes against the grain of the abstract individual endowed with natural rights that figures in liberal theory. In the famous Bangkok Declaration of 1993, issued by Asian governments in preparation for the Vienna World Conference on Human Rights (1993), the universality of rights was recognized, but their particular meanings and the methods of implementation were to be interpreted through a cultural prism:

> While human rights are universal in nature they must be considered in the context of a dynamic and evolving process of international norm-setting, bearing in mind the significance of national and regional particularities and various historical, cultural and religious backgrounds…
>
> (cited in Christie and Denny 2001: 10)

Second, a claim is made that Asian values orbit around a communitarian worldview, where the individual is obliged to the family and the community. Thus Asian culture is said to eschew individualism. Individual rights undermine social order and distract individuals from the fulfilment of social roles. Lee Kuan Yew, for instance, speaks of communities having precedence over individuals in Asia: 'Whether in periods of golden prosperity or in the depths of disorder, Asia has never valued the individual over society…. The society has always been more important than the individual' (cited in Christie and Denny 2001: 69). This form of thinking impacts on how one conceives of rights. For example, in response to an emerging LBGT movement in Singapore in the first decade of the 2000s, Lee was accommodating in saying that homosexuality was natural but argued that proselytizing for gay rights would upset conservative society. Rather, as senior statesmen and a pragmatic conservative he entrusted rights to the organic evolution of society:

> If I were the prime minister I would hesitate to push it through [decriminalization of homosexuality] against the prevailing sentiment, against the prevailing values of society. You're going against the current of the people, the underlying feeling…. It will evolve over time, as so many things have, because after a while my own sort of maturing process will take place with other people.
>
> (see Lee 2011: 377)

The communitarian perspective is one in which a social order is conceived as being held together by shared common values that bring people into a sense of togetherness and common identity. In this view, individuals are typically understood as emerging out of cultural contexts and being dependent on them; the community is reckoned as prior to the individual, while in the liberal perspective the individual is reckoned as prior to society and born with a bundle of rights that have precedence over society. This can take an extreme form in religious forms of communitarianism in Malaysia where leaving a faith community is viewed as apostasy and permission is required from religious authorities (Shah and Sani 2011: 664–7).

One consequence of this communitarian interpretation is that the Western stress on the rights of the individual as universally valid is perceived to flow from Western conceit, produced by the decadent individuals of Western capitalist and consumer societies. Again, Lee explains:

> The expansion of the right of the individual to behave or misbehave as he pleases has come at the expense of orderly society. In the East the main object is to have a well-ordered society so that everybody can have maximum enjoyment of his freedoms. This freedom can only exist in an ordered state and not in a natural state of contention and anarchy.
>
> (cited in Zakaria 1994: 111)

Third, a claim is made that, on the whole, Asians are predisposed to 'discipline' in order to serve the greater social good. Thus the political rights of the individual are secondary to the rights of the community and the nation's development. Development, properly pursued, secures overall wellbeing as a concrete outcome rather than being a product of compliance to the abstract rights of individuals. As one official from the Ministry of Foreign Affairs in Singapore has noted:

> Asian societies are now searching for their own distinctive configurations of market, state, and society.... The real debate is not about values of any particular geographic area, but about values per se; it is about which values, in what degree and in what proportion, are necessary for sustained development, the maintenance of social cohesion.
>
> (Kausikan 1998: 24–5)

Finally, a claim is made that the state is able to rule for the common good. It is assumed that state elites, endowed with national vision, are able to determine policies without the conflictive nature of public policy processes and interest groups. This is essentially an argument for the organic nature of state and society, which is to say that state and society are fused as if a single body, and act in unison as do the brain and body. In effect, the state is imagined as a benevolent patriarch, overseeing the interests of the common family, the nation. This position involves a critique of Western democracy and its perceived state of perennial conflict, excessive individualism and predatory interest group politics. The distaste for pluralist democracy in which conflict and adversarial politics abound is palpable in the Asian values position, as Mahathir sarcastically puts it: ‘Having multi-parties and holding elections are not enough. To be truly democratic we must change Governments with each election, endure civil strifes and frequent disruptive demos and generally verge on anarchy’ (Mahathir 1996b). Against this caricatured image of democracy Mahathir argues that:

> [o]nce a government has been elected, we believe it should be allowed to govern and to formulate and implement policies.... we believe that strong, stable governments...are a prerequisite for economic development.... When citizens understand that their right to choose also involves limits and responsibilities, democracy doesn’t deteriorate into an excess of freedom...
>
> (Mahathir 1995: 82)

In all of the above elements of so-called Asian values there is an implicit attack on liberal understanding of the state as a neutral mechanism through which the competing interests of society are articulated and given policy form. Contra the liberal-democratic view of the state, the democracy that is articulated to the Asian values position is characterized as having a strong leader who aggressively represses pluralistic contest and instead forges national visions and goals that are said to benefit all. A government’s legitimacy in this vision of democracy comes not from the consent of the people as such, although elections matter, but from effective government and economic development. While the proponents of Asian values do not necessarily dispense with the forms of democratic rule, they clearly interpret the nature of democracy in an authoritarian or illiberal manner (Bell and

Jayasuriya 1995). Moreover, obligations and duties of citizens to the state are put to the forefront while rights receive less emphasis.

Furthermore, as noted by Jacobsen and Bruun (2000: 3), the organic conception of the state implicit in the Asian values position 'has implications for foreign policy: the organic argument is expanded into an unyielding policy of state sovereignty and international non-interference, denying foreign governments and NGOs the right to monitor domestic human rights'.

Having described key features of the Asian values position, it is necessary to contextualize these ideas in the broader framework of an evolving international politics of democracy and human rights.

The international human rights regime

The expansion of international human rights agreements since the end of the Second World War has led to the formation of what many scholars describe as an 'international regime'. Following Krasner (1983: 2), an international regime is defined as 'implicit or explicit principles, norms, rules and decision making procedures around which actors' expectations converge in a given area of international relations'. While actors within the human rights regime profess a range of political ideologies and values, the normative core of this regime accords with dominant liberal understandings in the West on the rights of the person and the kind of political form that can best protect such rights. It is this particular interpretation that is invoked when there is talk about the promotion of democracy and human rights as aspects of Western foreign policy. It is also against the international regime, when liberally driven, that the proponents of Asian values position themselves, contesting the norms, rules and the locus of decision-making.

By using the term 'liberal', reference is being made to a longstanding interpretation of the so-called 'Western experience', in which political philosophers and historians posit that Western thought, dating back to the ancient Greeks, has long been concerned with elaborating a philosophy of the individual, and the conditions necessary for that individual's freedom. Relatedly, Western history is often presented as the struggle by concrete individuals to carve out a free space for the pursuit of individual lives. A necessary condition of this pursuit has been the limiting of the power of the state and of collectivities that might inhibit the freedom of the individual. Fred Dallmayr speaks of one particular discourse of rights in the West that runs 'from the assertion of baronial rights against kings in the Magna Carta to the proclamation of citizen rights against feudal absolutism in the French Revolution to the demand for social and economic rights in the era of industrial capitalism' (2002: 173). He also notes how rights can be a double-edged sword, used as 'weapons of aggression and domination in the hands of the powerful' (Dallmayr 2002: 173). The contradictory nature of rights is evident, for example, in the fact that rights to citizenship are used to exclude foreigners, and property rights can be used to maintain the luxurious lifestyles of the rich and to justify the poverty of the poor.

Germane to liberal conceptions of rights are two key elements, extracted from a particular reading of 'Western tradition'. First, human beings are said, by virtue of their humanity, to possess various rights: to life, to property, to liberty, to freedom of expression and so on. Rights are held to be inalienable and only under sanctioned conditions may they be violated. This understanding of rights is sometimes loosely described as the natural law position because it posits that the intrinsic nature of human beings requires that certain conditions be met for the fulfilment of each person's humanity. Rights flow from the natural state of being human and the limitation of these rights is deemed acceptable only so far as to protect the rights of others. Liberals argue that such rights are necessary for the fulfilment of each individual's potential as a rational agent. Generally speaking, these rights have been articulated to ideas about proper forms of government, which is to say that they are articulated to democracy, encapsulated in the notion of the right to representation. This coupling of rights and representation is generally described as liberal democracy. Legitimate government must function so as to protect the exercise of these rights by ensuring that all individuals have the opportunity to live full lives. The state positively protects freedoms by providing things such as education, health and equal opportunity. It is also the function of government, from a liberal perspective, to ensure that no nefarious institution emerges (tyranny, tyranny of the majority, a cumbersome welfare state, oligarchy, communism, absolutism or corruption) that would impinge on such rights. By circumscribing its own role, and that of other actors, the state protects freedoms by ensuring the absence of restraints on freedom: it limits as far as possible, for example, taxation that is viewed as a threat to individuals' property rights. Liberals are, of course, best described as a house divided, for they differ greatly on the role of the state in terms of providing the means by which freedom may be enhanced, including the role of welfare in lifting opportunity (see Freeden 1998). The history of Western governments from the mid to late 20th century is often the history of tension between competing modes of liberalism.

In the aftermath of the Second World War and with the establishment of the United Nations, a broad liberal vision has come to inform international practice related to human rights. The 1945 UN Charter declared 'respect for human rights and fundamental freedoms' as one of the organization's prime objectives. Notably the Charter also committed itself to the sovereign right of states to domestic jurisdiction; that is, control of subject populations within territorial borders. The tension between these two objectives is easily illustrated: to what extent does a nation's right to sovereignty override the international community's concern for state compliance with acceptable human rights practice? This question increasingly occupies the agenda of international politics and there is no easy fix.

Such intrusions on state sovereignty might be considered to undermine a principal realist premise that states alone are the sovereign holders of rights and responsibilities in the international system, for if internationally sanctioned bodies can now scrutinize state practice, sovereignty is diminished. A sense of this busy-body intrusion as it might express itself in everyday statecraft is nicely captured by law scholar David Kennedy:

> Governments have human rights departments, ombudsmen, special rapporteurs, and investigate divisions. If you are a diplomat, you can be assigned human rights as a specialty. If you are a law student you can aspire to a career in the field of human rights. We have human rights networks, human rights courts, non-governmental organizations, citizens initiatives, government bureaus, international institutions.... Diplomats denounce one another...and a cadre of professionals travels the world denouncing governments and promoting human rights.
>
> (Kennedy 2013: 19–20)

While the founders of the regime didn't fully anticipate the robust or selective manner in which states would sometimes hold each other to account, in the early years after the Second World War there was an agreed consensus on the need to challenge the model of unlimited sovereignty driving the Westphalian model (Dunne and Wheeler 1999: 1). The early UN system and its commitment to rights has thus been interpreted as a promise of cosmopolitan democracy in a world of post-sovereign states (Booth 1999: 65), or, put differently, a world where place of birth could not detract from each person's fundamental rights and freedoms. Certainly, the first few years after the Second World War inspired such visions.

For the first time in history an 'international bill of rights' came into existence strictly consisting of the Universal Declaration of Human Rights (UDHR) passed by the Western-dominated UN in 1948, the International Covenant on Economic, Social and Cultural Rights (1966), and the International Covenant on Civil and Political Rights (1966), as well as the latter's two optional protocols. Other conventions and related protocols have extended the Bill of Rights in practice, including the International Convention on the Elimination of Racial Discrimination (1965), the Convention on the Elimination of All Forms of Discrimination against Women (1979), the Convention against Torture and Other Cruel, Inhuman or Degrading Treatment (1984), the Convention on the Rights of the Child (1989), the International Convention on the Protection of the Rights of All Migrant Workers and Members of Their Families (1990) and the Convention on the Rights of Persons with Disabilities (2006).

However, after the UNDR was adopted, hopes for an emergent cosmopolitan order soon gave way to the logic of the Cold War and states' jealous guarding of national sovereignty. Initially, this meant that the human rights regime could only set aspirational normative standards. As Jack Donnelly writes:

> Work on a covenant to give greater legal force and specificity to the rights enumerated in the Universal Declaration became bogged down.... This reflected a more general return of human rights to the fringes of international relations. The rise of the Cold War...explains part of this recession. No less important, though, was the fact that most states were satisfied with an international human rights regime that included little more than a strong statement of norms.
>
> (Donnelly 1999: 73)

Despite this limitation, human rights did re-emerge on the international relations agenda. A gradual expansion of the role of international agencies in monitoring and promoting rights occurred. Drawing from Donnelly's periodization, this expansion can be traced through four key phases.

From abeyance (1950s to 1960s) to political codification (early 1960s to early 1970s)

As the Cold War heated up in the 1950s, human rights virtually disappeared from states' foreign policies. Instead, the terms of international discourse, or conflict, in relation to politics and social organization, were democracy, freedom, communism, imperialism, neocolonialism, etc. These terms indicated high-level ideological conflict. If a state was on the side of the US, and more generally the West, then it was considered a member of the free world, whatever its regime form might be. In such a world where state power was legitimated by its stance in relation to great power rivalry, the possibility of human rights protection was marginal. The instruments for protection in any case were very weak. After all, in 1947 the UN Commission on Human Rights had agreed that it held no power to 'take any action in regard to any complaints concerning human rights' (Donnelly 1999: 73).

In the early 1960s, the post-colonial states of Asia and Africa inspired a new round of human rights activism, especially around the Convention on the Elimination of All Forms of Racial Discrimination (1965). Further codification came with the passing of the ICCPR and the ICESCR in 1966. These two instruments reflected the ideological split in the United Nations, between the liberal capitalist democracies and their stress on political and civil rights (reflected in the ICCPR) and the ideological commitment of communist states and the practical development orientation of many Third World countries (reflected in the ICESCR). Indicating the slowness with which the human rights regime emerged, it took nearly a decade before the two covenants secured the 35 ratifications required to enter into force. It is worth noting too, that even when ratified, states were simply required to provide reports to the UN. As Donnelly puts it, 'Human rights norms had become fully internationalized. Implementation and enforcement, however, remained almost completely national' (1999: 75).

Revival and extension: 1970s to 1980s

Donnelly suggests that three major events triggered a revival in the fortunes of the international human rights regime. First, there was the 1973 *coup d'état* against President Allende in Chile. The human rights abuses that followed the coup led to the creation of a specific working group on human rights in Chile. Second, the Covenants of 1966 came into force in 1976 and a monitoring forum was established in the Human Rights Committee. Finally, the election of Jimmy Carter as President of the United States in 1977 led to human rights becoming a more forceful component of US foreign policy. These developments are said to have heralded a new era of human rights activism in the UN, with smaller states taking an active role in pushing new treaties and supporting higher levels of scrutiny (following the Chilean precedent). Moreover, the expansion of non-governmental organizations related to human rights promotion and protection further entrenched the importance of human rights in international politics. By the 1980s human rights had become common currency in international relations dialogue. It is in this period, too, that the United States government began to prefer limited democratic forms of government over the perennial civil wars waged between the leftist guerrillas they had opposed and the right-wing dictatorships they had supported. Accordingly, it began to selectively support efforts towards limited political democracy, where its interests were not threatened (Robinson 1996). However, in the Philippines, where it had important strategic military bases, the US maintained support for the notorious Filipino dictator Ferdinand Marcos until the 'people's power' movement overthrew him in 1986.

Post-Cold War: deepening of the international human rights regime

Freed from the politics of the Cold War, the UN has increasingly been able to address questions of human rights, within limits that states, ever protective of domestic sovereignty, will allow. The scope for intervention has widened however, and it is notable that in the 1990s there has been international support for interventions on humanitarian grounds where gross violations were judged as overriding a state's legitimate sovereign right to non-intervention. This shift occurred for several reasons, including the freeing of the UN system from the Cold War veto, and the increasing growth of the legitimacy of human rights discourse through the proliferation of struggles and organizations. One does well to remember that in the 1970s the international community fully condemned Tanzania's invasion of Uganda and Vietnam's invasion of Cambodia, despite those invasions ending the murderous rule of Idi Amin and Pol Pot respectively. As Hedley Bull put it:

> The reluctance evident in the international community even to experiment with the conception of a right of humanitarian intervention reflects not only an unwillingness to jeopardize the rules of sovereignty and non-intervention by conceding such a right to individual states, but also the lack of any agreed doctrine as to what human rights are…
>
> (cited in Dunne *et al*. 2001: 98)

The 1990s, however, saw UN peace-keeping operations carried out with reference to human rights in countries as varied as Namibia, Bosnia, Mozambique, Cambodia and Guatemala. Further, interventions or UN-endorsed interventions on humanitarian grounds in Iraq, Liberia, Somalia, Rwanda and East Timor have extended the horizon of when it is permissible to take action against states. All of these interventions, as well as those outside the UN system, have brought into focus the steadily eroding legitimacy of the absoluteness of the principle of non-intervention. This is not to say that rights have trumped states at this point in time;

the UN and states remain cautious in implementing intervention strategies. The situation remains fluid, but in many cases where intervention could be justified on humanitarian grounds, abusing states remain protected by abidance to the principles of sovereignty and non-intervention, and calculations by other states that it would not be in their interest to intervene. It arguably remains the case that the majority of foreign policy practitioners, within states, evince a certain agnosticism about the efficacy of international promotion and protection of human rights and have a keener regard for sovereignty as the key principle of international order. Even so, in matters of grievous abuse such as attempted genocide, war crimes, or ethnic cleansing, the United Nations declared a commitment to the principle of the 'responsibility to protect' in 2005.

Controlling and interpreting rights in an Asian values context

The principle of non-intervention has been jealously, if unevenly, guarded by the predominantly post-colonial states that comprise ASEAN (see Chapter 7), and by China and North Korea. The extension of the human rights regime is viewed as a threat where there are cultural and political 'traditions' and imperatives that differ greatly from the Western experience. This tension is reflected in how the states in the region relate to human rights instruments at the international level. For example, the First Optional Protocol to the International Covenant on Civil and Political Rights allows complaints to be made to the UN Human Rights Committee where individuals have exhausted all other avenues. Only South Korea and the Philippines have ratified the First Protocol among the states of East and Southeast Asia, while the states of the European Union, Australia and Canada have done so (see Bünte 2016). However, blurring this apparent Western/Asian polarity is the fact that the United States, for reasons related to contests between congressional and presidential power, and its privileged status as a hegemon, only ratified the Covenant in 1992, and has yet to ratify the optional protocols.

That the human rights regime in Asia is faltering is evidenced by the fact that it is the last major region to have an intergovernmental regional human rights mechanism, and even then this mechanism is best described as sub-regional. In 2009 ASEAN agreed to establish the ASEAN Intergovernmental Commission on Human Rights (AICHR). At that time only Thailand, the Philippines, Malaysia and Indonesia had what are known as National Human Rights Institutions (their national name varies). The establishment of the AICHR was expected to accelerate the formation of further national bodies. The AICHR grew out of a 1993 agreement that ASEAN would consider the formation of an intergovernmental human rights group. When it was formed the Commission embodied concern over the specific nature of rights and their relationship to state sovereignty. For example, the Terms of Reference (ASEAN 2009) governing the AICHR offers two opposed principles: 'To promote and protect human rights and fundamental freedoms of the peoples of ASEAN'. This includes upholding the Universal Declaration of Human Rights, and other human rights instruments to which states have agreed. However, circumscribing its human rights role is the principle of 'non-interference in the internal affairs of ASEAN Member States' (ibid.). To that end, AICHR is greatly restricted in its powers as demonstrated in a 'Score Card' administered by the civil society organization Forum-Asia to measure how closely the AICHR meets the requirements of the international human rights regimes, including the 1993 UN 'Principles Relating to the Status of National (Human Rights) Institutions' as well as the 'Principles for Regional Human Rights Mechanisms'. The AICHR receives a score of 27 per cent while the Inter-American Commission on Human Rights and the African Commission on Human and Peoples' Rights score 100 per cent (Forum Asia n.d). In practice what this means is that, unlike the latter two regional commissions, the AICHR is unable to visit countries of concern or receive complaints, it is not composed of elected members, nor can it hold hearings or compel state reporting on human rights performance.

In March 2010 the AICHR faced the first test of how it would deal with the contradictory principles present in its founding document. When relatives of 32 journalists killed in a massacre in the Philippines sought assistance, in the face of Filipino government indifference, the Commission responded by saying it would only receive thematic reports on human rights in ASEAN states and not receive individual complaints (see Amnesty International 2010). This stance has been challenged since, with organizations campaigning for complaints and specific reports to be receivable by the AICHR and for its powers to be expanded.

It is, however, possible to observe positive institutional development when considered against a very low starting point: ASEAN members states have ratified over two-thirds of available international human rights instruments (see Bünte 2016). But there has been a gap between these facts and the actual compliance or capacity to enforce observance of a full range of human rights. One explanation may be ASEAN's weak regional institutionalism and capacity (see Chapter 7). But that is only part of the story. For even when it comes to the application of nationally based state capacity in regards to the rights regime, ASEAN members have proved reluctant to drive institutionalization further. There has been remarkably strong resistance to the establishment of National Human Rights Institutions (NHRIs) which would make governments accountable. Myanmar was the only ASEAN member state to establish an NHRI after the formation of the AICHR. With Timor-Leste's expected accession to ASEAN in the coming years, a majority of ASEAN states will have an NHRI, but this will come about incidentally rather than by design. Existing NHRIs also face a range of political and budgetary pressures that diminish their independence. In some senses, the limits placed on the AICHR and resistance to the role of NHRIs reflect longstanding regional norms about appropriate forms of authoritarian governance and the secondary position of rights (see Rodan 2009). This is not to say that there is wide consensus about such norms but rather that these norms are fostered at elite levels. As Bünte (2016: 164) observes, the real conflict regarding the status of human rights in Southeast Asia is not between the West and Asia but rather between 'local civil societies, human rights institutions, and the various authoritarian governments in Southeast Asia'.

Critiques of the Asian values position

The Asian values position has attracted an enormous response from academics, and in the following section three basic critiques are discussed, as they remain relevant to the ongoing debate about regime form. The first critique, reflected in Bünte's observation above, focuses on the extent to which the Asian values position resonates with Western conservatism. Just as Western conservative ideas in the 18th and 19th centuries were a defensive response to rapid economic, social and cultural change, Asian values express, in the face of destabilizing tendencies brought on by profound economic transformation, a desire for cultural continuity, so that the social order has some sense of unity. Hewison and Rodan (1996) argue, for example, that the themes of Western conservatism are reprised in the Asian context. Some of these themes include: the evils of human nature and the need for discipline and a strong state to repress individual vice; the importance of hierarchical order and authority to ensure social order in the face of impending social chaos; the role of traditional values in promoting social solidarity and unity of purpose. By identifying commensurability between Asian values and Western conservatism it becomes possible to think of the Asian values position as being not so much about the expression of a separate civilizational identity, but rather a temporally and geographically contingent expression of modernizing elites seeking to advance economic development and change while maintaining selected traditional values.

A second critique focuses on the instrumental use of Asian values by elites. The defence of hierarchy, social order and social harmony essentially serves the consolidation of state power, in its economic development projects, enabling it to marginalize dissent and resistance (Robison 1996). A strong state is able to repress labour 'strife' and alternative economic or social visions. In essence, the constant promotion of Asian values serves to place a smokescreen around the government's real intent – which is largely to maintain its authority against other claimants, by advancing its moral claims to power over a disorderly population. Consider for example how a pro-government Chinese columnist writing for the official newspaper *People's Daily* expresses concern about the democracy movement in Hong Kong:

> if a society has yet to form a common sense of social morality, individuals will always need someone to look over their shoulders and to keep them in line…. The Chinese mainland is generally a society in which government still plays an instructive or even enlightening role in standardizing the public conduct. The reason may lie in both history and reality: the whole decade of the so-called 'cultural revolution' wrought untold havoc to the time-honored Chinese civilizations, suffocating almost all the human ethics and courtesies. Even today, more and more Chinese are getting rich, as a result of the galloping economic growth, merely in wealth, not equally in morality.
>
> (Li 2009)

The suggestion of a hierarchy of morality among citizens is rarely stated explicitly in defence of authoritarian rule, but the sentiment often lurks in the background. It is a classic conservative predisposition to believe in the necessary existence of a social aristocracy that has superior virtue or skill in matters of government.

A final, constructivist, critique rests on a critical reading of the politics of identity. Those who take this position are interested in the way that particular identities are articulated in international relations and the consequences of such identities. In the long history of Western global ascendancy, from the 17th century onwards, Western intellectuals began to sketch out civilizational and racial stereotypes. One particular sketching was that of the Orient. In his book *Orientalism*, Edward Said (1978) notes how 'Orientalism', or the positing of certain attributes about Orientals, functioned to provide the 'West' with a foil against which it could sketch its own identity. Travel books, poetry, novels and political tracts of the 19th century, for example, present an image of the typical 'Oriental' man who was irrational, lazy, undisciplined and feminine, while the typical Western man was celebrated as rational, masculine, disciplined and, consequently, able to rule and guide the natives. In effect, representations of the Oriental strengthened European identity, and this strengthening of identity provided spiritual sustenance for projects of domination over non-Western parts of the world.

Given this background to the politics of identity, it would seem unfortunate that some Asian leaders have seemingly appropriated the polarizing logic of civilizational identity and seem to fall into the trap of assuming an 'Asian' and 'Western' identity. Of course, these leaders do not subscribe to historical images of the Orient, but positively revalue Asian identity and contrast it to the West. However, as Callahan (1996: 3) notes, this reconstruction of Asian identity is 'not for the progressive project of dismantling dominance, but to try and beat imperialism at its own game by scripting a discourse of domination in terms of democracy: *Asian* democracy'.

Asian values redux and authoritarian persistence?

That the Asian values position became marginal after the economic crisis of the late 1990s has already been noted. The issue that now confronts us is how 'Asian values' as an argument for authoritarian rule has been rejuvenated in the context of a changing Asia-Pacific balance of power. It may be noted that the kind of ideas lying behind the Asian values position remain broadly popular among the political elites of Singapore and Malaysia, but cheerleaders can be found across the whole of Asia. To illustrate this, consider three examples from countries currently or formerly associated with democratic forms of rule.

Within Japan, conservatives have long espoused ideas that resonate with the concerns of Mahathir and Lee. The persistence of Liberal Democrat Party rule in Japan from 1955, with one minor exception, until the election of the Democrat Party in 2009, signals that the country most associated with liberal forms of democracy in Asia was in some respects 'different'. Many see that difference as reflecting traditional values of deference, obedience and the power of group identity, in line with a long tradition of literature and arts concerned with 'being Japanese' (see Sugimoto and Mouer 1990). A recent example of this genre is *The Dignity of the Nation* by Mashiko Fujiwara, which was a bestseller in 2006, beaten only by Harry Potter. Among other things, Fujiwara questions the appropriateness of Western forms of democracy and promotes the validity of Asian values. More specifically, he embraces Japanese values as embodied in the samurai (see James 2007, Rankin 2007). It is important not to see such publications as idiosyncratic; rather, they reflect the way some Japanese see themselves. As the critic Rankin (2007) puts it: 'You can listen to most of Fujiwara's other ideas for free at any noodle stand in Japan' – or indeed in parliament, where conservative identity politics are becoming more pronounced under the prime-ministership of Shinzō Abe (2012–).

There has long been a movement to revise the Japanese constitution which Abe actively promotes. Internationally, this has largely been perceived as a movement primarily about Article 9 and the constitutional prohibition on waging war (see Chapter 4). However, there are deeper identity politics in play in this issue. For example, the nation-wide organization Japan Conference, of which close to 40 per cent of Japanese MPs are associates, and to which Prime Minister Abe serves as an advisor, seeks a new constitution to replace the liberal constitution which many conservatives view, given its origins during post-war occupation by the Allied Powers, as a Western liberal imposition. The Japan Conference's Secretary General, explains what is at stake:

> The Constitution of the Great Empire of Japan has the preamble to explicitly show respect to the ancestors of the Imperial family and the Japanese deceased. However, the preamble of the current Constitution never respects Japan's traditions, the Emperor, or the ancestors of the Imperial family.... the Japanese people have become the non-Japanese people [due to the current Constitution]. Therefore, revising the Constitution is the pillar [of our movement].
>
> (cited in Sonoda 2016)

In democratizing Indonesia (1998–), echoes of the Asian values position are to be found among highly influential politicians, not to speak of religious leaders. For example, Jusuf Kalla, who served as vice president of Indonesia from 2004–09 and returned to that office in 2014, clearly admires Chinese authoritarianism as an effective development model. On an official visit to Beijing in 2007 Kalla noted, 'China's strength is that it can plan and implement. Our system, which is too democratic with too much individual freedom that often disregards the rights of others, has made it difficult for us to build infrastructure...'. He went on to explain that '[a]s long as individual right is above public responsibility, we will not progress...' (cited in Suparno 2007). Kalla is not a maverick figure. He is deeply embedded in the Indonesian political party Golkar, whose lineage may be traced to the authoritarian Suharto regime. His views reflect those of conservative elites troubled by the fractious politics of an open democratic system. As Indonesia responds to various challenges in its democratic development, Golkar or an offshoot can be expected to be waiting in the aisles to steer politics back to a more ordered conservative authoritarian centre.

While Japan and Indonesia possess radical conservative tendencies that may yet reverse liberal institutional forms, it is in Thailand where a full reversal has been experienced. After an uneven political opening from the late 1980s onwards, and the adoption of a broadly liberal constitution in 1997, Thailand began to shift towards a dominant party hegemonic system under prime minister Thaksin Shinawatra (2001–06). Thaksin moved to restrict freedom of expression and press rights, and his government presided over a number of human rights violations (see Pasuk and Baker 2009). Moreover, since the *coup d'état* that overthrew Thaksin in 2006, the country has been in political turmoil. In the face of continued turbulence a significant segment of Thailand's political elites have now concluded that it is necessary to restrict the power of the electorate (the majority of which supported Thaksin) and political contest in the interests of order and development (see Veerayooth and Hewison 2016, Pavin 2014). Such elites, in the military, bureaucracy and their popular support base, supported the second coup of 2014 and the strikingly authoritarian constitution of 2016. Commentators have for some time noted the aggressive re-emergence of a discourse of Thai-style democracy (see Hewison and Kengkij 2010) that is broadly consistent with 'Asian values'. Such democratic rollbacks, differently expressed, are being felt elsewhere, from the Philippines to Hong Kong.

These examples reflect the uneven political landscape of Asia and suggest that the Asian values discourse, however expressed, has fertile soil in which to grow. And Chinese intellectuals are eager to plough that soil. They have capitalized on Thailand's political instability to highlight the superiority of the Chinese system, and hope for a demonstration effect elsewhere. For example, Yin Jiwu, a researcher from the prestigious School of International Relations and Diplomacy, Beijing Foreign Studies University, writing in the official *China Daily* uses Thailand to poke holes in liberal-democratic models.

> Developing countries pursuing political modernization should learn some lessons from what happened in Thailand. The most important and urgent of them is that instead of putting too many Western democratic thoughts into action, they should concentrate their efforts on maintaining order in society.... To solve their problem, they need a strong legitimate government more than democratic principles.
>
> (Yin 2010)

That China is now a major pole of attraction within the Asia-Pacific is without doubt. Consider for example the revelations that emerged from WikiLeaks regarding how Thailand's military brass, sick of Western criticism regarding human rights after the coup of 2006, warmed to China. In a US embassy cable from 2010, officials reported a drift by the Thai military towards China:

> A U.S.-educated Thai Army Colonel at the National Defense College shocked a group of U.S. one-star officers visiting…by stating bluntly: 'The Thai perceive regional power dynamics as follows: China is rising; the U.S. is distracted/declining; and Thailand will adjust its policies accordingly'…. In comments to close aides after one trip in early 2009, [General] Anupong favorably compared the treatment he receives in China to the 'big brother' approach of his U.S. counterparts, whom he viewed as at times more interested in pursuing potential concerns over human rights and democracy than in building relationships…
>
> (US Embassy, Thailand 2010)

Even so, if China's endurance provides succour to those who seek to maintain or build authoritarian state forms in Asia, few would view its system of government as exemplary or culturally appropriate to their own national circumstance. Chinese intellectuals and officials are, of course, eager to present their country as a role model for developing states, but only in the broadest of terms. If commentators have spoken of a 'China Model' or the 'Beijing Consensus', the reality is that there are a plurality of political forms through which conservative Asian values may be expressed, and China does not aspire to spread its governing model. So, instead of a model, it is the case that in the past decade China's authoritarian endurance has provided a counter-hegemonic ideational structure in which a recalibrated Asian values position could emerge. It is indeed telling that Chinese intellectuals close to the state have studied the Singapore model as part of their long-term project of modernizing the ideological component of their own regime (Thompson 2015). This process of cultural and political learnings and potential adaptations suggests that China's relative success, despite its unevenness and costs, provides a platform for the propagation of ideas and practices that legitimate the continuation of illiberal and restricted democratic practices. The Western project of liberal democracy had always faced resistance. That it is now further diminished by the emergence of a new political and economic zeitgeist is exactly what some have been hoping for.

This new zeitgeist, understood principally as a re-evaluation of authoritarian forms of government, finds some Western support. There is general disenchantment with democracy as it is practised in the West. While there have been many criticisms of the inadequacies of Western democracies – and well before the crisis of the mid-2010s, as noted in the Freedom House report cited above – such critiques were largely ineffective until political forces began to successfully challenge the post-Cold War consensus on neoliberal globalization. Strikingly, the largely stable politics of Western Europe and Northern America are now facing their own legitimacy problems, that cannot be explored here. The fragility of democracy was something that was normally viewed as a problem only in developing countries or those engaging in processes of democratic transition. Now such concerns are present in commentary on Western Europe and the United States where there has been a resurgence of illiberal or anti-democratic values. In a report on various political values surveys, scholars Roberto Stefan Foa and

Yascha Mounk (2017) observe how support for democracy among young citizens across the West has reached dangerously low proportions. So alarmed are they that they speak of the deconsolidation of democracy in the West.

Given the politics of Britain's referendum on its European Union membership, the election of President Trump, and the blossoming of ethno-nationalism in Europe, it may be that a new global politics of economic nationalism accompanied by the emergence of populist, illiberal democracies in the West is eviscerating the role of regime change politics. A non-liberal West, or a splintered West, is less likely to promote its erstwhile universal aspirations. This drawdown from liberal democracy promotion, should it happen, could move states to more realist premises, concerned not with issues of values and norms but rather with power relativities, gains and losses.

Conclusion

Arguments made for Asian values represent a distinctive claim not necessarily about the absoluteness of Asian values, but about their appropriateness given the circumstances in which Asian societies exist. This circumstantial pragmatism also informs the China model. This is an important point because much ink has been spilt on an endless debate about the universality of liberally interpreted rights, as if it were possible to ground notions of the rights in the abstract individual that liberals invoke. The liberal vision, as has been noted, is contested within Western societies. Instead of granting either liberalism or the Asian values position status as 'right' or 'wrong', it might be more useful to think of them as particular projects promoting particular ways of being (Dallmayr 2002). At the same time, these projects cannot be seen to exist in a vacuum: the actors and states that promote them have particular interests related to their position in terms of state and economy and the global order. Both positions, insofar as they are articulated by people and agencies in power, tend to serve definable ends of state order differently conceived. Second, it is possible to also suggest that far from being a civilizational clash, the Asian values debate and its echoes in the 2000s may be taken as a more general debate about the kind of political and social forms relevant to the globalizing age from differential positions of economic, military and civilizational power. Taking the debate outside of its geographic confines, Hewison and Rodan (1996) suggested that the debate points to a global convergence among national elites around particular political positions: defined essentially as liberal and conservative. This is an observation that has renewed application with the rise of illiberalism in the West. A final observation is that hopes of a liberal international order are now at their lowest pitch since the end of the Cold War. If arguments that a new order of great powers is emerging are proven correct, the universalist politics of regime change will no longer be so much about sustaining a liberal international order as a second-order issue subject to a great power's sphere of influence. Under a counter-hegemonic authoritarian order, a hundred particular regime forms may blossom.

References

Amnesty International (2010) 'ASEAN human rights commission stumbles at first hurdle', 31 March, www.amnesty.org.au/news/comments/22792/.

ASEAN (2009) *Terms of Reference of ASEAN Intergovernmental Commission on Human Rights*, www.aseansec. org/DOC-TOR-AHRB.pdf.

Barr, M. D. (2002) *Cultural Politics and Asian Values: The Tepid War*, New York: Routledge.

Bell, D. A. and K. Jayasuriya (1995) 'Understanding illiberal democracy' in D. A. Bell, D. Brown, K. Jayasuriya and D. Jones (eds), *Towards Illiberal Democracy in Pacific Asia*, New York: St Martin's Press.

Booth, K. (1999) 'Three tyrannies' in T. Dunne and N. J. Wheeler (eds), *Human Rights in Global Politics*, New York: Cambridge University Press.

Bünte, M. (2016) 'Human rights in Southeast Asia: from contestation to compliance?' in M. Bünte and B. Dressel (eds), *Politics and Constitutions in Southeast Asia*, London: Routledge.

Callahan, W. (1996) 'Rescripting East/West relations, rethinking Asian democracy', *Pacifica Review*, 8: 1–25.

Carothers, T. (2015) 'Democracy aid at 25: time to choose', *Journal of Democracy*, 26 (1): 59–73.

Christie, K. and R. Denny (2001) *Politics of Human Rights in East Asia*, London: Pluto Press.

Connors, M. K. (2003) *Democracy and National Identity in Thailand*, London: Routledge.

Dallmayr, F. (2002) 'Asian values and global human rights', *Philosophy East and West*, 52: 173–89.

Diamond, L. (2003) 'Universal democracy?' *Policy Review*, 119 (June 2003), www.hoover.org/publications/policy review/3448571.html.

Donnelly, J. (1999) 'The social construction of human rights' in T. Dunne and N. J. Wheeler (eds), *Human Rights in Global Politics*, New York: Cambridge University Press.

Dunne, T. and N. J. Wheeler (1999) 'Introduction: human rights and the fifty years' crisis' in T. Dunne and N. J. Wheeler (eds), *Human Rights in Global Politics*, New York: Cambridge University Press.

Dunne, T., C. Hill and M. Hanson (2001) 'The new humanitarian interventionism' in M. Hanson and W. T. Tow (eds), *International Relations in the New Century: An Australian Perspective*, South Melbourne: Oxford University Press.

Foa, F. S. and Y. Mounk (2017) 'The signs of deconsolidation', *Journal of Democracy*, 28 (1): 5–16.

Forum Asia (n.d.) 'ASEAN Intergovernmental Commission on Human Rights – Scorecard', http://humanrightsinasean.info/asean-intergovernmental-commission-human-rights/score-card.html.

Freeden, M. (1998) *Ideologies and Political Theory: A Conceptual Approach*, Oxford: Oxford University Press.

Freedom House (2016) *Freedom in the World – 2016*, https://freedomhouse.org/sites/default/files/FH_FITW_Report_2016.pdf.

Hewison, K. and Kengkij Kitirianglarp (2010) '"Thai-style democracy": the royalist struggle for Thailand's politics' in S. Ivarsson and L. Isager (eds), *Saying the Unsayable: Monarchy and Democracy in Thailand*, Copenhagen: NIAS Press.

Hewison, K. and G. Rodan (1996) 'A "clash of cultures" or the convergence of political ideology?' in R. Robison (ed.), *Pathways to Asia*, St Leonards: Allen & Unwin.

Ikenberry, G. J. (2012) *Liberal Leviathan: The Origins, Crisis, and Transformation of the American World Order*, Princeton, NJ: Princeton University Press.

Jacobsen, M. and O. Bruun (2000) *Human Rights and Asian Values: Contesting National Identities and Cultural Representations in Asia*, Richmond: Curzon.

James, H. (2007) 'The return of Asian values', *Policy Innovations*, May, www.policyinnovations.org/ideas/commentary/data/asian_values.

Kahn, J. (1997) 'Malaysian modern or anti-anti-Asian values', *Thesis Eleven*, 50: 15–34.

Kausikan, B. (1998) 'The Asian values debate' in L. Diamond and M. Plattner (eds), *Democracy in East Asia*, Baltimore, MD: Johns Hopkins University Press.

Kennedy, D. (2013) 'The international human rights regime: still part of the problem?' in R. Dickinson, E. Katselli, C. Murray and O. Pedersen (eds), *Examining Critical Perspectives on Human Rights*, Cambridge: Cambridge University Press.

Kim Dae-jung (1994) 'Is culture destiny?' *Foreign Affairs*, 73: 189–94.

Krasner, S. (1983) 'Structural causes and regime consequences: regimes as intervening variables' in S. Krasner (ed.), *International Regimes*, Ithaca, NY: Cornell University Press.

Lee, K. Y. (2011) *Hard Truths to Keep Singapore Going*, Singapore: Straits Times Press.

Li Hongmei (2009) 'Elaborating on freedom and discipline', *People's Daily*, 24 April.

Mahathir, Mohamad (1995) 'Western modernism vs. Eastern thought' in M. Mohamad and S. Ishihara (eds), *The Voice of Asia*, Tokyo: Kodansha International, paper presented at the ECPR Joint Sessions of Workshops.

Mahathir, Mohamad (1996a) 'Speech presented at the 29th International General Meeting of the Pacific Basin Council', 21 May, www.smpke.jpm.my/gn-data/ucapan.pm/1996/960521.htm.

Mahathir, Mohamad (1996b) 'Speech presented at the Third Pacific Dialogue', Hotel Istana, Kuala Lumpur, 21 November, www.smpke.jpm.my/gn-data/ucapan.pm/1996/961121.htm.

Pasuk Phongpaichit and C. Baker (2009) *Thaksin*, Chiang Mai: Silkworm Books.

Pavin Chachavalpongpun (ed.) (2014) *Good Coup Gone Bad: Thailand's Political Developments since Thaksin's Downfall*, Singapore: ISEAS.

Puddington, A. (2016) 'Discarding democracy: a return to the iron fist' in *Freedom in the World 2015*, London: Rowman & Littlefield.

Rankin, A. (2007) 'A question of dignity or cause for embarrassment', *Japan Times*, 8 July.

Robinson, W. (1996) *Promoting Polyarchy: Globalization, US Intervention, and Hegemony*, Cambridge: Cambridge University Press.

Robison, R. (1996) 'The politics of "Asian values"', *The Pacific Review*, 9: 309–27.

Rodan, G. (2009) 'Accountability and authoritarianism: human rights in Malaysia and Singapore', *Journal of Contemporary Asia*, 39 (2): 180–203.

Ryan, A. (2012) *The Making of Modern Liberalism*, Princeton, NJ: Princeton University Press.

Said, E. W. (1978) *Orientalism*, London: Routledge & Kegan Paul.

Shah, D. and M. Sani (2011) 'Freedom of religion in Malaysia: a tangled web of legal, political, and social issues', *North Carolina Journal of International Law*, 36 (3): 647–87.

Sonoda, K. (2016) 'The quest to revise Japan's constitution', *The Diplomat*, 2 June.

Sugimoto, Y. and R. Mouer (1990) *Images of Japanese Society: A Study in the Social Construction of Reality*, London: Kegan Paul International.

Suparno, R. (2007) 'RI "too democratic" to progress, says Kalla', *The Jakarta Post*, 6 August.

Thompson, M. R. (1999) 'Asian values as Zivilisationaskritik?' paper presented at Workshop No. 4: Conservative Politics and the Nature of Consensus in the 1990s, Mannheim, 26–31 March.

Thompson, M. R. (2001) 'Whatever happened to "Asian values"?' *Journal of Democracy*, 12 (4): 154–65.

Thompson, M. R. (2015) 'Democracy with Asian characteristics', *Journal of Asian Studies*, 74 (4): 875–87.

US Embassy, Thailand (2010) 'China's sustained, successful efforts to court Southeast Asia and Thailand', *Wikileaks Cable*: 10BANGKOK269_a, 2 March, https://wikileaks.org/plusd/cables/10BANGKOK269_a.html.

Veerayooth Kanchoochat and K. Hewison (2016) *Military, Monarchy and Repression: Assessing Thailand's Authoritarian Turn*, special Issue of *Journal of Contemporary Asia*, 46 (3).

Wright-Neville, D. (1995) 'The politics of pan-Asianism: culture, capitalism and diplomacy in East Asia', *Pacifica Review*, 7: 1–26.

Yin, J. (2010) 'Thai dilemma of Western democracy', *China Daily*, 2 June, www.chinadaily.com.cn/opinion/2010-06/02/content_9920561.htm.

Zakaria, F. (1994) 'Culture is destiny: a conversation with Lee Kuan Yew', *Foreign Affairs*, 73: 109–26.

Index

Page numbers in *italic* refer to tables, and page numbers in **bold** refer to figures.